Marxism, Cultural Studies and Sport

The cultural ubi... nificance of contemporary sport pre al analysis. From
corporate and me events like the Olympic Games, to state
programmes for nation-building and health promotion, to the cultural politics
of 'race', gender, sexuality, age and disability, sport is so profoundly marked by
relations of power that it lends itself to critique and deconstruction.

Marxism, Cultural Studies and Sport brings together leading experts on sport
to address these issues and to reflect on the continued appeal of sport to people
across the globe, as well as on the forms of inequality that sport both produces and
highlights. Including a Foreword by Harry Cleaver and Afterword by Michael
Bérubé, this book assesses the impact of this work on the fields of 'mainstream'
Marxism and Cultural Studies. *Marxism, Cultural Studies and Sport* is centred on
three vital questions:

- Is Marxism still relevant for understanding sport in the twenty-first century?
- Has Marxism been preserved or transcended by Cultural Studies?
- What is the relationship between theory and intervention in the politics of
  sport?

The result is a unique and diverse examination of modern sports culture. The
first book published on the relationship between sport and Marxism for over
twenty years, *Marxism, Cultural Studies and Sport* is an invaluable resource for
students of sport sociology, Marxism and Cultural Studies at all levels.

Ben Carrington teaches sociology at the University of Texas at Austin, USA, and
is a Carnegie Visiting Research Fellow at Leeds Metropolitan University, UK.

Ian McDonald teaches the sociology and politics of sport at the University of
Brighton, UK. He is the co-editor (also with Ben Carrington) of *'Race', Sport and
British Society* (Routledge, 2001).

Routledge Critical Studies in Sport
Series Editors
Jennifer Hargreaves and Ian McDonald
University of Brighton

The Routledge Critical Studies in Sport series aims to lead the way in developing the multi-disciplinary field of Sport Studies by producing books that are interrogative, interventionist and innovative. By providing theoretically sophisticated and empirically grounded texts, the series will make sense of the changes and challenges facing sport globally. The series aspires to maintain the commitment and promise of the critical paradigm by contributing to a more inclusive and less exploitative culture of sport.

Also available in this series:

Marxism, Cultural Studies and Sport

Edited by Ben Carrington and
Ian McDonald

Routledge
Taylor & Francis Group

LONDON AND NEW YORK

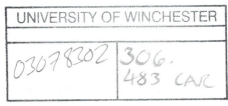
First published 2009
by Routledge
2 Park Square, Milton Park, Abingdon, Oxon, OX14 4RN

Simultaneously published in the USA and Canada
by Routledge
270 Madison Avenue, New York, NY 10016

Routledge is an imprint of the Taylor & Francis Group, an Informa business

© 2009 Ben Carrington and Ian McDonald selection and editorial
matter; © individual chapters the contributors

Typeset in Goudy by
Keystroke, 28 High Street, Tettenhall, Wolverhampton
Printed and bound in Great Britain by
CPI Antony Rowe, Chippenham, Wiltshire

British Library Cataloguing in Publication Data
A catalogue record for this book is available from the British Library

Library of Congress Cataloging-in-Publication Data
  Marxism, cultural studies and sport / edited by Ben Carrington
and Ian McDonald.
      p. cm.
   1. Sports–Social aspects. 2. Sports and state. 3. Philosophy, Marxist.
I. Carrington, Ben, 1972– . II. McDonald, Ian, 1965–
   GV706.5.M364 2009
   306.483–dc22   2008020760

ISBN10: 0–415–37540–1 hbk
ISBN10: 0–415–37541–X pbk
ISBN10: 0–203–09905–2 ebk

ISBN13: 978–0–415–37540–5 hbk
ISBN13: 978–0–415–37541–2 pbk
ISBN13: 978–0–203–09905–6 ebk

Contents

Notes on contributors

David L. Andrews is Professor of Physical Cultural Studies at the University of Maryland, College Park, USA and is one of the leading international scholars currently writing on the intersection of sport and contemporary culture. His books include *Michael Jordan, Inc.: Corporate Sport, Media Culture, and Late-Modern America* (SUNY Press, 2001), *Manchester United: A Thematic Study* (Routledge, 2004) and *Sport-Commerce-Culture: Essays on Sport in Late Capitalist America* (Peter Lang, 2006). With Steven J. Jackson, he is the editor of *Sports Stars: The Cultural Politics of Sporting Celebrity* (Routledge, 2001) and *Sport, Culture, and Advertising* (Routledge, 2003); with Stephen Wagg he is the editor of *East Meets West: Sport and the Cold War* (Routledge, 2007); and with C.L. Cole and Michael Silk, he is editor of *Corporate Nationalism(s): Cultural Identity and Transnational Marketing* (Berg, 2005). He is currently on the editorial board of the *Sociology of Sport Journal*, and an associate editor of the *Journal of Sport and Social Issues*.

Alan Bairner is Professor of Sport and Social Theory at Loughborough University, UK, having previously held the position of Professor in Sports Studies at the University of Ulster. His doctoral thesis, which was completed at the University of Hull, was entitled 'An Examination of the Origins, Development and Analytical Applicability of Antonio Gramsci's Theory of the State'. He is the author of *Sport, Nationalism, and Globalization: European and North American Perspectives* (SUNY Press, 2001), co-author (with John Sugden) of *Sport, Sectarianism and Society in a Divided Ireland* (Leicester University Press, 1993) and joint editor (with John Sugden) of *Sport in Divided Societies* (Meyer and Meyer, 1999). He has written widely on the politics of sport with a particular focus on such issues as national identity, social democracy, masculinity and sectarianism.

Rob Beamish is Head of the Sociology Department, Queen's University, Kingston, Canada. He was among the founders of the Centre for Sport Studies at Queen's which, in the 1970s, initiated in Canada the systematic study of sport using Marxist and Critical Theory. He has published widely in numerous sport studies journals and recently co-authored, with Ian Ritchie, *Fastest, Highest, Strongest: A Critique of High-Performance Sport* (Routledge, 2006). His theoretical work includes *Marx, Method and the Division of Labour* and 'The Making of the Manifesto' in *The Socialist Register*.

Anouk Bélanger is Professor of Sociology at the Université du Québec à Montréal, Canada. Her work focuses on urban popular cultures, sports and collective memory. She earned her Ph.D. from Simon Fraser University which was entitled 'Marketing Memories: Sport Venues and the Political Economy of Memory in Montreal'. She has published widely on sport, spectacle and political economy in journals such as the *International Review for the Sociology of Sport*, *Canadian Journal of Urban Research* and *Sociology and Society*. Currently she is part of the executive board of an international research group, the Culture of Cities Project, through which she runs a project on urban popular cultures.

Ben Carrington teaches Sociology at the University of Texas at Austin, USA, where he is also the Associate Director of the Center for European Studies and is a Carnegie Visiting Research Fellow at Leeds Metropolitan University, UK. He is the co-editor (with Ian McDonald) of *'Race', Sport and British Society* (Routledge, 2001).

Grant Farred is Professor of Africana Studies and English at Cornell University, USA. He is author of *What's My Name? Black Vernacular Intellectuals* (University of Minnesota Press, 2003), *Phantom Calls: Race and the Globalization of the NBA* (Prickly Paradigm Press, 2006) and *Long Distance Love: A Passion for Football* (Temple University Press, 2008). His forthcoming works include *Bodies at Rest, Bodies in Motion: The Event of the Athlete* (University of Minnesota Press, 2009) and *The Politizen* (Cornell University Press, forthcoming). He is the general editor of the journal *South Atlantic Quarterly*.

Jayne O. Ifekwunigwe is a Visiting Research Fellow in Africana Women's Studies at Bennett College, USA, having previously held the positions of Reader in Anthropology at the University of East London, UK, and, more recently, Visiting Scholar in the Cultural Anthropology Department at Duke University, USA. Her scholarly interests include comparative 'mixed race' theories and identities politics; feminist (post)colonial and transnational genealogies of the African Diaspora; global youth cultures and the politics of appropriation and authenticity; and the discrepant management of public memories in cultural and heritage tourism (Cape Town, South Africa). Among her publications are *Scattered Belongings: Cultural Paradoxes of 'Race', Nation and Gender* (Routledge, 1999) and the edited *'Mixed Race' Studies: A Reader* (Routledge, 2004). She is currently working on a new book project provisionally entitled *Out of Africa ('By Any Means Necessary'): Recent Clandestine West African Migrations and the Gendered Politics of Survival*, which seeks to resituate these contemporary migration processes within the African Diaspora paradigm and to force a reassessment of what constitutes volition and victimization.

Ian McDonald teaches Sociology and Politics of Sport at the University of Brighton, UK. He is the co-editor (with Ben Carrington) of *'Race', Sport and British Society* (Routledge, 2001). He is also co-editor (with Jennifer Hargreaves) of the Routledge 'Critical Studies in Sport' Series.

Toby Miller is Chair of the Department of Media and Cultural Studies at the University of California, Riverside, USA. He is the author and editor of over twenty books, including *The Well-Tempered Self: Citizenship, Culture, and the Postmodern Subject* (Johns Hopkins University Press, 1993); *Contemporary Australian Television* (University of New South Wales Press, 1994; with Stuart Cunningham); *Technologies of Truth: Cultural Citizenship and the Popular Media* (University of Minnesota Press, 1998); *Popular Culture and Everyday Life* (Sage Publications, 1998; with Alec McHoul); *Film and Theory: An Anthology* (Basil Blackwell, 2000; edited with Robert Stam); *Global Hollywood* (British Film Institute/Indiana University Press, 2001; with Nitin Govil, John McMurria and Richard Maxwell); *Globalization and Sport: Playing the World* (Sage, 2001; with Geoffrey Lawrence, Jim McKay and David Rowe); *SportSex* (Temple University Press, 2001); *Cultural Policy* (Sage Publications, 2002; with George Yudice); *Critical Cultural Policy Studies: A Reader* (Basil Blackwell, 2003; edited with Justin Lewis); and *Cultural Citizenship: Cosmopolitanism, Consumerism, and Television in a Neoliberal Age* (Temple University Press, 2007). His work has been translated into Spanish, Chinese, German, Japanese and Swedish.

Brett St Louis is a sociologist who teaches at Goldsmiths College, University of London, UK. He has written extensively on social theory, 'race' and culture and has published articles in a range of journals, including *Body and Society*, *Ethnic and Racial Studies*, *Ethnicities*, *new formations* and *Sociology of Sport Journal*. He is the author of *Rethinking Race, Politics, and Poetics: C.L.R. James' Critique of Modernity* (Routledge, 2007).

Garry Whannel is Professor of Media Cultures, and Director of the Centre for International Media Analysis in the Department of Media Arts at the University of Bedfordshire, UK. He has been writing and researching on the theme of media and sport for over twenty years and his most recent published work includes *Media Sport Stars, Masculinities and Moralities* (Routledge, 2001) and (with John Horne and Alan Tomlinson) *Understanding Sport* (E. and F.N. Spon, 1999). Previous books include *Fields in Vision: Television Sport and Cultural Transformation* (Routledge, 1992) and *Blowing the Whistle: The Politics of Sport* (Pluto, 1983). He also edited *Consumption and Participation: Leisure, Culture and Commerce* (LSA, 2000) and has previously co-edited collections on television, leisure cultures, the Olympic Games and the World Cup. His current research interests include the politics of the Olympic bidding process and the growth of commercial sponsorship.

Series editors' preface

Marxism, Cultural Studies and Sport, edited by Ben Carrington and Ian McDonald, is the eleventh book to be published in the Routledge Critical Studies in Sport Series. The series was launched in 2004 with Belinda Wheaton's edited collection *Understanding Lifestyle Sport* which, in common with the other nine books, closely reflects our aims. From the outset we had a clear sense of purpose for the series: to publish texts that are interrogative, interventionist and innovative. We want the books to challenge commonsense ideas and expose relations of power in sport; to highlight relationships between theory and practice and provide arguments and analyses of topical and polemical issues; and to develop new areas of research and new ways of thinking about and studying sport. The series will thus help to shape the direction of Sport Studies as a discipline, and encourage students to become critical scholars. While any series will be judged by the quality of the individual texts, we feel that collectively the books in our series constitute a strong body of scholarship about, and critique of, the social and cultural significance of sport in a fast-changing and challenging global world.

We have published searing critiques of contemporary sport by established authors in Sport Studies such as *Why Sports Morally Matter* (2006) by William Morgan (shortlisted for the prestigious North American Society for the Study of Sports (NASSS) 2006 Book Award); *Fastest Highest Strongest: A Critique of High-Performance Sport* (2006) by Rob Beamish and Ian Ritchie; and *Culture, Politics and Sport: Blowing the Whistle, Revisited* (2008) by Garry Whannel. The series has also given opportunities for already well-established and widely respected authors to explore lesser-known aspects of familiar subjects, such as Gary Armstrong's and Jon Mitchell's anthropological observations on football in Malta, *Global and Local Football: Politics and Europeanization on the Fringes of the EU* (2008). Meanwhile, Jennifer Hargreaves and Patricia Vertinsky's edited collection on *Physical Culture, Power, and the Body* (2006) represents a reminder of the importance of locating the sporting body within a wider context of physical culture.

However, the series is not simply about publishing the work of established authors. We have also published texts by rising scholars in the field. These include research monographs such as *British Asians and Football: Culture, Identity, Exclusion* (2006) by Daniel Burdsey (also shortlisted for the NASSS 2006 Book Award); *The Cultural Politics of the Paralympic Movement: Through an*

Anthropological Lens (2008) by P. David Howe; and *Olympic Media: Inside the Biggest Show on Television* (2008) by Andrew Billings. In addition to research monographs, we have published edited collections that push the disciplinary boundaries of sport into new and exciting areas of research. These include *Understanding Lifestyle Sports: Consumption, Identity and Difference* (2004) edited by Belinda Wheaton, and *Sport, Sexualities and Queer/Theory* (2006) edited by Jayne Caudwell.

And now, in keeping with the tradition established by the ten previous publications, we are delighted to introduce this edited text, *Marxism, Cultural Studies and Sport*. The purpose of *Marxism, Cultural Studies and Sport* is essentially threefold. First, it is to introduce students to the richness and relevance of Marxist and Marxist-inflected Cultural Studies approaches to studying contemporary sporting cultures. And with an impressive line-up of authors, each a key figure in the fields of Sport Studies, Literary Studies and Anthropology, the text certainly offers a key resource for students looking for contemporary justifications, applications and critiques of Marxism and Cultural Studies of sport. Second, it is a provocation to radical and critical scholars in Sport Studies to connect their research and analysis to the transformative potential of sport. A theme that permeates the text is the problematic of intervention – the question of what it actually means to be engaged in radical theory and social research. Third, the text is also an intervention into the mainstream disciplines of Sociology, Marxist Theory and Cultural Studies. As Ben Carrington and Ian McDonald note in their acknowledgements, a key motivation that initiated the book was 'the desire to advance discussions on critical social theory *within* Sport Studies *and* to attempt to insert sport as an object of study into mainstream debates within Marxist scholarship and Cultural Studies'. Thus, many readers familiar with the Sport Studies literature will recognize and appreciate the high quality of the contributing authors: David Andrews, Alan Bairner, Rob Beamish, Anouk Bélanger, Toby Miller and Garry Whannel. The editors, who each have a contributing chapter of their own, have also included contributions from scholars outside of Sport Studies, namely Grant Farred (Professor of Africana Studies and English at Cornell University, USA), Jayne O. Ifekwunigwe (Visiting Research Fellow in Africana Women's Studies at Bennett College, USA) and Brett St Louis (Lecturer in Sociology at Goldsmiths College, University of London, UK). Furthermore, in a clear indication of Carrington and McDonald's desire to bring sport to the attention of mainstream disciplines, the Foreword is by Harry Cleaver (Professor of Economics at the University of Texas at Austin, USA), and the Afterword by Michael Bérubé (Paterno Family Professor in English Literature at Pennsylvania State University, USA). We hope that their contributions signal that the study of sport need not and must not be consigned to the margins of academic debate and discussion.

Finally, it is appropriate in this reflective overview of the series to acknowledge the support and encouragement of the two commissioning editors with whom we have worked over the past five years: Simon Whitmore and Samantha Grant. They have shared our vision for the series. They understand and back our commitment to further the humanistic ideals of nurturing intellectual curiosity, of promoting progressive ideas in sport that serve the cause of social justice, human rights, equality and respect. Simon and Samantha have been crucial in allowing the series to evolve into what we hope is now considered in the academic community to be one of distinctiveness and distinction.

Jennifer Hargreaves and Ian McDonald
University of Brighton, UK

Acknowledgements

This book has been a long time in the making. Originally conceived in 2004, when we were colleagues at the University of Brighton in the UK, our proposal was enthusiastically received and supported by Samantha Grant at Routledge and is included as part of the Critical Studies in Sport Series. Since then, Ben has moved to the University of Texas at Austin, Samantha has moved to a different post within Routledge, and a lot of transatlantic communication and exchanges have taken place. Throughout this period, Samantha has remained positive and supportive, and we owe her a debt of thanks for her patience and professionalism. The final stages of the book's production were overseen by the expert eye of Simon Whitmore, who also happened to be the commissioning editor for our first edited collection, 'Race', Sport and British Society (2001).

Part of the reason for the length of time it has taken to go from conception to publication is that we wanted an edited collection that was more than simply a series of discrete or isolated chapters. We were clear from the outset that we wanted a collection in which the contributing authors would have a strong engagement with the central problematic of the book and with each other's perspectives, so as to give a sense of the book as a collaborative product in which the totality was as important, if not greater, than the sum of the parts. Furthermore, we wanted the contributing authors, all of whom are eminent scholars in their fields, to situate their own theoretical trajectory and politics more explicitly in their chapters. Some took to this exercise in reflexivity more easily than others, but all acknowledged the value of such an approach. We thank all of the contributors for the quality of their work, for their patience with us as editors, and for the critical but friendly exchanges that resonate through the pages of this book.

To assist us in achieving this coherence, we set about organizing a symposium in Austin, Texas, that brought the contributing authors together to facilitate dialogue and debate. We were grateful to receive funding to support the symposium from Routledge, UK, the Chelsea School at the University of Brighton, and the Center for Women's and Gender Studies, the Center for African and African American Studies as well as the Department of Sociology, all at the University of Texas in Austin. For two days in April 2005, most of the contributors to this volume sat around a table at UT and delivered their work in progress;

discussion and debate flowed. The value of this scholarly exercise is we hope reflected in the overall quality of the text. In addition to thanking our current institutions and Routledge for sponsoring the symposium we'd like to thank the ever-insightful contribution of Ross Dawson, who joined us in Austin.

The Austin symposium was capped by a one-day public conference entitled 'The Politics of Sport', where the contributing authors were able to rehearse their arguments to a broader academic audience. The critical feedback by the conference delegates was greatly appreciated, especially the sharp observations of John Hoberman and Harry Cleaver, the latter of whom kindly agreed to write the Foreword for this collection. We'd also like to extend a deep thanks to Michael Bérubé for agreeing to write the Afterword. One of the key motivations that initiated the project back in 2004 was the desire to advance discussions on critical social theory *within* Sport Studies *and* to attempt to insert sport as an object of study into mainstream debates within Marxist scholarship and Cultural Studies. In that regard, having writers of the quality and stature of Cleaver and Bérubé write on sport for the first time significantly helps us to achieve that goal.

Finally, the Austin conference also became something more. For it was around the mid-morning break on Friday, 15 April 2005, that news filtered through of the death of Alan Ingham, one of the pioneers of the critical sociology of sport. The afternoon session commenced in sombre mood, but with a renewed sense of perspective and purpose about the promise of the critical sociology of sport, thanks to an impromptu yet powerful and moving personal tribute to Alan by Rob Beamish. Rob spoke about Alan's intellectual rigour and generosity of spirit, and of his important contribution and passionate commitment to a genuinely critical sociology of sport.

It is wholly appropriate then, that we dedicate this collection to the memory and work of Alan Ingham (1947–2005).

Foreword

Sports?

Harry Cleaver

First off: a disclaimer. Although I've worked on and used Marxist theory for many years and have learned a great deal from several prominent contributors to 'Cultural Studies', for most of my life I have been largely an outsider to sports – not playing competitive sports, nor working in some aspect of the sports industry, nor even involved as a fan. My own intellectual and political work has never involved either 'sports scholarship' or political mobilization around some dimension of sports. Therefore, I was surprised to be asked to write this Foreword and accepted partly out of friendship and partly out of curiosity to see what kinds of relationships these authors have found, or imagined, among these three partially distinct domains of intellectual and political activity.

As I was satisfying my curiosity reading the essays in this collection, it gradually dawned on me that not only were all of the authors academics, like myself, but almost all appeared to be writing from *outside* the entire world that they were analysing. The one exception, I finally found, was Grant Farred, who, towards the end of his essay, proudly professed to being one of 'the most pathologically loyal' fans of the object of his study: Liverpool Football Club. What about all the others, I wondered? Were the others writing here also passionate fans? Were they actively engaged in some other way with the sports industry? Were they weekend players? Had they ever been? When I turned to the brief biographies at the start of the book I was no more enlightened as to their own direct experience in the world of sport. Hmmm. For a change of pace, and so no one be left in the dark about the origins of my comments, I decided to explain my reactions to the texts included here within a personal narrative. (If, like Toby Miller, you are contemptuous of such narratives as merely *banal fetishizations of the self*, then I invite you to go directly to the essays and skip this Foreword.)

Play, work and sports

When I was young, *sports* seemed to be just an organized form of *play*, and therefore something fun. *Play*, for me, was also quite distinct from *work*. I considered myself to be playing when I was free to exercise my imagination, skills and creativity with few constraints. Work was when those things were subordinated to activities imposed upon me by forces beyond my control – most immediately my parents but behind them, I would eventually realize, lay the many coercive structures of capitalist society.

A country boy, growing up in the 1950s and early 1960s among the cultivated fields and wild forests of Ohio, both my work and my play were strenuous and physically demanding. When I was five my parents purchased some land where we built a house, cultivated a half-acre vegetable garden, landscaped some two acres of yard, planted and managed an evergreen nursery and grew wheat on the rest of the land. All of those projects involved work, often hard manual labour: hauling construction materials, cutting and shaping them, nailing or screwing or bolting them together, cultivating, planting, watering, weeding, harvesting, canning and freezing, pruning, digging and balling trees and so on. The older I got, the more numerous the tasks I was assigned and the harder the work. Every day after school and for some of each weekend, I worked, often until evening. Vacations from school were usual and regular; vacation from all this work at home were brief annual events – in good years.

All of these activities were *work* in several senses. First, they were work in the vernacular sense of activities that took a lot of effort. Second, as a child, I also experienced them as work in the sense of undesired, onerous, imposed labour – things I had to do but had no desire to. Third, although in those years I didn't think in such terms, they were also work, or labour, as defined by Marx in Chapter 7 of Volume I of *Capital* where he analyses 'the labour process': people using tools to transform some elements of the non-human world into objectifications of human intentions, or will. Finally, all that work was also – to far too high a degree – the work of producing and reproducing labour power: the ability and willingness to work. We worked to supplement my father's low Air Force wage – with food from the garden and money from selling the wheat and evergreen bushes and trees. We worked to reproduce his labour power that he was selling to the Air Force, but we also reproduced that of my mother, my brother and myself. None of us thought of this work as play; we just did what we had to do. We worked to live.

So my early childhood 'leisure time' – mostly evenings and weekends – was largely made up of reading and play, which were often closely interconnected. I was an avid reader of adventure stories such as Howard Pyle's *Robin Hood*, Rafael Sabatini's *Scaramouche*, James Fenimore Cooper's *Last of the Mohicans*, Jack London's *White Fang*, Zane Gray's *The Last Trail* and Robert Louis Stevenson's *Treasure Island*. My play, sometimes alone, sometimes with friends, often involved strenuous play-acting inspired by those novels, including such activities as archery, making and wielding wooden swords and cudgels, hunting with bow or rifle in forests with my dogs, building make-believe forts, tree houses, ships, and so on. Long before anyone thought to create role-playing games like Dungeons and Dragons, much less video games such as World of Warcraft and the Age of Conan, my friends and I imagined and crafted our own worlds of rebels, medieval knights, pirates and frontier pathfinders.

Now, clearly, some of this play involved work in Marx's sense of the labour process: we crafted sticks into cudgels, scrap lumber into forts and tree houses.

Some of this play did not: role-playing Robin Hood and Little John with those cudgels, creating fantasy scenarios in those forts and so on. What work there was, however, was clearly subordinated to play. All of this unfolded at a time in our lives before any of the many 'functionaries of capital', as Marx called them, would try to structure and shape our play into the work of producing labour power. Other than the odd hour playing cards, or Scrabble, or assembling jigsaw puzzles, such was our *play* and much of it was quite strenuous, very 'athletic' – but it wasn't *sport*.

Sport was something organized by schools, such as basketball, baseball or (American) football. Although such activities struck me as more formal, less imaginative ways to *play*, they nevertheless seemed like fun. So I played them all and did, at least at first, have some fun. I had fun playing and I had fun watching my friends play. I also watched others play, at school and on television, to learn from them. Elementary school sports – in those days, where I grew up – were organized games and most of those who bothered to watch were other players or players' friends and parents. There were no *fans* in the sense of people who lived vicariously through the actions of others, people whose lives were organized around the activities of *their* teams, whose moods shifted up or down with success or failure. (Well, maybe there were a few parents overly invested in their kids' success, but we saw very little of the kind of fanatical parental behaviour – sometimes leading to violence – that has become far too familiar these days.)

That kind of sport was certainly more fun than the obnoxious discipline imposed in classrooms, more fun than school*work*: that is, having to sit still, be silent, do what we were told, the way we were told to do it and subordinate our curiosity to someone else's curriculum. It was also more fun than home*work* – where what would have been free time, time for play, was usurped by more imposed work. In the classroom the imposition of discipline was obvious; at home it was worse – we were supposed to impose it on ourselves. Because the ideology of schooling pretended that school was for students, to prepare us for citizenship, to expose us to the cultural legacies of civilization, it would be a long time before I recognized that schoolwork, like the work I was doing at home, was the work of producing labour power. Instead, I just thought schools were doing a lousy job of all those things they claimed to be doing. Organized sports such as baseball or basketball may have had rules, but for a few years it didn't seem weird to speak of 'playing' those games.

In junior high school, however, organized sports began to be transformed from play into something else. On the one hand, they began to take on, more and more, the character of a deadly serious, ferociously competitive endeavour in which fanatic coaches insisted on such frequent and intense 'practices' as to suck up all our available energy and leave us physically and emotionally exhausted. On the other hand, they were increasingly transformed into a spectacle whose primary purposes seemed to be to provide a distraction from issues 'better left to experts' and a training ground for future fans – spectators who repeatedly invest time, energy, money and emotions.

For those of us who participated in various athletic activities, we were, less and less, allowed to *play* games; we had to *work* at them. All of us little *homo ludens* were being reshaped into *homo fabers*. Coaches didn't just make friendly, useful, constructive comments on what we did; they designed strategies and 'plays' that we had to memorize and execute under their direction. We were being driven, step by step, into that world of alienated sports that Rob Beamish analyses in Chapter 6. Little by little, our will was subordinated to that of the coach. Beneath an inspiring ideology of rising to our potentials and developing strong group bonds lay a repressive reality of meeting someone else's goals and competing with each other to be part of the 'starting line-up' and not bench-warmers.

We were worked by coaches, but we were also supposed to learn to work ourselves. School sport, it turned out, was just like the rest of school. Just as in the classroom, 'practices', 'workouts' and games involved the imposition of supervised discipline; just as with homework, all of us budding athletes were also supposed to craft our bodies (by working out and managing our diets – alcohol was the taboo in those days, not steroids) and hone our skills at home. Years later I would appreciate Foucault's distinction between incarceration and centralized discipline, on the one hand, and decentralized biopower, on the other, because of these experiences in both classrooms and sports. Toby Miller's essay here on Foucault and the critique of sport provides a nice doorway to what seems to be a whole literature exploring these relationships.

Winning, whether in contests among ourselves or with teams from other schools, was the overriding preoccupation and passion of coaches. They, in turn, sought to inspire or intimidate us into the same focused fanaticism – whether by forcing us to pray together for God's help in whipping the other team or by yelling and berating us to try harder, play smarter. Growing up with a father in the Air Force, I couldn't help but see the frequent resemblance between the behaviour of our coaches and that of drill sergeants browbeating new recruits. Among those of us who were actually playing, competition was used by coaches to get us to drive both ourselves and each other to work harder.

Beginning in junior high but fully developed only in high school, all that competition, whether imposed or internalized, provided the drama of an elaborate spectacle, whether under 'Friday night lights' (football or baseball) or those of a gymnasium (basketball, wrestling, gymnastics) or the glare of the sun (track and field). I never ceased to be amazed at the number of students drawn to these spectacles – a few on stage (the players, the coaches, marching bands, drill teams and cheerleaders), most in the stands or bleachers (fans). Those on the field were easier to understand; they had the satisfaction of exercising their skill, and were performing for a big crowd and hoping for recognition and appreciation. Given the popularity of sports, performing well almost guaranteed enhanced social status in school. This was primarily the case for boys (male sports were the most valorized in those days) but also for girls who stood out in cheerleading and organizing pep club activities.

The thing that puzzled me the most were the fans. Whether at pep rallies or at the games themselves, how could so many people get so excited about what a handful of other people were doing? A few were friends of players or kids who played the various games informally among themselves – I could understand them. But the vast majority were not – and their enthusiasm was a mystery. Vicarious participation? Need for community being satisfied by participation in what Sartre called a 'serial group' – a group only because of a common point of reference? Yet, clearly, over time, fans knit themselves into something more than that through repeated interaction related to their team and its successes and failures.

What did seem apparent to me at the time was why the school administration supported and ploughed so many resources into these spectacles: they kept very large numbers of students busy – either involved in or worrying about their team's future chances. They were also a central mechanism for inculcating school spirit and identity among students who, in reality, had no control over the repressive organization of their schools, their curriculum or their time. Keep in mind that I'm talking about sports in rural Ohio where most folks either earned their income from farming or from working at the local Air Force base. It was a world much closer to the one portrayed in George Lucas's film *American Graffiti* (1973) than the big city world Grant Farred analyses in his account of Liverpool and Liverpool Football Club.

By that time my reading had widened considerably. While I had read Homer's *Odyssey* as an adventure story, that was impossible with Plato's *Republic*. Because by then I was working hard at being a receiving end in the fall, a center in the winter and a first baseman in the spring, Plato's emphasis on how athletic training could be good for something beyond mere play or amusement – for example, training for leadership – made some sense to me and gave historical perspective to some of the claims made by our coaches as to the virtues of personal hard work in sports. More and more, however, Aristotle's critique, in his *Politics*, of the Lacedaemonians for brutalizing their children through the imposition of excessive athletic exercise seemed all too relevant to what I was experiencing. The pitting of one team against another team increasingly reminded me of the ancient Greeks and their use of competitive athletics to prepare citizens for war. The spaces in which these so-called 'games' took place looked less and less like 'playing' fields and more and more like bootcamps and spaces of incarceration. After two years of trying to balance the demands by coaches on my time and energy with my other, more intellectual and playful interests, I called it quits and abandoned organized sports.

In my high school Latin courses we read the usual obligatory material, such as Caesar, Virgil and Cicero, but that literature led me to other Roman writers, including Catullus (poems) and Petronius (*The Satyricon*), as well as writers of historical fiction about the period such as Shakespeare (*Julius Caesar*, *Coriolanus*), Lew Wallace (*Ben Hur*), Howard Fast (*Spartacus*) and Henryk Sienkiewicz (*Quo Vadis*). One result was that, alongside a suspicion that high school sports and school spirit were conditioning for patriotism and war, the conviction grew that the sports spectacle and everything associated with it were more closely akin to the circuses of ancient Rome than anyone around me was willing to admit: vehicles of social control. When Stanley Kubrick's film *Spartacus* came out in 1960 (my sophomore year in high school) I fantasized about the revolt of an entire football team tearing off their uniforms at half-time, declaring their freedom and charging out of the stadium. Alas, it was not to be.

In high school I also became as hostile to competition in the classroom as I had become towards competition in sports. Like coaches, teachers and administrators encouraged competition, systematically pitted student against student and rank ordered us in a grade hierarchy. Where others studied hard for grades, I blew off such work, preferring to read for pleasure (including the Beats and French poets such as Rimbaud and Baudelaire), to listen to music (not rock 'n' roll but cool jazz, especially Miles Davis), to pursue biochemical research (on closed ecological systems) and, of course, to hang out with my friends. Sports events by that time were merely an excuse to get out of the house and were usually bypassed in favour of long conversations with my friends or sexual frolics with my girlfriend. I wasn't exactly Holden Caulfield but I was certainly deviant and not about to be a jock. Years later, after reading Foucault's *Discipline and Punish* (1975) and Peter Linebaugh's antidote to Foucault's top-down focus on control – his chapter in *The London Hanged* (1991) on eighteenth-century jail-breaker Jack Shepard – I rediscovered Caulfield and my own act of excarceration vis-à-vis sports. Reading Doug Foley's account of the 'Great American Football Ritual' in his book *Learning Capitalist Culture* (1990) made me realize that my friends and I were not the only ones who used sports events to escape school and parental control to enjoy brief times of freedom.

During my first year or so in college, I continued to eschew sports. Although there were no intercollegiate sports at the school I attended (Antioch College in Yellow Springs, Ohio), there were plenty of intramural sports like baseball, basketball and football. Self-organization and the absence of authoritarian coaches did something to restore the element of play to such activities and remove the character of spectacle, but I continued to prefer long rambles in the local nature preserve, science research, intellectual and political arguments and, eventually, political action in the Civil Rights Movement.

It was not until a year of study in France that I returned to any kind of serious athletic activity: I discovered the traditional culture of mountain climbing in the Alps. In that tradition, mountain climbing was overwhelmingly a non-competitive team activity of intimate cooperation and mutual aid in a startlingly beautiful but also frequently dangerous environment. Climbing the rock, ice and snow of the high mountains was physically demanding but not, in those days, a *sport* (unlike contemporary rock climbing). Achievement was celebrated but there was no hierarchical rank-ordering typical of competitive sports. As I had done when I did play sports, I learned from others (famous climbers such as Gaston Rebuffat and Lionel Terray) by watching their films and reading their books, but it was the beauty of the environment and the intellectual and physical challenge of dealing with the complexities of the high mountains that motivated me; there was no competition and no winning or losing other than succeeding or not succeeding in doing something you set out to do. Later, upon returning to Antioch, I would teach both archery and rock climbing – without any competition.

Spectacle and fandom, patriotism and war

Later, at Stanford University during graduate school, my personal athletic activities (mostly non-competitive mountain climbing in the Sierra Nevada Mountains) contrasted sharply with the Stanford administration's heavy investment in highly competitive intercollegiate sports of all sorts, but especially football. For the first time since high school I couldn't avoid seeing, once again, the twin phenomena of the sports spectacle and mobilization of enthusiastic fans. But this time it was on a much larger and much more commercialized scale and within a very different historical context.

The only commercial operations I can remember during the years that I was in high school were the selling of tickets and refreshments at sporting events and of annual school pictures and yearbooks. At Stanford and, I soon realized, at every university involved in intercollegiate sports, commercialization was rampant. Ticket and refreshment sales were limited by the number of games, but the merchandizing of T-shirts, sweatshirts, hats and all kinds of other junk to fans went on continuously. And while the university profited from such small-scale sales to individuals, it profited far more from the millions of dollars contributed by alumni whose school spirit was carefully kept alive through the sports spectacle. Universities like Stanford are non-profit in name and law only; they maximize their net revenues and, like openly profit-making corporations, plough those revenues into expansion. Spending money on sports was, among other things, just one more investment strategy. Although new to me, I soon realized it was not at all new in US universities. Thorstein Veblen and Upton Sinclair wrote eloquently of the subordination of 'higher learning' to business goals early in the twentieth century, long before the Trotskyist Ernest Mandell (whose 1972 book *Late Capitalism* inspired Frederic Jameson and is discussed here by David Andrews) decided that 'late' capitalism was driven by monopoly profits to invest in universities. (Economist Paul Baran of Stanford and Paul Sweezy, editor of *Monthly Review*, made an argument similar to Mandel's in their 1964 book *Monopoly Capital*.)

But if all this is true, then it also means, as Anouk Bélanger and Rob Beamish separately emphasize, that among the 'products' of the work of sports – in universities as well as in the professional sports industry – are not only labour power but the spectacle itself. And while the players (and even the fans) who produce those spectacles never earn a surplus value on their efforts, universities most definitely do profit. Moreover, as Brett St Louis makes clear, this profitability is not just a matter of individual colleges but of networks, organized in the National Collegiate Athletics Association and in conjunction with the out-and-out big business of professional sports leagues like the National Football League and the National Basketball Association. And finally, as Jayne Ifekwunigwe details, all this profit-making has become racialized and gendered through the mobilization of celebrity athletes such as Michael Jordan, Tiger Woods and the Williams sisters.

The Vietnam War build-up made linkages between competitive sports, school spirit and patriotism both more obvious and more immediate. In the midst of war the obligatory standing and singing of the national anthem at every game smacked of political conditioning in a way I hadn't noticed in high school. For many of us, football drills in the Stanford Stadium and ROTC drills outside it seemed frightfully parallel. So did the apparent ignorance of fans and patriots. Later I would realize that when it came to historical knowledge, fans were generally far more informed about their team's past activity than most patriots were about US history. As essays such as Grant Farred's demonstrate, the investment of fans in their consumption of organized sports generally involves not only money and the commitment of time and energy but the accumulation of a wealth of sports history – far more than most patriots' investment in learning about domestic conflicts and foreign interventions by their own governments. By the end of the 1960s, despite the Civil Rights Movement, the inner-city uprisings in places such as Watts, Newark and Detroit and the ongoing struggles against racism by groups such as the Black Panthers and Brown Berets, most self-proclaimed patriots could respond to demands for an end to the war in Southeast Asia only with pathetic chants of 'America, love it or leave it', or the even more moronic 'Commies go home.'

As such struggles unfolded on and off campus, the efficacy of sports discipline and sports spectacle-as-distraction was, at least partially, undermined. As millions of students mobilized against the war and against racism, a few athletes, like a few Hollywood actors, spoke up or took stands against the injustices of the day. Even those of us uninvolved with sports took notice and cheered the courage of medal-winning John Carlos and Tommie Smith when they raised black-gloved fists in protest at the Mexico Olympics in 1968. I say *partially* undermined because unfortunately, while millions saw the protest of those two athletes, their focus on the Olympics *per se* blinded observers to widespread repression taking place in Mexico at that time, including the Tlatelolco Massacre, which had taken place in Mexico City only ten days before the Games began – a massacre in which police and military shot 200–300 student protesters.

This year (2008) thousands are trying very hard to prevent the Chinese government from using the Games to distract attention from its widespread repression of protests in Tibet and elsewhere. As Garry Whannel makes clear, the Chinese government – like so many others before it – has been doing its best to 'market itself' through the Games. It has been refreshing to see how the Torch Relay – originating with the Nazis in 1936 (see Beamish's essay) – has been repeatedly subverted by protests all across the world.

The Stanford administration would have 1970 remembered primarily as the year Mexican-American quarterback Jim Plunkett won the coveted Heisman Trophy (and on New Year's Day 1971 Stanford beat Ohio State at the Rose Bowl), but for others it would be remembered as a year of struggle: of the anti-war movement and, later that year, of a Native American student intervention into Stanford sports.

For many Stanford students 1970 is remembered as the year of the Cambodian invasion and of the creation of the April 3rd Movement. That moment of creation occurred when several thousand students came together in Dinkelspiel

Auditorium to discuss what actions to take next to subvert Stanford's role in the war. It was one of those moments, evoked by Anouk Bélanger in her essay, when a space designed for spectacle was appropriated and transformed – in this case into a space of dialogue and collective self-determination. After much debate about the university's Applied Electronics Laboratory (AEL), where classified war research was being carried on to find electronic measures to counter Vietnamese ground-to-air missiles defending against US carpet bombing of cities and rice fields, the massed students voted to occupy it and shut down the research. Roughly 800 of those students rose up, trooped across campus to the AEL and did just that – holding it for eight days and converting it, as they had done with the auditorium, from a place of work for the capitalist state into another space of self-organization and action. Locks were picked, files were exposed, hidden research was made public, conference rooms were converted into daycare centres, and a commercial printing press in the basement was appropriated to produce a daily *Street Wall Journal* of revelations that was plastered up around campus.

For Native American students, 1970 is remembered as the year they created an autonomous group (Stanford American Indian Organization) and launched a struggle to remove the *Indian* as the school's sporting mascot – graphically portrayed as the profile of a Native American wearing a feather headdress – and acted out in costumed flesh at sporting events. While Alan Bairner in this volume, discussing Gramsci's Marxism, cautions about the limitations of such efforts, within the context of the university and the time, those efforts should be seen as only one terrain of struggle within a larger series of actions to open spaces and gain resources for students' self-determination. Not only did the struggle at Stanford succeed (after only two years the university administration capitulated and the Stanford *Indians* became the Stanford *Cardinals*), but it was only one thrust in a broader campaign that resulted in the creation of a Native American cultural centre, a new programme of Native American Studies, the hiring of professors for that programme and the mobilization of funding for students wishing to pursue such studies.

Those actions, and those results, must also be seen within two broader movements: an emerging Indigenous Renaissance that was happening not only in the United States but elsewhere in the world; and parallel struggles of other students for Black Studies, Women's Studies, Chicano Studies, and so on. Such efforts have often been linked and mutually supportive. Obviously, such struggles proliferated across academia in the 1970s, forcing university after university to better meet the needs of many of its more militant students.

That said, the degree to which such struggles and their success have retained their autonomy and continue to play an important role in the efforts to transform society or have been co-opted and neutralized by the educational system requires closer examination than I have given it. As a university professor myself, I am keenly aware of just how such co-optation works, as well as how the pressures to work (study for students, write and publish for professors) limit the time and energy available to pursue social change, on campus or off. From what I have been able to observe, within the university where I work as well as elsewhere, resistance to such repressive pressures and the struggle to use campus resources for autonomous purposes continue.

Marx

It was participation in the struggles of the 1960s, the Civil Rights Movement and then the Anti-Vietnam War Movement, that drove me to explore Marx's writings and those of his interpreters and then to critique both. Most interpreters, I found, read Marx as a theorist of capitalist domination, whether through economic or cultural means. Although frequently useful in identifying mechanisms of domination, neither approach centred our struggles and our ability not only to challenge but sometimes to rupture those mechanisms. But by the end of the 1960s and early 1970s our struggles had ruptured those mechanisms, had thrown the Fordist social factory and the Keynesian management of exploitation into crisis and had launched an irreversible cultural revolution – the most powerful components of which were based on the prioritizing of our own needs: of the waged for unalienated work, of women for an end to patriarchy, of so-called minorities for an end to discrimination and for greater self-determination, and of many for more rewarding relationships among themselves and with nature – all of which required the liberation of time and energy from work both to understand better those needs and to find ways to meet them.

Thus, along with many others, I reread Marx to see to what degree the man himself centred our role as collective subjects, our desires and our ability to reshape the world. Was his labour theory of value an a-historical theory of labour as the unique source of value (and thus a totalizing analysis that ignored other factors of production and other values – such as freedom from ethnic, gender or racial discrimination) or was it a theory of how capital was able to convert our abilities into mechanisms of domination? I had been taught the former in a graduate course on the history of economic thought, but eventually concluded that the latter interpretation was not only more accurate but made sense. My write-up of my analysis was subsequently published as *Reading* Capital *Politically* (1978, 2000).

In my reading, Marx's *Capital* does *not* constitute the totalizing grand narrative it has often been accused of being, but rather a theory of capital's effort to totalize the world – human and non-human – within its peculiar way of organizing life around the endless imposition of work maintained through myriad means. In other words in *Capital*, and elsewhere in his work, capitalism is analysed as a social system in which human agency, both individual and collective, is subjected to a series of constraints which people have resisted from the beginning and from which we have repeatedly struggled to free ourselves ever since. At the heart of those constraints is imposed work (which still occupies the vast majority of most people's time and energy – a brutal fact ignored by those who have argued that control via work has been *replaced* by control via consumption and other cultural means) and thus work involves, as Beamish points out in his essay, alienation.

But Marx's analysis of alienation – of how people are alienated from their work, from the product of their work, from each other and from the ability to realize their potential as a species – can be applied not just to commodity-producing waged labour, but to all kinds of unwaged activities that capital has been able to shape into forms which produce and reproduce one very singular commodity: labour power. Education is reshaped as schoolwork. Preparing and sharing food or taking care of children are reshaped as housework. Athletic activity is reorganized as sport – some waged, some unwaged. Each cluster of activity becomes work and each kind of work involves alienation.

In Marx's day more and more people, men, women and children, were being forced into waged work, so that they all had less free time; but I take issue with Ben Carrington's assertion that for Marx 'the leisure field is simply assumed to be a space for the re-creation of labour power'. In Marx's writings there are two major situations of leisure: that of waged workers outside hours of paid work; and that of the unemployed. It is true that in Chapter 23 of Volume I of *Capital*, Marx says what while the reproduction of labour power is an essential part of the reproduction of capital as a whole, 'the capitalist may safely leave this to the workers' drives for self-preservation and propagation'. But he was also acutely aware of workers' struggles for less work and analysed the history of those struggles in great detail in Chapter 10. Success in gaining shorter working hours meant more hours of leisure. More hours of leisure, even at subsistence-level wages, meant more time for workers to do more than simply reproduce their labour power. Indeed, the success of workers in reducing the length of the working day was clearly due, as Marx well knew, to workers using their leisure time to organize themselves into unions and into movements to fight for that reduction. Moreover, Marx also knew that capitalists realized this and actively intervened to undermine such self-organization. For example, he saw how capitalists actively sought to pit Irish and English workers against each other: 'this antagonism is artificially kept alive and intensified by the press, the pulpit, the comic papers, in short by all the means at the disposal of the ruling classes'. Obviously, such use of the press and the Church was predicated on the working class using at least some of its leisure time to read and to worship.

Marx was also aware of, and despised, propagandistic writings, such as those of Harriet Martineau, designed to convince workers to accept their fate as dictated by 'political economy'. Most obviously, Marx himself spoke to gatherings of workers and wrote for them. Clearly he did not think his lectures or his *Communist Manifesto* were contributions to the reproduction of labour power, and was delighted when the French version of *Capital* was published serially in a workers' newspaper. It is true that Marx dealt little with workers' use of their leisure time, but not because he assumed all they could do was reproduce themselves as labour power for business. On the contrary, what we have in Marx are the bare bones of an analysis of struggles in the sphere of 'culture'. As workers succeeded in working fewer hours a day and fewer days a week, capital would intervene more and more to avoid leisure time being used to enhance struggle and to shape its activities in its own interests.

From this perspective, many of the discoveries of bottom-up labour historians and the insights of cultural theorists, from the Frankfurt School through Critical Theory to Cultural Studies have been vital in identifying just how such interventions have been carried out, how more and more domains of human activity have been transformed into work for capital. As several of the authors in this collection point out, much of that work can be appropriated to complement Marx's own writing.

Seeking further for other interpreters who had recognized and highlighted the centrality of our struggles – in Marxist jargon the self-activity of the working class (multitude?) writ large to include all kinds of waged and unwaged persons – I discovered a series of Marxist authors as well as some anarchists with strikingly similar perspectives. One of the most important, for me, especially with respect to sports, was C.L.R. James.

Originally from Trinidad, and a participant in the Trotskyist movement, James parted ways from orthodoxy in the 1940s around a number of issues including the nature of the Soviet Union, the role of the party and the particularity of black struggles. But at the heart of his interpretation of Marx and of his politics was the recognition and appreciation of the ability of people not merely to resist, but to take the initiative in struggle against the capitalist constraints on their lives. Whether in his *History of Negro Revolt* (1938) or his *Black Jacobins* (1938), the struggles of the exploited formed the heart of his historical studies. That centring of our struggles made his work, that of the various groups he helped organize (the Johnson–Forest Tendency, Correspondence, Facing Reality) and that of those influenced by him (Socialism ou Barbarie, the Italian New Left) of intense interest to me.

But as I researched his work – and the tradition I would come to call 'autonomist Marxism' – I was surprised to discover his intense involvement in *cricket*, first as a player and fan and then as a well-known cricket journalist. Widely played not only in Britain but in its colonies and ex-colonies, cricket was a terrain upon which colonizer and colonized, or ex-colonized, could meet and battle in an overt manner. Little by little, reading James's book on cricket, *Beyond a Boundary* (1963), despite my inability to make head nor tail of the subtleties of the game described in his book, I began to see how it was possible for someone – in this case a black Marxist intellectual – to be passionate about an organized sport, to be a player, a fan and a professional commentator while still analysing it in a critical manner, taking into account race, class and the whole cultural, ethical and political context within which it has been played. Because, to me, it was a revelation, I must admit to being somewhat disappointed to find the book largely ignored in this collection. Ben Carrington and Ian McDonald relegate it to the 'pre-history' of Marxist analysis of sport, apparently because it does not 'explicitly draw upon Marxist categories' – despite Carrington's own recognition that, for James, sport 'could, under specific circumstances, offer a space through which oppositional politics could be fought and won'. It is not even mentioned in Brett St Louis's discussion of James's ideas in his chapter on 'Post-Marxism, Black Marxism and the Politics of Sport'. But this *is* a Marxist text, one written by a seasoned Marxist intellectual who had broken with his orthodox past, despite being written in the vernacular for popular consumption. As a book on the second most popular sport in the world, written by a Marxist deeply appreciative of the realities and potentialities of working-class autonomy, I would recommend it to anyone interested in exploring the relevance of Marxism to the political understanding of sports. I also can't help but wonder if there are any comparable analyses of other sports: for example, squash or rugby in colonial and ex-colonial areas.

Ian McDonald claims that the revolutionary element of Marx's work has been lost in contemporary cultural studies of sports. For me, this would be true to the degree that those studies fail to centre and analyse our self-activity and struggles to escape domination. The point, as the man said, and McDonald quotes, 'is not to interpret the world, but to change it', and changing it is only facilitated by theory when it helps us understand our own strengths as well as the obstacles that confront us. In Marx's own analysis, our living labour appears as the only source of whatever dynamism the system has. The possibility of our self-activity rupturing capitalist efforts to harness it appears as the only path to revolution: that is, getting beyond capitalism. Historically, resistance to being reduced to *mere workers*, as Marx says in the *Grundrisse*, forced capital repeatedly to innovate and find new methods of control: for example, by forcing people to work in factories where their work could be overseen and better controlled. Resistance in factories has repeatedly forced business to revamp the technological organization of work and the division of labour: for example, using machines to regulate the rhythm of work in order to decompose workers' self-organization. Workers' successful struggles at home for higher wages has forced the search for new markets, cheaper resources and new pools of more easily controlled labour abroad, through imperialism in the past, 'outsourcing' and Empire today (Hardt and Negri, 2000). It was workers' successful struggles to hammer down the length of the working day, week and year that freed children from mines, mills and factories and created mass leisure time, forcing capital to try to colonize that time through mass public schooling and entertainment of all sorts, including subordinating athletics to the sports spectacle. We have a consumerist capitalism and 'culture industries' only because workers have been successful in pushing up wages and other forms of income so that they have had money to spend, beyond subsistence, in the leisure time their struggles have freed from waged labour. In short, we have 'Cultural Studies' and the need for Marxist analyses to deal comprehensively with domain after domain of 'culture' because workers' struggles and capitalist responses have made them terrains of conflict.

Resistance and self-valorization

Resistance, properly speaking, involves people *resisting* phenomena such as exploitation and alienation. Workers *resisted* the extension of the working day; communities have *resisted* the destruction of homes to make way for the building of a sports stadium. But our struggles become more than resistance when we strive to find new ways of being and doing. Such struggles are acts of what Marxist Antonio Negri once called *self-valorization*, or moments in the exercise of what he more recently calls – following Spinoza – *constituent power*, or the power to create a radical newness beyond capitalism – newness capitalism must then try either to crush or co-opt. Almost always such radical newness (like all newness, even within capitalism) is crafted out of the existing elements and forms. Just as the history of capitalism has involved the capitalist takeover of (1) more and more human activities and their transformation into alienated work-for-capital and (2) more and more non-human parts of nature and their conversion into 'natural' resources and raw materials to be worked up by that alienated labour, so our struggles have involved, repeatedly, the liberation of activities and things from capitalist uses.

When nineteenth-century workers fought for the eight-hour day, one slogan was: 'Eight hours of work, eight hours of sleep and eight hours *for what we will.*' In other words eight hours for self-determined, self-valorizing activity of whatever kind they might desire. When communists from Germany emigrated to Texas in the wake of the failed revolutions of 1848 and created utopian communities in the Hill Country, they were not only continuing their struggles but trying to create seeds of a new world. When the children of those who stayed behind created workers' councils in Germany at the end of the First World War, they too were creating something new. When small groups of young people in the 1960s created 'communes' they were quite self-consciously creating spaces for *self-valorization* as well as launching pads for further struggle.

We need to be able to recognize, identify and understand such moments of self-valorization as they emerge within and against the constraints imposed by capital and the degree to which they are able, however temporarily, to break free of those constraints and craft something truly new. Such moments emerge repeatedly, all around us. It's just a matter of seeing them. How do children learn, despite being forced to do schoolwork? What have been the successes and failures of efforts to liberate learning from schools? How have people freed cooking and eating from the mere reproduction of their ability and willingness to work? How have people pursued athletic activities outside of capitalist organized sports?

These are not easy questions to answer. I have posed them to myself with regard to my own mountain climbing that most definitely took place outside the capitalist organization of sports. At first, climbing seemed like pure self-valorization; it heightened my awareness, developed me physically, provided an opportunity for close bonds with others, taught me about a part of the earth I had never known and I loved it. But further consideration forced me to realize that the degree to which my climbing might be judged to involve self-valorization depended not only on the content of the activity itself but its relationship to my other activities, especially work and political struggle. While climbing I was certainly diverting my time and energy from work, but what of the energy gained in climbing? When I came back from a climbing trip did I plough all that energy into work – in which case climbing, like daily sleep or weekend relaxation could be seen as reproducing my labour power – or did I use it for political struggle to resist work and explore other forms of self-valorization further? It was quickly obvious that I did some of both; it wasn't an either/or situation but a question of degree. And that realization made my use of that energy into a political project.

This collection provides a useful survey of capitalist methods in the management of sport for profit and for its own reproduction. Fortunately, it also contains a few references to resistance and even a couple of references to athletic activities that escape, to one degree or another, capitalist control.

The most sustained discussion of *resistance* is by Anouk Bélanger and concerns local reactions to things like capitalist investments in urban sports spectacles. She writes of resistance 'designed to insure more equal access, more democratic control of certain spaces, such as stadiums, arenas and parks, or in some instances, simply as a form of protest'. As she shows, such resistance may be narrowly focused or may be interlinked with movements against other capitalist investments involved in gentrification. Such resistance seems to have been widespread enough to force capital to negotiate 'with the local imaginary and popular culture'. She also points out, but does not explore, how 'spaces are also *used* by different people in various contexts, and these spaces can be put to use in divergent, potentially even subversive ways'. While things like our use of Dinkelspiel Auditorium at Stanford for anti-war organizing or the squatting of buildings in Italy for the construction of *centri sociali autogestiti* come immediately to mind, I wonder what kinds of subversive activity have been carried out in existing, capitalist-built sports facilities – other than the kind of momentary protests such as that by John Carlos and Tommie Smith mentioned above.

But such resistance has also proliferated outside of cities, contesting not urban but rural spaces. For example, resistance to the destruction of natural areas or farmland by investments in golf courses have occurred in Austin (Texas), Ragland (New Zealand), Sorowako (Indonesia), Avila (Spain), Mount Gyeyang (Korea), Pacaltsdorp (South Africa), Jalisco and Tepoztlan (Mexico), among many other places. Sometimes, such resistance has linked to struggles elsewhere: for example, the successful resistance of Austinites to the efforts of Freeport McMoran Corporation to build a golf course and luxury homes in the Barton Creek watershed drew not only upon the history of US government citations of Freeport for pollution violations in the United States but on the struggles of the indigenous Amungme in West Papua against Freeport's mining operations and resultant pollution to demonstrate Freeport's history of environmental (and human) destruction. Sometimes, such resistance has given rise to international campaigns of support, such as the case of the 'indigenous ecologists' in Mexico who were protesting Grupo KS's plans to build an eighteen-hole golf course and 800 luxury homes *inside* El Tepozteco National Park. The internet has been used to circulate news and mobilize support, across Mexico and across national borders, condemning the shooting and jailing of protesters and the sacrifice of nature to profit.

In many of the above cases the struggles have been truly those of resistance – of trying to *stem the expansion* of capitalist investment in sport complexes. But in some cases they have been aimed at *rolling back* previous losses. One such case was the successful campaign to reverse the loss of indigenous Maori land that had been taken from the Tainui Awhiro people in New Zealand and turned into first a military airfield and then a golf course. Protests and civil disobedience led to arrests and a series of court cases that ultimately culminated in the return of the land to the Maori for their own uses.

But beyond contestation over the space of sports lies the issue of the appropriation of athletic activities themselves. While capitalist organized sports spectacles seem omnipresent, do they truly succeed in instrumentalizing and totalizing all, or even most, athletic activity? Certainly some of the articles in this collection give that impression. For example, as David Andrews nears the end of his essay celebrating the theoretical insights of Mandel and Jameson, he laments: 'Thus currently there would appear to be no sustainable, viable, or, indeed, even imaginable alternatives to the late capitalist, corporatist, iteration of sport.' From what I can make out through this collection, there seems to be considerabley more attention paid to the resistance of the consumers (fans) and primary producers (athletes) of capitalist organized sporting events than to the appropriation of athletic activities by others.

Now, I don't know for sure, but I'd be willing to bet money that there are millions of people who engage in athletic activity *outside of capitalist management* – and by *outside* I mean outside of both professional sports and school sports at all levels. Some of that activity may, effectively, simply reproduce labour power; no doubt some people exercise just to be able to continue working, which is one reason why many businesses, from the nineteenth-century Krupp Steel Works to twenty-first-century Motorola Inc. have provided 'physical fitness' facilities for their workers. However, some, perhaps a great deal, of athletic activity provides both physical and mental energy that bolsters struggle rather than work for business. When waged workers use corporate facilities to regain energy lost on the job so that they can struggle for better working conditions, higher wages or less work, it's a nice piece of *détournement* (as the Situationists might say).

But most athletic activity that escapes capitalist management probably takes place beyond the walls of corporations. Perhaps not far beyond. According to Jeremy Brecher in his book *Strike!* (1972), Louis Adamic, the author of *Dynamite: The Story of Class Violence in America, 1830–1930* (1931) told how he visited Akron to find out how the great Depression Era wave of worker sit-downs had begun and learned that the first sit-down had occurred not in a rubber factory but at a baseball game when players from two factories sat down on the field to protest against a non-union umpire. The method was soon carried by the workers into their factories. Clearly not only was playing baseball helping those workers survive their obnoxious, unregulated conditions of work but it sparked an idea of struggle that swept through and beyond the US labour movement to become a worldwide tactic on all kinds of terrain.

As Ian McDonald points out, Marx's analysis of alienation *implies* the possibility of non-alienated self activity, including that of an 'empowering culture of sport and physical activity'. Reversing Marx's analysis of the four kinds of alienation, we can postulate that non-alienated athletics would presumably involve: (1) athletes' control over their own activity in individual and collective self-expression, (2) activity that creates bonds among players, (3) activity whose 'product', whether immediate satisfaction or spectacle, would be under the control of the players and (4) be organized as a creative realization of human species-being. Have such non-alienated athletics existed? Can we find moments of such non-alienated activity? When, where and to what degree? Determining the answers to these questions requires finding and analysing examples of self-organized sports. McDonald argues that 'sport does not have its equivalent of avant-garde artistic movements, or revolutionary cinematic and literature movements'. But does the absence of organized 'movements' mean the absence of self-organized athletic activity that contributes to social struggle, and potentially to revolutionary struggle? I don't think so.

Because I never played intramural sports in college, I'm not sure exactly how those self-organized athletic activities are appropriated by students. I don't know to what degree they merely contribute to the recreation of the students' labour power and to what degree they contribute to resistance to schoolwork. But I did see, in the 1960s, how within the Anti-War Movement, as well as among black and Chicano struggles, collective revitalization that built solidarity among protesters came in the form of pick-up games of baseball, basketball or soccer.

I have also discovered, in more recent years, how self-organized games have played a role on other terrains of struggle. Two examples. First, to avoid having the *migra* called in by growers, undocumented farm workers in Maricopa County, Arizona, launched a *huelga de tortuga* or partial slow-down strike in which they picked fruit in the morning but then played soccer in the afternoon. Not only were they having fun but playing clearly contributed to solidarity. Second, within the indigenous Zapatista Movement in the southern Mexican state of Chiapas, soccer is a common form of re-creation – not just of labour power but of a spirit of struggle that has not only challenged neoliberalism and demanded radical democracy, an end to racial discrimination and indigenous cultural autonomy in Mexico but catalysed the emergence of the alter-globalization movement around the world.

With soccer the most popular game in the world, I would encourage radical sports theorists to investigate what I can easily imagine to be similar uses of it in struggles elsewhere. And the same goes for other sports. What has been the role of pick-up basketball on inner-city courts across the United States with regard to the struggles going on in those neighbourhoods? What contribution has self-organized cricket made to struggles in Africa? Beyond the media-amplified spectacle of capitalist organized sports that seems to have preoccupied a great many 'cultural theorists', are self-organized athletic activities important parts of social movements and moments of what Félix Guattari called 'molecular revolutions' all over the world? I don't know. But I would like to know before I succumb to David Andrews' and others' pessimism about the possibilities of 'viable' alternatives to capitalist organized sports.

To radical sports theorists who say that they cannot even 'imagine' alternatives, I would recommend both the investigation of what people are doing right now, on their own, and what they have done in the past – the exploration of those attitudes and practices of human athletic and sports activity across the globe that were not or have not been instrumentalized by capital. The kind of research I am thinking of is the sort carried out by those who have searched for alternatives to Western attitudes and practices vis-à-vis the rest of nature. Dissatisfied not only with capitalism's rapacious exploitation of nature but with Judaeo–Christian–Islamic and Enlightenment traditions of an anthropocentric tendency to view the rest of nature as just resources for human use, self-described 'deep ecologists' have sought sources of stimulation for their efforts to imagine more biocentric approaches to the human–nature relationship. It is obvious to me that those explorations have been fruitful and have contributed much to the struggles to save the earth, and humankind, from capitalist exploitation and destruction. I suspect that similar research in the domain of athletic and sports activity might also be fruitful.

To conclude: coming from years of working with Marxist theory, but from outside the domain of Sport Studies, I have found this collection of essays to provide a rich and provocative introduction to what is clearly a wide-ranging critical literature. Beyond the insights offered by the essays themselves – interventions into that literature – is the abundant material referenced by each of the authors. Many are the articles that I marked 'Ref' in the margins; some I have already looked up, downloaded and read; many more I will explore in the future. I began reading this collection curious about what I might find. Reading has left me more curious than ever, not only about what else has been written but about the subject itself: the actuality and potential of sports as a terrain of struggle against capitalism and as one interesting form of self-valorization beyond it.

Reference

Hardt, M. and Negri, A. (2000) *Empire*, Cambridge, MA: Harvard University Press.

1 Marxism, Cultural Studies and sport

Mapping the field

Ben Carrington and Ian McDonald

Introduction

The cultural ubiquity, political prominence and economic significance of contemporary sport in global capitalist society present fertile terrain for its critical
socio-cultural analysis. Whether it's corporate and media dominated mega-events
like the winter and summer Olympic Games, state programmes for nation-
building and health promotion, or the cultural politics of 'race', gender, sexuality,
age and disability, sport is so profoundly marked by relations of power that it lends
itself to critique and deconstruction. Foremost in this critical scholarship are
Marxist and Cultural Studies approaches. The key issues addressed from these
perspectives concern not simply how we are to make sense of sport as a social
phenomenon but, as importantly, how we might effect social changes that could
challenge and undermine dominant relations of power. That is, these perspectives
are defined in large part by their emphasis on the dialectic of *interpretation* and
transformation of sporting cultures, institutions and practices.

Marxism and Cultural Studies represent contested and heterogeneous bodies
of thought and their application to the study of sport has not been conducted in
any uniform or systematic way. Furthermore, as theoretical traditions, Marxism
and Cultural Studies are not necessarily synonymous, although there are clear
overlaps between the two. Within Sport Studies, for example, the main thrust of
Cultural Studies emerges out of a critique of orthodox Marxist approaches which
raises the question as to what extent and in what ways do scholars working within
an explicitly Cultural Studies framework remain within the Marxist problematic
of interpretation and transformation. The aim of this introduction is to provide a
brief historical overview of the development of Marxist approaches within Sport
Studies and the subsequent growth of a Marxist inflected Cultural Studies of
Sport. It concludes by situating each chapter in this volume in relation to the key
problematics that have emerged from this history.

Three moments of Marxist and Cultural Studies approaches to sport

In this vein, it is possible retrospectively to posit three distinct but overlapping
'moments' or phases in the development of Marxist and Cultural Studies

approaches to the study of sport, all preceded in sound Marxist logic with a 'pre-history' moment. The 'pre-history' of a Marxist and Cultural Studies of Sport is represented by C.L.R. James's *Beyond a Boundary* (2000), first published in 1963 and a classic statement on the relationship between cricket, anti-colonialism and Caribbean society during the 1950s and early 1960s. The text remains an important marker for any discussion of the political significance of sport. Though the Marxism of James is well established (see Farred, 1996), *Beyond a Boundary* is not an explicitly Marxist critique, in the sense that it does not draw directly upon Marxist categories nor develop a theoretical framework for a 'Marxism of sport'. Rather, it is in its understanding of the role of the individual in history, the relation between colonialism and the social structures of the Caribbean, and the constitutive role of cricket as culture in the politics of resistance that James reveals his epistemological commitment to Marxism.

However, the first phase in the more formal Marxist-influenced approaches to the study of sport and society emerged in the wake of cultural and political radicalism of the mid- to late 1960s. This decade was the 'high point' for forms of anti-colonial resistance and Third Worldist nationalism that had emerged during the 1950s. It was a period marked by worldwide student revolt, Civil Rights protests, workers' strikes, anti-war movements and general civil unrest. In many areas of society, millions of people were actively engaged in exposing exploitative social structures, values and ideologies, in critiquing different forms of power, in searching for strategies of resistance and debating alternatives (Harman, 1988). It was out of this political ferment that the radical critique of sport emerged, led by North American academic sport activists like Harry Edwards (1969), Jack Scott (1971), Paul Hoch (1972) and European Marxists such as Jean-Marie Brohm (1978) and Bero Rigauer (1981).

Variously labelled as 'neo-Marxism' (McKay, 1986), 'Frankfurt Marxism' (Morgan, 1994) and 'Structural Marxism' (Young, 1986), writers from the nascent Marxist sociology of sport eschewed the false neutrality of extant positivist paradigms. They sought, instead, to connect sport to the radical movements that were confronting traditional, oppressive and imperialist structures of power. Howeyer, save for the ongoing struggles of black athletes for civil rights within US college and professional sports, culminating in the genuinely heroic and iconic 'black gloved' salute by Tommie Smith and John Carlos at the 1968 Mexico City Olympic Games (Edwards, 1969), the culture and institutions of sport were relatively untouched by the spirit of radicalism (Brohm, 1978). Yet, a significant body of work was produced under the banner of Marxism. First and probably most importantly, the complacent idea that sport was simply and only a positive force in society was debunked. Indeed, sport was condemned as ideological, divisive, alienating and exploitative. As the culturally and historically specific expression of physical culture under the conditions of capitalism, few redemptive qualities were seen to be present in sport. The limiting and damaging culture of sport was contrasted with the expansive and liberating qualities of play. Sport was, as the title of Jean-Marie Brohm's seminal book so evocatively captured, 'a prison of measured time'.

If the first 'moment of Marxism' identified the fundamentally exploitative and ideological nature of sport in capitalist society, then the second was more concerned with the limits and possibilities of resistance and transformation of these exploitative and ideological structures. Spanning a period of two decades from the late 1970s to the late 1980s, this was the formative phase in the establishment of the critical sociology of sport within the academy. It is useful to conceive of this moment as constituted by an early period and a late period: the early period was marked by an engagement and critique of neo-Marxism, while the latter period developed a more Cultural Studies-inflected Gramscian analysis of sport.

The early period of the second moment of Marxism – from the late 1970s to the mid-1980s – produced a sophisticated and complex materialist theory of culture as the basis for a (neo-)Marxist perspective of sport. Its leading theorists were Canadian academics such as Rob Beamish (1981, 1982, 1985), Hart Cantelon and Rick Gruneau (1982), as well as Alan Ingham (1982). The hallmark of this scholarship was a concern to comprehensively challenge the tradition of positivism and functionalism that were characteristic of approaches to studying sport. Influenced by debates on Marxism and critical theory in the social sciences, these scholars turned their attention to a critical analysis of the state and sport, highlighting the rootedness of sport within social relations of power, its ideological potency, its alienating effects and questioning its place in the project for social transformation. These writers (to differing degrees) maintained an explicit commitment to the politics of class and to the use of classical Marxist categories such as the labour process and alienation.

The later period of this second moment represented a shift away from such classical Marxist theory. Spanning the mid-1980s to the 1990s, and coterminous with the emergence of the post-Marxist turn in mainstream social theory (see Hall, 1983; Laclau and Mouffe, 1985; McDonald, Chapter 3, this volume), it signalled the influence of an explicitly Gramscian Cultural Studies that took as its point of departure the need to critique the perceived philosophical determinism and sociological reductionism of neo-Marxism. Key proponents of Gramscianism were British scholars such as John Hargreaves (1986), Alan Tomlinson (1999), Garry Whannel (1983, 1992), Jennifer Hargreaves (1994), as well as Australian-based academics such as Jim McKay (1986) and David Rowe (1995).

These scholars looked in particular to appropriations of Gramsci by Raymond Williams and Stuart Hall (with perhaps the work of Chas Critcher among others being an important conduit of Cultural Studies work into Sport Studies) and concepts like 'hegemony', 'cultural materialism' and 'cultural contestation' that seemed to permit a means of overcoming the limitations of 'vulgar' Marxism in favour of a non-structuralist and agency-oriented reading of Marx. As Alan Ingham outlined, signalling the shift that was taking place, Antonio Gramsci provided a way of synthesizing the dynamics of structure and agency (1982: 205–6):

A dialectical Marxism would require both a theoretical concern for the logic of capital and an empirical concern for experience. The logic, surely, is ever

4 Ben Carrington and Ian McDonald

present and cannot be relegated to some last instance of determination and experience, the mediator of culture, is not purely independent of the logic. Is not a concern for the relationships between capital's logic and lived experience integral to an adequate analysis of social formation, social being and social consciousness? Is this concern not the crux of Gramsci's contribution?

It was argued that although sport and society were of course mutually constitutive, the nature of this relationship was better conceived as part of the contested terrain of capitalist culture in the 'war of position' between different social groups and blocs. The key concerns related to understanding relations of power, exposing forms of domination and crucially highlighting 'spaces of resistance'. 'Gramsci's humanism', argues David Rowe (2004: 102), 'appealed especially to those Left-leaning social scientists and cultural critics made uneasy by the dismissal of the working class for being insufficiently revolutionary. Gramsci encourages intellectuals to "feel" as well as to "know" . . . therefore licenses critical analysts of sport to share – with reservations – the thrill of the sports stadium and the *frisson* of sports fandom'. The rise of Gramscian Cultural Studies of Sport during this period did much to shape the interdisciplinary field of Sport Studies itself. It attained a near-hegemonic position within the academy, but in the process assumed the status of commonsense thinking such that concepts like 'contestation' and 'hegemony' were gradually drained of any historical materialist framing. It was partly in a response to this expansive and increasingly depoliticized use of Gramscian concepts that the third moment in the historiography of Marxism and Cultural Studies of Sport needs to be located.

The third moment, developed in the mid- to late 1990s, represents an attempt to substantially rework and develop the cultural Marxism of the (late) second moment phase by drawing on non-Marxist perspectives in contemporary social theory while maintaining a grounded and engaged critique of relations of power in sport. As exemplified in the various writings of, for example, Toby Miller, C.L. Cole and David Andrews, a new generation of Cultural Studies scholars emerged. This work was characterized by an openness to developments in contemporary social and political theory, and particularly to forms of post-structuralist theorizing, while stressing the need for grounded analysis that revitalizes the interventionist 'spirit' of Marxism. This attempt at a kind of *rapprochement* between Marxism and contemporary social and political theory reflects the very different economic and political conjunctures between the mid-1980s, the high tide of New Right radicalism, and the late 1990s, which saw the 'return of Marx' to public and academic debates (Martin, 2002). It is notable and significant then that in contemporary developments in Cultural Studies of Sport there is an explicit engagement with 'political economy', 'late-capital' and forms of 'cultural praxis'. This latest, theoretically eclectic phase is an ambitious attempt to stride contrasting epistemic and metaphysical positions, around, for example, the question of language and subjectivity, as well as the critical issues of political change and social agency.

In outlining these moments or phases, we are not attempting a nuanced historiography of ideas. Rather, our aim is to identify the contours within which perspectives emerged, overlapped, became established, and were then superseded. Thus, while we argue for the analytical salience of these three phases, we are aware that any schematic historical mapping runs the risk of occluding other important moments and key theorists and that our reading is premised on a *particular* account of Sport Studies' encounter with *Western* Marxism. Significant omissions here would include, for example, the occasional commentaries on sport found in Theodor Adorno and perhaps more substantially within Pierre Bourdieu (and their own implicit 'dialogue' with the writings of Norbert Elias). There is also a strong degree of overlap between the Canadian theorists such as Gruneau, Beamish and Cantelon whom we place in the early period of the second moment or phase, and what their, primarily British, counterparts were doing in the late period of the second phase. These caveats aside, we still believe that the three moments of an academic-activist approach in the 1960s–70s, to a more critical and somewhat classical materialist critique of sport in the 1970s–early 1980s leading to the mid-1980s 'embrace' of Gramscian theorizing and hegemony theory, to, finally, the 1990s shift towards a post-structuralist inflected form of post-Marxism can be useful as a way to think about the developmental shifts within critical Sport Studies. In short, while discrete breaks rarely occur, these general shifts in the theoretical and political landscape can still be discerned.

Sport studies, capital and the absence of Marxism

Given the rich history of Marxist and Cultural Studies approaches to sport and the renewed interest in questions of political economy, labour and capital, if not of the writings of Karl Marx himself, it is surprising that there have been so few books in recent times that have explicitly brought these issues and perspectives together in one collection. Despite much theoretically innovative work within recent Marxist scholarship, sport has remained a marginal and often neglected subject matter. Similarly 'mainstream' Cultural Studies has yet to develop as sophisticated a body of knowledge on sport as it has done on other aspects of popular culture, such as music, film or television.

In fact it could be argued, somewhat provocatively, that the 'leading edge' work on sport and capital is being produced by professors of Economics, often found within business schools and departments of Marketing and Advertising. That is, the economic impact and social significance of sport have not been lost on those who seek to accelerate the effects of sports globalization. The reorganization of sport in accordance with the strictures of economic rationality, as David L. Andrews (Chapter 12) puts it, is being pursued as rigorously within business-orientated academia as it is within the boardrooms of the world's multinational companies. Recent examples here would include John Forster and Nigel Pope's (2004) *The Political Economy of Global Sporting Organisations*, Frank Jozsa's (2004) *Sports Capitalism*, Robert Sandy, Peter Sloane and Mark Rosentraub's (2004) *The Economics of Sport: An International Perspective*, and Aaron Smith and Hans

Westerbeek's (2004) *The Sport Business Future*. Indeed, it is not surprising that in 2000, Sage launched the *Journal of Sports Economics*, the first academic journal specifically dedicated to the economics of sport. However, the critical reader will search in vain for any serious discussion, let alone acknowledgement, of the relevance of the writings of Karl Marx, Marxist theorists or Marxian concepts within this literature, even though such texts are often founded upon an analysis of the global economic system that is profoundly indebted to Marxist thought and categories. Instead, discerning students will learn about economic growth cycles, elasticity of demand, profit maximization and effective market penetration strategies with passing references to the insights of Adam Smith and Milton Friedman – but alas, no Marx.

While there are books that have attempted to provide a more critical reading of these developments, that is to locate the emergence and growth of 'sports capitalism' as an active and deliberate process with often contradictory and damaging human results – as opposed to being the natural and spontaneous growth of the 'free market' based on the autonomous behaviour of rational actors – even these texts have generally given only token attention to Marxism as a body of thought. Recent examples would include the edited collection by Trevor Slack (2004), *The Commercialisation of Sport*, as well as Michael Silk, David Andrews and C.L. Cole's (2005) *Sport and Corporate Nationalisms* and John Amis and Bettina Cornwell's (2005) *Global Sport Sponsorship*. An account of sport that explicitly brings together questions of capital and labour, economics and culture, Marxism and Cultural Studies, is long overdue.

Marxism, Cultural Studies and Sport: rationale and overview

With the possible exception of Morgan's (1994) *Leftist Theories of Sport*, a meticulously argued, philosophically based liberal critique of Marxist analyses of sport, there is no contemporary book that directly engages the Marxist tradition and its application to sports scholarship. Indeed, while Morgan's account is an essential read for any critical theorist of sport, it remains theoretically and politically problematic in important ways: for example, Morgan's dependence on the radical liberal tradition renders his critique essentially idealistic and social democratic. Also, as it was published well over a decade ago, it cannot account for recent developments in the field. *Marxism, Cultural Studies and Sport* is therefore intended to address this gap and we hope that it will ultimately make an important contribution to the fields of Marxism, Cultural Studies and, of course, Sport Studies. Central to the book's project is an attempt to draw out the tensions and convergences between Marxism and Cultural Studies as the respective authors set out their critiques and theoretical positions. Three themes or 'problematics' underlie the collection as a whole:

- The place of Marxism in contemporary critical Sport Studies: Is Marxism an unfashionable and simplistic theoretical straitjacket that has been superseded by more sophisticated approaches?

- The relationship of Marxism to Cultural Studies in Sport Studies: Has Marxism been preserved or transcended by Cultural Studies?
- The meaning of *praxis* in Marxist and Cultural Studies: How is the relationship between theory and intervention understood in relation to the politics of identity, resistance, social transformation and social reproduction in sport?

As will quickly become apparent, there is no 'party line' as to how Marxism is understood and its relationship to Cultural Studies approaches to the study of sport. Some authors argue that Cultural Studies has had a deleterious effect on critical approaches to sport and that only a reformulated approach, which retrieves rather than rejects the central tenets of Marxism, can help us understand and potentially change the exploitative structures of contemporary sport in the West. Others reject the very basis of a split between Marxism and Cultural Studies, arguing that the latter has always been a form of Marxist analysis and that the attempt to draw a line between 'true' Marxist accounts based on political economic analysis and 'false' Cultural Studies approaches is to misunderstand both what Marxism is and what Cultural Studies does. While others simply set about the business of usefully employing the critical concepts of Marxism in order to affect Cultural Studies analyses. The collection's strength lies precisely in the polyvocality of differing authors, from distinct disciplinary backgrounds, addressing the core themes of the book in their own disciplinary-specific yet rigorous way. Most contributions proceed via an examination of the contribution of non-Marxist radical perspectives in Sport Studies, such as post-colonial theory, feminism and post-structuralism, in order to show both the flexibility and at times limitations of Marxist frameworks.

Part I: Marxism, Cultural Studies and Sport: The key debates opens with two chapters from the editors that attempt to sketch the broad parameters of the debates (the thesis and antithesis, we might suggest) between and within Marxist and Cultural Studies approaches to sport, which the following chapters then, and in true dialectical fashion, work through. Ben Carrington (Chapter 2) locates the problematic positioning of sport within both the Marxist and Cultural Studies traditions. He argues that orthodox Marxist accounts have struggled to account for cultural formation as being constitutive as opposed to merely reflective of economic relations and social structures, thus rendering the study of the content of cultural forms such as sport largely redundant. Against this, he argues for a rethinking of the category of culture itself as being determined, following Stuart Hall, only in the first instance and as part of a broader historical process in which culture is seen not so much as a way of life but rather as a way of struggle. The determinate politics of sport thus cannot be known in advance and an implicitly 'open' theorization of sport's political potential held on to.

Ian McDonald (Chapter 3) reviews the development of Marxist theory in Sport Studies, and argues that despite important contributions to our understanding of the cultural politics of sport made by both Gramscian and post-Marxist Sport

Studies scholars, the revolutionary aspect of Marx's work and of Marxism as a political project has been lost. This 'retreat' from revolution within the field of Sport Studies (and in the social sciences more generally) is located in a socio-historical context of widespread disillusionment within the academy at the possibility of a politics that is able to transcend the existing coordinates of global capitalism. The provocation, then, in McDonald's critique lies both in an insistence on the revolutionary kernel of Marxist theory *and* in an assessment of the historically accommodative nature of sport. Thus, invoking Herbert Marcuse's *One Dimensional Man*, McDonald posits that modern sport – one-dimensional sport – produces its own 'mechanics of conformity' that merely confirms the irreformability of capitalism's fundamental structures yet calls for the necessity of a sustained revolutionary praxis.

The chapters in Part II: Political Economy, Commodification and Sport are rooted in case studies of particular manifestations of and contestations with political economy. Anouk Bélanger (Chapter 4) provides an account of the spectacularization of city sporting spaces by urban developers. In a telling critique of extant theories of the spectacle, Bélanger presents a powerful case of how 'resistance' is played out within the sport spectacle, revealing the need for scholars to transcend the pitfalls of a sociology of denunciation on the one hand and an immersion in idiosyncratic details of the particular on the other hand. She insists on the need for a nuanced and multidimensional concept of spectacle that is capable of engaging with the paradoxes and ambiguities of cultural practices set in motion by the new urban entertainment economy. In concluding what she calls 'a critical political economy of sport as popular culture' she highlights the dialetical relationship between the urban sport spectacle and local popular cultures, thus recognizing the constitutive place of struggle in and over the spectacle.

Along similar lines, Garry Whannel's (Chapter 5) account of the power of the corporate media–sport nexus argues for the continuing relevance of Marxian analysis in a world in which media and reality appear to have collapsed into each other, in ways which place the fetishized commodity, the consuming individual and the promotional culture at the centre of human experience. Whannel critiques what he sees as the negative impact of the divergence of economic and cultural analysis in Western cultural analysis and calls for a return to a mode of analysis built upon a dialectical relationship of abstract theorization and empirical exemplification.

Rob Beamish (Chapter 6) uses the Olympic Games as a way to look at the political economy of sport within capitalist societies and the institutional frameworks within which elite athletes perform. Via a detailed and scholarly excavation of Marx's method and theory, Beamish develops a highly original account of high-performance sport as a particular form of alienated labour and so reveals the impossibility of Pierre de Coubertin's deeply humanist, albeit compromised, sporting vision. In addition, Beamish calls for a greater understanding of how sporting labour is 'deformed' in and through capitalist production: a call that raises the continuing relevance of Marx's key work on the commodity form, and the importance of *Capital* itself, for understanding the production of sport in contemporary society.

In Part III: The Sporting Poetics of Class, Race and Gender the authors focus on particular sporting texts and athletes, and work back towards a general theoretical evaluation of their mediated construction and political significance. Brett St Louis (Chapter 7) provides an analysis of the position of African-American 'student-athletes' by drawing and expanding upon what we might loosely describe as the 'black Marxist tradition'. St Louis reads C.L.R. James, and other radical black intellectuals, against the insights of post-Marxist thinkers such as Laclau and Mouffe in order to produce a complex Bourdieuian analysis of race, class and sport. He shows how racism is reproduced in articulation with class and in so doing retrieves James from the 'pre-history' of a Marxism of sport and places him firmly in the present. The tragic tale of how Maurice Clarett, a National Football Champion with Ohio State University who tried to challenge the National Football League's (NFL) draft policy, went from being considered one of America's top football talents to being sentenced in 2006 to over seven years in prison for aggravated robbery and carrying a concealed weapon shows both the limits to resisting the 'capitalist-athletic complex' and what consequences can befall those who try.

Jayne Ifekwunigwe (Chapter 8) provides an account of the lives and careers of the tennis stars Venus and Serena Williams. Ifekwunigwe examines how the Williams sisters have come to embody a new hip-hop black feminist world view that simultaneously presents a confident and emboldened model of black femininity while simultaneously acquiescing to transnational corporate patronage. The chapter provides a novel reading of the ethical dilemmas and contradictory positions that the 'Ghetto Cinderellas' pose for progressive politics in the post-Civil Rights era and the age of celebrity.

Grant Farred (Chapter 9) develops a literary Cultural Studies approach in order to produce an ethical mediation on the relationship between capital and sport. Farred achieves this through a novel and idiosyncratic reading of the city of Liverpool, Liverpool Football Club, its home ground of Anfield, and the heroic figures of two 'local boys made good': the players Steven Gerrard and Robbie Fowler. The Socratic moment of solitude is imaginatively used as a means to think through the ways in which class is spatialized, the importance of locality, belonging and solidarity to working-class fan cultures, the ethical relationship between the public sporting and the private selves, and how sporting spaces may still offer tangible if contradictory moments for the realization of class consciousness and solidarity, even amid growing and rampant hyper-commercialization.

Finally, in Part IV: Key Concepts, Critical Theorists three of the leading contemporary social theorists of sport and popular culture revisit some of the key Marxist concepts and thinkers that have been central to Sport Studies' development over the past two decades. Toby Miller (Chapter 10) provides a systematic exegesis of perhaps *the* pivotal figure in the debates over the post-structuralist turn from (classical) Marxism to (post-Marxist) Cultural Studies, namely

Michel Foucault. Miller calls for a revaluation of Foucault's latent Marxism, making a robust and powerful argument for the continued need and relevance of post-structuralist modes of theorizing. Contrary to many orthodox accounts of Foucault that read the French theorist as *anti*-Marxist, Miller suggests that Foucault's work was always in dialogue with Marxism and that Sport Studies scholars, among others, can usefully draw upon the legacy of this 'post-industrial Marx'.

If Foucault can be seen as the pivotal *theorist* in producing the 'linguistic shift' within social theory and the turn to questions of discourse and subjectivity, then a similar argument can be made for 'hegemony' in marking the *conceptual* moment of post-Marxism. Alan Bairner (Chapter 11) attempts to recover the Marxist Gramsci from his modern-day (mis)appropriators by examining how the concept of 'hegemony' fits within Antonio Gramsci's wider writings and theoretical framework. Bairner argues that within Cultural Studies in general and Sport Studies in particular the concept of hegemony has been detached, with disastrous effects, from its necessary mooring within a radical, revolutionary Marxist tradition and then reduced to little more than a way to describe any form of cultural 'resistance'. This, Bairner suggests, ultimately devalues both the concept of resistance and the actual, real world politics of class struggle against capitalism.

In the final chapter of this volume David Andrews (Chapter 12) provides a detailed rereading of the Marxist cultural critic and theorist Frederic Jameson and his work on 'late capitalism', via a detour through the earlier writings of Ernest Mandel. Andrews suggests that sport has become the leading example of the hyper-commercialization of the contemporary culture industry. Returning to the concept of the spectacle that Bélanger examines in the beginning of Part II, Andrews suggests that the colonization of sporting cultures by the market is now so complete that corporate sport spectacle has become, somewhat pessimistically, the logical and maybe only viable option for the production and consumption of sport in the US and much of the overdeveloped West. If there is hope for another (sporting) world, Andrews suggests that the intellectual tools for reconstituting the optimism of the intellect are to be found in the type of critical cultural Marxism that Jameson offers.

Given the wider tensions within social theory between Marxism and those forms of Cultural Studies associated with the post-Marxist moment, we asked our contributors to be more explicit than they may have been until now on how they envisioned *their own work* in relation to these debates. Some authors were more successful than others in meeting this 'request'. Regardless, all the contributions to this volume help to clarify, delineate and extend our understanding of the continuing relevance of Marxism, its relationship to Cultural Studies and how each can be productively used to help make sense of contemporary sporting cultures. Thus each of these chapters, though self-contained, contributes to a dialogue over the status and meaning of Marxism and Cultural Studies in a radical theory of sport, both within and beyond the disciplinary boundaries of Sport

Studies, and collectively mark the next stage in the (r)evolution of critical approaches to sport, society and social change.

References

Beamish, R. (1981) 'Central Issues in the Materialist Study of Sport as Cultural Practice', in S. Greendorfer and A. Yiannakis (eds) *Sociology of Sport: Diverse Perspectives*. New York: Leisure Press, pp. 38–55.

Beamish, R. (1982) 'Sport and the Logic of Capitalism', in H. Cantelon and R. Gruneau (eds) *Sport, Culture and the Modern State*. Toronto: University of Toronto Press, pp. 141–97.

Beamish, R. (1985) 'Understanding Labor as a Concept for the Study of Sport', *Sociology of Sport Journal* 2, pp. 357–64.

Brohm, J.M. (1978) *Sport: A Prison of Measured Time*. London: Ink Links.

Cantelon, H. and Gruneau, R. (eds) (1982) *Sport, Culture and the Modern State*. Toronto: University of Toronto Press.

Edwards, H. (1969) *The Revolt of the Black Athlete*. New York: Free Press.

Farred, G. (ed.) (1996) *Rethinking C.L.R. James*. Cambridge: Blackwell.

Gruneau, R. (1983) *Class, Sports and Social Development*. Amherst: University of Massachusetts Press.

Hall, S. (1983) 'The Problem of Ideology – Marxism without guarantees', in B. Matthews (ed.) *Marx: A Hundred Years on*. London: Lawrence and Wishart, pp. 57–84.

Hargreaves, J.A. (1994) *Sporting Females*. London: Routledge.

Hargreaves, J.E. (1986) *Sport, Power and Culture*. Cambridge: Polity Press.

Harman, C. (1988) *1968: The Fire Last Time*. London: Bookmarks.

Hoch, P. (1972) *Rip off the Big Game*. New York: Anchor Books.

Howell, J.W., Andrews, D.L. and Jackson, S.J. (2002) 'Cultural and Sport Studies: An Interventionist Practice', in J. Maguire and K. Young (eds) *Theory, Sport and Society*. Oxford: JAI Press, pp. 151–77.

Ingham, A. (1982) 'Sport, Hegemony and the Logic of Capitalism: Response to Hargreaves and Beamish', in H. Cantelon and R. Gruneau (eds) *Sport, Culture and the Modern State*. Toronto: University of Toronto Press, pp. 198–208.

James, C.L.R (2000) *Beyond a Boundary*. London: Serpent's Tail.

Laclau, E. and Mouffe, C. (1985) *Hegemony and Socialist Strategy: Towards a Radical Democratic Politics*. London: Verso.

Martin, R. (2002) *On Your Marx: Relinking Socialism and the Left*. Minneapolis: University of Minnesota Press.

McKay, J. (1986) 'Marxism as a Way of Seeing: Beyond the Limits of Current "Critical" Approaches to Sport', *Sociology of Sport Journal* 3, pp. 261–72.

Morgan, W. (1994) *Leftist Theories of Sport: A Critique and Reconstruction*. Illinois: University of Illinois Press.

Rigauer, B. (1981) *Sport and Work*. New York: Columbia University Press.

Rowe, D. (1995) *Popular Cultures: Rock Music, Sport and the Politics of Pleasure*. London: Sage.

Rowe, D. (2004) 'Antonio Gramsci: Sport, Hegemony and the National-Popular', in R. Guilianotti (ed.) *Sport and Modern Social Theorists*. London: Polity, pp. 97–110.

Scott, J. (1971) *The Athletic Revolution*. New York: Free Press.

Tomlinson, A. (1999) *The Game's up: Essays in the Cultural Analysis of Sport, Leisure and Popular Culture*. Aldershot: Arena.

Vinnai, G. (1973) *Football Mania*. London: Ocean Books.

Whannel, G. (1983) *Blowing the Whistle: The Politics of Sport*. London: Pluto Press.

Whannel, G. (1992) *Fields in Vision*. London: Routledge.

Young, T.R. (1986) 'The Sociology of Sport: Structural Marxist and Cultural Marxist Approaches', *Sociological Perspectives* 29(1), pp. 3–28.

Part I

Marxism, Cultural Studies and sport

The key debates

2 Sport without final guarantees
Cultural Studies/Marxism/sport

Ben Carrington

> Must we still cite Marx as an authority in order to say 'I am not a Marxist'? What is the distinguishing trait of a Marxist statement? And who can still say 'I am a Marxist'?
>
> Jacques Derrida, *Spectres of Marx*

> Had Marxism not existed, 'post-Marxism' would have had to invent it, so that 'deconstructing' it once more would give the 'deconstructionists' something further to do. All this gives Marxism a curious life-after-death quality. It is constantly being 'transcended' and 'preserved'.
>
> Stuart Hall, 'The Problem of Ideology'

Introduction

This chapter provides a schematic outline of the relationship between Cultural Studies and Marxism. It seeks to clarify both the points of departure and moments of convergence between these two intellectual and political projects, particularly as they pertain to an analysis of contemporary (sporting) cultures. It is suggested that the claims of Marxism's death have been much overstated. In fact, while it might be somewhat of an exaggeration to claim that 'Marxism is experiencing a rebirth' (D'Amato, 2006: 11), it is certainly the case that there has recently been something approaching a revival of interest in Marxist *theory* as well as related questions concerning political economy and class (for example, see Cleaver, 2000, Edensor, 2000, Burawoy and Wright, 2001, Martin, 2002, Wilson, 2002, Ray, 2003, Aronowitz, 2003, Byrne, 2005, Lawler, 2005, Joseph, 2006, Chan and Goldthorpe, 2007 and Dworkin, 2007).[1]

As argued in the introduction to this volume, while we can trace a linear, if uneven, series of 'moments' in the critical history of Marxist-influenced work on sport, whether we as yet have a coherent and integrated body of work that could be labelled 'a Marxism of sport' is questionable. This is not to suggest that writers self-identified as Marxist (as well as perhaps a larger number of fellow travellers) have not produced insightful accounts and critiques of sport within capitalist societies. They have done and continue to do so, as this collection itself shows. The point, rather, concerns the problematic ontological status that culture in general and sport in particular hold within what is often labelled as orthodox or classical Marxism. I suggest that Cultural Studies, properly understood, becomes productive at precisely that moment where we reach the limits of orthodox Marxist analysis. Whether that moment is read as a rupture/break or an extension/ revision depends on which side of the 'divide' one is located. This chapter does not resolve this tension. Merely, it is an attempt at clarifying what is at stake within such arguments in the hope that writers and theorists of the left will engage in less dogmatic rejections of each other's work as either being not properly 'critical' or as in some sense redundant and anachronistic. More specifically for this project, such an approach will help towards more engaged analyses that appreciate sport's protean, dialectic nature as a site of everyday domination *and* resistance; a space of joy and creativity *and* routine mechanized existence. That is, to develop ways to conceptualize sport's potential for (embodied) emancipation and freedom but without any final guarantees as to its political effectivity.[2]

Marxism/culture

In 2005 BBC Radio 4 ran a poll to find the 'world's greatest philosopher'. To the bemusement and surprise of some, the British middle-class listeners voted Karl Marx as the clear winner, with 28 per cent of the vote, ahead of David Hume with 13 per cent and Ludwig Wittgenstein with 7 per cent.[3] As Francis Wheen noted, the poll results indicated 'that Marx's portrayal of the forces that govern our lives – and of the instability, alienation and exploitation they produce – still resonates, and can still bring the world into focus. Far from being buried under the rubble of the Berlin Wall, he may only now be emerging in his true significance' (2005: 27; see also Wheen, 2006). In short, Marx(ism) still matters.

It is undoubtedly the case that with the latest phase of global capitalism, we have not in fact witnessed the end of ideological evolution and history and with it the so-called triumph of neo-liberal democratic capitalism. The globe appears as fractured and as riven by conflict over scarce resources and the politics of wealth distribution as at any stage in its recent history. Divisions within societies between the wealthiest few and the overworked rest continue to expand, with many countries, such as the USA, experiencing real-term declines in the average wages of workers, despite increases in productivity, while at the same time the top 10 per cent have seen their incomes grow and the super-rich accumulate even greater levels of wealth.[4] In 2006 the top twenty Wall Street fund managers earned an *average* of $658 million, with Renaissance Technologies' James Simons topping the list with *personal* annual earnings of $1.5 billion (Ozanian and Schwartz, 2007). With the 2007 publication of *Forbes* magazine's 'Forbes 400', for the first time $1 billion was not enough even to make it on to the list of the richest Americans. The collective wealth of the top 400 was estimated at a staggering $1.54 trillion (Miller, 2007). The American investor Warren Buffett topped *Forbes'* 2008 list of the world's super-rich with a personal wealth of some $62 billion (Miller, 2008). With such concentration of wealth in the hands of the few and as multinational corporations report record profits despite, and in some cases because of, global economic uncertainty, Marx's notion of the 'wealth of the nation and the poverty of the people' (Marx, 1990: 886) has rarely rung as true. The expansion of capital continues, the relative autonomy of civil society shrinks, citizens become consumers, 'choice' itself is fetishized and competition displaces equity as the *modus operandi* for how public services should be evaluated.

Yet counterveiling forces of (global) protest and resistance 'from below', be they non-state actors and the (new) social movements of various types, or the more traditional forms of organized labour and their aligned parties, continue to offer alternative visions of how another world is possible (Piven, 2008). The legitimacy of the global economic structures installed by capital, underpinned by a military-industrial complex based upon pre-emptive wars, torture and a repudiation of human rights, is increasingly being brought into question on the grounds of justice and equality, environmental damage and sustainability. In this context it is not surprising that Marxist thought and concepts remain indispensible as guiding tools in understanding and potentially changing the current global malaise.

'Culture', of course, has not escaped these tumultuous changes. Indeed, it could be argued that sport is one site where these broader transformations and processes – and the varied oppositions to them – can be most clearly witnessed: as David Andrews (see Chapter 12) puts it, this domain is the most evocative of the current late capitalist condition. But what does a Marxist theory of sport look like, and is a truly orthodox, revolutionary account even possible? An obvious starting point would be to go back to the writings of Marx himself as a way to reconstruct a unified and fully developed theory of culture from which we could 'read off' the position of (popular) culture in general and then of sport. However, there are a number of limitations to this approach. It is unlikely that such an account would be sensitive to the complexity and nuances of contemporary culture. Marx remains pre-eminent as a theorist of capitalist (economic) production but his writings offer little in the way of an analysis of cultural reproduction. The leisure field is simply assumed to be a space for the *re*-creation of labour power. Beyond that 'function' culture ceases to do anything much more than prepare the working classes for wage-labour. Further, such an approach in trying to work out what Marx *himself* said on the matter of culture, as opposed to political economy, while of historical interest, is not as important as the attempt to work with and *extend* the analytical and conceptual tools that Marxism provides: it is the notions of class formation and consciousness, ideological reproduction, commodity fetishization, labour power and alienation, surplus, use and exchange value, and the nature of political struggle itself that remain of paramount significance.

The latter theoretical discussions, of course, require us to go 'back to Marx' in the sense of understanding the contingent historical context of the emergence of such terms and to be careful that our reading of them is consistent with Marx's overall theoretical framework. However, what needs to be resisted is the notion that simply extracting those concepts out of that moment of European industrial capitalism and applying them to our current twenty-first-century cultural condition can be done without any remodelling. As Raymond Williams (1983: 265) noted:

Marx himself outlined, but never fully developed, a cultural theory. His casual comments on literature, for example, are those of a learned, intelligent man of his period, rather than what we now know as Marxist literary criticism. On occasion, his extraordinary social insight extends a comment, but one never feels that he is applying a theory. Not only is the tone of his discussion of these matters normally undogmatic, but also he is quick to restrain, whether in literary theory or practice, what he evidently regarded as an over-enthusiastic, mechanical extension of his political, economic and historical conclusions to other kind of fact.

To reiterate, this does *not* mean we should not go back to Marx's own writings in order to see what can usefully be retrieved from his extensive *oeuvre*. It is precisely this type of dedicated scholarship and careful, systematic rereading of 'Marx in the original' that underpins Rob Beamish's contribution to this collection (see Chapter 6) which at its best avoids the pitfalls of a mechanistic reading of Marx. Similarly, Alan Bairner's (Chapter 11) diligent rereading of Antonio Gramsci shows that the selective extraction of concepts such as hegemony that are divorced from Gramsci's political project and his other key writings can lead to an impoverished understanding of what Gramsci intended, and our own ability to make productive use of him.

Put simply, Marx's writings, the key concepts that have emerged from his work, and the debates that have ensued from theorists self-identified as Marxist represent a body of knowledge that demands a recognition of its full complexity. This is important in order to avoid slipping too readily into an account that homogenizes all Marxist-inspired scholarship as 'deterministic' due to a narrow reading of the preface of 'A Contribution to the Critique of Political Economy', where Marx (2000) briefly outlines how the relations of production constitute an economic structure of society providing the 'real' foundation upon which all other 'superstructural' forms of social, political and spiritual consciousness rise.[5] The key question, as Williams reminds us, is whether the 'formula' of the base/superstructure – which in various formulations has framed Marxist accounts of culture – was meant as a literal reading or 'no more than an analogy' (1983: 267), both of which pose very different implications as to how we should view 'superstructural' activities such as sport, as well as their ideological effects and political possibilities. As Engels emphatically stated in his letter to Joseph Bloch:

> According to the materialist conception of history, the determining element in history is *ultimately* the production and reproduction in real life. More than this neither Marx nor I have ever asserted. If therefore somebody twists this into the statement that the economic element is the *only* determining one, he transforms it into a meaningless, abstract and absurd phrase.
>
> (Cited in Williams, 1983: 267)

It was precisely this complexity of determinations, the attempt to map, in more concrete detail, the precise ways in which these 'interactions' between differing levels of society play out, that formed the intellectual and conceptual basis for Cultural Studies as it began to emerge out of adult and workers' educational associations in Britain during the 1940s and 1950s and latterly materialized in the writings of Richard Hoggart, E.P. Thompson and especially Raymond Williams and Stuart Hall (Carrington, 2001). I would argue therefore that Cultural Studies has always worked within and against a Marxist problematic (see also Miller, Chapter 10). It is precisely this attempt to construct a nuanced and non-mechanistic reading of (popular) culture and ideology that draws upon but cannot be reduced to Marx's early formulations that underpins both Williams' notion of 'cultural materialism', with its acknowledgement of the importance of avoiding any idealist conceptualization of culture, and Hall's account of the 'problem of ideology'. To jettison, in other words, the 'dogmatic retention' (Williams, 1977: 68) of an account of ideology as simply 'false consciousness' towards a formulation that acknowledges complexity. As Hall (1981: 232–3) argued in his essay 'Notes on Deconstructing "The Popular"':

> The study of popular culture keeps shifting between these two, quite unacceptable, poles: pure 'autonomy' or total incapsulation . . . I think there is a continuous and necessarily uneven and unequal struggle, by the dominant culture, constantly to disorganise and reorganise popular culture; to enclose and confine its definitions and forms within a more inclusive range of dominant forms. There are points of resistance; there are also moments of supersession. This is the dialectic of cultural struggle. In our times, it goes on continuously, in the complex lines of resistance and acceptance, refusal and capitulation, which make the field of culture a sort of constant battlefield. A battlefield where no once-for-all victories are obtained but where there are always strategic positions to be won and lost.

In part, this shift – or what some may call a break – with(in) Marxism was at once political as well as theoretical. That is, neither Williams nor Hall believed that a breakdown in the capitalist order was imminent and both believed that culture should be accorded a constitutive, not merely reflective, role in forming class consciousness. Williams arguably held on to the view that the working class could perhaps still be a revolutionary agent and that the long revolution of social change had not ended (see Williams, 1989). Hall, on the other hand, and certainly by the 1980s, is clear that the social structures of Western societies had become so complex that a self-conscious and revolutionary working-class subject – as represented in structuralist terms – no longer existed and that the terrain and nature of politics itself had fundamentally shifted.[6] Yet for Hall the serious intellectual work of reading Marx was never about a simple rejection or repudiation. In contrast to some rather one-sided readings of Hall, the project was, as his essay 'The Problem of Ideology: Marxism without Guarantees' makes clear, an attempt at *reconstructing* and not merely deconstructing a materialist theory of ideology. It necessitated understanding that the mystifying and 'distorting' effects of ideology did not necessarily mean that such beliefs were 'false'. That in fact we could develop a 'Marxist' conceptualization of ideology that instead understood the distortions produced by dominant ideologies as *partial accounts* and the forces of production as 'real' only in the sense of the analytical primacy given to the economic within the broader circuits of capitalist production and reproduction. A Marxism without (final) guarantees understands 'determinacy' as the setting of limits and parameters, an attempt to shape the conditions of material existence within which politics becomes possible, but without the 'absolute predictability of particular outcomes' (Hall, 1996: 45) or the possibility of finite conceptual closure: a determination, in other words and *contra* Althusser, of the economic over the social only in the *first instance*. This is the socio-historical and theoretical moment of Cultural Studies.

And Marx is claiming that it was offside . . .

Sport occupies a somewhat problematic position within revolutionary Marxist accounts of culture. This was especially so within the context of the early British workers' movement, which, unlike its continental and especially German counterparts, did not develop alternative socialist sporting structures and spaces as a counter to the bourgeois model offered (Holt, 1989: 145–8; Rigauer, 2000: 34–6).[7] After watching a game of cricket, Karl Marx is said to have concluded that a revolution in England was improbable. If the masses could be so easily subdued by such a resolutely sedate game with its mores of bourgeois Englishness dripping from every rule and expression, then all was lost for the socialist cause. Regardless of its veracity, the fact that the no doubt apocryphal story continues to be told as if it were true (for example, see Gerard, 2007: 11) highlights the widely held perception concerning the inherent incompatibility of sport with politics, and especially of sport with any genuinely revolutionary form of political struggle.

Monty Python mercilessly played on just such assumptions in numerous sketches, such as the political debate show 'World Forum', where Marx, Lenin, Mao Zedong and Che Guevara are asked questions not about world politics but about popular culture and sport. In the 'special gift section', Eric Idle, as the game-show host, asks Karl Marx a series of questions on his chosen topic, the workers' control of factories, as Marx attempts to win a 'beautiful lounge suite':

Idle: The development of the industrial proletariat is conditioned by what other development?
Marx: The development of the industrial bourgeoisie.
Idle: Yes, yes it is indeed. You're on your way to your lounge suite, Karl! Question number two: The struggle of class against class is a *what* struggle?
Marx: A political struggle.
Idle: Yes, yes! One final question, Karl, and the beautiful lounge suite will be yours. You gonna have a go? You're a brave man. Karl Marx, your final question: Who won the Cup Final in 1949?

Marx: Er, the workers control the means of production? The struggle of the urban proletariat?

Idle: No, it was in fact Wolverhampton Wanderers, who beat Leicester 3–1.

In another equally memorable sketch an international philosophy football match takes place between Germany and Greece: Germany fielding the likes of Hegel, Kant and Nietzsche, the Greeks with Plato, Socrates and Aristotle, among others. The game consists of the philosophers pondering the meaning of life and existence, never once actually touching the ball. Even here, Karl Marx can't make it on to the pitch and is sidelined on the German bench – figuratively and literally not playing the game. In the final minute of the game, and shortly after Marx replaces Wittgenstein in a late substitution, the commentator narrates:

> There's Archimedes, and I think he's had an idea! 'Eureka!' Archimedes, out to Socrates. Socrates back to Archimedes. Archimedes out to Heraclitus who beats Hegel. Heraclitus a little flick. Here he comes, on the far post. Socrates is there! Socrates heads it in! Socrates has scored! The Greeks are going mad! The Greeks are going mad! Socrates scores! What a beautiful cross from Archimedes. The Germans are disputing it! Hegel is arguing that the reality is merely an *a priori* adjunct of non-naturalistic ethics. Kant, via the categorical imperative, is holding that ontologic exists only in the imagination. And Marx is claiming that it was offside.[8]

It is sport, not music or film, nor any other popular culture form, that makes these sketches possible, makes the joke 'work'. The impossible moment of cultural suture: politics and high theory simply cannot be articulated with sport, and certainly not football, and in that improbable, ironic conjuncture lies the humour.

In this context sport is not merely seen to be apolitical – as conservative and some liberal accounts tend to argue – but actively *anti*-political. As Karl Kautsky lamented, the English labouring classes had rejected revolutionary struggle at the altar of bourgeois games and pleasures in their 'spiritless manner of killing their leisure time' (1902: 101–2). Disillusioned with the lack of socialist consciousness found among the English working class, Kautsky continued that their class emancipation 'appears to them as a foolish dream. Consequently, it is foot-ball, boxing, horse racing and opportunities for gambling which move them the deepest and to which their entire leisure time, their individual powers, and their material means are devoted' (*ibid.*: 102). Such views no doubt helped to perpetuate what Richard Gruneau labels the 'somewhat unfair stereotype of socialists as all work and no play' (1988: 11).

Within such a framework sport can have no redeeming features other than being a conduit for dominant ideology, thereby weakening the revolutionary spirit. The working classes must simply be taught to see through the candy spectacle of sports. As the comedian Mark Steel (2003: 222) notes:

[The] left can be bafflingly puritanical at times. I once heard a lecture entitled 'Will There Be Sport under Socialism?' The speaker informed us there wouldn't be any desire for sport in a socialist society, as everyone would seek more fulfilling desires, such as hill-walking. So all the struggle through the centuries will be worthwhile in the end, when our prize is to spend all day up the Cotswolds with a thermos and a fucking haversack.[9]

But this is to view sport, and by default most forms of popular culture that can be read as extensions of the cultural industries, in an overly structurally determined way. It fails to consider precisely those aspects of the indeterminacy of cultural forms whose *content* needs to be studied in complex relation to the wider historical conjuncture and the contingent set of social relations that produce it. Thus C.L.R. James understood that even a sport as 'overdetermined' as cricket was both partially autonomous from the capitalistic and colonial structures from which it was born and that it could, under specific circumstances, offer a space through which oppositional politics could be fought and won. As James (1994: 153) empathetically stated, 'Trotsky had said that the workers were deflected from politics by sports. With my past I simply could not accept that.'[10]

This, perhaps, is where those Cultural Studies scholars who would describe themselves as being on the left and most probably socialist would part company with those who would self-identify as Marxist and who believe that in the last instance all relevant theoretical work must ultimately lead to an increase in class consciousness, aimed at advancing political struggle and eventually revolutionary change. Anything short of that, however well intentioned, is at best reformist and at worst complicit with the very oppressive conditions of existence that capital produces. However, a truly revolutionary Marxism would seem, in the end, to have little need to study sport other than to expose it – in Jean Marie Brohm fashion – as a form of ideological manipulation. That is, sport is so complicit and devoid of any counter-cultural elements, let alone transformative potential, that it becomes pointless to study the *content* of particular sports formations. We may still need to show *why* sport is such a restricted popular cultural practice but once this is done the intellectual work is over. Popular culture in general and sport in particular are viewed in this context 'either as politically irredeemable or as strategically irrelevant' (Gruneau, 1988: 14). Thus any radical Marxist theory of sport becomes at once redundant and eventually oxymoronic.

Cell phones for goal posts

The attempt, in 2008, by English football's Premier League to initiate a series of regular-season games that would be played *outside* of England can be used, if only illustratively, to show what a critical Cultural Studies analysis can bring to bear on a topic that is at once both economically determined and yet culturally constrained. In February 2008, the Premier League's chief executive Richard Scudamore announced that the league, with the approval of the twenty club owners, was planning to extend the regular season. Starting in 2010–11, an additional overseas round of games would be added, with the extra matches being played in five locations around the world and with cities bidding to host 'game 39'. Acknowledging the irresistible logic of globalization, Scudamore was quoted by the BBC as saying, 'Globalization is a challenge for all sports because the whole world seems to be interested in the very best of sport wherever it comes from . . . Through modern media exposure there is a globalization [sic] and we need to do something to make sure we are at the forefront of that and making sure we turn that into positive benefits for the game at all levels in this country' (BBC Sport, 2008). Sensing that many fans would be unhappy by this surprise announcement that risked delinking the local bonds of attachment to the clubs that have structured association football in Britain since its emergence in the nineteenth century, Scudamore added, with mixed metaphors and analogies: 'You can't stand still and if we don't do this then somebody else is going to do it, whether it be football or another sport. Therefore it's trying to ride the crest of that wave at the same [time] as protecting what is good and great about what we do. Every time there is an evolutionary step, the reaction of the fans is not always great but I would ask them to take a step back and look at the positives' (*ibid.*). The model for such 'extra-national' games has already been established by North American sports leagues, most noticeably baseball, which for a number of years has been experimenting with holding games outside of the US and Canada (see Macur, 2008). On 28 October 2007, the New York Giants (the eventual winners of the 2008 Super Bowl) beat the Miami Dolphins 13–10 on a rain-soaked evening at Wembley Stadium, the first regular-season NFL game to be played in Europe.

The (economic) logic to such expansion is inescapable: there are limits to the fan base that any national sport can attract within its own country, competing as it is with other 'local' sports and the finite supply of people who watch games, buy T-shirts and other merchandise, and generally 'consume' the sport. International markets are difficult to penetrate but licensing and image merchandising deals have enabled sports to be 'exported' around the globe, wherever there is a potential, consuming market. But spectator sport as commodity has a problem. The 'product' is relatively fixed in time and, more importantly, by location. As Grant Farred's account of Liverpool FC (see Chapter 9) demonstrates, locality has until this moment come to define and constitute the footballing experience, generating a powerful series of emotional bonds of identification and attachment that cannot easily be disentangled in order to produce 'pure' market relations of producer and consumer. The drive to develop new scopic techniques – replays, dramatic camera angles, during-match interviews, etc. – by the televisual (and increasingly internet and mobile phone) media is undermined by the fact that no matter how great the sound, picture and 'shot', the medium cannot ever fully reproduce the 'authenticity' of the actual sporting moment and experience. A 'real' game played in the 'local' (that is international) market thus helps to anchor the development of these new technologies of spectatorship and expanding sporting markets.

However, while the logic of late capital may compel 'traditional fans' to turn their creative commitments into those of active consumers (and of course many fans do, and always have, become consumers of club paraphernalia), this does not *necessarily* mean that the object of desire becomes commodified in any simple sense with the resultant market relations of producer and consumer. For one, the very notion of 'ownership' outstrips the simple categories of legal, exclusive property rights. While football clubs do have owners in this sense, the very premise and legitimacy of exclusivity are called into question by active fan groups and independent supporter associations. While some critics dismiss these forms of resistance as either naïve or misplaced, the important insight that needs to be recognized is that such fans generate powerful sets of counter-hegemonic dis- courses that challenge the legitimacy of the private commercial claims that are made. The fans know who the legal majority shareholders are. The fans are not stupid. Rather, they are aware of the limits to capital and are therefore able to contest the discourse concerning who owns 'the people's game' by articulating their own symbolic ownership claims over the club (see Free and Hughson, 2006). They provide a challenge to the notion that social relations, cultural practices, collective memory and, in the last instance, identity itself can be commodified, commercialized, packaged and sold as if it were a product whose value can be realized only as an outcome of market exchange. Thus 'Not for sale!' is a moment, a fragile one perhaps, temporary for sure, limited for certain, but a moment none the less of economic, political *and* cultural resistance.

To be clear, this is not an argument against acknowledging the full force of economic relations in transforming sport in general, and professional men's football in particular. As the journalist Barney Ronay (2007) has argued:

> The top tier of British football stands as an extreme expression of a certain kind of politics, rampant capitalism with the volume turned up to 11. A Premiership socialist? It might not even be possible . . . Various forces have been working on this relationship between supporters and players: the repacking of the game as televised entertainment and the dilution of the idea of a geographical fanbase; the hyper-inflationary hikes in ticket prices and the emphasis on football as a corporate hospitality product. Going to watch a game at Arsenal's new Emirates ground feels more like attending a stadium rock concert or visiting the Ideal Homes exhibition. Your relationship to everyone else inside the stadium has changed. You're united by consumer choice. The people performing in front of you are skilled entertainers.[11]

It is, rather, to remind us of the limits of capital and the opportunities for contes- tation and change that always reside within such spaces. So, when Scudamore's plan was revealed it did not have the winds of global economic change – the crest of the wave – behind it but the force of oppositional cultural resistance against it. Fans, many sports writers and the odd manager (Alex Ferguson notable among them) and player expressed either concern or outright opposition. Malcolm Clarke of the Football Supporters' Association was quoted by the *Guardian* as saying, 'We challenge the Premier League to scrap these plans if the majority of football fans in this country don't want matches to be played abroad . . . The FSF has no doubt whatsoever that the vast majority of supporters are against this, and believe it would drag the Premier League into the realms of farce' (Kelso and Adamson, 2008). Clarke continued:

> Are we going to see local derbies played in a foreign country thousands of miles away? Are supporters supposed to accept missing the biggest games of their season because it's being played on the other side of the planet? Let's face facts, the sole motivation for this is the Premier League to make more money – aren't they making enough already? This displays a complete disregard for the proud traditions of the English game as well as a crass lack of consideration for football supporters in general.

Significantly the Labour government, ever keen to boost its populist credentials, sensed the growing opposition to the proposal and let it be known that it had 'serious reservations' about the development (*ibid.*).

Within days Michel Platini, president of UEFA, had branded the idea 'comical', and more seriously Sepp Blatter, president of FIFA, football's world governing body, made it clear that he would not support the proposal. The FA, who until then had welcomed the Premier League's idea, suddenly realized that England's bid to host the 2018 World Cup was in jeopardy and subsequently rejected Scudamore's proposal. In order to avoid a humiliating rejection, a meeting that was due to be held at the end of February 2008 at FIFA's Zurich headquarters was cancelled at the last minute when it became apparent that the lack of consultation and the generally negative reaction to the idea meant that FIFA would attempt to block the round of international matches. In an attempt to save face, the Premier League acknowledged that it could not proceed without FIFA's approval and that it was now committed to 'consulting widely' before taking the proposal forward at some unspecified future date. In less than a month 'game 39' had gone from being, as many commentators argued, 'inevitable' to a dead proposal that increasingly lacked the support of even some of the clubs who had been behind the idea in the first place (Kelso, 2008).

Any analysis worth listening to has to do more than simply say that the 'game 39' episode was an example of the 'free market' further encroaching into the sporting lifeworld in order to render all non-market-place values redundant as capital seeks to extract surplus value from the game and further accumulate wealth for the owners of the clubs. This is, of course, true, but it is not the full story. Any critical analysis having *started* here, from the economic, would then have to provide an account of the following: of the attributes of the specific actors involved and their various public and private roles, to link this with an institutional analysis that would map the competition between different sections of the sporting infrastructure – between the FA and the Football League, the Football League and UEFA and particularly FIFA – as well as the various national associations sensitive to an English colonization of their own domestic leagues, and the sets of power plays between these bodies. We would need to understand the role of the different stakeholders, ranging from fans and players, managers and owners, and the tensions within these groups, to an account of the role of media companies (and in this case the role of Rupert Murdoch's BSkyB) in initiating and shaping the proposed changes, and the desire to expand into 'overseas markets' linked to a broader analysis of the global market place for merchandising, sponsorship and licensing. Also central would be the extent to which the Premier League now sees itself in competition with MLB, the NBA and the NFL for coveted global markets, especially the large ones in China and increasingly India.

Within all of this, an account of the state, of politicians, and their relationships (both formal and informal) to capital and various social movements and pressure groups would have to be considered. We would then have to return to the basic questions of how and why American sporting cultures with equally fervent and committed fan bases seem at best reluctant to engage in active supportor-based protest or, worse, appear to be apathetically indifferent about why their teams play some of their games overseas. This would require an account of differing national sporting cultures (and how they have changed over time), the ways in which capital operates in different countries, and even that there are different and sometimes competing logics of capital at play. It would require too a reading of specificity – of those few, exceptional sporting cultures in the US that do come close to replicating the vociferous nature of localized identification found in sporting (and particularly footballing) culture around the world and the deeply gendered configuration of these cultures. A return, also, to an account of class formation and football, its origins, 'diffusions' and reconfigurations from the moment of nineteenth-century imperial industrialism to the hyper-mediated, information age of the twenty-first-century global postmodern. A space in which questions of identity and belonging, of place and locality, of symbolic ownership in the midst of the corporate sport spectacle, are now powerfully colliding and contesting.

At the end of this multidimensional analysis, which would include a discourse analysis of the media and how the proposal was discursively framed by both its protagonists and detractors, within which nothing was guaranteed from the start other than an attempt to map the flow of the economic imperative, we would return to the contingent relationships between culture and economy, having traced their intertwining and interpenetrating effects upon each other through all levels of the social structure, drawing on the historical conditions that make the sociological outcomes possible. We would have an understanding at that moment as to why the initial proposal ultimately failed. And why, almost certainly, it will be resurrected with new and improved clothes the next season, or the season after that. There is a term for this type of analysis, which, at its best, does all of these things simultaneously and more: Cultural Studies.

Conclusion

A critical approach to sport needs, ultimately, to hold on to and to wrestle with the strongest aspects of both the Marxist and Cultural Studies traditions – namely, a deep appreciation of the complexity and polyvocal nature of cultural formation, in the context of an evolving and powerful set of constraints framed by an increasingly militarized world economic system, aligned to analyses that at some level seek to demystify, critique and potentially change the conditions of social inequality, economic exploitation and human injustice that are found. Such an approach brings into question the artificial distinction that is created by the notion of there being any credible analysis of culture that is not at the same time engaged with questions of political economy and an economic analysis that understands society only through numbers and abstracted determinations of 'the market'.

Although the chapters contained in this volume speak from different stand-points, and occasionally, as the careful reader will note, *against* each other, they do share and exemplify an underlying commitment for engaged scholarship that seeks both to make sense and to make a difference. In this regard they contribute to a deepening of our understanding of sport, an activity that while central to the lives and passions of hundreds of millions around the globe remains stubbornly under-theorized within 'mainstream' Marxist theory – compared to, say, the copious writings about and on Marxist literary criticism – and even within the pages of the 'major' Cultural Studies theorists – despite their self-professed openness towards the popular.

We might think of sport, therefore, not only as a 'way of life' but as a 'way of struggle'. Sport, in this context, does not have some a-historical, transcendental quality that makes it inherently 'resistant', as some Cultural Studies-inflected modes of thought sometimes imply, and neither is it irrevocably 'complicit', as some orthodox Marxist positions often state. The question that any universalizing claim has to ask is: which sports? Practised where and by whom? And under what conditions? The geographical location of particular sports practices and their temporal delimitations should require of us greater specificity and caution, even as we work towards generalizable statements about the contemporary sporting condition: 'The very uniqueness of the historical moment, or conjuncture, means there is a condition of no necessary correspondence, or indeed noncorre-spondence, between sport and particular forces (i.e. the economic): Forces do determine the *givenness* of sporting practices, their determinacy just cannot be guaranteed in advance' (Andrews, 2002: 116). Or, to end where I started, and to paraphrase and follow the insights of both Hall and Andrews, this necessitates a contextual and contingent account of sport without *final* guarantees.

Notes

1 It might be argued that the revival and/or continuing interest in class can be more readily seen in British, and perhaps European, social science than within American social science, where the category of 'class' has a more problematic status. Mainstream American sociology in particular has largely stopped using the term, which has been displaced by the notion of socio-economic status or SES. As the phrasing implies, this is, to all intents and purposes, a proxy for class and signals the attempt to map the complex relationship between economic forms of stratification linked to income and occupational 'status' and the various sociological dimensions of class related to

education, lifestyle and so on. The benefit of producing SES-indexes is the ability to measure how the different variables included impact upon each other and the life chances of those studied. In short, 'class' can be quantified allowing for important statistical forms of analysis, prediction and causal relationships to be shown. A problem occurs, however, when SES status is seen purely as a continuum. The point at which lines are drawn to differentiate groups becomes arbitrary, especially so with interval variables, what gets included or excluded from the index itself is often a subjective judgement, and the relative power of different (often adversarial) groups vis-à-vis each other is elided. The underlying conditions of capitalism, the political struggles that result and that in a sense 'produce' class, tend to get written out of the conceptual schema of analyses reliant upon a rigid SES framework. In other words, capitalism as system, power as both institutional and relational, and political struggle (and its effects) are difficult to measure in this way, so often disappear from the analysis and with it the concept of class and class consciousness.

2 My title deliberately plays off (or less charitably steals) both Stuart Hall's 1986 essay 'The Problem of Ideology: Marxism without Guarantees' and David Andrews' (2002) programmatic article 'Coming to Terms with Cultural Studies', which ends with a clarion call for an engaged, contextual Cultural Studies premised upon an understanding of 'sport without guarantees'. I use these two sophisticated and erudite theorists of, respectively, culture and sport as interlocutors in order to stage the terms of the debate that follow in this collection and as a critical but friendly rejoinder to Ian McDonald's powerfully argued chapter that follows this. Although I may be accused of semantics, the claim to a politics of *final* guarantees is a stronger statement that implies a knowing and knowable (in advance) political end point. This is the strong/absolute sense of 'determinacy' that I am arguing against. However, this is *not* the same as claiming that politics should be 'infinitely dispersed' in which there is an endless deferral of any standpoint. We still need to take positions, however contingent and arbitrary, in order to make any sort of claim upon power. There is no *final* guarantee of the correctness of any position, but not to attempt any closure leads to a form of deconstructionism for its own sake and political inertia.

3 The final top ten positions were: 1. Marx, 2. Hume, 3. Wittgenstein, 4. Nietzsche, 5. Plato, 6. Kant, 7. Aquinas, 8. Socrates, 9. Aristotle, 10. Popper. Interestingly, at the same time as the BBC poll was published, the American right-wing magazine *Human Events* published its own top ten list of the 'most harmful books of the past two centuries'. Paradoxically demonstrating the continuing relevance of Marxism, Marx and Engel's *The Communist Manifesto* just edged out Adolf Hitler's *Mein Kampf* for top spot. The full list, which any self-respecting progressive would want to appear on (the company of *Mein Kampf* excluded), was: 1. Marx and Engels' *The Communist Manifesto*, 2. Hitler's *Mein Kampf*, 3. Mao Zedong's *Quotations from Chairman Mao Tse-Tung*, 4. Alfred Kinsey's Kinsey Reports, 5. John Dewey's *Democracy and Education*, 6. Marx's *Das Kapital*, 7. Betty Freidman's *The Feminine Mystique*, 8. Auguste Comte's *Introduction to Positive Philosophy*, 9. Nietzche's *Beyond Good and Evil*, 10. John Maynard Keynes' *The General Theory of Employment, Interest and Money* (see 'Bound for trouble', *Chronicle of Higher Education*, 17 June 2005: A5). It would be tempting to see this list as a *Python*-esque spoof. Sadly, as an example of the poverty of conservative 'thought' in the US, it was serious.

4 For contrasting positions on the complex relationship between rising wage inequality, changing occupational structures and class, see Weeden *et al.* (2007) and Kim and Sakamoto (2008).

5 There is, of course, a similar tendency 'the other way', in which *all* of Cultural Studies scholarship is denigrated for its populist, pro-consumer-capitalist and anti-political tendencies due to a misreading of something John Fiske may or may not have said in the late 1980s and/or a narrow reading of what Jacques Derrida meant by the notion that there is no meaning outside of the text.

6 This is perhaps why many Marxists seem to hold Hall personally at fault for acceler-ating the move away from Marxist scholarship into a post- or even anti-Marxist position while generally being more sympathetic to Williams.

7 There is some dispute as to the true extent of the British workers' movement's successful engagement with sport. See, for example, Hargreaves (1992: 150), who argues, 'Strictly speaking, British socialism cannot be said to have failed with sport because, in retrospect, it never seriously tried'; for a counter-view, see Jones (1988). Without wishing to get drawn into this debate, it is *generally* true to say that alterna-tive and autonomous working-class sporting structures seemed to be more successful on the continent than in Britain.

8 It should be noted that Marx was right: the replay shows that Socrates was clearly in an offside position.

9 For just such a utopian, post-capitalist vision without sport, where the boundary between work and play has dissolved, and where people instead engage in 'Gardening and orchard management' (p. 273), among other exciting and suitably socialist activ-ities, see 'Appendix: Edilia, or "Make of it what you will"' in David Harvey's (2000) *Spaces of Hope*.

10 Gruneau notes that while condemning sport, Trotsky still held out the possibility that other popular cultural forms, such as film, might not be redundant to the socialist cause (Gruneau, 1988: 13).

11 David Conn and Tom Bowyer both make convincing arguments that due to the British government and Football Association's weak regulatory structure, English football clubs are now more susceptible to hostile takeovers, increasingly from overseas 'investors' with little knowledge of or intrinsic interest in the game. The new owners can then 'leverage' the costs of the buy-out back on to the club's assets, thus leaving the likes of Manchester United and Liverpool with huge debts to service, as compared to some European counterparts, such as Barcelona, which are collectively owned by the fans (see Conn, 2007; Bower, 2007).

References

Andrews, D.L. (2002) 'Coming to terms with cultural studies', *Journal of Sport and Social Issues* 26(1), pp. 110–17.

Aronowitz, S. (2003) *How Class Works: Power and Social Movements*, New Haven: Yale University Press.

BBC Sport (2008) 'Top clubs consider overseas games', 2 February, http://news.bbc.co.uk/sport1/hi/football/eng_prem/7232390.stm (accessed 10 March 2008).

Bower, D. (2007) 'The big sell out', *Observer*, 29 July, http://football.guardian.co.uk/News_Story/0,,2134482,00.html (accessed 10 March 2008).

Brohm, J.M. (1978) *Sport: A Prison of Measured Time*, London: Ink Links.

Burawoy, M. and Wright, E.O. (2001) 'Sociological Marxism', in J. Turner (ed.) *Handbook of Sociological Theory*, New York: Kluwer Academic/Plenum Publishers, pp. 459–86.

Byrne, D. (2005) 'Class, culture and identity: A reflection on absences against presences', *Sociology* 39(5), pp. 807–16.

Carrington, B. (2001) 'Decentering the Centre: Cultural studies in Britain and its legacy', in T. Miller (ed.) *A Companion to Cultural Studies*, Oxford: Blackwell , pp. 275–97.

Chan, T. and Goldthorpe, J. (2007) 'Class and status: The conceptual distinction and its empirical relevance', *American Sociological Review* 72(4), pp. 512–32.

Cleaver, H. (2000) *Reading Capital Politically*, 2nd edn, Leeds: Anti/Theses/AK Press.

Conn, D. (2007) 'What money can't buy', *Observer Sport Monthly*, 29 July, http://football.guardian.co.uk/News_Story/0,,2134516,00.html (accessed 10 March 2008).

D'Amato, P. (2006) *The Meaning of Marxism*, Chicago: Haymarket Books.

Derrida, J. (1994) *Spectres of Marx*, London: Routledge.

Dworkin, D. (2007) *Class Struggles*, London: Pearson Longman.

Edensor, T. (2000) 'A welcome back to the working class', *Sociology* 34(4), pp. 805–10.

Free, M. and Hughson, J. (2006) 'Common culture, commodity fetishism and the cultural contradictions of sport', *International Journal of Cultural Studies* 9(1), pp. 83–104.

Gerard, J. (2007) 'Opinion', *Observer*, 1 July, p. 11.

Gruneau, R. (1988) 'Introduction: Notes on popular cultures and political practices', in R. Gruneau (ed.) *Popular Cultural and Political Practices*, Toronto: Garamond Press, pp. 11–32.

Hall, S. (1981) 'Notes on deconstructing the "popular"', in R. Samuel (ed.) *People's History and Socialist Theory*, London: Routledge and Kegan Paul.

Hall, S. (1996 [1986]) 'The problem of ideology: Marxism without guarantees', in D. Morley and K.-H. Chen (eds) *Stuart Hall: Critical Dialogues in Cultural Studies*, London: Routledge, pp. 25–46.

Hargreaves, J. (1992) 'Sport and socialism in Britain', *Sociology of Sport* 9(2), pp. 131–53.

Harvey, D. (2000) *Space of Hope*, Edinburgh: Edinburgh University Press.

Holt, R. (1989) *Sport and the British: A Modern History*, Oxford: Clarendon Press.

Hutton, W. (2007) 'Greed will be the death of football', *Observer*, 30 September, http://www.guardian.co.uk/commentisfree/2007/sep/30/comment.football (accessed 10 March 2008).

James, C.L.R (1994 [1963]) *Beyond a Boundary*, London: Serpent's Tail.

Jones, S. (1988) *Sport, Politics and the Working Class*, Manchester: Manchester University Press.

Joseph, J. (2006) *Marxism and Social Theory*, Basingstoke: Palgrave Macmillan.

Kautsky, K. (1902) *The Social Revolution*, Chicago: Charles H. Kerr and Company.

Kelso, P. (2008) 'Scudamore forced to climb down over game 39', *Guardian*, 27 February, http://football.guardian.co.uk/comment/story/0,,2260181,00.html (accessed 10 March 2008).

Kelso, P. and Adamson, M. (2008) 'Government has reservations about Premier League's plans to go global', *Guardian Unlimited*, 7 February, http://football.guardian.co.uk/News_Story/0,,2254032,00.html (accessed 10 March 2008).

Kim, C.H., and Sakamoto, A. (2008) 'The rise of intra-occupational wage inequality in the United States, 1983 to 2002', *American Sociological Review* 73(1), pp. 129–57.

Lawler, S. (2005) 'Introduction: Class, culture and identity', *Sociology* 39(5), pp. 797–806.

Macur, J. (2008) 'Playing in China, chipping at a wall', *New York Times*, 16 March, http://www.nytimes.com/2008/03/16/sports/baseball/16china.html?pagewanted=1&ref=sports (accessed 21 March 2008).

Martin, R. (2002) *On Your Marx: Relinking Socialism and the Left*, Minneapolis: University of Minnesota Press.

Marx, K. (1990 [1867]) *Capital: A Critique of Political Economy*, Vol. 1, London: Penguin.

Marx, K. (2000 [1859]) 'A Contribution to the Critique of Political Economy', in D. McLellan (ed.) *Karl Marx: Selected Writings*, 2nd edn, Oxford: Oxford University Press, pp. 424–8.

Miller, M. (2007) 'The Forbes 400', *Forbes*, 20 September, http://www.forbes.com/2007/09/19/forbes-400-introduction-lists-richlist07-cx_mm_0920richintro.html (accessed 16 March 2008).

Miller, M. (2008) 'Gates no longer world's richest man', *Forbes*, 5 March, http://www.

forbes.com/2008/03/05/buffett-worlds-richest-cx_mm_0229buffetrichest.html (accessed 16 March 2008).

Mirza, H. (ed.) (1997) *Black British Feminism*, London: Routledge.

Ozanian, M. and Schwartz, P. (2007) 'Top guns', *Forbes*, 21 May, pp. 102–7.

Piven, F. (2008) 'Can power from below change the world?', *American Sociological Review* 73(1), pp. 1–14.

Ray, L. (2003) 'Review essay: Capitalism, class and social progress', *Current Sociology* 51(2), pp. 163–9.

Rigauer, B. (2000) 'Marxist theories', in J. Coakley and E. Dunning (eds) *Handbook of Sports Studies*, London: Sage, pp. 28–47.

Ronay, B. (2007) 'Anyone want to play on the left?', *Guardian*, 25 April, http://football.guardian.co.uk/comment/story/0,,2064827,00.html (accessed 10 March 2008).

Steel, M. (2003) *Vive le Revolution: A Stand-up History of the French Revolution*, London: Scribner.

Weedon, K., Kim, Y.-M., Carlo, M. and Grusky, D. (2007) 'Social class and earnings inequality', *American Behavioral Scientist* 50(5), pp. 702–36.

Wheen, F. (2005) 'Why Marx is the man of the moment', *Observer*, 17 July, p. 27.

Wheen, F. (2006) *Marx's Das Kapital: A Biography*, London: Atlantic Books.

Williams, R. (1977) *Marxism and Literature*, Oxford: Oxford University Press.

Williams, R. (1983 [1958]) *Culture and Society: 1780–1950*, New York: Columbia University Press.

Williams, R. (1989 [1975]) 'You're a Marxist, aren't you?', in R. Williams (ed. R. Gable) *Resources of Hope: Culture, Democracy, Socialism*, London: Verso, pp. 65–76.

Wilson, T. (2002) 'The paradox of social class and sports involvement: The roles of cultural and economic capital', *International Review for the Sociology of Sport* 37(1), pp. 5–16.

3 One-dimensional sport
Revolutionary Marxism and the critique of sport

Ian McDonald

Introduction

Karl Marx died in 1883. Yet, the fact that the political ideology that was to bear his name endured through the twentieth century and continues, 125 years after his death, to shape political movements, ideas and academic disciplines in the twenty-first is testimony to the scope and depth of the work of Marx. Contrary to expectations of writers like Francis Fukuyama (1992), the political revolutions that swept across the Soviet Union and Eastern Europe from 1989 did not consign Marxism to the proverbial dustbin of history. Indeed, the disintegration of the Communist Bloc, far from heralding the 'end of history', has merely paved the way for a new phase of war, crises and instability in what is now commonly referred to as the new global disorder (Amin, 2004). In response, a new spirit of radicalism has emerged on a mass scale. The development of the anti-globalization/capitalist/ war movements and the electoral successes of radical parties in Latin America have posed serious political challenges to the hegemony of neo-liberal ideology and economics. It's a challenge that is reflected in the academy in the waning intellectual dominance of postmodernism, and what has been referred to as the 'return to Marx' (Rees, 1998b). This 'waning' of postmodernism and the 'return' of Marx have rippled out to disciplines cast on the outer rings of the academy, such as the sociology of sport.[1]

This volume is partly a reflection of the renewed interest in Marxism within the sociology of sport. It is also intended as a contribution to developing the understanding and relevance of Marxism for a critique of the contemporary politics of sport. Significantly, the starting point for the majority of the contributors in this volume is a reading of Marx through the lens of Cultural Studies, hence the title of the book. The emphasis struck by those authors who attend to this relationship is on the continuities and overlaps between Marxism and Cultural Studies, or more precisely on the ways in which the latter serve to overcome, augment and develop the former, suffering as it does from a number of theoretical limitations and inadequacies.

However, the argument that I will make in this chapter is that we need to think more about the *discontinuities* between Marxism and Cultural Studies than has hitherto been the case. That instead of assuming an alignment between temporal and theoretical advances (that because Cultural Studies emerged as a critique of classical Marxism it must be an advance), we ought to consider the ways in which newer theoretical formulations might also be understood as diluting and diminishing, and may even represent a break rather than a continuity. This is the argument that I advance, as I set about reiterating the revolutionary essence of Marxism. There is an element here of 'bending the stick', as Lenin would say, but the polemical tone and disruptive nature of this chapter are necessary given the dominance of a Cultural Studies-inflected form of Marxism that permeates the sociology of sport. Thus the purpose of this chapter is first to outline and defend the nature of Marxism as a revolutionary political project, and second to assess, from this perspective, the politics of Marxism in the sociology of sport. Particular attention will be paid to the post-Marxist turn in the sociology of sport, via a critique of Laclau and Mouffe's influential text, *Hegemony and Socialist Strategy*. The chapter concludes with some suggestions for how a revolutionary Marxist approach to Sport Studies might be developed, drawing on the key arguments about the containment of alternatives outlined by Herbert Marcuse in *One Dimensional Man* to make an analogous case for 'one-dimensional sport'.

The revolutionary Marx

Speaking at the funeral of his lifelong friend and collaborator, Friedrich Engels declared, 'Marx was before all else a revolutionist' (cited in Foot, 2004: 14). Theory was, for Marx, a means to understand the social world, as a necessary step to transforming the same. This is why Grant Jarvie and Joe Maguire (1994: 110) are correct to assert that 'one cannot accept Marx's scientific theory and reject his revolutionary politics'. Marx's life work – the materialist conception of history and the studies of capital – is dedicated to one goal: to do away with the exploitation, suffering and violence that are built into the capitalist system. As Engels continued in his funeral speech, '[Marx's] real mission in life was to contribute, in one way or another, to the overthrow of capitalist society and of the state institutions which it had brought into being, to contribute to the liberation of the modern proletariat' (cited in Foot, 2004: 14). The essence of Marxism is rooted in the unity of theory and practice of the proletarian revolution. In this sense, the peculiarity of Marxism is that it is both an analysis of what he called the laws of motion of the capitalist system as well as a political project. The scientific and the philosophic, on the one hand, and the interventionist politics, on the other, are distinct but necessary elements of the Marxist totality. This is suggested by Gramsci's phrase 'the philosophy of practice' and stated without any ambiguity in the attack on the idealism of the young Hegelians in the oft-quoted 11th Thesis on Feuerbach: 'The philosophers have only interpreted the world in various ways: the point is to change it' (Marx, 1984: 423). Within the academy it is the philosophical and theoretical aspects of Marxism that tend to take precedence. As a form of division of labour, premised on a commitment to Marxism as irredeemably a politics of activism, such privileging is not as corrosive as approaches that define theoretical engagement itself as the primary locus of activism and struggle.

A useful way to distinguish and defend my approach to Marxism is to identify other traditions that in theory if not in practice reject the revolutionary project as the definitional core of Marxism. First, there are the distortions produced by the enemies of Marxism. Contemporary versions of explicitly anti-Marxist accounts present revolutions as monstrous ideologically driven efforts to change history: Simon Schama's (1989) account of the French Revolution and Orlando Figes (1997) on the Russian Revolution epitomize this perspective. Second, there are the distortions and derivations that have emerged within the Marxist camp. In general terms, we can note three broad sources of this: reformism; Stalinism; and academicism.

Reformism

In the political struggles of the international labour movement, Marxism has been used to support *reformist* paths to socialism, achieved by using the institutions of existing society, such as the state and the apparatus of bourgeois democracy. Examples of such reformist formulations of Marxism include the German 'Father of Marxist Revisionism', Eduard Bernstein, at the turn of the twentieth century, who argued that there was an evolutionary road to socialism (Bernstein, 1961), to the British Communist Party's adoption of the Parliamentary Road to Socialism in the post-war period (CPGB, 1951).

Stalinism

Arguably the most damaging distortion was effected by the regime that emerged in the USSR out of the disintegration of the Bolshevik Revolution of 1917. Marxism, filtered through the *realpolitik* of the USSR, or Stalinism, slaughtered, persecuted and imprisoned millions of people all under the banner of Marxism. Socialist revolutions were no longer created by the self-emancipation of the working class, but could be imposed by the military power of tanks. While the catastrophic Soviet ideology of 'Marxism–Leninism' (known as Stalinism) has crumbled, the legacy is still with us, because Stalinist Marxism with its crude economism and philosophical catechisms disoriented at least two generations of socialist activists. Stalinist Marxism also framed attempts by Marxists in more advanced capitalist societies of the West to rescue Marxist theory from its economistic and deterministic straitjacket by shifting to the analysis of ideology and culture (Anderson, 1976). This highlights the third aspect of what I am describing as a distortion of Marx's revolutionary legacy: Western Marxism which is characterized by what I call academicism, or the non-dialectical privileging of ideas over action.

Academicism

Western Marxism is a broad category that embraces both the Frankfurt School and Cultural Studies. It constituted an attempt to mould Marxism to the conditions of Western capitalist societies with mature, dense civil society networks that rendered utopian the goal of revolutionary change. With its emphasis on theory, ideology and culture, Western Marxism was particularly attractive to the growing number of radically inclined academics in the rapidly expanding universities in Western societies in the post-Second World War period. In assessing the *politics* of Western Marxism, it is important to acknowledge that it emerged as a historical and political reaction against the rigid economism and determinism of Stalinism. As such, though Western Marxism tended to eschew revolutionary change, it offered some important theoretical innovations. As Terry Eagleton (2003: 30) notes, it reminded the political left of what it flouted: 'Art, pleasure, gender, power, sexuality, language, madness, desire, spirituality, the family, the body, the ecosystem, the unconscious, ethnicity, life-style, hegemony [to which we could add, sport]. This on any estimate was a sizeable slice of human existence.'

Thus it was out of the fertile discussions of culture and ideology that defined Western Marxism that the sociology of sport was to emerge. But as Eagleton notes, much of Western Marxism was also defined by its disavowal of revolution. The shift in Western Marxism to culture was partly borne out of political impotence and disenchantment. Caught between capitalism and Stalinism, groups like the Frankfurt School could compensate for their political homelessness by turning to cultural and philosophical questions. As Eagleton notes (2003: 31):

> much Western Marxism ended up as a somewhat gentrified version of its militant revolutionary forebears, academicists, disillusioned and politically toothless. This too, it passed on to its successors in cultural studies, for whom such thinkers as Antonio Gramsci came to mean theories of subjectivity rather than workers' revolution.

Each of these three distortions – reformism, Stalinism, academicism – vary in their theoretical significance, and their practical effects. But they are all united in their antipathy to what Hal Draper (2004) called 'socialism from below', and thus repeat the standard bourgeois hostility to working-class revolution. In Stalinist Marxism, the discourse of revolution is used to buttress reactionary regimes. In the labour and trade union movement, revolutionary strategy is replaced by reformist compromises, while in Western Marxism, cultural resistance has masked a retreat from workers' revolution. As it is the tradition of Western Marxism that is of most significance for the sociology of sport, the remainder of the chapter will focus on its impact in the sociology of sport, in particular on the influence of what is known as post-Marxism.

Post-Marxism and the abandonment of revolution

In their 1985 landmark study, *Hegemony and Socialist Strategy*, Ernesto Laclau and Chantal Mouffe marked the emergence of what became known as post-Marxism.

It was an enormously influential text in setting out a new agenda for Marxist theory and practice; and it has proved to be a highly contentious text, acclaimed on the one hand as an innovative rendering of Marxism for the modern age, while condemned on the other for waging a 'war of manoeuvre' on classical Marxist theory (Townshend, 2004). While the debate about the status of Laclau and Mouffe's Marxism was not felt as keenly in Sport Studies as in mainstream social theory, there can be no doubting that it had a major influence on how a generation of leftist scholars came to conceive of Marxism in their work. Therefore, in order to understand the problematic nature of Marxist theorizing in Sport Studies, it is necessary to engage with key aspects of Laclau and Mouffe's arguments. In particular I want to focus on their concept of society as a totality and the place of hegemony within this, and then relate these ideas to their influence on Marxist sport sociology.

Hegemony and Socialist Strategy was written at the time of a 'crisis of the Left' (Laclau and Mouffe, 1985: 2). In the face of the onslaught of neo-liberal economics and social conservatism, the book argued for a reorientation of Marxism so as to take account of the apparent failure of the working class to play its revolutionary role and the marginal impact of Marxist politics on the burgeoning new social movements (such as the women's movement, the environmentalist movement, and the struggles of gays, lesbians and ethnic minorities). If Marxism were to be relevant to contemporary reality, it was necessary to make the shift from the politics of production to the politics of recognition. Writing in 2000, in a debate with Judith Butler and Slavoj Žižek about the contemporary legacy of Gramsci's hegemony, Laclau (2000: 8) states: 'Today, we tend to speak of emancipations (in the plural), which start from a diversity of social demands, and to identify democratic practice with the negotiated consensus among a plurality of social actors. What notion of social agency is compatible with this transformed approach?' Actually, this is more of a rhetorical question. Laclau and Mouffe argue that the struggle for society as a totality is beyond the capabilities of a historically restructured and muted working class. Furthermore, by drawing on the Saussurean structuralist notion of discourse, which is read via Derrida's poststructuralist concept of *différance*, they deny the possibilities for any social agent to institute a closed synchronic social totality. Laclau and Mouffe maintain that a given society or discourse is always prevented from becoming a fixed totality because of the ontological necessity that 'all discourse (totality) is subverted by a field of discursivity, which overflows it' (Laclau and Mouffe, 1985: 113). Society is conceived as irredeemably open and indeterminant, thus rendering a fully rational totality, free from social antagonisms and power relations, an impossibility. As Mark Wenman (2003: 588) puts it: 'For Laclau the actual form that social relations take at any given time is always unstable, unintended, and a precarious byproduct of the discord between what are understood as explicit attempts to construct the object society-as-totality and the discursive conditions of (im)possibility of that object.'

Where does Gramsci's theory of hegemony feature in this framework? Gramsci argued that the success of the proletarian struggle depended upon the working class's capacity to construct a contingent hegemonic formation, which would enlist the consent of other subordinate social sectors in the formation of a new historical bloc. In post-Marxism, Gramscianism is shorn of its revolutionary politics, but it does provide Laclau and Mouffe with two key terms – contingency and articulation – and also a means of adhering to a concept of the universal. Hegemonic practices are understood as the strategic means by which different and competing particularisms (feminism, anti-racism, the gay movement) become equivalent terms in their mutual antagonism to the external oppressive force (such as the state) and seek to find expression in the substitution of a collective social identity for the particular demands of each of the social struggles. The moment of hegemony is the widespread acceptance of the contiguity of the concrete demands of some particular social sector with the new collective identity and consequently with society as a totality. This process, referred to by Laclau (2000: 303) as 'the logic of equivalence', is countered by 'the transformatic operation' of the dominant powers which seek to neutralize the equivalent potential and so prevent the formation of counter-hegemonic blocs. Universality is the universality of the empty signifier:

> Emptiness, as a result, presupposes the concrete. Both because the general equivalent will be, at the same time, above the chain (as its representative) and inside it, and because the chain will include some equivalences but not others, the universality obtainable through equivalential logics will always be a universality contaminated by particularity.
>
> (*Ibid*.: 304)

Laclau's theoretical rendering of the universal–particular problematic results in an incomplete, indeterminate and impossible totality. It effectively undercuts the political quest for a revolutionary change through a unitary subject such as the working class, as this singular subjectivity can be achieved only through the denial of other subjectivities. Such theorizing is expressed programmatically in the rejection of revolutionary politics in favour of popular democractic struggles, hence the subtitle to *Hegemony and Socialist Strategy* is *Towards a Radical Democratic Politics*. However, in severing the struggle for democracy from revolutionary transformation, Laclau and Mouffe are not charting an alternative path to the goal of a socialist society; rather they are signalling an acceptance of capitalism as the ultimate horizon of social thought and political change.

> How is it possible to maintain a market economy which is compatible with a high degree of social control of the productive process? What restructuration of the liberal democratic institutions is necessary so that democratic control becomes effective, and does not degenerate into regulation by an all powerful bureaucracy? How should democratisation be conceived so that it makes possible global politics effects which are, however, incompatible with the social and cultural pluralism existing in a given society?
>
> (*Ibid*.: 293)

These are key questions, but they are social democratic ones framed with the existing coordinates of liberal democracy, not revolutionary questions seeking transcendence. Gallant and intellectually weighty challenges were made to this capitulation to reformist politics, most notably by Ellen Meiksins Wood (1986) to defend the centrality of class and by Norman Geras (1990) to engage with key philosophical and methodological issues raised by Laclau and Mouffe. Yet the mood of pessimism that dominated the left in the 1980s was not fruitful terrain for these critics, especially when Laclau and Mouffe had held out a privileged space for intellectuals through their emphasis on the discursive construct of subjectivity.

What is certain is that Laclau and Mouffe helped to create an intellectual terrain that opened the door to the deconstructionist currents of postmodernism, signalling, in the words of Anthony Giddens (1994: 10), 'a move away from Marxist thinking in cultural studies'. For Fredric Jameson (1993), too, this was the moment when Cultural Studies became a substitute for Marxism. For his part, Jameson demonstrated that taking postmodernism seriously need not involve a political capitulation to its logic. In his analysis of postmodernism as 'a cultural dominant', Jameson (1984: 88) insisted on the necessity for a theory of the 'social totality' in which the mode of production acts as a 'final horizon' and in which 'Marxism subsumes other interpretive modes of systems'. In other words, as Žižek (2004: 191), another theorist hostile to the post-Marxist project, comments, 'Marxism is not the all-encompassing interpretative horizon, but the matrix which enables us to account for (to generate) the multiplicity of narratives and/or interpretations.'

The deleterious impact of post-Marxism on the Marxist sociology of sport

The influence of post-Marxism on Cultural Studies provides the context for an important intervention by David Andrews with two articles published in 2002: one single-authored piece titled 'Coming to Terms with Cultural Studies'; the other co-authored, titled 'Cultural and Sport Studies: An Interventionist Practice' (Howell *et al.*, 2002). A critique of the arguments presented in these articles follows, as they represent the most serious attempt to delineate the cultural studies of sport by authors who have all been central to advancing this project since the early 1990s.

Andrews' sole-authored article reflects a concern that Cultural Studies scholarship on sport had expanded to the point where it was in danger of losing its distinctiveness as a political project. He warned that Cultural Studies was 'oftentimes used as an empty cultural metaphor . . . there is a real danger that among sport scholars, cultural studies is reduced to being a caricatured and banal intellectual practice', and he called for a need to reconsider 'the specificities of cultural studies . . . to preserve the integrity of the cultural studies project' (Andrews, 2002: 110–11). A key influence on Andrews is Larry Grossberg's take on the Cultural Studies project, in particular Grossberg's identification of 'radical contextualism' – a contextual theory of contexts – as the definitional core of Cultural Studies:

> Cultural studies can be and needs to be defined or delineated; that it is not so broad as to encompass any critical approach to culture nor so narrow as to be identified with a specific paradigm or tradition. This is not a matter of a proprietary definition, or of 'the proper' form of cultural studies, but of holding on to the specificity of particular intellectual trajectories.
>
> (Grossberg, 1997: 245)

This is, as Andrews notes, a type of 'intellectual sensibility' rather than a theoretical or methodological injunction. It takes its inspiration from Stuart Hall's 1983 essay 'The Problem of Ideology: Marxism without Guarantees'. Andrews takes Hall's revised notion of determinacy, 'in the sense of setting the limits, the establishment of parameters, the defining of the space of operations, the concrete conditions of existence . . . rather than in terms of the absolute predictability of particular outcomes' (Hall, cited in Andrews, 2002: 113) as being sensitive to the constraining influence of the social structure, and the creative impulses of human agents, thus avoiding the economic determinism of vulgar Marxism and the romanticism of cultural humanism. Marxism without guarantees states that the meaning and effects between one level of social formation and another, or between the social structure and the human agent, are never guaranteed, but, as Grossberg says, 'The specificity of any conjuncture, at whatever level of abstraction, is always produced, determinate' (cited in Andrews, 2002: 113). As Andrews (2002: 116) concludes:

> The structure and influence of sport in any given conjuncture is a product of intersecting, multidirectional lines of articulation between the forces and practices that compose the social contexts. The very uniqueness of the historical moment, or conjuncture, means there is a condition of no necessary correspondence, or indeed noncorrespondence, between sport and particular forces (i.e., the economic). Forces do determine the *givenness* of sporting practices, their determinacy just cannot be guaranteed in advance.

As references to 'no necessary correspondence' reveal, Andrews advances a distinctly Grossbergian inflection of Hall's notion of determinacy, rendering his theoretical position as rather more eclectic, open-ended and post-structuralist – in short, closer to post-Marxism than to Hall's Marxism (at least as Hall outlined it in the 1983 essay). However, Hall has already set the slippage towards post-Marxism in motion. Hall's position itself, which is an attempt to marry a conception of Marxism with the insights of post-structuralism, especially in the form of identity politics, is problematic. His essay is an argument against forms of *determinism* – 'the absolute predictability of particular outcomes' (Hall, 1983: 98). Given that the resolution to such a conception of determinism is found within non-Marxist traditions there is a collapsing of Marxism *per se* with determinism.

However, within the broad Marxist tradition, only the most fatalistically naïve Second Internationalist, or the most ideologically driven Stalinist, would insist on the 'absolute predictability of particular outcomes'. There are many currents within Marxism that could have been drawn upon to construct a determinate but non-deterministic theory of social development, which eschewed fatalism without abandoning the revolutionary kernel of Marxism (Rees, 1998b).

In the co-authored article, Andrews and his colleagues present three case studies as exemplars of this Cultural Studies practice. As stated in this piece, the Cultural Studies project is predicated on 'the failure of the Marxist Left to comprehend, in theoretical, strategic, interventionist, and political terms' (Howell et al., 2002: 153) the changed realities of a post-war consumer society. This 'failure' to adapt to the changed socio-cultural conditions of 'late-capitalism', of which the Conservative Party-voting working class was symptomatic, signalled a need for the left to shift from class-based economistic analyses to critical cultural theorizing, first to understand the cultural ramifications of consumer capitalism, and thereby to open up the cultural sphere as a 'new political and intellectual space' for 'academics and public intellectuals to *intervene* into the historical context of post-war Britain' (*ibid.*).

Scholars within Cultural Studies then attached themselves to what they saw as the new progressive social forces in society, known broadly as the new social movements. They developed cultural critiques of the rise of neo-conservative social and political formations and advocated new forms of cultural politics around the growth of consumerism, globalization and the politics of diaspora. The key concept centred on Stuart Hall's notion of articulation, the ongoing production of contexts, which is explained by Howell et al. (2002: 155) thus:

> The strategic, interventionist, and methodological implication of articulation is partly found in the struggle to uncover the way in which particular sporting practices are positioned into specific contexts . . . questioning how sporting practices get their meaning and identity through the power structures and relationships to which they are connected. It is an attempt to contextually destabilise connections that appear natural and extremely stable in any given historical context.

Cultural Studies, then, is 'at its core, an interventionist intellectual practice' (Howell et al., 2002: 170). However, the specific case studies provided in the article highlight the limited kind of interventionist strategies offered, and they do not make clear in what sense they are illustrative of a Cultural Studies intervention. One case study is an account of the development of a charity cycle ride to raise money for AIDS research, heralded as an alternative model of lifestyle fitness discourse. Such events may be apposite examples of the benefits of civic engagement through sport, but it could be argued that they are complicit in what Pierre Bourdieu calls the withdrawal of the 'left hand of the state' from its welfare obligations (Bourdieu, 1998: 2). Also, in what sense was the cycle ride reflective of an interventionist intellectual practice? There is no indication that the authors were involved in the event, either as organizers or as cyclists. The second case study is an analysis of soccer in American suburbia. This case study is certainly an informative account of social status struggles of this section of middle-class Americans, and stands up as a fine application of the aforementioned Bourdieu's framework. However, is it distinctively Cultural Studies? The third case study concerns the banning of a Nike advert from New Zealand television following two complaints that it encouraged violence. This is taken as a form of local resistance to Americanized globalization, which is read *a priori* as a progressive political act. However, rather than being taken as an exemplar of Cultural Studies interventionism (again it is not clear where the intervention lies, apart from supporting the protests, or maybe the authors were the complainants), I would suggest that this case study raises the problematic and complex notion of intervention. Certainly different readings of this event are possible, and not all are necessarily progressive (though there is not sufficient detail in the case study to arrive at any firm conclusion on the politics of this episode). Local resistance to Americanization, particularly by nation states on the periphery of the global capitalist economy, can be as much reactionary as progressive.[2]

While the spirit underpinning the desire to politicize Cultural Studies as an 'interventionist intellectual practice' deserves support, it is not clear how such an approach takes concrete form from the case studies. The problem is one of politics rather than methodology. Over the past decade or more, as critical theory travelled from neo-Marxism, via Gramscianism, to the hegemonic influence of post-Marxism, critical sport sociology has been noticeably detached from a significant leftist (or, better, revolutionary Marxist) politics. It is the absence of just such a vision of the necessity of revolution, of transcending the existing order, from the politics of Cultural Studies interventions that weakens its analysis of different instances of resistance.

The relevance of the classical Marxist tradition

The classical Marxist tradition offers some very useful concepts for analysing sport. For example, as Rob Beamish ably demonstrates in Chapter 6 (this volume), the Marxist concept of labour is indispensable in critiquing alienation in sporting practices. A proper understanding of the Marxist concept of labour will reveal that alienation is not an inevitable result of sport as a bodily practice, but a consequence of sport within a specific socio-historical conjuncture. Labour becomes an alienating activity in the context of a class society, because what should be her life activity through which she affirms her species-being or her humanity becomes a mere means to an end. Such a concept not only provides the basis for negative critique, but also provides the point of departure for discerning the conditions of possibility for a non-alienating, empowering culture of sport and physical activity.

Marx's materialist analysis of alienation is rooted in the social conditions of life, and not, as Hegel said, in the minds of people. The same idealist–materialist distinction between Marx and Hegel exists over the dialectical method. For

Hegel, the dialectic was idealist and teleological; whereas for Marx, it was materialist and propelled by conflict. Dialectical materialism proceeds from the real conflicts between individuals, their activity and the material conditions of their life. But Marx was no empiricist. He distinguishes between the real but concealed and the apparent but misleading behaviour of objects. This distinction, between what he calls the essence, or inner structure, and the phenomenon, or outward appearance of things, runs right through *Das Kapital*. To penetrate beneath the surfaces, Marx appeals to the 'powers of abstraction' – to concepts that capture the most basic and general features of reality, removing all secondary and irrelevant matters. Then we must explain how these features are related to what we can observe empirically in the actually existing world. Marx called the process of explaining appearance by starting from abstractions, and working through a number of intermediary stages, 'the method of rising from the abstract to the concrete' (Marx, 1973: 101).

The Marxist method moves from sport as it appears phenomenologically to the abstract, which breaks down the concrete into its simplest determinations: such as alienation or commodification, for example. Then we move back from the abstract to the concrete, using these to reconstruct the whole. Marx calls concrete reality, despite its complexity, a 'totality' and a 'unity of the diverse'. Thus sport can be understood only as a complex, differentiated totality, a rich totality of many determinations and relations in relation to the whole of society. This leads to a consideration of the base and superstructure model of society, which offers just such a way of analysing the relationship and role of sport in society – its political and ideological dimensions – without collapsing into idealism. The base and superstructure model of society is often derided for its determinism, but as Engels reveals in a letter to Bloch (1972 [1895]), such criticisms have a long lineage:

> According to the materialist conception of history the ultimately deter-mining element in history is the production and reproduction of real life. More than this neither Marx nor I have ever asserted. Hence if somebody twists this into saying that the economic element is the only determining one, he transforms that proposition into a meaningless, abstract, senseless phrase. The economic situation is the basis, but the various elements of the superstructure – political forms of the class struggle and its results, to wit: constitutions established by the victorious classes after a successful battle etc., juridical forms, and even the reflexes of all these actual struggles in the brains of the participants, political, juristic, philosophical theories, religious views and their further development into systems of dogma – also exercise their influence upon the course of the historical struggles and in many cases preponderate in determining their form. There is an interaction of all these elements, in which, amid all the endless host of accidents . . . the economy.

Far from reductive, the base and superstructure allows for the interplay of the structural and the contingent, the conjunctural and the organic. However, what sets it apart from providing the conceptual and analytical resources for doing good sociology is a commitment to the goal of social transformation, a necessarily revolutionary transformation from capitalism to socialism. In short, it is a theoretical tradition with a substantive political content. A commitment to the goal of socialist transformation of society is no guarantee of a properly dialectical materialist Marxist theory; but without it, it is vulnerable to the distorting and diluting effects of reformism, Stalinism and academicism.

Conclusion: one-dimensional sport

The preceding notes on labour, alienation, the dialectic and base and super-structure are only offered as reminders of the utility of well-known Marxist concepts for an analysis of sport. But I would like to conclude with some observations about the relationship between sport, socialism and the revolutionary Marxist project, particularly as it relates to the historically conservative function played by sport in society. Perhaps the most significant step forward made by critical perspectives in the sociology for sport (including but extending beyond Marxism to forms of post-structuralism and figurational sociology) is winning the argument that sport is political: that there is a politics *of* sport and there is politics *in* sport. However, in terms of the contribution that these politics make to the cause of socialism, little can be advanced beyond notions of sport as, at best, a form of cultural resistance to the logic of capitalist, imperialist or any expression of dominant ideology. More often than not, sport serves to buttress, if not actively promote, rather than undermine dominant ideologies.

In *One Dimensional Man* Herbert Marcuse (2002) portrays a theory of advanced industrial society in which a 'mechanics of conformity' systematically effaced critical thought and behaviour to produce a 'society without opposition'. Marcuse claims that the mass media, industrial management and uncritical modes of thought had created false needs that serve to integrate individuals into the system of production and consumption. Resistance could only come from social forces outside of and marginalized from 'one-dimensional society' that in their 'great refusal' of repression and domination display the liberatory potential of critical and dialectical thinking. Is there an intriguing parallel between Marcuse's 'one-dimensional society' and the institutions and culture of modern sport? Does modern sport – one-dimensional sport – produce its own 'mechanics of conformity' in which alternative and oppositional cultures are ultimately negated?

The fact that competitive high-performance sport, the dominant culture of sport in most parts of the world today, can be characterized economically by commodification, politically by bureaucratization (especially under the shadow of nation states) and ideologically by linear record does not mean that there are struggles that haven't been fought and still need to be waged over various forms of oppression and exploitative practice in sport. But these are essentially struggles within the existing and highly limited discourse of high-performance sport. Alternative cultures or dimensions of sport have been suggested as offering more potential for progressive politics. I am thinking here of Henning Eichberg's (1998) important work of the trialectics of body culture, which relativizes the dominant culture of sport by naming it 'high-performance sport' and contrasting it to recreational/fitness sport, and what we might call body culture, incorporating a range of expressive or lifestyle physical pursuits. However, to the extent that these other dimensions of sport become avenues of political activity, they offer only limited possibilities for challenging organizational and structural power. Indeed, if we take lifestyle sport as one example: what started off as a radical challenge to the dominant values of sport has been easily if unevenly incorporated (Wheaton, 2001), thus confirming Žižek's observation: 'Is not the history of capitalism a long history of how the predominant ideologico-political framework was able to accommodate (and soften the subversive edge of) the movements and demands that seemed to threaten its survival . . . ?' (Žižek, 2004: 225).

The conservatism of modern sport is not surprising, given that its emergence was not as a form of rebellion against capitalist society that then had to be co-opted. It was from the beginning more a form of catharsis than a challenge. Sport thrived because it was experienced by the masses as a means of temporarily escaping or coping with the demands of life. The history of previous attempts by socialists to intervene systematically in the culture of sport demonstrates the limited contribution that sport can make to advancing the socialist movement (Jones, 1986). At most, it seems that all we can and must do is engage in rearguard and defensive strategies: such as exposing relations of power, engaging in campaigns for equality, formulating critiques. Sport does not have equivalents of avant-garde artistic movements, or revolutionary cinematic and literature movements. However, unlike its more radical cultural counterparts, it does have a public profile and presence that suggest political possibilities, particularly for those of us involved in teaching critical sport sociology in universities. This perspective is eloquently developed by Brett St Louis in the concluding section Chapter 7 (this volume), and it is one that I wholeheartedly endorse.

Given the inherently political nature of sport, its culpability in the reproduction of oppressive and exploitative social relations, and its limited utility as a form of practice to challenge the structures of power, the aim for Marxists in sport must be twofold. First, to continue to subject sport to rigorous critique – to understand its limitations *and* its potential. Philosophically speaking, sport is inherently paradoxical. That is, the structured nature of sport as expressed through the elaboration of gratuitous rules presupposes a necessary though (in terms of high-performance sport) subordinate communicative imperative to sport that exists alongside the dominant instrumental values and relationships. Thus, concealed within the structure of sport is an inherent utopian dimension, a promise of different sets of possibilities between humans in play. When set alongside the essentially conservative role played by sport vis-à-vis revolutionary change, it points towards the need for a dialectical approach to sport in modernity. Such an approach has been summed up by Frederic Jameson in his comments on culture in general. The methodological conclusion to be drawn, the view of culture as something more than a mere epiphenomenon, 'Is that we must denounce culture (as an idea but also as a phenomenon) all the while we continue to perpetuate it, and perpetuate it while continuing tirelessly to denounce it' (Jameson, 1990: 47–8). Based on the notion of critique set within a revolutionary Marxist politics, I suggest that a properly dialectical approach involves denouncing sport while continuing to perpetuate it. It is the idea that sport must be simultaneously preserved and overcome: preserved because its paradoxical nature contains within it an inherent criticality that we can articulate as the utopian dimension of sport; overcome because sport contributes to the legitimacy of extant social relations of power, and serves to incorporate us into a system that causes immense human suffering. So, comrades, to invoke once more Marx's famous 11th Thesis on Feuerbach: sociologists have hitherto only interpreted the world of sport; the point is to denounce and perpetuate it.

Second, in the spirit of Marx's thesis on Feuerbach, the other task facing Marxists is to develop an activist orientation by making the links between sport and a wider set of political questions outside of sport. That is, to insert the politics *of* and *in* sport back into the discussions and movements on pressing political issues of the day. For example, given the way in which the US government has sought to exploit sport to drum up a spirit of patriotic support for the war in Iraq, ought radicals in sport be arguing and campaigning for a movement of athletes against war? Sports radicalism lies in exploiting the opportunities given by its cultural centrality to raise awareness and consciousness of political issues outside of sport. Given the increasingly crisis-ridden nature of contemporary global capitalist society, there is still plenty to do for those who self-identify as revolutionary Marxists working in Sport Studies.

Notes

1 A concrete example of this resurgence of interest in Marxist theory and sport is the formation in 2006 of the International Network for the Marxist Study of Sport (see http://marxistsport.pbwiki.com/FrontPage).
2 Over the past few years, it has become routine on 14 February for right-wing Hindu fundamentalists to protest against Valentine's Day – deemed yet another Western import undermining 'traditional' Indian culture. This sort of protest against Western and especially American culture is common, and is more often than not political territory captured most readily by backward and reactionary forces.

References

Amin, S. (2004) *Obsolescent Capitalism: Contemporary Politics and Global Disorder*, London: Zed Books.

Anderson, P. (1976) *Considerations on Western Marxism*, London: Verso.

Andrews, D.L. (2002) 'Coming to Terms with Cultural Studies', *Journal of Sport and Social Issues* 26(1), pp. 110–17.

Beamish, R. (1981) 'Central Issues in the Materialist Study of Sport as Cultural Practice', in S. Greendorfer and A. Yiannakis (eds) *Sociology of Sport: Diverse Perspectives*, New York: Leisure Press, pp. 38–55.

Beamish, R. (1982) 'Sport and the Logic of Capitalism', in H. Cantelon and R. Gruneau (eds) *Sport, Culture and the Modern State*, Toronto: University of Toronto Press, pp. 141–97.

Beamish, R. (1985) 'Understanding Labor as a Concept for the Study of Sport', *Sociology of Sport Journal* 2, pp. 357–64.

Bernstein, E. (1961) *Evolutionary Socialism: A Criticism and Affirmation*, London: Random House.

Bourdieu, P. (1998) 'The Left Hand and the Right Hand of the State', in *idem*, *Acts of Resistance: Against the New Myths of Our Time*, Cambridge: Polity Press, pp. 1–10.

Brohm, J.M. (1978) *Sport: A Prison of Measured Time*, London: Ink Links.

Butler, J., Laclau, E. and Žižek, S. (2000) *Contingency, Hegemony, Universality: Contemporary Dialogues on the Left*, London: Verso.

Callinicos, A. (1983) *The Revolutionary Ideas of Marx*, London: Bookmarks.

Cantelon, H. and Gruneau, R. (eds) (1982) *Sport, Culture and the Modern State*, Toronto: University of Toronto Press.

CPGB (Communist Party of Great Britain) (1951) *The British Road to Socialism: The Programme Adopted by the Executive Committee of the Communist Party*, London: CPGB.

Draper, H. (2004) *Socialism from Below*, Alameda: Center for Socialist History.

Eagleton, T. (2003) *After Theory*, London: Allen Lane.

Edwards, H. (1960) *The Revolt of the Black Athlete*, New York: Free Press.

Eichberg, H. (1998) *Body Culture: Essays on Sport, Space and Identity*, London: Routledge.

Engels, F. (1972 [1895]) Letter to J.Bloch, http://www.marxists.org/archive/marx/works/1890/letters/90_09_21.htm (accessed 17 October 2007).

Figes, O. (1997) *A People's Tragedy: Russian Revolution, 1891–1924*, London: Pimlico.

Foot, P. (2004) 'Karl Marx: The Best Hated Man', *Socialist Review* 282, pp. 14–16.

Fukuyama, F. (1992) *The End of History and the Last Man*, New York: Free Press.

Geras, N. (1990) *Discourses of Extremity: Radical Ethics and Post-Marxist Extravagances*, London: Verso.

Giddens, A. (1994) 'Living in a Post-Traditional Society', in U. Bech, A. Giddens and S. Lash (eds) *Reflexive Modernization*, Cambridge: Polity Press.

Grossberg, L. (1996) 'History, Politics and Postmodernism', in D. Morley and K.H. Chen (eds) *Stuart Hall: Critical Dialogues in Cultural Studies*, London: Routledge, pp. 151–73.

Grossberg, L. (1997) *Bringing It All back Home: Essays on Cultural Studies*, Durham, NC: Duke University Press.

Gruneau, R. (1983) *Class, Sports, and Social Development*, Amherst: University of Massachusetts Press.

Hall, S. (1983) 'The Problem of Ideology – Marxism without Guarantees', in B. Mathews (ed.) *Marx: A Hundred Years on*, London: Lawrence and Wishart, pp. 57–86.

Hargreaves, J.A. (ed.) (1982) *Sport, Culture and Ideology*, London: Routledge and Kegan Paul.

Hargreaves, J.E. (1986) *Sport, Power and Culture*, Cambridge: Polity Press.

Harman, C. (1989) *1968: The Fire Last Time*, London: Bookmarks.

Hoch, P. (1972) *Rip off the Big Game*, London: Anchor Books.

Howell, J.W., Andrews, D.L. and Jackson, S.J. (2002) 'Cultural and Sport Studies: An Interventionist Practice', in J. Maguire and K. Young (eds) *Theory, Sport and Society*, Oxford: JAI Press, pp. 151–77.

James, C.L.R. (2000 [1963]) *Beyond a Boundary*, London: Serpent's Tail.

Jameson, F. (1984) 'Postmodernism or the Cultural Logic of Late Capitalism', *New Left Review* 146, pp. 52–92.

Jameson, F. (1990) *Late Marxism: Adorno, or, the Persistence of the Dialectic*, London: Verso.

Jameson, F. (1993) 'On "Cultural Studies"', *Social Text* 34, pp. 17–52.

Jarvie, G. and Maguire, J. (1994) *Sport and Leisure in Social Thought*, London: Routledge.

Jones, S. (1986) *Workers at Play: A Social and Economic History of Leisure 1918–1939*, London: Routledge and Kegan Paul.

Laclau, E. (2000) 'Identity and Hegemony: The Role of Universality in the Constitution of Political Logics', in J. Butler, E. Laclau and S. Žižek, *Contingency, Hegemony, Universality: Contemporary Dialogues on the Left*, London: Verso, pp. 44–89.

Laclau, E. and Mouffe, C. (1985) *Hegemony and Socialist Strategy: Towards a Radical Democratic Politics*, London: Verso.

Marcuse, H. (2002 [1964]) *One Dimensional Man: Studies in the Ideology of Advanced Industrial Society*, London: Routledge.

Marx, K. (1973) *Grundrisse: Foundations to the Critique of Political Economy*, Harmondsworth: Penguin.

Marx, K. (1984) *Early Writings*, London: Penguin.

Marx, K. and Engels, F. (1973) *Selected Works*, Moscow: Progress.

McKay, J. (1986) 'Marxism as a Way of Seeing: Beyond the Limits of Current "Critical" Approaches to Sport', *Sociology of Sport Journal* 3, pp. 261–72.

Meiksins Wood, E. (1986) *The Retreat from Class*, London: Verso.

Morgan, W. (1994) *Leftist Theories of Sport: A Critique and Reconstruction*, Illinois: University of Illinois Press.

Rees, J. (1998a) 'The Return of Marx?', *International Socialism Journal* 79(3), pp. 3–11.

Rees, J. (1998b) *The Algebra of Revolution: Dialectic and the Classical Marxist Tradition*, London: Routledge.

Rigauer, B. (1981) *Sport and Work*, New York: Columbia University Press.

Rowe, D. (2004) 'Antonio Gramsci: Sport, Hegemony and the National-Popular', in R. Gulianotti (ed.) *Sport and Modern Social Theorists*, London: Polity, pp. 97–110.

Schama, S. (1989) *Citizens: A Chronicle of the French Revolution*, New York: Alfred Knopf.

Scott, J. (1971) *The Athletic Revolution*, Free Press: New York.

Thompson, E.P. (1978) *The Poverty of Theory and Other Essays*, London: Merlin Press.

Tomlinson, A. (1999) *The Game's up: Essays in the Cultural Analysis of Sport, Leisure and Popular Culture*, Aldershot: Arena.

Townshend, J. (2004) 'Laclau and Mouffe's Hegemonic Project: The Story so Far', *Political Studies* 52(2), pp. 269–88.

Vinnai, G. (1973) *Football Mania*, London: Ocean Books.

Wenman, M. (2003) 'Laclau or Mouffe? Splitting the Difference', *Philosophy and Social Criticism* 29(5), pp. 581–606.

Whannel, G. (1983) *Blowing the Whistle: The Politics of Sport*, London: Pluto Press.

Whannel, G. (1992) *Fields in Vision*, London: Routledge.

Wheaton, B. (ed.) (2001) *Understanding Lifestyle Sport: Consumption, Identity and Difference*, London: Routledge.

Žižek, S. (2004) *Revolution at the Gates: Žižek on Lenin, the 1917 Writings*, London: Verso.

Part II

Political economy, commodification and sport

4 The urban sport spectacle

Towards a critical political economy of sports

Anouk Bélanger

Introduction

The leisure and entertainment industries became increasingly significant components of transnational capitalism in the late 1980s and have also, arguably, 'helped generate popular consent for the current gospel of free trade, deregulated markets, economic competitiveness, and the privatizations of public goods and services' (Gruneau and Whitson, 1997: 360). In the networks of transnational flows of capital and information, these industries are integrated players for cities now competing intensely for spectacular urban entertainment as a strategy for growth and re-imaging as world-class cities of culture. Major League sports and sport mega-events are prime commodities of growing importance in this international entertainment economy. In many cases, they are central expressions of the contemporary mobilization of spectacle as they merge with an entrepreneurial urban economy in the economic and socio-cultural regeneration of cities.

The financing and building of new arenas, stadiums and various sports complexes by private firms as part of initiatives in urban development are by no means isolated phenomena. In fact, these developments – where nearly every major multinational entertainment company in North America has established a development team to evaluate, plan and initiate 'urban entertainment destination projects' (Hannigan, 1998: 1), such as large-scale sporting and cultural events – are indicative of the integration of the new entertainment economy with a new urban economy and the centrality of sport in this conjuncture. In an inter-urban global competition, urban leaders try, both implicitly and explicitly, to:

> kill the two birds of economic and socio-cultural regeneration with one stone by prioritising one particular local economic sector and by using one particular kind of strategy to develop this sector. The local economic sector is that of the 'popular cultural' consumer economy, broadly understood to include such industries as sport, tourism, leisure entertainment and retailing. And the strategy involves the use of large-scale sporting and cultural events, and the construction of large-scale visitor attractions like sport facilities.
>
> (Roche and France, 1998: 140)

If sport has become a key player in the recent mobilization of the spectacle in cities, the urban sport spectacle has also come to occupy a central place within contemporary sport sociology. There have been many case studies of the urban sport spectacle over the last decade, providing compelling stories, revealing sets of data and critical discourses. This growing body of literature helps us to understand how sport is often put to work as an expression of recent political economic transformation towards the mobilization of spectacle in urban centres across the Western world, contributing to the commercialization and corporatization of sport (for example, see Gruneau and Whitson, 1997, 2001; Whitson and MacIntosh, 1996; Bélanger, 2000; Lowes, 2002, 2004; Silk, 2002, 2005; and Smith and Ingham, 2003).

In this chapter, I suggest that a political economy of sport implies both a consideration of how political economy is important to the development of sport and to its critical study, *and* a consideration of how sport itself is important to political economy. In other words, I wish to underscore the value of an iterative approach between political economy and sport. Following this, I shall argue that in order to create fertile ground for a critical understanding of the urban sport spectacle, we need to treat it as more than a manifestation or an expression of something else: as a multidimensional concept. In fact, the expression 'urban sport spectacle' is not merely evocative or descriptive; it evokes as well a sense of *critique*, or a way to rediscover the complex set of relations between political and economic changes and sport.

This chapter, which aims to offer a few propositions towards a political economy of the urban sport spectacle, begins with a mapping of the existing critique of the urban sport spectacle. I then outline a conceptualization of the urban sport spectacle, which provides the basis to move towards a critical (multidimensional) political economy of the urban sport spectacle.

The tyranny of the urban sport spectacle: mapping an existing critique

The mobilization of the urban sport spectacle in a competitive global environment has raised a number of concerns among sport sociologists and critical urban scholars. A first area of critique could broadly be identified as the 'paradox of distinctiveness'. Some critics argue that the urban spectacle produces spaces that are too similar in their design and content and can therefore be easily interchanged. Urban landscapes are often sold on the basis of their distinctiveness yet they are often redeveloped in favour of a singular North American generic model. Thus, Zukin (1998: 239) argues that what is being created in urban spaces is a 'national middle class culture as represented by a coast-to-coast chain of red-brick shopping centers with their standardized assortment of gourmet and ethnic food shops, crafts boutiques, [and] bookstores'. According to Robins (1997), this situation typically involves the promotion or valorization of a specific history and heritage, on the one hand, and the devaluation of these things through their commodification, on the other.

A second area of critique takes issue with how the spectacular redevelopment of the urban fabric transforms and sanitizes the urban imaginary – that is, the narrative about the city as presented to outsiders as well as for insiders. It seems that urban elites utilize urban redevelopment towards the forging of a coherent and distinctive sense of place – one that carefully selects a particular vision of the city's history and then imposes this vision as a unifying theme that then determines future development in the key city spaces (Gotham, 2002; Kearns and Philo, 1993). The concern often expressed is that the themes chosen by city leaders frequently narrate a dominant (Debord (1967) would say 'banalized') urban imaginary stripped of all references to any counter-narratives that might be told from the perspective of workers, residents and marginalized minorities (Boyer, 1992; Hannigan, 1998; Silk, 2002; Bélanger, 2000). This line of critique identifies a tension between vernacular and spectacular uses of urban history, and views the projection of a sanitized urban imaginary as an explicit repression of the vernacular culture and the obscuring of the historical reality of inequality and urban struggle.

The urban sport spectacle therefore works to transform and sanitize specific urban spaces as well as their experiences. In their playful arrangement of sights, sounds and activities, these new entertainment and consumption spaces offer upscale target markets for a spectacular urban experience, but it is an experience that is orchestrated, scripted and, in the end, sealed off from contact with the realities of daily life outside of those specific spaces (Hannigan, 1998). Within these spaces upmarket consumers/spectators wander through a carefully constructed series of thematic, and usually branded, consumption experiences. Here, the paradox of surface diversity and underlying monotony marks the cleavage between the style of the spectacle and the actual content and historical context of the new urban experience. For critics, then, this inevitably overwhelms and obscures the underlying denotative reality of coldly calculated exchange values and profit-taking (Kearns and Philo, 1993; Gotham, 2002; Silk, 2002; Gottdiener, 2001). As Gibson (2005: 182) so graphically puts it, 'What offends, in other words, is how the spectacular façade of the modern "fantasy city" mystifies the true purpose of its design: grabbing patrons by the ankles, turning them upside down, and then shaking them vigorously until their money falls out.'

In a sense, these areas of critique echo the cultural analysis of the Frankfurt School. It also evokes the way in which political economists have engaged popular culture in studies of determinism and domination. In the same way, the literature on urban sport spectacle sometimes overemphasizes a single focus of analysis on the exchange value of the urban sport spectacle. In addition, these critiques are not too far from the work of Guy Debord in *The Society of the Spectacle*, which is most often considered as the 'starting point' for understanding the economic dimensions of the contemporary spectacle, and the overlapping dimensions of the economic and the symbolic in such an event. According to Alan Tomlinson (2002: 59), Debord's text situated 'cultural analysis and a kind of social psychology of the individual at the centre of political economy. It represents a metatheoretical tradition, in the spirit of Hegel, and demonstrates its persisting resonance for the cultural critic of advanced capitalism and its culture.' Certainly, *The Society of the Spectacle* needs to be considered seriously, as it powerfully demonstrates and denunciates the emerging and suffocating power of the commodity form. As Debord (1967: 42) asserts, 'The spectacle is the moment when the commodity has attained the total occupation of social life.' Still, there are problems with Debord's work (or at least with the dominant interpretation of his work), in that it tends, at best, to trivialize human agency and, at worst, to deny it.

As Tomlinson (2002) has rightfully pointed out, some researchers (myself included) might have jumped into an easy association of Debord's presentation of spectacle as the intensified passivity of human agency that overdetermines the analysis and more or less readily categorizes his work as some kind of theoretical shorthand. Yet, Debord's legacy seems to direct us to focus on an imposition of the spectacle and specific forms of entertainment and consumption which do not strongly lead towards a dialectical view of agency or mobilization, thus concealing not only possibilities of spectacular resistance but of day-to-day usages and tactics working to mould the spectacle to the local scene and cultures. In other words, these lines of critiques leave us with a necessary analysis of the exchange value of the urban sport spectacle, yet this analysis remains incomplete if it does not take into account the relation between the exchange value *and* the use value of such spectacle and the ambiguities of the latter. In my view, the specific conjunctural articulations at play in the process of developing and integrating various urban sports spectacles and mega-events in local cultures and imaginaries are key to a complex understanding of these events. It is important to gain a sense of the specific cultures that might characterize the spectacle. In this sense, it could be argued that Debord deals with culture in a perfunctory way that does not lead to an iterative political economy of the urban sport spectacle. He denies an appreciation of the *resistance to the spectacle* that paradoxically is constantly reasserted in his interventions as a Situationist. As Gibson (2005: 184) notes, following Peter Jackson's comments on the popular appropriation and transformation of urban spaces which recall a curious contradiction within Debord's theory of spectacle:

> On the one hand, Debord is a profound pessimist. The spectacle not only extends alienation and fragmentation into the once-protected realms of home and leisure, but its flood of compelling fantasies and images serve to anaesthetize individuals against the knowledge of their repression. At the same time, Debord was himself an activist and founding member of the *Situationist Internationale*, a small but influential group of French artists straddling the historic leftist divide between Marxism and Anarchism. For the Situationists, the appropriate response to modern alienation was not to pine for 'the revolution' but to take control of everyday life and to liberate oneself from the boredom and banality of late capitalist society.

I wonder if critiques that either implicitly or explicitly condemn 'the masses' for immersing themselves in the fakery of urban spectacle might not lead to a conceptual and political cul-de-sac. For one thing, spectacle and simulacra have always been important features of sport and urban life (Fainstein, 1998; Gruneau, 1988). Second, fantasy, play and spectacle are not only undeniable, but they should not be readily excluded from any progressive definition of the urban good life and of Major League sports and sport mega-events. Dismissing the pleasures of consumption, sport spectatorship and commercialized leisure along with the pleasures of large gatherings as inherently retrograde might underestimate the contradictory political meanings that inhere in popular cultural practices such as sport (Gruneau, 1988).

A third area of critique focuses on the way in which the mobilization of the spectacle contributes to a new sense of 'publicness' constructed by and for the urban spectacle. In some instances, the idea of public space can be extended culturally to certain spaces that are privately owned, but where the public over long years of use has come to assume that the space actually belongs to them. These are spaces – such as the Montreal Forum and the Maple Leaf Garden in Canada – through which people move and are addressed more as citizens, or community members, than as consumers. In the urban sport spectacle both of these senses of the publicness of spaces are undermined. A new set of private–public partnerships and strategic alliances that have been developing over the past three decades has eroded the distinction between public and private by linking public investment with the interests of capital accumulation. These permanent spaces – sport and entertainment complexes – and even single events, such as car-driving events, reconstruct the very idea of public space by replacing the traditional practices of citizenship with the practices of citizen-consumership. This was strikingly clear in the discourses of the Coalition des Amis du Parc Jarry organized and active in Montreal around the renovation project of Jarry Park Stadium, proposed in 2002, to host an international pro-tennis tournament. The association was not lobbying for a right of access and use of the park. Instead, it was re-vindicating 'their right of ownership' of the park. This, I believe, is a powerful expression of the process of formation of a 'new sense of publicness' in which the urban sport spectacle is very present and active in Western cities.

This area of critique also addresses the works of collective memory and nostalgia in the orchestration and the reception of the urban spectacle. In many cases of urban sport spectacle, local memories and nostalgia have come to play an important role for capital in the selling of places (new arenas and stadiums), not only as a resource for economic gain but, in a Gramscian sense, as a way of generalizing hegemonic interpretations of history and society so that these interpretations come to be widely seen as a matter of common sense. The case of the new Molson Centre/Bell Centre (supported by a strategic alliance with the local government and facilitated by their established beer–hockey synergy) sought to produce for Montrealers a particular version of the past, invoking particular nostalgia, not only to legitimate their new arena project but more importantly to convince the public to 'let go' of the old one.

A fourth area of critique tackles the idea that resistance takes place only in the context of certain predictable geographies. Resistance can be found in other

spaces from the ones where power relations are at play, or on the actual sites of the urban sport spectacle. On this point, Steve Pile (1997: 2) argues that 'Geographies of resistance do not mirror geographies of domination' and that resistance, or movements of oppositions around urban development, can have their own spatiality. For instance, the actions of a corporation might provide community resistance, but sometimes the resistance can spill into other areas or form elsewhere then to cross paths with the urban sport spectacle. In the case of the renovation of the tennis stadium at Park Jarry in Montreal, the above-mentioned coalition operated on the ground of the actual park, yet also networked with other local movements and associations lobbying for similar rights in their districts (to slow down rapid gentrification) or in other parks of the city (to protect green spaces), forming in the end a growing presence and a growing voice which was increasingly present in the media coverage of various development projects around Montreal. In this case, then, the resistance could be found not only on the site of the urban sport spectacle.

Similarly, these complexities in expressions of resistance are equally evident in the process of building new arenas and stadiums (Bélanger, 2000). In most cases, we rarely see a pattern of a coherent class force in opposition to a simple act of corporate domination. The issue is far more complex and muddled. At the same time, however, resistant interpretations are not completely random. By engaging in any socio-political struggle people articulate the identities and memories that are active in their social life, but in so doing they often also articulate the social relations that these identities and memories entail. In addition, resistance is not something that necessarily comes together in reaction to every act of domination. Resistance, or movements of critical opinions and culture, is part of a process of understanding a space, a community, and trying to take part in the reorganization of it. In this sense, resistance is always connected to memory and the imagination: memory of a place that has been lost, or memory as an imaginative force of becoming that will defend and advance particular common interests. Pile (1997: 2) puts it this way: 'resistant political subjectivities are constituted through positions taken up not only in relation to authority but also through experiences which are not so quickly labelled "power", such as desire and anger, capacity and ability, happiness and fear, dreaming and forgetting'.

If political economy is important to the understanding of popular culture, it is also true that popular culture is important to political economy. Leisure and entertainment are now among the fastest growing and most publicly visible industries in the world and can be seen as playing a defining role in a new phase of capitalist accumulation – variously described as 'postfordism', 'postmodernism' or 'disorganized capitalism'. The production of images and the marketing of pleasures have become so significant that political struggles centred in and through popular culture may now be as crucial as the more traditional struggle against class domination at the workplace or in state policy (Gruneau and Whitson, 1997). Such arguments, by no means universally accepted either in political economy or in Cultural Studies, are put forward here, through the specific case of the urban sport spectacle, in order to stimulate debate about the relevance of a political economy of sport. More specifically, a critical political economy of sport as popular culture begins by taking sports, or in this case the urban sport spectacle, 'seriously', which means going beyond understanding it as mere manifestation to appreciate its multidimensionality.

The dominant themes of the urban sport spectacle

One of the limiting aspects of many case studies on sport spectacles is the fact that the spectacle is mainly conceptualized as a simple manifestation. Rarely is the spectacle treated in its multidimensionality, thus keeping analysis from a thorough understanding of the emerging and sustained ambiguities at play in the urban sport spectacle. Therefore, presenting the urban spectacle as a critical concept implies unpacking the urban sport spectacle and addressing its dimensions in their specificity, in order to allow a more nuanced and complex critical understanding. In this regard, Gibson's (2005) work, drawing on David Harvey, outlines three related but distinct dimensions – mobilization of spectacle; spectacle of the commodity; and spectacular urban resistance – and so offers a useful point of departure on the urban spectacle. However, in order to address the notion of resistance in its dialectical character, I propose integrating to Gibson's third dimension the notion of resistance to the spectacular.

The mobilization of spectacle

The mobilization of spectacle relates to the recent wave of postfordist urban redevelopment through which new multi-megaplexes of shopping and entertainment, theme parks, theme restaurants, arenas and stadiums have sprung up across cities in the Western world. This recent trend of urban development projects echoes David Harvey's arguments about the mobilization of spectacle. Harvey (1990: 92) termed this wave 'the mobilization of spectacle' and noted that 'imaging a city through the organization of spectacular urban spaces [has become] a means to attract capital and people (of the right sort) in a period (since 1973) of intensified interurban competition and urban entrepreneurialism'.

With the development of global communication and transportation networks as well as the enhanced mobility of corporations, cities now compete on a global field for future growth and investment (Castells, 2000; Judd and Fainstein, 1999; Judd and Swanstrom, 1994; Robins, 1997; Sassen, 1991). For individual cities embroiled in this global competition, the stakes are enormous; and, to this end, city officials and civic boosters across North America have searched for strategies that can secure for their cities a favourable position in the international market place. In this sense, Roche and France (1998: 139) have noted that the achievement of economic regeneration and restructuring requires more than the purely economic: 'It has increasingly come to be connected with cultural and political development.' Moreover, as many sport sociologists have shown (Gruneau and Whitson, 2001; Roche and France, 1998; Whitson and MacIntosh, 1996; Lowes, 2002, 2004; Silk, 2002; Bélanger, 2000), Major League sport and international pro-sport mega-events have become key in these strategies to attract promoters, investors, tourists and consumers back to cities. Sport is central to these strategies and therefore to the new spirit of entrepreneurialism underlying this mobilization of the spectacle.

Many of the urban development projects (sport complexes, arenas and international competitions) put forward in this context are largely symbolic and ideological. In fact, 'new developments like sports arenas, concert halls, and spectacular retail emporia are being conceived, planned, and constructed not merely for the tangible economic benefits they might generate, but also, and perhaps most importantly, for their more nebulous symbolic advantages' (Gibson, 2005: 175). The construction of 'world-class' retail–cultural developments, in other words, helps urban leaders project a powerful image of urban vitality into the international market place, thereby improving their city's chances in the intense competition for tourism, consumption dollars and new capital investment (Hannigan, 1998).

Development initiatives as part of this spirit of entrepreneurialism are expressed concretely in various forms of sporting realities and events that should be distinguished following broad categories. In fact, there are differences between a single spectacular event, a semi-permanent event and a permanent type of spectacle. These differences are important to the degree that each type of urban sport spectacle comes with specific implications for the relation between sport mega-events, Major League sport and local cultures (fans, citizens and consumers) in the short and long term.

The urban sport spectacle can come in the form of a single event. These forms of spectacles are the sporting events that will occur only once, as part of an international tour, and that will operate mainly through non-permanent installations. For example, Michael Silk (2002) examined how the Malaysian government explicitly directed the national broadcaster to use the 1998 Commonwealth Games as a vehicle both for showcasing Kuala Lumpur as a sleek, modern technopole and for narrating a particular version of the Malaysian national story. Mark Lowes (2002, 2004) has studied single-event sport spectacles – 'world-class' motorsport events – and their role in the promotional strategies of cities in Canada and Australia.

There are also forms of semi-permanent urban sport spectacles. Olympic installations and 'villages' are examples of such kinds of spectacle. In fact, the 2006 winter Olympic Games occurred in a postfordist city – Turin in Italy – attempting to reconstruct and re-image itself after a long period of deindustrialization precipitated by the decline of the automobile manufacturer Fiat.

Other forms of urban sport spectacle require the construction of elaborate, permanent sports amenities that promise either to retain or attract a much-coveted professional sport franchise (Bélanger, 2000; Gruneau and Whitson, 2001; Whitson and MacIntosh, 1996), which necessarily comes with many forms of profits and attractions. These permanent installations, often the result of public–private initiatives, have been the object of much criticism. Such private–public partnerships are also legitimated as viable uses of public funds through the argument that the enhancement of a city's status and, indeed, new development projects themselves will result in economic dividends for all citizens.[1] In Canada, sports owners have also tried to pressure city governments into large subsidies for arenas in recent years. Demands for new arenas were made in Edmonton, Winnipeg and Quebec City, based on threats to move the teams to economically 'friendlier' US cities. Stadium and arena boosters argue that these significant public–private investments will have a broader 'public' pay-off. The argument put forward is that the fans who crowd into a sports stadium or arena also stay at local hotels, eat at local restaurants and otherwise generate economic activity far beyond the ticket revenue earned by the building itself.

The spectacle of the commodity

A second dimension of the concept of urban spectacle shifts the analytical focus from the mobilization of the spectacle in an inter-urban competition for investment to the kinds of social and cultural experiences cultivated within the spectacle itself. As Gibson (2005: 180) notes:

> If the 'mobilization of spectacle' focused on the production of urban space to help reposition localities within the global economy, the spectacle of the commodity directs our attention to the textual characteristics of contemporary consumption environments – including theme parks and redeveloped urban shopping districts – and how the design of such spectacular spaces evokes images of adventure, fantasy, and play within a regimented architecture of surveillance and control.

The commercial production of urban popular culture in this context fuels a seemingly limitless proliferation of cultural goods and experiences, thereby creating an unprecedented global field of possibilities for consumer satisfaction and identity formation. But at the same time, these sources of satisfaction become even more closely tied to the market, to the need to find meaning through consumption.

Newly built festival market places come with elaborated iconographies and promotional discourses. These elements are supposed to sell the urban sport spectacle through the idea of a memorable 'experience' minimizing at the same time the consuming aspect of the place and its managed, controlled, orchestrated dimensions as well as certain regularly critiqued politics and effects of exclusion. Thus, the most notable trend here is the construction of elaborate 'urban entertainment destinations' which attempt to weave the process of buying and selling into a seamless experience of spectacle and entertainment (Hannigan, 1998). Often, as many scholars have noted, this merging of consumption and entertainment is organized around a specific and carefully orchestrated visual theme (Zukin, 1995; Davis, 1996, 1997; Hannigan, 1998; Gottdiener, 2001). Examples of this are shopping complexes such as Niketown or outdoor shopping areas set up for events such as motor races where fans/consumers are led through a series of carefully controlled spaces in which every textual element reflects and reinforces the more general narrative embodied in the space. Following theme park types of design and logic, the ultimate goal is to create places where fans/consumers are encouraged to play out certain fantasies (to feel empowered, excited and seduced) in a context drained of negative references to the day-to-day lives of most consumers (Davis, 1996, 1997; Sorkin, 1992; Zukin, 1991, 1995).

Spectacular resistance and resistance to the spectacle

According to Harvey (1989, 1990), the post-war urban spectacle has been transformed from counter-cultural events, anti-war demonstrations, street riots and the inner-city revolutions of the 1960s to more managed, accumulation-oriented spectacles to make the city a more attractive centre for tourism, consumption and leisure. In this transformation, the post-war urban spectacle – when it arises – has become a spectacular resistance to different, more recent forms of urban spectacle. Therefore, the concept focuses on occasions when the routine administration of daily urban life is ruptured by moments of spectacular resistance to either the plans and aims of policy and property elites or to specific events, such as international political meetings. Harvey (1989, 1990), for his part, has called such moments 'the spectacle of the street' and noted that the history of capitalist urbanization has long been punctuated by explosions of popular discontent. For example, Deluca and Peeples argue that the protests in Seattle outside the World Trade Organization summit in 1999 'make a compelling case of spectacular urban-based protests that [do] more than [simply] wage localized struggles over urban space' (Deluca and Peeples quoted in Gibson, 2005: 185). They argue that urban-based protests, like the kind that swept up and down the streets of Seattle, can also offer insight into a new, and potentially explosive, brand of progressive, global and image-savvy politics. Yet, acts or events of spectacular resistance are only a part of what can be generally understood as responses to spectacular development. This analytical dimension of the urban spectacle has not found regular expression in the sport or urban entertainment industry. However, an interest in exploring moments of resistance in the singular logics of commodification and accumulation informs another dimension of the concept: resistance to the spectacular.

This dimension aims at integrating the local symbolic and political forms of negotiations with the urban spectacle that do not 'add up' as spectacular types of resistance. Yet it seems to constitute most of the resistance around these new types of spectacular development project within the realm of sports or otherwise. This dimension comes out of the observation that many corporations, and public–private strategic alliances 'producing' the urban sport spectacle, have acknowledged that securing a profitable global presence necessitates negotiating with the local imaginary and popular culture. In other words, every spectacular redevelopment project more or less has to find a way to interpellate local sport fans and find ways to integrate itself rapidly in the social, political and cultural fabric of the city. The work of Smith and Ingham (2003) makes this point in arguing that funding new professional sport stadiums with public money in the United States centres upon the notion of community – fans' connection with the teams and the money that teams bring into the community. Their work also suggests that the urban sport spectacle, although often used in civic boosterism discourses, does not (re)generate a community-as-a-whole, but indeed may further divide residents, hinting then at the importance of the resistance to the spectacle in our analyses.

The resistance to the spectacular needs to be understood as an integrated part of the concept of the urban sport spectacle and not just a 'response' to it. Furthermore, this analytical focus is more than a typology of resistance to the spectacle: it includes the concrete expressions of the dialectical articulation between the mobilization of the spectacle, and the spectacle of the commodity and local popular cultures. If the first two dimensions focused on the production of the spectacle and the well-orchestrated, sanitized consumer spaces that they produce, this aspect of the third dimension (resistance to the spectacular) really shifts the focus to the uses and the vernacular appropriations of the spectacle, thus opening analysis to the ways in which this spectacle does not provoke resistance in the traditional sense, but goes through a process of short- and long-term nego-tiations with local cultures, imaginaries and practices.

In this vein, Peter Jackson (1993) argues that although environments like Niketown are built with the singular intent of accumulation and profit, these motives of production do not completely determine the moment and ways of 'consumption', that is, experience and interpretation of such spaces by members of the public themselves. Spaces are thus not merely produced by capital. Spaces are also *used* by different people in various contexts, and these spaces can be put to use in divergent, potentially even subversive ways (Bélanger, 2002). In some instances, the actual meanings and uses generated in such commodified, branded and themed consumption spaces spill over the tidy symbolic boundaries preferred by their private corporate controllers. I would add that in the case of the urban sport spectacle, the uses and meaning also spill over the boundaries of the 'world of sport'.

The mobilization of the urban sport spectacle often prompts resistance, designed to ensure more equal access, more democratic control of certain spaces such as stadiums, arenas and parks, or, in some instances, simply as a form of protest. It is important to note here that more often than not the response to the urban sport spectacle is a reaction as the mobilization of the spectacle does not often allow local fans/residents/consumers to formulate anything more than an 'after-the-fact reaction', prompting Roche and France (1998) to write about a disempowered view of the dynamics at play in the reception of such mega-events and spectacles.

Yet, we should keep in mind that if movements of opinions and resisting acts are fragile and fragmented, dominant powers are not always consistent and completely coherent either. As Gramsci (1971) showed in his complex analyses of class alliances and re-alliances in Italian history, the construction of a hegemonic bloc of shared capitalist interests can also be somewhat fragile and is filled with gaps and contradictions. These gaps and contradictions are important to take into consideration from a critical point of view, because they provide spaces for potential counter-hegemonic energies and practices. This last analytical focus allows empirical cases to start feeding theoretical understanding of the dialectics at play in the urban sport spectacle, in order to locate those spaces for counter-hegemonic energies and practices.

Towards a critical political economy of sport as popular culture

The powerful and significant relation between local sport fans and Major League sport or sport mega-events of various kinds has never been 'stable'. It is always in a constant state of re-articulating itself amid various contextual forces at play. The urban sport spectacle and the changes provoked do not eradicate the deep feeling and attachment sport fans have for certain teams and certain sports, rather it re-articulates it – albeit sometimes in problematic ways (Gruneau, 1988; Smith and Ingham, 2003). A critical analysis of contemporary urban sport spectacle should start with this premise. There is a great deal of work to be done to clarify exactly what is old and what is new about the recent restructuring of the entertainment and sport industries and the promotional discourses that sustain them. There is also a need to examine when and how current forms and prac-tices of symbolic production in the urban sport spectacle sustain ideology – and mobilize meaning on behalf of dominant interests – and when they do not.

I would argue that a striking characteristic of sport sociology in regards to the urban sport spectacle is a tendency to remain a sociology of denunciation in either readily adopting somewhat generalizing abstractions, or in delving too deep in the idiosyncratic details of a specific case-study without using it to inform the ongoing theoretical understanding of such events and developments. However, the concrete expressions of urban sport spectacle are a product of many deter-minations and interests; they come with many ambiguities and are always subject to change and 'realignment'.

Developing a critical political economy of sport as popular culture aiming at theorizing and understanding the meeting point between political economic forces and cultural practices and forms through the urban sport spectacle needs to come out of a perspective using the urban sport spectacle as a multidimen-sional concept rather than a series of generally likeable events (see Hall, 1981). In doing so, it allows us to acknowledge the strengths and limitations of the existing critiques. For example, I agree with Roche and France (1998) when they 'take side' with a disempowerment view (one that understands the spectacle as rather autocratic in character by provoking reactions as opposed to generating participation in the process of mobilization and construction) of the urban sport spectacle in their study of Sheffield's World Student Games multi-sport mega-event. This is particularly so in the mobilization of the spectacle and the spectacle of the commodity. These two dimensions are autocratic in character yet they are articulated in short and long term with experiences, resistances, attitudes of indifference and antipathy. In addition, considering the reaction/resistance to a specific urban sport spectacle yet also more generally reactions/resistance to events to come might stimulate an understanding of these reactions as something that works in the short and long term and that can be more empowering. A coalition of residents reacting in force after the construction of a larger stadium or a new sport–entertainment complex taking up a large part of 'their' public space does not offer much to the analysis of empowering uses of this specific park, yet this strong and convincing reaction 'sends a message' to upcoming promoters and developers. The Coalition des Amis du Parc Jarry is one convincing example of how networking between associations and coalitions can render their claims and critiques constructive and useful for a series of other related local causes. In this case specifically, they actively built and promoted an association to protect Montreal's green spaces and wrote an official report that was presented to city officials. This report is used to this day in many local causes of resistance to gentrification and redevelopment projects.

Generally speaking, core to a critical political economy of the urban sport spectacle is a focus on conjunctural articulations in ways that will not merely see a disempowered point of view slip into a condemnation of the tyranny of the urban sport spectacle; not seek apolitical empowerment in postmodern analysis of the sovereign consumers of these spectacles as creative or political appropriation; not rely on or seek a kind of traditional class-based resistance movement, politically and geographically; not contribute to a dis-alignment between context and critique; but consider a constant historicization of the urban sport spectacle as well as the approach it offers through interpretations of a struggle in its own context.

Throughout the formation and development of industrial capitalism and then in the transition towards post-industrial capitalism, there is a struggle over popular culture. 'This fact must be the starting point of any study', writes Stuart Hall (1981: 227) when he argues that:

> the changing balance and relations of social forces throughout that history reveal themselves, time and again, in struggles over the forms of the culture, traditions and ways of life of the working class because the constitution of the whole new social order required a more or less continuous, if intermittent, process or re-education, in the broadest sense.

In this sense a critical political economy of the urban sport spectacle as popular culture should consider sport as a practice formed in articulation with various indeterminate economic, political and ideological forces and seek to clarify the possibilities of sport as politicized cultural form and a space for struggle over popular culture.

The integration of empirical political economy and theoretical political economy is crucial, considering that one is often mistaken for the other and one does not always come to inform the other, as a way to continue constructing a critique that is always seeking transformative contexts rather than final and set changes. As Hall (1981: 227) observes, 'Time and again what we are really looking at is both the attempt of active destruction of particular ways of life and their ambiguous transformation into something new.'

Concluding remarks

The recognition of sport as spectacle is nothing new, but the 'nature' of these spectacles, their changing forms and ambiguous cultural, social and political meanings, remains surprisingly underemphasized. And this, as I have argued, is not simply a matter of empirical importance but one of opening up revealing avenues of theoretical significance and conceptual terrain. In this sense, if the concept of urban sport spectacle has any critical utility, it is not because it offers yet another opportunity to condemn the public for being the dupes of consumer society or solely to condemn the processes of production of such events and spaces. The concept of urban sport spectacle works best when it reminds us that the current monolithic drive to build spaces of upscale consumption and international sport mega-events represents only one dimension of the ongoing relation between professional sport and Major League sports with the fans, locals and consumers. To this end, the concept of urban spectacle reminds us that, rather than passively accepting the subordination of all social values to the singular pursuit of upscale retail and leisure, we should assert and analyse the urban sport spectacle spaces and events as multidimensional and ambiguous realities transforming over time and between localities.

Based on this, I call for a critical political economy that would aim at the conjunctural cracks of the fusion between urban development, consumerism, entertainment and sport, not in a naïve hope of finding a politically liberating potential of this form but to trace places and moments where we may observe, in these invested cities, active participation and resistances, albeit most often divided and dispersed. The aim is to be able to locate the core ambiguities in the state of play of the urban sport spectacle and therefore locate the struggles that do offer potential for change in order to orient theory and practice, and this requires considering the urban sport spectacle not simply as an expression or a manifestation of something else.

Such a perspective will facilitate understanding the ambiguous and dialectical integration of the urban sport spectacle into local cultures and imaginaries and addressing the following questions. What are the emerging paradoxes or ambiguities of the relation between political economy and cultural practices in what has been set in motion by the new urban entertainment economy – and in which sport has a central place? What is the dialectical relationship between the urban sport spectacle and local popular cultures? Is the importance of the urban sport spectacle for urban regeneration and for the international entertainment and leisure industries merely an empirical fact or is it also a matter of theoretical significance?

Sport sociologists often claim that sport has been left on the margin of mainstream Sociology, Cultural Studies and Political Economy, yet we tend to frame our analysis and theoretical perspective too often within the sport cosmology. A critical comprehension of the urban sport spectacle, especially one directed towards potential changes, should open the field to the multidimensional relations of the spectacle and its resistance to the urban sport spectacle which we could also call the dialectical processes of local integration (Bélanger, 2005). All forms of urban sport spectacles are contradictory, composed of antagonistic and unstable elements. The meaning of the urban sport spectacle is not inscribed inside its events and locations. Nor is its position fixed once and for ever. Paraphrasing Hall (1981: 285), we could say that what matters is not the historically fixed expression of the spectacle but the state of play in its constitutive dimensions and relations; or, to put it bluntly, what counts, in a critical political economy of the urban sport spectacle, is the struggle in and over the spectacle.

Acknowledgements

This argument borrows from the recent work of Tim A. Gibson, who was part of the 'Jolly Tax Payer Reading Group on the Urban Spectacle' set up by Rick Gruneau at Simon Fraser University in 1998 (with Mark Lowes, James Compton and myself).

Note

1 Many recently built sports stadiums in the USA illustrate this case. In Buffalo, for example, taxpayers will contribute up to $55 million of the $122.5 million necessary to construct a new home for the Sabers – a club in the National Hockey League. It is the same story for the Tampa Bay Lightning, where the city and the State of Florida were significantly involved in the financing of the Ice Palace.

References

Bélanger, A. (2000) 'Sports Venues and the Spectacularization of Urban Spaces in North America: The Case of the Molson Centre in Montreal', *International Review for the Sociology of Sport* 35, pp. 378–97.

Bélanger, A. (2002) 'Urban Space and Collective Memory: Analysing the Various Dimensions of the Production of Memory', *Canadian Journal of Urban Research, Special Issue: Space, Place and the Culture of Cities* 11(1), pp. 69–92.

Bélanger, A. (2005) 'Montréal vernaculaire/Montréal spectaculaire: Dialectique de l'imaginaire urbain', *Sociologie et Sociétés* 37(1), pp. 13–34.

Boyer, M.C. (1992) 'Cities for Sale: Merchandising History at South Street Seaport', in Michael Sorkin (ed.) *Variations on a Theme Park*, New York: Hill and Wang, pp. 181–204.

Castells, M. (2000) *The Rise of the Network Society*, 2nd edn, Oxford: Blackwell.

Davis, S.G. (1996) 'The Theme Park: Global Industry and Cultural Form', *Media, Culture, and Society* 18, pp. 399–422.

Davis, S.G. (1997) *Spectacular Nature: Corporate Culture and the Sea World Experience*, Berkeley: University of California Press.

Debord, G. (1967) *The Society of the Spectacle*, Detroit: Red and Black Books.

DeLuca, K.M. and Peeples, J. (2002) 'From Public Sphere to Public Screen: Democracy, Activism, and the "violence" in Seattle', *Critical Studies in Media Communication* 19, pp. 125–51.

Eckstein, R. and Delaney, K. (2002) 'New Sports Stadiums, Community Self-esteem, and Community Collective Conscience', *Journal of Sport and Social Issues* 26(3), pp. 236–48.

Fainstein, S. (1998) 'Justice, Nature, and the Geography of Difference' [book review], *International Journal of Urban and Regional Research* 22, pp. 339–41.

Gibson, T.A. (2003) 'The Trope of the Organic City: Discourses of Decay and Rebirth in Downtown Seattle', *Space and Culture* 6, pp. 429–48.

Gibson, T.A. (2004) *Securing the Spectacular City: The Politics of Homelessness and Revitalization in Downtown Seattle*, Lanham: Lexington Books.

Gibson, T.A. (2005) 'La ville et le "spectacle": Commentaires sur l'utilisation du "spectacle" dans la sociologie urbaine contemporaine', *Sociologie et Sociétés* 37(1), pp. 171–96.

Gotham, K. (2002) 'Marketing "Mardi Gras": Commodification, Spectacle, and the Political Economy of Tourism in New Orleans', *Urban Studies* 39(10), pp. 1735–56.

Gottdiener, M. (2001) *The Theming of America: American Dreams, Media Fantasies, and Themed Environments*, Boulder: Westview Press.

Gramsci, A. (1971) *Selections from the Prison Notebooks*, ed. Quintin Hoare and Geoffrey Nowell Smith, London: Lawrence and Wishart.

Gruneau, R. (ed.) (1988) *Popular Culture and Political Practices*, Toronto: Garamond Press.

Gruneau, R. and Whitson, D. (1997) 'The (Real) Integrated Circus: Political Economy, Popular Culture, and "Major League" Sport', in Wallace Clement (ed.) *Understanding Canada: Building on the New Canadian Political Economy*, Montreal and Kingston: McGill-Queen's University Press, pp. 359–85.

Gruneau, R. and Whitson, D. (2001) 'Upmarket Continentalism: Major League Sport, Promotional Culture, and Corporate Integration', in V. Mosco and D. Schiller (eds) *Continental Order? Integrating North America for Cyber-Capital*, Lanham: Roman and Littlefield, pp. 235–64.

Hall, S. (1981) 'Notes on Deconstructing the Popular', in S. Raphaël (ed.) *People's History and Socialist Theory*, London: Routledge, pp. 227–40.

Hall, S. and Jefferson, T. (eds) (1976) *Resistance through rituals: Youth subcultures in post-war Britain*, London, Hutchinson.

Hannigan, J. (1998) *Fantasy city: Pleasure and Profit in the Postmodern Metropolis*, London: Routledge.

Harvey, D. (1989) *The Urban Experience*, Baltimore: Johns Hopkins University Press.

Harvey, D. (1990) *The Condition of Postmodernity*, Oxford: Blackwell.

Hebdige, D. (1979) *Subculture: The Meaning of Style*, London, Methuen.

Ingham, A. and McDonald, M. (2003) 'Sport and Community/communitas', in R. Wilcox, D. Andrews, R. Irwin and R. Pitter (eds) *Sporting Dystopias: The Making and Meaning of Urban Sport Cultures*, Albany: State University of New York Press, pp. 17–33.

Jackson, P. (1993) 'Towards a Cultural Politics of Consumption', in J. Bird et al. (eds) *Mapping the Futures: Local Cultures, Global Change*, London: Routledge, pp. 207–28.

Judd, D. and Fainstein, S. (eds) (1999) *The Tourist City*, New Haven: Yale University Press.

Judd, D. and Swanstrom, T. (1994) *City Politics: Private Power and Public Policy*, New York: HarperCollins.

Kearns, G. and Philo, C. (1993) *Selling Places: The City as Cultural Capital, Past and Present*, Oxford: Pergamon Press.

Lowes, M. (2002) *Indy Dreams and Urban Nightmares: Speed Merchants, Spectacle, and the Struggle over Public Space in the World-Class City*, Toronto: University of Toronto Press.

Lowes, M. (2004) 'Neoliberal Power Politics and the Controversial Siting of the Australian Grand Prix Motorsport Event in an Urban Park', *Society and Leisure* 27, pp. 69–88.

Pile, S. (1997) 'Oppositional, Political Identities and Spaces of Resistance', in S. Pile and M. Keith (eds) *Geographies of Resistance*, London and New York: Routledge, pp. 1–32.

Robins, K. (1997) 'What in the World is Going on?', in P. Du Gay (ed.) *Production of Culture/Cultures of Production*, London: Sage, pp. 12–61.

Roche, M. and France, A. (1998) 'Sport Mega-Events, Urban Policy and Youth Identity', in Roche, M. (ed.) *Sport, Popular Culture and Identity*, Aachen: Meyer & Meyer, pp. 139–66.

Rothman, H. and Davis, M. (eds) (2002) *The Grit beneath the Glitter: Tales from the Real Las Vegas*, Berkeley: University of California Press.

Sassen, S. (1991) *The Global City: New York, London, Tokyo*, Princeton: Princeton University Press.

Shields, R. (1989) 'Social Spatialization and the Built Environment: The West Edmonton Mall', *Environment and Planning D: Society and Space* 7, pp. 147–64.

Shropshire, K.L. (1995) *The Sports Franchise Game: Cities in Pursuit of Sports Franchises, Events, Stadiums*, Philadelphia: University of Pennsylvania Press.

Silk, M. (2002) '"Banga Malaysia": Global Sport, the City, and the Mediated Refurbishment of Local Identities', *Media, Culture, and Society* 24, pp. 775–94.

Smith, J. and Ingham, A. (2003) 'On the Waterfront: Retrospectives on the Relationship between Sport and Communities', *Sociology of Sport Journal* 20(3), pp. 252–75.

Sorkin, M. (ed.) (1992) *Variations on a Theme Park: The New American City and the End of Public Space*, New York: Hill and Wang.

Tomlinson, A. (2002) 'Theorizing Spectacle, beyond DeBord', in J. Sugden and A. Tomlinson (eds) *Power Games: A Critical Sociology of Sport*, London: Routledge, pp. 44–60.

Von Borries, F. (2004) *Who's Afraid of Niketown? Nike-Urbanism, Branding and the City of Tomorrow*, Rotterdam: Episode.

Whitson, M. and MacIntosh, D. (1996) 'The Global Circus: International Sport, Tourism, and the Marketing of Cities', *Journal of Sport and Social Issues* 20, pp. 239–57.

Williams, R. (1983) *Dreamworlds: Mass Consumption in the Late Nineteenth Century*, Berkeley: University of California Press.

Zukin, S. (1991) *Landscapes of Power: From Detroit to Disneyland*, Berkeley: University of California Press.

Zukin, S. (1995) *The Cultures of Cities*, Cambridge: Basil Blackwell.

Zukin, S. (1998) 'Urban Lifestyles: Diversity and Standardization in Spaces of Consumption', *Urban Studies* 35(5–6), pp. 825–40.

5 Between culture and economy

Understanding the politics of media sport

Garry Whannel

Introduction

The day before I finished writing this chapter I stood at a bus stop surrounded by people who were listening to iPods, making mobile phone calls, texting or playing electronic games. At one end of the shelter an electronic advert played trailers and music for a forthcoming film. On the bus, as an alternative to gazing out of the window (at the 'real' world?), there was a screen with news, weather, forthcoming attractions and other promotional material. It would be an exaggeration to say that the world has collapsed into 'the media' but fair to recognize that culture, social exchange and everyday life are thoroughly saturated by media representation. Advertising and promotion are significant, indeed, dynamic elements in this constant media penetration of new areas of the public landscape. In trying to understand media sport politically, I am searching for modes of analysis that enable an understanding of signification *and* commodification both separately and together, recognizing both their separateness and their interconnectedness, while avoiding collapsing one into the other. It is necessary here to trace developments in cultural theory in order to outline why this project is both imperative and difficult.

This chapter argues for the continuing relevance of Marxian analysis in a world in which media and reality appear to have collapsed into each other, in ways which place the fetishized commodity, the consuming individual and the promotional culture at the centre of human experience. It will examine the damaging impact of the divergence of economic and cultural analysis in Western cultural analysis and will sketch out ways that we might begin to reintegrate the two in concrete critical analysis.

Cultural Studies and Marxist theory

Marxism poses a relation between culture and economy that is one of determinacy, albeit in 'the last instance'. In Marx's own writing, however, it is clear that this was not simply a reductive model. The relations between economic relations and cultural production are necessarily complex and contradictory, as are those between economic relations, classes and political parties. Marx never got round to developing further upon his schematic accounts of the relation between culture and economy; and his work in this area remained suggestive rather than fully elaborated. Developments in Western Marxism sought to explore further the nature of ideology (Anderson, 1976). Writing in this tradition sought to avoid reductionist and economistic modes of analysis, and attempted to elaborate upon, interpret and revise Marx's work, in order to develop a Marxist theory of ideology, focused on concepts of determination in the last instance, reciprocal effectivity and relative autonomy (CCCS, 1977).

Althusser's influence on the field of Cultural Studies was profound, in changing the ways in which ideology was conceptualized, emphasizing its all-pervasive character (see Althusser, 1971, 1977, and Althusser and Balibar, 1968). But the attempt, following Althusser, to hold on to both determination in the last instance and relative autonomy proved an unstable equilibrium (Hall, 1980). Even as it crystallized into an embryonic 'tradition', the Cultural Studies perspective began to fragment, torn between post-structuralist, sociological and anthropological directions. Althusserian Marxism was criticized for its neglect of the economic level (Murdock and Golding, 1977). Stuart Hall's work was said to overemphasize the role of the state and underemphasize capitalist entrepreneurship (Garnham, 1977, 1979). It was certainly true that much of the work emanating from the Centre for Contemporary Cultural Studies paid closer attention to the nature of the state in capitalist societies than it did to the structure of capitalist enterprise. Debates over the best means of analysing cultural production in this period were rich and lively, and served to outline an agenda which foregrounds the need for a viable non-reductionist theory of cultural production (see, for example, Barrett *et al.*, 1979).

The rising influence of discourse theory, Lacanian psycho-analysis and post-structuralism generally produced a focus upon the processes of entry into language, the construction of subjectivity, and the ceaseless productivity of signification, pushing at the limits of Marxist-derived models of ideology (Coward and Ellis, 1977). The Birmingham model of Cultural Studies was criticized in *Screen* for being reductionist, for having an essentialist model of class subjectivity, and for privileging class politics over gender relations (Coward, 1977; Chambers *et al.*, 1977). A second trajectory, influenced by the ethnographic tradition, consisted of a growth in small-scale qualitative and participant-observational research on audiences. Economic relations, and their relation to cultural production, became first marginalized and then repressed as the great unspoken of Cultural Studies.

The growing influence of new modes of theorizing culture, influenced by Foucault, Lacan, Kristeva and Hindess and Hirst, marked a departure from the terrain of the 'determinations' problematic. Post-structuralist developments in theories of language emphasized the endless productivity of the sign, the independence of signifiers from any signified, and a tendency to conceptualize the autonomy of culture and language as total rather than 'relative'. Foucault's work on power and discourse retained a concept of power relations but posited a model in which power relations were imbricated in all social exchange and were dispersed throughout society. While the model was not intrinsically inimical to the theorizing of economic relations, in much Foucauldian work the question of the economic relations underpinning power relations tended to be marginalized (Foucault, 1972).

One notable legacy of post-war debates on culture was that terms such as 'reductionism' and 'economic determinism' became derogatory labels in a way that contributed to a marginalization of the economic in analysis. Indeed, Timpanaro (1975: 29) dryly pointed out that, 'Perhaps the sole characteristic common to virtually all contemporary varieties of western Marxism is their concern to defend themselves against the accusation of materialism.' The fear of being thought reductionist continues to haunt cultural analysis, to the extent that studies of consumption often appear to avoid the integration of such a basic concept as 'profit'.

For those who perceived problems with Althusser's two ends of the chain but wished to pursue questions of the relation between economy and culture, Gramsci offered potential. Gramscian Marxism offered a distinct way of theorizing such problems as agency, the relation between theory and practice and the relation between the economic and the cultural (see Boggs, 1976; Mouffe, 1979; Sassoon, 1980, 1982). The concept of hegemony provided a means of retaining economic and cultural levels within the same analysis without collapsing one into the other. However, much commentary on Gramsci focused on politics as distinct from economics, and upon the role of Gramsci as a 'theoretician of the superstructures' (see Mouffe, 1979; Sassoon, 1980). The full value of hegemony as a concept that allowed examination of the ways in which economic relations, common-sense and organized political discourse were related was not fully realized. Marxist analyses of the late 1970s and early 1980s took their cue from the work of Althusser and the growing influence of Gramsci, and tended to focus more on the state than on enterprise, and more on politics than on economics. Raymond Williams' discussion of determination – arguing that determination involves both setting limits and exerting pressures – is suggestive of a different mode of analysis in which relations between economics and culture can be both immediate and distant at the same time. This approach acknowledges cultural production as both a cultural–ideological and an economic practice. It recognizes a relative autonomy of the cultural while also insisting that the economic relations underpinning cultural production constantly set limits and exert pressures (Williams, 1977: 83–9).

The principle of the economic setting limits and exerting pressures is suggestive of modes of analysis that can encompass more direct and immediate relations than implied by 'determination in the last instance' without becoming reductionist. The formula does not, however, provide any firm methodological guarantees, and a lot then depends upon the quality of interpretation and attention to the empirical detail of specific examples. The innovative interdisciplinary Open University Popular Culture course (U203), although including work on the cutural industries, on practices and on institutions, as well as retaining an emphasis on the text and ideology, and the conceptual frame, remained one in which economic relations tended to be assigned to a last instance that never came. The underlying theoretical model did not promote easy integration of the ideological analyses of texts and the contextual material on industries, practices and institutions (see Bennett *et al.*, 1981a; Bennett *et al.*, 1981b; and Waites *et al.*, 1982).

In the wake of the moment of high theory (the period in the late 1970s when Cultural Studies debate became dominated by issues in abstract theory), and the failure of any one theoretical synthesis to hold the middle ground, the developing but fragmenting field of Cultural Studies turned its attention back towards concrete empirical studies. Such studies, frequently eclectic in spirit, often found ways of making connections in concrete analysis even if these connections were not adequately theorized. Yet, it was possible to detect the gradual disappearance, with a few notable exceptions, of the problem of the relation between economic relations and cultural production as an element in Cultural Studies theorizing. Textual analysis became a dominant methodological approach; the inadequacies that some perceived textual analysis to have were addressed by a growing commitment to audience research. Studies of institutions, and institutional practices that gave attention not just to power and discourse but to economic relations, were less common within Cultural Studies.

While the Cultural Studies community, in neo-philiac fashion, embarked on a frenetic period of intellectual importation, the external political context began to shift dramatically. These shifts, outlined by Hall (1983) as 'The Great Moving Right Show', included the exhaustion in the West of the social democratic repertoire, the rise of monetarism, Thatcherism and Reaganomics, a confrontational stance towards the USSR, and the sudden and dramatic collapse of Eastern Bloc communism. Eric Hobsbawm (1978) declared that the 'forward march of Labour' had been halted. The new ascendant political analyses talked of the post-industrial society, post-Fordism, the consumption-based society, and the 'end of history' (Bell, 1960; Fukuyama, 1992).

One central tenet of one of the key texts of postmodern analysis, Lyotard's *The Postmodern Condition* (1984), argues that the old totalizing narratives of the Enlightenment have lost their force, and that there are no longer grand narratives. This has been used in critiques of Marxism that usually seek to place emphasis on its teleological and historicist aspects. One problem of the premature obituaries for Marxism based on an attempt to consign grand narratives to the dustbin of history is that grand narratives clearly do still exist and have immense social and political force. Modes of fundamentalism, both Christian and Islamic, have dominated the growing political tensions between the USA and the Middle East states. Fundamentalist Christians in the USA have acquired considerable political power, influencing the highest levels of policy formation. The political cluster that brings together environmental campaigners, eco-warriors, anti-globalization and anti-capitalist activists draws on an environmental grand narrative about the life-threatening impact of climate change. Of course, they tend to be narratives of salvation and doom rather than the progressive grand narratives of Enlightenment rationality and optimism, but these are totalizing narratives that successfully hail many millions of adherents. Few now might want to accept the historical projections of Marx but the analysis of capitalism still seems to have considerable force. Clearly there have been profound changes, not always foreseen by Marx, such as the expansion of the state, the growth of a service sector, the growth of a salaried but affluent middle class. Yet, many of the fundamental mechanisms identified and dissected in *Capital* are still in operation.

Transformative processes have markedly reshaped the urban cultural and economic landscape over the last thirty years. Walk down any high street, or shopping mall, sit in an airport or railway station, and the manifestations of depth-lessness, the domination of surface appearance over substance, self-referentiality, pastiche and irony, the dilution of difference into diversity, seem all too apparent. Insightful as much postmodern analysis has been, it also appears to have delivered us into an anchorless and rudderless miasma – relativist, de-totalizing and ulti-mately anti-analytic. This in turn has served to foster a de-politicization of cultural commentary. The denial of history is a dangerous business, as events since 2001 illustrate. Baudrillard's (1998) proclamation of the illusion of history has no more explanatory value in the end than Fukuyama's (1992) proclamation of the end of history. The year 2000 *did* happen, as did 2001.

There is a younger generation of scholars – the children of Baudrillard – who have suggested that those who cling on to earlier theorists, from Marx to Althusser, are like drivers who navigate by gazing in the rear-view mirror. Manifestly this is not a safe way to drive, and one needs to look forward. However, driving only by gazing excitedly through the windscreen is not a sound tactic either. To know where you are going, it helps to know where you have been. Simon Clarke (Clarke *et al.*, 1980: 11) commented that reading *For Marx* had become a substitute for reading Marx, and reading Althusser's *Reading Capital* had become a substitute for reading *Capital*. It seems to me that, today, reading Baudrillard has become a substitute for reading Barthes for many scholars. While, for too many students, surfing the net has become a substitute for reading.

New Times, new theories?

The impact of Thatcherism during the 1980s prompted a reassessment of left positions on culture in which attention was focused on consumption and the construction of identities (Clarke, 1991; McRobbie, 1991; Norris, 1992; Murdock, 1994). Angela McRobbie (1991) warned of the tendency to celebrate consumption while severing it from the context of social practices and called for a return to integrative modes of analysis that tracked the social and ideological relations prevailing at every level between cultural production and consumption. This meant examining all of those processes that accompany the production of meaning in culture, and not just the end product. The impact of the 1980s did prompt a refocus of analysis, and a greater concern to analyse the processes of production and consumption of culture (see, for examples, Tomlinson, 1990; Corner and Harvey, 1991).

During the 1990s the Cultural Studies tradition was subject to critical reassess-ment and proposals for new agendas. Yet, it was striking that the reintegration of the economic remained marginal. Of the eleven texts discussed in detail in *Reading into Cultural Studies* (Barker and Beezer, 1992) none foreground the issue of the relation between economic relations and cultural production, and in only a handful does it intrude as a significant element in the explanatory schema. But this was not a lacuna that the editors sought to highlight. Barker and Beezer, in their introduction, identify the gradual marginalization of the concept of class in cultural analysis, but do not discuss economic relations. So the core texts of the Cultural Studies tradition, as seen at the start of the 1990s, were studies in which the economy/culture issue was marginal. The essays in *Relocating Cultural Studies*, offered as a critique of the Anglocentricism of British Cultural Studies, discussed the boundaries of Cultural Studies from feminist, post-colonial and ethnographic contexts, but none placed back on the agenda the issue of the economic (Blundell *et al.*, 1993).

Jim McGuigan's *Cultural Populism* (1992) offered a constructive critique of the reassessment of consumption, and refocusing on identity politics that grew out of the New Times debates and the repositioning of left critical intellectual work during the 1980s. McGuigan does reopen the issue of the political economy of culture, although the absence of analyses of economic relations is not identified as a major lacuna in the Cultural Studies trajectory. Post-colonial theory asserted the importance of processes of diaspora and hybridity, criticized the Euro-centricism of much Cultural Studies theory, but did not bridge, indeed contributed to, the gulf between textual reading and economic analysis. Similarly, the growing centrality of debates on globalization, while producing a greater attention to economic relations, has yet to narrow the gap in the middle of media study. However, both post-colonialism analyses and globalization analyses required a re-engagement with the complex relationships between culture and economy. During the 1990s, the ground became fertile for a new regeneration of critical media analysis that could grow out of an engagement with such challenges.

Of course, the rise of postmodern theory, its adherents claim, renders Marxist Cultural Studies old fashioned and redundant. Baudrillard's (1972) insight that the symbolic value of commodities dominates makes discussion based on Marxist concepts of use value and exchange value superfluous. The appropriation and eclipse of 'the real' by simulacra and by hyper-reality makes a philosophy of social change based on the unmasking of 'real relations' irrelevant. The supersession of production by consumption means that Marxism is no longer focused at the cutting edge of analysis.

Yet, little in postmodern analysis allows us any superior purchase on the power of the giant corporations of this age of consumption. We can acknowledge that we live in an era in which culture has become overwhelmingly self-referential and saturated with pastiche, and still ask the old questions about ideology, economic relations and power. We do not have to maintain that Marxism, as a totalizing system, accounts for every aspect of the social totality in order to use, develop and apply its modes of analysis. Indeed, the commercialization and globalization of culture would appear to make Marxism more, rather than less, relevant.

An interesting feature of Cultural Studies analysis in the 1990s has been the re-emergence of attempts to bring economy and culture together in specific focused, empirically based analyses. As Du Gay (Du Gay *et al.*, 1997: 3) proposes: 'contemporary material culture is predominantly "manufactured" . . . everyday cultural lives are bound up with mass-produced material artefacts to such an extent that a principled opposition between the economic and industrial, on the one hand, and the cultural, on the other, is simply untenable.'

Rather, the 'economic' and the 'cultural' are posited as irrevocably 'hybrid' categories: so what we think of as purely 'economic' processes and practices are in an important sense cultural phenomena. Du Gay (*ibid.*) refers to the term 'cultural economy' as a way of suggesting 'both continuity and rupture with deterministic approaches to the study of "economic life"'. The concept is a productive and useful one, although, as the emphasis remains on language, representation and meaning, it has a tendency to collapse 'economy' upwards into 'culture', such that 'the economic has been thoroughly culturalized' (*ibid.*: 5).

What is in the mainstream of culture today? Hollywood cinema, a global-ized television system, major spectacular sport such as the World Cup and the Olympics, soap opera, women's magazines, Coca-Cola and McDonald's. All of this cultural production is predominantly in the hands of major multimedia, multinational companies. If it is valid to claim that the economic has been thoroughly culturalized, the reverse is also a tenable model. It is not wise to believe that culture can be analysed without attention to the economic relations underpinning cultural production, or to analyse texts without a proper attempt to contextualize this analysis with an understanding of their conditions of exis-tence. Analysis needs to pay close attention to the ways in which diverse dynamic processes – hybridity and diaspora, the relation between the global and the local, the rise of the new media and digitalization, the celebrity culture and vortextuality – interact within the complex and contradictory social formation. More recently, Mike Wayne (2003) has argued for a reassertion of the base–superstructure model. He argues that this model has to be seen as a dynamic process rather than a static determining structure. It is worth revisiting Marx's own description of this relationship:

> In the social production of their life, men enter into definite relations that are indispensable and independent of their will, relations of production which correspond to a definite stage of development of their material pro-ductive forces. The sum total of these relations of production constitutes the economic structure of society, the real foundation, on which rises a legal and political superstructure, and to which correspond definite forms of social consciousness. The mode of production of material life conditions the social political and intellectual life process in general.
>
> (Marx, 1968: 181)

Wayne is quite right to remind us that this is a description of process, in which people 'enter into' definite relations, and in which the mode of production 'conditions' the life process. Marx does not, here, refer to this as a base, and the emphasis on the 'legal and political' superstructure became rather displaced by the attempts in 'Western Marxism' to elaborate a theory of ideology in general. Wayne suggests that the base includes both mode of production and, in drawing on Castells, mode of development; and suggests a model with several interacting but analytically distinct elements in the superstructure. This returns to the problematic of 'determination in the last instance', along with 'relative autonomy', and, as I read it, allows for 'reciprocal effectivity', without reducing economy and culture to equally and mutually determining elements or, as in the OU model, tending to project 'production' upwards into culture.

Analysing mediated sport and culture now

Understanding the media demands both semiological and sociological analysis. It involves an analysis of the circuit of production–text–consumption in the media system. This involves two analytically distinct but connected processes. In the first, at the level of signification, media texts are composed through signs that acquire their meanings through codes and conventions, structured by the configuration of pre-existing and emergent discourses. In the second, texts are produced in an institutional context in which structures, practices and ideologies govern the nature of the production process. They reach an audience through socially structured practices of distribution that play a key role in determining which texts most readily reach an audience. Both legal–political structures and economic relations serve to set limits and exert pressures on this process. The two levels are analytically distinct, but it is also a task of analysis to understand how these two levels are embedded together in the process of the production and consumption of media texts.

To illustrate, briefly, with an example. An analysis of the film *Bend It Like Beckham* might start with textual analysis, exploring the ways in which discourses of masculinity and femininity, celebrity and fame, Asian-ness and British-ness are mobilized within a 'triumph over obstacles' narrative structure. This in turn requires some attention to be paid to the broader structure of these discourses and the ways in which they are dispersed across a range of texts. Questions of hybridity and diaspora are central here to understanding the particular British-Asian configuration that has generated a particular set of cultural manifestations, and how these manifestations find an audience.

Analysis also needs to ask about the conditions of existence through which British cinema survives, the circumstances under which a film project of this kind can find finance, get made and be distributed. Crucially, in this case, the question of how this film found a large market in the USA is of great interest. These questions are both economic and cultural. They require us to examine the ways in which a globalizing culture, local specificities and hybridized and diasporized identities combine to produce the unlikely commercial success of the film. This is not to say, of course, that every analysis has to operate at all these levels; but any programme of research that does not at some point consider the levels and their relation is to some degree limited. This, it seems to me, is exactly what the best Marxist-inspired cultural analysis has been doing and still does. The project remains that of finding a non-reductionist, materialist theory of culture, in which there can be a productive relation between theory and concrete detailed empirical analysis.

After such a lengthy period of driving while looking in the rear-view mirror, we should turn our attention to the view through the windscreen of the road ahead. I want to outline three aspects of media sport linked to three themes of analysis by way of example. The first considers sports chatter and sports information as a form of disarticulation and rearticulation; the second considers the commodification of celebrity as a convergence of cultural and economic aspects of the commodity; and the third considers the dynamic force of advertising and the promotional culture.

Sports chatter on planet sport

Considered as a form of disarticulation (separation from the wider social world) and rearticulation (the production of imaginary coherences, such as fandom, the nation) sports chatter and sports information serve both to demarcate one narrow domain and to provide it with a place, a meaning and a significance. A significant percentage of the broadcast time devoted to sport does not feature live or recorded action, but rather discussion, analysis, debate and statistical information (see Rowe, 1992). One could suggest here two categories of material: sports chatter and sports information.

Sports chatter (see Eco, 1986) is a form of exchange, largely between men and tending to exclude women, in which analysis of events, tactics, players and perfor- mances blends with anecdote, banter and reminiscence. It serves to underpin the separateness of sport (a world of its own), to promote the circulation of an alternative masculine cultural capital, to reinforce and bind the coherence of those within this masculinist and heterosexist culture, while excluding and distancing those outside it. Of course, it is also a potentially contradictory practice. Radio soccer phone-ins, for example, contain a range of contributions, including some that are deeply critical. Sometimes this criticism is limited to rants at particular referees, clubs or players, but often too it has constituted a more structured attack on the directors (owners) of football, and the governance of the game. Such a discourse has fed into the group consciousness of fans, and the rise of a more assertive fan power, and the establishment of supporters' trusts. The gatekeepers of such programmes – the presenters and producers – then wield a degree of cultural power in their ability to inflect discussion in particular direc- tions. There is nothing guaranteed about ideological reproduction – hegemony is a process in permanent contestation. In the proliferation of channels on radio and television, and the continued expansion of the internet, there is a voracious appetite for media content and an imperative that this content be cheap. The voice of the fan has been incorporated – providing chat on the radio, alternative football reports in newspapers and many gigabytes of internet content.

The representation and social practices of sport have always offered a distillation, a positivist and quantitative map of the sport world in wh thing is measured, counted, assessed and ranked. The new technologic; – computers, the internet, and digitalization – have greatly enhanced u.. to perform this distillation; the Opta Index for quantifying football performance is just one instance. Brohm (1978) commented on this process in the pertinently titled *Sport: A Prison of Measured Time*. Mewshaw (1983) drew attention to the impact of ranking in tennis, recalling that when asked how they were, tennis professionals replied with their place in the rankings.

Dedicated sports channels, like Sky Sports in the UK and ESPN in the US, have borrowed an internet aesthetic for television, with multiple windows and crawling and scrolling text, enabling a non-linear representation of statistics and information. Visually sports news and financial news are now very similar – compare Sky Sports with the financial channel and website Bloomberg. Marx regarded money as an abstract system of equivalence, reducing economic relations to an abstract system that enabled the comparison of value. Sport has its own abstract systems of equivalence that enable the constant ranking and re-ranking of performance. Knowledge of these systems of statistics and information in turn feeds into male cultural capital, uniting and binding those men within the cultures of sport, providing an easy mode of exchange, while excluding outsiders (mostly women, but also many men). The combination of chat and statistic, which we could dub 'waffle 'n' info', while appearing ephemeral, provides the structure of a core alternative virtual world – planet sport. Planet sport severs its links from the everyday – from the world of work, from the domestic sphere, from politics and even from sexuality. It is a space with its own values, rituals and symbols. Stars, action, gossip, anecdote and banter are all profoundly inward looking and self-referential.

Commodity sport celebrities

Baudrillard's (1972) discussion of the political economy of the sign drew attention to the rising significance of the symbolic value of goods, which he regarded as eclipsing their use value. The convergence of sport stardom and the celebrity culture has fostered an objectification of the body and a commodification of the self. The intensity of media attention paid to major sporting events produces a vortextual effect that draws people in, builds an audience, and greatly enhances the economic opportunities associated with television rights, sponsorship, corporate entertainment and marketing (Whannel, 2002). Top stars now utilize the services of platoons of pseudo-professionals – public relations advisers, image consultants, personal shoppers and marketeers. The appearances of such stars in the media are carefully planned to link to promotional opportunities for books, clothing, films and personal appearances. Michael Jordan and David Beckham are two of those who have most successfully accomplished the branding of the self. Brand Beckham, skilfully managed, has become his own symbolic form, available at a price to attach to your product, whether it is designer sunglasses or a major football team (see Cashmore, 2004).

The symbolic form, though, is not entirely in the control of those who seek to transform symbolic capital back into financial capital. Image is inherently unstable. Note the prevalence of style guides which divide the world into the 'cool' and the 'uncool'; the 'hip' and the 'naff'; that divide celebrities into 'heroes' and 'zeroes'; or that constantly pose questions like 'What's hot? What's not?' The saturation of culture with image and celebrity demands turnover, innovation and the thrill of the new; and so old celebrities must constantly be jettisoned to make way for new ones. The process whereby a star loses their luster is a mysterious one: an ill-judged remark, a poorly chosen outfit, being caught by photographers on a bad hair day – all can precipitate a draining away of public enthusiasm. Paul Gascoigne went from being the focal point of Gazzamania to sad, fat clown in a matter of months; rugby player Jonny Wilkinson won a nation's attention but had no desire to be a marketing tool; only the almost complete lack of British competition kept Tim Henman, despite his inherent dullness, at the epicentre of tennis fandom, until Andrew Murray arrived. The trajectories of stars like Tiger Woods, Mike Tyson, Denis Rodman, Paula Radcliffe and Michael Schumacher serve to illustrate that public image is a complex and unpredictable form that is always uncertain and can never be completely controlled. Modern media culture, it seems to me, cannot be understood without analysing the complex interplay of symbolic form and economic relationship.

Advertising and promotional culture

In analyses of sport, the processes of commercialization and commodification have been a central theme (for recent examples, see Sugden and Tomlinson 1998; Miller *et al.*, 2001; Slack, 2004; Jackson and Andrews, 2005; Horne, 2006). The media-scape is heavily influenced by the practices of public relations consultants, media managers, image consultants, advertisers and spin doctors, and these practices have yet to receive as much critical analysis as they warrant. Let me illustrate this with two examples from online gambling and the Olympic Games.

Online gambling has extended the lure of betting beyond the walls of the casino and now hails a global audience. Gambling is a highly profitable form, offering one of the few commodities in which people will pay for the mere possibility of a return, and have to accept that they may well pay out for no gain. Online gambling is widely advertised, frequently accompanied with sexualized images of showgirls and female croupiers. Spread betting, a model derived from city trading, long established in the USA, has extended its reach to other parts of the world. With its technological base and city trader image, such forms of gambling constitute an addition to the repertoire of toys for the boys, or at least toys for the heterosexual boys. Rather like the mythologized heroin dealer at the school gate, from whom the first taste was always free, the online poker sites offer free taster games, and then cash floats to start you off. Once registered, if you fail to play, regular email invitations will come your way. Gambling is an inevitable process of attrition: in the long run the players lose and the house wins. As a means of getting the audience to meet the full cost of the entertainment and provide the profit, online gambling is a perfect media form. If Brecht were writing his play *Mahagonny* today, he might well elect to set it in the virtual city of online gambling. This is another instance of capital seeking new areas to penetrate. The moment, only a few years in the past, when the internet was being proclaimed by some as a wonderful new collectivized and socialized space where free interaction could take place already seems a long time ago.

The Olympic Games has never been innocent of commerce, but the extent to which marketing has moved from periphery to core in the last twenty years is remarkable. The strategies and styles of marketing have become globalized. The marketing strategy for the Beijing Olympics used a rhetoric and structure virtually indistinguishable from that employed in Athens 2004, Sydney 2000 or Atlanta 1996. It is instructive to examine the language of the Beijing 2008 *Marketing Plan Launch* (2003). Two things are striking. First, that the systematic global marketing of the Olympic Games and its symbols to corporate sponsors, which was still controversial in the mid-1980s (see Whannel, 1994a), has become absolutely routinized and taken for granted. Second, despite the unique and extraordinary character of China, a dynamic market economy presided over by an authoritarian communist state, there is virtually nothing culturally distinct about the language, which could have emanated from any corporate marketing culture anywhere in the world.

The International Olympic Committee President Jacques Rogge called the Games 'an unprecedented marketing opportunity for China' which will 'provide a unique global platform, a powerful international stage for building brands and market share'. The President of the Beijing Organizing Committee outlines the way that 'the unique format of the marketing operations of the Olympic Games and its global brand impact will provide an effective way for Chinese enterprises to raise their international reputation and credibility and for Chinese products to move to the world'. The President of the Chinese Olympic Committee asserts that 'successful marketing is a vital guarantee for the success of an Olympic Games'. The Mayor of Beijing says that 'preparations for the Beijing 2008 Olympics have created a very favorable environment for the development of Chinese enterprises and provided a new driving force for enterprises to enter international markets'. The Chairman of the IOC Marketing Commission proclaims that 'we expect the power of this enduring marketing partnership to reach new heights and generate a new level of benefits . . . in 2008 the unity of humanity will reach a new crescendo'.[1]

The symbolic force of Olympism is condensed on to one of the world's most recognized logos and the *Marketing Plan* comments that 'The power of Olympic Marketing starts with the fundamental value of the symbol of the five rings' (Beijing 2008, 2003: 23). Never was Baudrillard's (1972) assertion about the rise of symbolic value more applicable. Staging an Olympic Games enables a further condensation of the image of city and of country on to the five-ring symbol. The *Marketing Plan* (*ibid.*: 35) refers to:

> The Powerhouse combination of Beijing 2008: an integration of Brand
> China, Brand Beijing, the COC and Chinese Olympic Team . . . showcases
> the heritage, the culture and the spirit of its people . . . an unrivalled mar-
> keting platform for building the national brand, and clearly communicating
> the image of China . . . the full integration of Brand China into Beijing 2008
> will infuse the Games with cohesive expressive and emotive brand attributes
> essential to the overall success of the event and its marketing programmes.

Indeed, this relationship provides a promotional dream, linking city, country, idealism and enterprise: 'In short, Beijing 2008 represents the full potential of Brand China, Brand Beijing and the Chinese Olympic team which are joined as seamless components in the unmatched long-term marketing platform offered by the Games' (*ibid.*: 39).

In this discourse, the Olympic Games has become 'an unrivalled marketing platform from which to build an unmatched competitive advantage by max-imising the power of the Olympic Image' (*ibid.*: 59). The Games provides sponsors with 'powerful opportunities to reach consumers in a multitude of ways', and, as a bonus, 'By supporting Olympic athletes, sponsors also demonstrate a commit-ment to noble and enduring values, convey good corporate citizenship, and communicate a dedication to success, excellence and goodwill' (*ibid.*). The discourse offers its readers, potential sponsors, a flattering self-image of their benevolent role: 'sponsors intimately communicate their commitment to the Olympic ideals, the Games, the athletes while helping to enhance the lives of consumers everywhere' (*ibid.*: 63).

After the rings, the second most marketable symbol is the torch relay. The relay used to be simply a symbolic linking of the site of the current Games and the site of the ancient Games in Olympia in Greece, passing through many other countries en route. It has now become another sponsorship opportunity and one that provides links between the local and the global: 'Olympic partners and sponsors who also support the Olympic Torch Relay can maximise this highly effective platform on practical and emotional levels, bringing the excitement and anticipation of the Games to local communities, foster intense consumer goodwill while reaching consumers on the street in their hometowns' (*ibid.*). In short, the stakeholders of the Olympic family are univocal in their performance of a unified and unifying discourse, suturing together Olympism and enterprise, goodwill and profit, identity and brand. This, then, is the new Olympic spirit.

Reflections on the cultural economy of mediated sport

In recent work on sport the concepts of commercialization, commodification and globalization have rightly played a central role. It is reasonable to regard this work as being in the lineage of Marxian political economy. Clearly commodification is a valuable explanatory and analytic device for understanding the transformations of late twentieth-century sport. Commodification as a process is at once economic and cultural, and in the best analyses efforts are made to explicate the complex ways in which this happens.

I wonder, though, if 'commodification' and 'globalization' are in danger of becoming ritual incantations through which, once labelled, a social practice eludes more precise analysis. It may be that analysis has developed a dangerous one-dimensionality, in which the complex contradictions and tensions in and around the practices of sport are not fully deconstructed. In addition, and despite the Marxist lineage of commodification, Marxism itself is often absent, as if writers have become coy and defensive, or wish to put clear blue water between themselves and Marx as the 'father' of the philosophy of praxis. It is important to remember that a commodity is only a moment in the circuit of capital, and that commodification is a process, not an object. Miller *et al.* (2001: 30) rightly warn of the danger of allowing 'globalization' to become a mere brand name and transcendental signifier. They sketch out a protocol, which calls for analysis of:

> the ways in which trans-national capital is commodifying and corporatizing sport, evaluating the attempts of nation-states – successful or otherwise – to control capital and information flows, including the pressures on them to adopt neoliberal policies. It should be sensitive to the growth of extra-state bodies that monitor and regulate production and exchange in sport. At the local level, it is essential to acknowledge differentiated impacts in the face of global culture. The interconnectedness of locations around the world reduces the importance of space and time and allows for an increase in the flows of people across national boundaries – a process of major significance for sport.

Such an approach allows for examination of tensions, contradictions, unevennesses and discontinuities. A similar approach needs to be taken to the central question of the commodity form. This concept presupposes the construction of an object that can be traded, through the abstract system of equivalence of money, in order that surplus value may be extracted in the form of profit. The term has come to be used too often as an oversimplified label and requires a degree of deconstruction in order that it continues to be productive.

Who buys sport? The cash nexus intervenes in numerous ways. People buy individual tickets, season tickets, executive boxes and hospitality packages. They also purchase television sets, digital boxes and satellite decoders; and may rent access to dedicated sport channels. They may buy newspapers for the sport sections, or dedicated sports magazines. Some also purchase merchandise, most notably replica shirts. This is not the only source of revenue for sport, of course. Television companies pay huge sums to acquire rights. Sponsors and advertisers pay, but sometimes they are buying from a sports club or stadium owner, sometimes from a club, and sometimes from a governing body. There has risen a whole new tier of expertise – sport agents, sponsorship brokers, event managers, public relations consultants – who also make money from sport, albeit in and through another set of economic relations.

If the customer appears in diverse forms, so too does the vendor. Who is 'selling' sport? Sport clubs and stadium owners sell admission at a variety of price levels. Catering is often franchised, with clubs and/or stadiums taking a cut. Merchandising may be in the hands of a club, a governing body or a licensed retailer. Television companies are both buying and selling sport. Commentators and experts sell their expertise to television, which purchases it to enhance the value and audience appeal of their product. Sponsors and advertisers buy sport in order to boost sales, and in doing so are investing in image association.

Clearly, then, there is not one simple 'commodity' here but rather a set of overlapping commodities, embedded in a diverse but linked set of economic relations. Equally, we are not dealing with a unitary commodified object, but rather a complex set of objects, practices, processes and symbolic forms, which all too easily become condensed together in the category 'sport'. We are never simply dealing with monetary capital, but also with cultural capital, with symbolic value, with icons, with stars, with narratives and with discourses.

Signification has its own history, sedimented common sense, popular memories, cultural sensibilities and structures of feeling. Adherence to and involvement in the processes of sports spectatorship have their own historically shaped and formed sensibilities, in which the shared memories, values and commitments continue to form and re-form the experience of 'consuming' sport. When people purchase 'sport', what are they purchasing? At the level of basic economics, people buy entrance to a stadium, or subscribe to a sports channel, in order to view a spectacle. More broadly, though, as J.B. Priestley famously described in a much-quoted passage of *The Good Companions*, they are also buying a rich cultural experience, which provides a basis for conversation during the subsequent week.

Why do television companies buy rights? Why 'do' sport? The most obvious answer, of course, is that they wish to win audiences, although apart from a few major events, sport is not an especially prominent means of winning audiences. In the case of companies who make their own revenue from selling advertising, it may seem that the sporting commodity is simply 'sold on'. However, as Dallas Smythe (1977) pointed out, advertisers are not buying the programmes; they are buying audiences – in short, they are buying us. The programmes, from this perspective, are not the commodity but simply the means of producing the commodity of audiences. We, the viewers, are the commodities which advertisers purchase. This provocative refocusing of analysis offered by Smythe provides a means of analysing an advertising-based television channel, but does not account as effectively for public service broadcasting or subscription television. It also constructs an over-passive model of audience. Clearly, then, in analysing television sport, we are not dealing with one simple commodity or one simple set of economic relations. Public service broadcasting, dependent on public finance, is typically assessed not on a programme-by-programme basis, but on its whole service. This has usually involved the requirement to provide a range of programming for a range of audiences, and endeavouring to ensure that minority audiences are not ignored merely because their lack of spending power makes them an unattractive niche market for advertising. In the case of a public service model such as the BBC, as consumers we are buying a whole service, and it is this whole service that constitutes the commodity. Conversely, with subscription channels, a niche market has been developed, and those who select to subscribe are purchasing the channel. The experience of BSkyB suggests strongly that live soccer is the element that drives the market, with audiences for most other sports considerably lower. Smythe's argument gives us some purchase on sponsors and advertisers who are buying access to audiences; but in order to capitalize on their access to us, they seek to associate their products with the connotative resonances of sport events, sometimes in quite complex ways. It is no coincidence that those far from nutritious products Coca-Cola and McDonald's have been among the most keen to associate with the youthful and healthy images that sport facilitates.

Brookes (2002) refers to the argument that the most significant economic relation in entertainment is not the selling of commodities but the licensing of rights and argues that sporting rights are licensed rather than sold. The economic relations through which the new professionals of the sports world – sport agents, sponsorship brokers, event managers and public relations consultants – operate adds another dimension to the commercialization of sport. Their income is usually based on receiving percentages of the revenue they can generate for their client, or the size of the rights payments they negotiate. On a simple level, they are selling their negotiating skills. This skill involves the inflation of value, or, to put it another way, the ability to increase surplus value. The potential income of a client, though, has become rooted in symbolic value. David Beckham's value to Real Madrid, while growing out of his football ability, was greatly enhanced by the Beckham brand – the commodification of self – that means merchandising of shirts emblazoned with his name is a highly profitable enterprise. Beckham contributes even more in symbolic value than he does through his football. It is striking that, even towards the end of his career, his symbolic value, and consequent marketing value, is able to secure millions of dollars in a contract to play out the rest of his football career in Los Angeles.

All of these forms of economic relation, though, depend ultimately upon the performativity of sport – the spectacle is initially not an object but a process. Indeed, it is an unpredictable and unscripted process, and therein, precisely, is its specific appeal. The capitalization of sport involves exactly the process of transforming this process into commodity forms. This, however, is not a single simple or unitary process, but a complex layering of economic relations that do not work together neatly. At the cultural level, the tensions and contradictions are even more apparent.

Take football spectatorship, which can now occur in a variety of forms – at the stadium, at home, in a bar, or in a city square. Each cultural context has its own practices and conventions. In stadiums, tensions can arise between the predominant segmented and ordered all-seated geography and the historically shaped desire of fans for fluidity, carnival and disorder, all of which suggest standing. Stewards are instructed to ensure that fans remain seated. The home can be a site of gender and generational tensions over control of the remote, and sport in particular tends to polarize gendered viewing habits. The viewing context of bar and city square, ironically, has reproduced many of the historically shaped rituals of fandom, now rendered difficult within stadiums. Bar and city centre, as well as reproducing, in transformed form, a residual and threatened set of spectatorship practices, also apparently subvert the commodification of television, in that they can enable the viewing of subscription channels. Of course, in a bar, we are paying for it through alcohol, but we feel we just might have consumed those drinks anyway. The struggle between different modes of provision and consumption of televised football has not simply imposed a new, more regulated and disciplined spectatorship, but has generated new cultural practices and rituals of consumption.

Conclusion

To sum up, I am suggesting that while commodification is of central value for any Marxian attempt to analyse media sport and culture, if we are to continue to build on existing work, we need to avoid the tendency towards one-dimensionality by paying close attention to the multiple levels in which it occurs, to the unevenness, the lack of fit, the discontinuities, the tensions and the contradictions. Further, we need to remember that at the heart of the process lies a set of relations between the performative spectacle and the gaze of the spectator which can never be totally subsumed by commodity, and retains on occasion an ability to offer the sublime and transcendent moment (see Whannel, 1994b). I am suggesting here a reassertion of one of the core methodological principles underlying the best work in critical Cultural Studies – the dialectical relationship of abstract theorization and empirical exemplification. We cannot simply construct a version of the world from our selection and organization of evidence, but must, inevitably, draw on and utilize, implicitly or explicitly, theorized models of that world. However, abstract models are only models – which must constantly be tested, adjusted and challenged by the complex ambiguities of representations, social relations and economic relations. It is only by so doing, I would suggest, that we can begin to understand why the 'triumph' of a globalized commodification can never be totally secured but will always be a contested and uneven process.

Note

1 All of the above quotes are from the introductory section of Beijing 2008 (2003).

References

Anderson, P. (1976) *Considerations on Western Marxism*, London: NLB.
Althusser, L. (1971) *Lenin and Philosophy and Other Essays*, London: NLB.
Althusser, L. (1977) *For Marx*, London: NLB.

Althusser, L. and Balibar, E. (1968) *Reading Capital*, London: NLB.

Barker, M. and Beezer, A. (eds) (1992) *Reading into Cultural Studies*, London: Routledge.

Barrett, M., Corrigan, P., Kuhn, A. and Wolff, J. (eds) (1979) *Ideology and Cultural Production*, London: Croom Helm.

Baudrillard, J. (1972) *Pour une Critique de l'Économie Politque du Signe*, Paris: Gallimard.

Baudrillard, J. (1998) 'The End of the Millennium or the Countdown', *Theory Culture and Society* 15(1), pp. 1–9.

Beijing 2008 (2003) *Marketing Plan Launch*, Beijing: Beijing Olympic Games Organizing Committee.

Bell, D. (1960) *The End of Ideology: On the Exhaustion of Political Ideas in the Fifties*, New York: The Free Press.

Bennett, T., Boyd-Bowman, S., Mercer, C. and Woollacott, J. (1981a) *Popular Television and Film*, London: BFI/OU.

Bennett, T., Martin, G., Mercer, G. and Woollacott, J. (eds) (1981b) *Culture, Ideology and Social Process*, London: Batsford.

Blundell, V., Shepherd, J. and Taylor, I. (eds) (1993) *Relocating Cultural Studies: Developments in Theory and Research*, London: Routledge.

Boggs, C. (1976) *Gramsci's Marxism*, London: Pluto.

Brick, C. (2000) 'Taking Offence: Modern Moralities and the Perception of the Football Fan', *Soccer and Society* 1(1), pp. 158–72.

Brick, C., (2001) 'Anti-Consumption or "New" Consumption? Commodification, Identity and "New" Football', in J. Horne (ed.) *Leisure: Culture, Consumption and Commodification*, Eastbourne: Leisure Studies Journal, pp. 3–15.

Brohm, J.M. (1978) *Sport: A Prison of Measured Time*, London: Ink Links.

Brookes, R. (2002) *Representing Sport*, London: Arnold.

Cashmore, E. (2004) *Beckham*, Oxford: Polity.

CCCS (1977) *On Ideology*, Working Papers in Cultural Studies 10, Birmingham: CCCS.

Chambers, I., Clarke, J., Connell, I., Curti, L., Hall, S. and Jefferson, T. (1977) 'Marxism and Culture', *Screen* 18(4), pp. 109–19.

Clarke, J. (1991) *New Times and Old Enemies: Essays on Cultural Studies and America*, London: HarperCollins Academic.

Clarke, S., Lovell, T., McDonnell, K., Robins, K. and Seidler, V.J. (1980) *One Dimensional Marxism: Althusser and the Politics of Culture*, London: Allison and Busby.

Corner, J. and Harvey, S. (eds) (1991) *Enterprise and Heritage*, London: Routledge.

Coward, R. (1977) 'Class, "Culture" and the Social Formation', *Screen* 18(1), pp. 75–105.

Coward, R. and Ellis, J. (1977) *Language and Materialism*, London: RKP.

Du Gay, P., Hall, S., Mackay, H. and Negus, K. (eds) (1997) *Doing Cultural Studies: The Story of the Sony Walkman* [part of the Open University course D318, Culture, Media and Identities], London: Sage.

Eco, U. (1986) 'Sports Chatter', in idem, *Travels in Hyper-Reality*, New York: Harcourt Brace Jovanovich.

Foucault, M. (1972) *The Archaeology of Knowledge*, London: Tavistock.

Fukuyama, F. (1992) *The End of History and the Last Man*, London: Hamish Hamilton.

Garnham, N. (1977) 'Towards a Political Economy of Culture', *New Universities Quarterly* Summer, pp. 340–57.

Garnham, N. (1979) 'Contribution to a Political Economy of Mass Communication', *Media Culture and Society* 1(2), pp. 123–46.

Giulianotti, R., Bonney, N. and Hepworth, M. (eds) (1994) *Football, Violence and Social Identity*, London: Routledge.

Hall, S. (1977) 'Culture, Media and the Ideological Effect', in J. Curran, M. Gurevitch and J. Woolacott (eds) *Mass Communication and Society*, London: Arnold, pp. 315–48.

Hall, S. (1980) 'Cultural Studies: Two Paradigms', *Media Culture and Society* 2(1), pp. 57–72.

Hall, S. (1983) 'The Great Moving Right Show', in *idem, The Politics of Thatcherism*, London: Lawrence and Wishart.

Hobsbawm, E. (1978) 'The Forward March of Labour Halted?', *Marxism Today* 22, p. 279.

Horne, J. (2006) *Sport in Consumer Culture*, London: Palgrave.

Jackson, S. and Andrews, D.L. (eds) (2005) *Sport, Culture and Advertising: Identities, Commodities and the Politics of Representation*, London: Routledge.

Jhally, S. (1982) 'Probing the Blindspot: The Audience Commodity', *Canadian Journal of Political and Social Theory* 6(1–2), pp. 204–10.

Lyotard, J.-F. (1984) *The Postmodern Condition*, Manchester: Manchester University Press.

Marx, K. (1968) 'Preface to A *Critique of Political Economy*', in *Karl Marx and Frederick Engels: Selected Works*, London: Lawrence and Wishart.

McGuigan, J. (1992) *Cultural Populism*, London: Routledge.

McRobbie, A. (1991) 'New Times in Cultural Studies', *New Formations* 13, pp. 1–18.

Mewshaw, M. (1983) *Short Circuit*, London: Collins.

Miller, T., Lawrence, G., McKay, J. and Rowe, D. (2001) *Globalization and Sport*, London: Sage.

Mouffe, C. (ed.) (1979) *Gramsci and Marxist Theory*, London: RKP.

Murdock, G. (1978) 'Blindspots about Western Marxism: A Reply to Dallas Smythe', *Canadian Journal of Political and Social Theory* 2(2), pp. 109–19.

Murdock, G. (1994) 'New Times/Hard Times: Leisure, Participation and the Common Good', *Leisure Studies* 13(4), pp. 239–48

Murdock, G. and Golding, P. (1977) 'Capitalism, Communications and Class Relations', in J. Curran, M. Gurevitch and J. Woolacott (eds) *Mass Communication and Society*, London: Arnold, pp. 12–43.

Norris, C. (1992) 'Old Themes for New Times', *New Formations* 18, pp. 1–25.

Rowe, D. (1992) 'Modes of Sports Writing', in P. Dahlgren and C. Sparks (eds) *Journalism and Popular Culture*, London: Sage, pp. 64–83.

Sassoon, A.S. (1980) *Gramsci's Politics*, London: Croom Helm.

Sassoon, A.S. (1982) *Approaches to Gramsci*, London: Writers and Readers.

Slack, T. (2004) *The Commercialisation of Sport*, Abingdon: Routledge.

Smythe, D. (1977) 'Communications: Blindspot of Western Marxism', *Canadian Journal of Political and Social Theory* 12(3), pp. 1–27.

Smythe, D. (1978) 'Rejoinder to Graham Murdock', *Canadian Journal of Political and Social Theory* 2(2), pp. 120–9.

Sugden, J. and Tomlinson, A. (1998) *FIFA and the Contest for World Football: Who Rules the People's Game?*, London: Polity.

Timpanaro, S. (1975) *On Materialism*, London: NLB.

Tomlinson, A. (ed.) (1990) *Consumption, Identity and Style*, London: Comedia.

Waites, B., Bennett, T. and Martin, G. (1982) *Popular Culture: Past and Present*, London: Croom Helm.

Wayne, M. (2003) *Marxism and Media Studies: Key Concepts and Contemporary Trends*, London: Pluto Press.

Whannel, G. (1994a) 'Profiting by the Presence of Ideals: Sponsorship and Olympism', in *International Olympic Academy: 32nd Session*, Olympia: International Olympic Academy.

Whannel, G. (1994b) 'Sport and Popular Culture: The Temporary Triumph of Process over Product', *Innovations* 6(3), pp. 341–50.

Whannel, G. (2002) *Media Sport Stars, Masculinities and Moralities*, London: Routledge.

Williams, R. (1977) *Marxism and Literature*, Oxford: Oxford University Press.

6 Marxism, alienation and Coubertin's Olympic project

Rob Beamish

Introduction

Sport provides the modern world with some of its most inspiring images and metaphors – images of power, courage, dedication and resolve in the face of adversity. Sport evokes notions of beauty, creativity and transcendental freedom. To many, sport stands above the crude, crass materialism of everyday life; while to others, sport is more – it is the antidote to those debasing realities. Baron Pierre de Coubertin's revival of the Olympic Games remains the most celebrated, and to some most inspirational, project in which sport would bring about major social change. For Coubertin, the modern Olympics would transform European society and return it to the traditional values which capitalism had supplanted and replaced with overtly materialist ones.

As a project – both its means and ends – Coubertin's modern Olympic Games are truly inspirational but that alone is not enough, no matter how inspiring, to realize his objectives. Coubertin and his followers were never able to actualize the transformative potential they saw in the Olympic Games. Why did the project fail? Where would one begin fully to understand the social dynamics that militated against the success of Coubertin's dream?

In this chapter, Marx's theory of alienation is used to establish the framework with which one can begin to examine Coubertin's Olympic project critically and understand why it failed. The discussion begins by locating Marx's conception of alienation within his work as a whole and notes why the theme remains an important part of his *oeuvre*. The chapter then focuses upon Marx's conception of alienation *per se*, noting its essential features and how they are interrelated. Finally the chapter examines Coubertin's Olympic project and indicates how the forces that Marx identified as central to alienated existence within capitalist societies prevented the project from ever actualizing Coubertin's fervent aspirations to oppose the crass materialism of capitalist society as it consolidated itself on an expanding scale in the early twentieth century.

Marx's critique of capital and capitalist society

Karl Marx spent his entire adult life working towards the formulation of his own unique critique of capitalist society. Over the course of almost half a century, his plans grew in scope and complexity as he discovered, while organizing and consolidating his ideas at various points in time, questions or critical aspects of his analysis that he still needed to explore and develop more fully.[1] Marx's research drew upon a wide range of ideas: he used insights from classical Greek philosophy, German idealism, European history, political economy, a host of different and divergent socialist thinkers, as well as his own personal experiences within an emerging and active communist movement. The scope of Marx's research also included material ranging from classical and contemporary European literature to the ethnological analyses of different early social formations. His critique stemmed from a genuinely impressive breadth and depth of knowledge.[2]

Throughout forty years of active intellectual and political engagement, Marx continually struggled with how to bring coherence to the prodigious volume of work he was generating. The difficulties he encountered at the very outset would continue to plague him over the next four decades. His first step in demystifying the reality of capitalist society was an 1843 draft critique of Hegel's *Philosophy of Law* but he quickly realized that 'the wealth and diversity of the different objects to be handled' could only be compressed into a single work by adopting 'a highly aphoristic style'. As a result, he decided to present 'the critique of law, morals, politics, etc. . . . [in] different, independent pamphlets' after which he would, in a 'special work', 'present the interrelation of the whole, the relation of the individual parts'. He also planned 'a critique of the speculative treatment of that material' (Marx and Engels, 1982: Pt. I, Vol. 2: 325).[3] By 1 February 1845 Marx had revised his plan again but was sure enough of his direction that he signed a contract with publisher Carl Leske to produce a two-volume *Critique of Politics and Political Economy*. Once again, as Marx immersed himself in the project, it outgrew his original framework and forced him to rethink his presentation.[4]

The economic crisis of 1857–8 gave Marx a renewed, now urgent motivation to publish his ongoing critique 'before the deluge' (Marx and Engels, 1990: Pt. III, Vol. 8: 210). He quickly sketched a new plan for presenting the material with which he had struggled for almost fifteen years. Marx (Marx and Engels, 1976: Pt. II, Vol. 1.1: 41) noted that:

> In all forms of society there is a determinate production which directs all the others, and whose relations therefore assign rank and influence to all the others. It is a general illumination into which all the others are plunged and it modifies their particularity. It is a specific ether which determines the specific importance of everything under its predominant presence.

'Capital', Marx (*ibid.*: 42) continued, 'is the all-dominating economic power of bourgeois society' and since it was bourgeois society that Marx wanted to examine critically, capital 'must form the departure-point and the end-point' of his analysis.

Within a couple of paragraphs, Marx appeared to settle on the following order for his critical analysis of capitalist society:

(1) the general, abstract determinants which are found, more or less, in all forms of society, but in the form discussed above. (2) The categories which make up the inner structure of bourgeois society and on which the fundamental classes rest. Capital, wage-labour, landed property. Their relationship to one another. Town and country. The 3 great social classes. Exchange between them. Circulation. Credit system (private). (3) Concentration of bourgeois society in the form of the state. Viewed in relation to itself. The 'unproductive' classes. Taxes. State debt. Public credit. The population. The colonies. Emigration. (4) The international relation of production. International division of labour. International exchange. Export and import. Rate of exchange. (5) The world market and crises.

Between this outline and the publication of *Towards a Critique of Political Economy* in 1859, Marx drafted at least ten different plans and outlines for his project (Beamish, 1992: 54–9; Rubel, 1968: lxxvi–cxxi). By April 1858, for example, he had decided that his work would consist of six books – capital, landed property, wage-labour, the state, international trade and the world market. The book on capital would have four sections – capital in general, competition (the action of many capitals on each other), credit, and share capital. By May, Marx had decided that the treatment of capital in general would require two volumes; when he finally delivered the manuscript for the *Critique* to Franz Duncker in January 1859 the text consisted of a chapter on the commodity and another on money as simple circulation. Despite the *Critique*'s opening subtitle 'Section One: Capital in General', the 1859 *Critique* did not contain any of the copious material Marx had already written on capital! From 1859 to 1867, when the first volume of *Capital* appeared, Marx's plan underwent further refinement and massive expansion – his treatment of the production and circulation processes alone had grown into thousands of manuscript pages and Marx would continue to struggle with the presentation of the process of circulation until at least 1878 – never completing a final draft of volume two of *Capital* before his death in 1883.[5]

The points to note from the above are the following. First, Marx changed his plans numerous times over the course of his adult life and each change was precipitated by his desire for a deeper and more detailed examination of particular aspects of political economy. Second, as Marx progressed towards the final drafting and revising of volume one of *Capital*, he continued to refine and expand both his theoretical and empirical insights into the economic infrastructure of the capitalist relations of production (see Beamish, 1992). Finally, and most important, in the evolution of his expanding critique of political economy, Marx's intellectual energies became increasingly focused upon the essential relations of capital; capital would serve as the departure point for his critique of capitalist society but the detailed presentation of that departure point had become a life's work (and more). Attention to detail drew Marx slowly but surely away from the larger, broad dimensions of his critique of capitalist society as a whole and focused his attention upon increasingly specific aspects of a highly detailed critique of the economic infrastructure of capitalist society. As a result, Marx's later works are so precisely focused on the critique of political economy that they do not serve as well as his earlier works for insight into his overall critique of capitalist society as a whole. The general framework for Marx's critique of capitalist society is dispersed throughout his voluminous manuscripts and correspondence or within certain drafts of his early work. It is for this reason that a return to Marx's early works, despite the lifetime of scholarship that he dedicated to his emerging critique of capital and bourgeois political economy, is a useful strategy for initiating an analysis of how the broad dimensions of capitalist society shape, contour and constrain a wide variety of human productive activities, including high-performance sport.

Marx's early work and the questions of freedom and self-determination

Marx's entry into the political arena of Prussia in the 1840s occurred within the context of an ongoing struggle by Prussian liberals to reduce the restrictions that the state, religion and tradition had placed upon society as a whole. Marx's critique of Hegel's *Philosophy of Law*, which served to legitimate the existing Prussian state, was threefold. First, Marx noted that Hegel had made the 'real predicate' of the individual/state relationship – that is, the state – into the 'subject'. As a result, rather than real individuals determining the actions of the state, Hegel's *Philosophy of Law* justified the numerous controls the Prussian state exerted over its citizens. Hegel, Marx argued, had reversed subject and predicate; it was real, active humans who generated and created the state and they should exercise control over their creation rather than a ruling minority, through the power of the state, controlling and dominating all of civil society.

Second, Marx's analysis indicated that by reversing subject and predicate, Hegel had undermined the active essence he had attributed to humanity in one of his most important works – *The Phenomenology of Mind*. In the *Phenomenology*, Hegel had demonstrated how the human mind progressively discovered, over the course of history, its active, creative capacities as it overcame its state of alienation – or separation – from an accurate and absolute knowledge of the real world. A central aspect to Marx's critique of Hegel's *Philosophy of Law* in particular and Prussian society more generally stemmed from Marx's transcendence of the alienation theme within German idealist philosophy such that the real, material causes, located in the everyday practices of capitalist society, could be seen.

Finally, Marx argued that real material humans, themselves, would carry forward the actual critique of Hegel's *Philosophy of Law*. Their actions would not only return the real subject to its proper place but free humanity from the oppressive control that the Prussian state, through its various agents, exercised. Marx argued that a particular class would undertake the transformation of Prussian society. Revolutionary change would be found

> In the formation of a class with *radical chains*, a class of bourgeois society that is no class of bourgeois society, a rank which is the dissolution of all ranks,

which possesses a universal character because of its universal suffering, and claims no *particular right* because no *particular wrong* but *wrong generally* is perpetrated on it, which can invoke not only an *historical* but also a *human* title, which does not stand in a one-sided opposition to the consequences [of state oppression] but stands rather in a comprehensive opposition to the assumptions of the German state, a sphere, finally, which cannot emancipate itself without emancipating itself from all other spheres of society and thereby emancipating all the other spheres of society, [a sphere] which is, in a word, the *complete loss* of humanity and thus can only redeem itself through the *full redemption of humanity.*

(Marx and Engels, 1982: Pt. I, Vol. 2: 181–2)

The class that would make this revolutionary transformation of Prussia was the proletariat. To understand the working class more fully and to grasp the social forces which shaped it and would influence its actions, Marx – following Engels' lead – began to immerse himself in the study of political economy.[6]

Political economy and alienated existence

The early political economists – Adam Ferguson, Adam Smith, James Mill, Jean Baptiste Say, Frédéric Skarbek, David Ricardo, J.R. MacCulloch and Pierre Boisguillebert – the writers Marx read in the early 1840s, did not hesitate to make a connection between the economy and the broader contours of society. In fact, they studied political economy to recommend policy that would shape bourgeois societies as a whole. In his early study of political economy, Marx could also see the connections between political economy – the production of the means of life under the private ownership of the means of production – and people's broader social conditions. While preparing the manuscript promised to Leske, Marx drew upon the work of a number of political economists to understand how production, under conditions of private ownership, affected people's lives. After setting out at some length the findings of various political economists, Marx (Marx and Engels, 1982: Pt. I, Vol. 3: 363) noted:

We have proceeded from political economy's assumptions. We have accepted its language and its laws. We have presupposed private property, the separation of labour, capital and land, likewise wages of labour, the profit of capital and ground rent, similarly the division of labour, competition, the concept of exchange-value, etc. From political economy itself, with its own words, we have shown that the worker is reduced to a commodity, to the most impoverished commodity, that the poverty of the worker stands in an inverse relation to the power and size of the worker's production, that the necessary result of competition is the accumulation of capital in fewer hands, thus the frightening re-establishment of monopoly, that finally the distinction between capitalist and landowner like that of the farm worker and manu-facturing worker disappears and the entire society must divide into the two classes of *owner* and property-less *worker.*

On the basis of the given facts of political economy, Marx continued, workers become poorer the more their productive power grows and the more wealth they create. The more workers produce, Marx argued, the more they produce themselves as commodities – commodities that become cheaper as the wealth they produce stands in opposition to them. Work under the conditions of private property had a very specific outcome:

> The object which the worker produces, his product, confronts him as an *alien Being* as an *independent power* of the producer. The product of labour is labour which fixes itself in an object, has become material, it is the *objectification* [*Vergegenständlichung*] of labour. The actualization [*Verwirklichung*] of labour is its objectification. [But] the actualization of labour under the conditions of political economy appears as the *diminution* [*Entwirklichung*] of the worker, objectification as the *loss and bondage to the object*, the appropriation [of the object] as *estrangement* [*Entfremdung*], as *alienation* [*Entäußerung*].
>
> (*Ibid.*: 364–5)[7]

There are two major points in this part of Marx's analysis and they are deeply intertwined within each other. First and foremost, Marx argued that workers producing under conditions of political economy – where the means of production are privately owned and controlled – create not only products and profit; they simultaneously create the very system that confronts them. Workers working under the conditions of bourgeois society live and work under conditions of alienation and estrangement; they are dominated by the end product of their own labour. Intertwined with this concrete manifestation of alienation is the deeper reality that labour, which should actualize human potential, does the opposite – it diminishes workers and progressively estranges them from their full human potential, their 'Being' as humans. These are two of the central themes of Marx's draft text for Leske and constitute the overarching theme of Marx's early critique of political economy in particular and capitalist society in general.

Over the course of his draft text, Marx (*ibid.*: 327–37, 363–76) had argued that four specific, interrelated, moments of production were involved in the conditions of alienated existence. First, while producing under the conditions of private property, workers are separated, alienated and estranged from the products they produce. Second, they are alienated from and have no control over the production process (see *ibid.*: 365–7). These are very concrete, material aspects of alienated production under the conditions of capitalism but they are crucial because it is through these very mundane, material practices that the system of private property is produced and reproduced on an expanding scale. Without control over the product and the production process, capital could not pursue profit and could not ensure the expansion of its influence into all aspects of people's lives.

The third aspect of alienated production is less palpable and readily obvious but its implications are far reaching as a key material component of capitalist production. Marx argued that production under the conditions of political economy separates the workers from their human potential, from their 'Being' as humans.

Alienation from 'Species-Being' is critical to Marx's argument and merits some elaboration.

Human production meets what is required to sustain life materially – it is life-activity [*Lebenstätigkeit*] that serves as the basic means to physical existence. But, Marx argued, productive life is also 'life generating life' in a much more profound sense. 'In the nature of life-activity lies the whole character of a species, its species-character, and free, conscious activity is the species character of human-kind' (*ibid.*: 369). The potential for free, conscious activity – for free, creative labour – sets humankind apart from all other species (see also Schmidt, 1962).

'It is in the creation of the objective world that humankind actually proves itself as a *Species-Being*', Marx (Marx and Engels, 1982: Pt. I, Vol. 3: 370) argued in one of the text's most important passages:

> This production is its active species-life. Through it nature appears as *its work* and its actuality. The object of labour is therefore the *objectification of the species-life of humankind*: for humankind doubles itself not only, as in consciousness, intellectually, but in working, actually, and it can therefore view itself in a world created by it. Insofar therefore as alienated labour tears humankind from the object of its production, it tears humankind from its *species-life*, its actual species-objectivity [*Gattungsgegenständlichkeit*] and transforms its advantage over animals into a disadvantage; its inorganic life, nature, is taken away from it.

In the inverted world of bourgeois production, the centrally creative process – labour – through which workers could and should be able to actualize their human potential, diminishes them instead and labour is torn away from its potential to realize the full scope of humankind's species-life. 'The actualization of labour is its objectification' but under the conditions of private property – that is, 'the actualization of labour under the conditions of political economy' – the *Entwirklichung* (the de-actualization, diminution) of the worker takes place (*ibid.*: 365). This *Entwirklichung* is the exact opposite of the *Verwirklichung* – of the potential actualization of the worker – that exists in the labour process. Under conditions of private property, production alienates workers from their genuine species-character and full species-potential. This leads to the fourth aspect of alienated existence:

> Every self-alienation of humankind from itself and nature appears in a rela-tionship that there is between it and nature and between different individuals . . . Through *estranged, alienated labour* the worker creates the relation to work of one who is estranged from labour and stands outside it. The relation of the worker to labour creates the relation of the capitalist to labour, or whatever one wants to term the one who oversees labour. *Private property* is thus the product, the result, the necessary consequence of *alienated labour*, the estranged relations of labour to nature and to itself.

(*Ibid.*: 372)

To summarize the above, there are four key aspects to the alienated existence Marx detailed in his early critique of political economy and capitalist society more generally. The first two are seemingly mundane and are obviously part of the material-practical dimensions of production under conditions of the private ownership of the means of production: workers neither own nor control the products of their labour and they do not control the production process; their alienation is an economic relation but it also has significant social implications which emerge in the next two moments of alienated production. It extends into the most far-reaching aspects of alienation as Marx conceptualized it. The third moment draws one deeper into Marx's analysis of alienated existence: it addresses alienation as well as key dimensions to his materialist ontology. Production within a capitalist political economy alienates humankind from the full creative potential of labour; production under those specific social relations of production tears humankind from the actualization of its full species-potential. Finally, alienated production not only separates workers from the products they produce, the production process, and their full creative potential, but creates specific social and production relations of opposition – alienated labour perpetuates and produces on an expanding scale the relations of bourgeois political economy; it produces the class opposition of workers and capitalists.

For Marx, the conditions of alienation are rooted in the social relations of production – they are a set of real, objective, social conditions that exist in societies where the means of production are owned and controlled by a minority within civil society. They are not a psychological state of mind – indeed, one might not even be consciously aware of the objective class antagonisms, the real and potential conflicts that alienated labour produces, or feel any unhappiness, anxiety or concern about producing under capitalist relations of production. Irrespective of subjective awareness, the objective social conditions of alienated labour exist and they can be overcome only by changes in the material, social relations of production.

As an organizing framework for understanding the human costs associated with the labour process and production under specific social relations of production, Marx's conception of alienation has many significant implications. As a framework for assessing the potential of different human practices that might permit the full expression of humankind's creative potential, Marx's conception of alienation can be an important analytical framework. For sport sociologists, his alienation theme is particularly useful because, of all human practices, sport is continually raised as one that permits individuals and groups to explore their physical potential, to develop strong team and social bonds, and to aid in the fulfilment of their individual personal needs. Sport is often seen as a panacea for much that ails modern society and it is against a framework like Marx's conception of alienation that one may assess the extent to which sport in contemporary society meets those high aspirations. Moreover, if contemporary sport forms do not help people realize their full human potential – if it serves as an impediment to human fulfilment – then the alienation theme also allows one to focus upon those aspects of sport which must be changed if it is ever to deliver upon its implicit promise.

The Olympic project and human development

While Baron Pierre de Coubertin and Karl Marx had little in common, both recognized that nineteenth-century capitalism promoted the highly skewed, one-sided development of people. Youth in nineteenth-century Europe, Coubertin (2000: 559) argued, were excessively specialized; critical minds, he argued, were 'debased by an overwhelming mass of facts'. 'Trained into the mentality of the anthill', youth was 'surrounded by the artificial and the accepted, with categories and statistics, a fetish for numbers, an unhealthy search for detail and the exception'.

For Coubertin, the remedy to Europe's intellectual and associated moral decline lay in the ideals of ancient Greece and the 'muscular Christian' philosophies of Canon Kingsley and the Reverend Thomas Arnold (ibid.: 294–5). Believing that humans consist of mind, body and character, where character was formed through the interaction of mind and body, Coubertin believed that sport, appropriately structured, was the perfect vehicle for building a strong, resilient character in European youth and reversing the moral decline initiated by industrial capitalism (*ibid.*: 308, 532).

Coubertin's image of sport and his aspirations for what it could accomplish were genuinely inspiring. He celebrated the internal dimensions of sport. 'The athlete', he argued (*ibid.*: 552), 'enjoys his effort. He likes the constraint that he imposes on his muscles and nerves, through which he comes close to victory even if he does not manage to achieve it. This enjoyment remains internal, egotistical in a way.' What truly inspired Coubertin was the idea that one could capture those inner elements and project them to a broader audience – inspiring an entire generation to identify with and embrace the personal strengths of true 'brothers-in-arms' engaged in athletic contests (see Beamish and Ritchie, 2004).

'Imagine', Coubertin (2000: 552) continued, if the athlete's internal experiences and enjoyment 'were to expand outward, becoming intertwined with the joy of nature and the flights of art . . . Picture it', he enthused, 'radiant with sunlight, exalted by music, framed in the architecture of porticoes. It was thus that the glittering dream of ancient Olympism was born on the banks of the Alphaeus, the vision of which dominated ancient society for so many centuries.' Coubertin believed that through the proper sporting experience, he could build social leaders who would inspire others and guide Europe towards the political structures needed for humanity to fulfil its vast potential. The sporting experience he had in mind was, of course, very different from the increasingly commercial, overtly competitive sport that had already begun to characterize athletic competitions in late nineteenth-century Europe.

Although Coubertin did not use the term or conception of alienation and did not draw upon idealist philosophy or Marx's work to sharpen his critique of nineteenth-century Europe, he shared the view with Marx and others that capitalist society was misdirecting human energy, human resources and human aspirations away from where they should be invested. Capitalist Europe was becoming increasingly characterized by the pursuit of wealth, power and economic domination. A unique, sport-based, educational movement would, in Coubertin's mind, end this misdirection of human energy and potential. Sport, in the form of the Olympic Games, would reverse the conditions of alienation that Marx had been examining over the course of Coubertin's lifetime; and while Marx would never have advocated sport or education as the solution to alienated existence in the late nineteenth century, he would, nevertheless, have recognized the creative potential they held as productive, material activities. More important, even though Marx might not have endorsed sport as a force for liberation, there is a long line of scholars, philosophers and policy-makers who have.[8]

Sport, most often thought of in the abstract – as an ideal to be made real – is regarded as a highly creative human practice that is separate from, and can therefore resist, the mundane, material realities of our everyday work lives. It is seen as an ideal process through which character can be developed as young boys and girls explore their physical capacities, meet in 'non-serious', competitive situations, and work together in the pursuit of team goals and objectives. Discipline, cooperation, creativity under pressure, the experiences of joy, disappointment and personal perseverance all hold out the potential that, through sport, participants may experience a broad range of human emotions and physical demands within a single social activity. It is this form of non-alienated activity that Coubertin and sport policy-makers after him have put forward as the inner essence of sport and the reason why it can play a transformative role in human experience (see Gruneau, 1980).

To meet the objectives he had set, Coubertin would have had to insulate the Olympic movement, at least during its initial stages, from the powerful forces of the capitalist economy in the late nineteenth century; but irrespective of how hard he may or may not have tried, that could not and did not happen. On the contrary, from the very outset, Coubertin's Olympic project was inescapably tied to the dominance of the market economy in Europe.

To launch the first Games, for example, Coubertin required the largesse of wealthy businessman George Averoff to renovate the ancient stadium in Athens where the Games were held (Guttmann, 2002: 15–16). More important, rather than resisting capitalism's crass materialism, the International Olympic Committee (IOC) had no choice but to hold the Paris, St Louis and London Games (1900, 1904 and 1908, respectively) in conjunction with the World's Fair which celebrated technology, science, industrial capitalism and modern culture – the forces causing the demise of traditional European values. As a movement that was separate from, and potentially opposed, the dominant political economy of Europe, the Games were not at all viable. As a result, by 1928 the IOC had inescapably tied the Games to the political economy of Europe by securing sponsorships from large corporations like Coca-Cola. Rather than resisting the ethos of capitalism, Coubertin's project increasingly had to embrace capitalism in ways that were both large and small.

While the participants in the initial Games might have felt they controlled the product of their athletic labour and produced it within a context that they embraced, shaped and accepted, the reality was quite different. From 1896 onwards, on a growing scale, the athletes of the Games created a product – the Olympic spectacle – that they did not and could not control, under conditions they did not determine, within a system that prevented them from exploring and fulfilling their full human potential through their athletic endeavours. Despite Coubertin's inspiring vision and lofty goals, Olympic sport, like other forms of alienated labour in the late nineteenth and early twentieth centuries, pitted athlete against athlete in a system where sport entrepreneurs and bureaucrats owned and controlled the undertaking. More important, rather than representing a set of early compromises that were needed to launch the project and would be overcome as the Games established themselves, the reality of Olympic sport consolidated its alienated form and substance. Over the course of the next fifty years three forces in particular solidified the alienated relations of athletic production in the Olympic Games: nationalism; the unrestrained implementation of instrumental rationality; and the commercialization and professionalization of high-performance sport.

Even during their early history, the modern Olympic Games never escaped the divisive power of nationalism and political ambition, but the political significance of the Games became abundantly clear during the 1936 summer Olympics in Nazi Germany. Despite claims to the contrary, the Olympic Games have never been above politics: the IOC's decision to award the 1936 Games to a republican Germany was in itself an overt, politically motivated decision, as was the ensuing debate about whether the IOC should withdraw the Games from Germany once Hitler came to power in 1933. But it was the fully conscious, systematic exploitation of the 1936 Games by Nazi Germany which clearly exemplified how athletes' immediate productive labour created a product over which they had no control – a wide-ranging, powerful political spectacle (see, for example, Beamish and Richie, 2006: 31–40; Teichler, 1975; Krüger and Murray, 2003).

Under the grandiose aspirations of Joseph Goebbels, the coldly calculating Minister of Public Enlightenment and Propaganda, and Albert Speer, Hitler's chief architect and ultimately the Minister for Armaments during the Second World War, Nazi propaganda operated on a massive scale (see Welch, 1993; Rentschler, 1996). Goebbels and Speer routinely used the most advanced technologies in the emerging field of mass communications to reach the widest audiences possible through media that brought the viewer or listener directly into the spectacle. The Nazis' trademark propaganda events combined dramatic music and the carefully choreographed movements of hundreds of performers inside imposing neoclassical stadiums before thousands of spectator-participants to produce powerful, emotion-laden *Gesamtkunstwerke* (total works of art). Music, choreography, drama and neoclassical architecture blended into captivating, exhilarating and emotionally draining experiences (Beamish and Ritchie, 2006: 31–40; Speer, 1969). This was the context within which the 1936 Games were produced. The Olympian stage upon which the athletes would produce the spectacle of the modern Games was elaborately set by the Ministry of Public Enlightenment and Propaganda. The athletes simply brought it to life and provided the organizational focal point for a carefully choreographed extravaganza that would celebrate the central themes of Hitler's Nazi empire, beginning with the torch relay, continuing through the course of the Games' athletic contests, and coming to a close that pointed forward to the glorious potential of Hitler's Thousand-Year Reich. The Berlin Games served as a prototype for several key aspects of future Olympiads.

At sport historian Karl Diem's suggestion, the Nazis introduced the Olympic torch relay which, on one level, would symbolically link the mythology of the ancient Games which Coubertin had so carefully cultivated with the grandeur of the modern project – the subordination of capitalist materialism and the return to the traditional values that ancient Greece had bequeathed to Western Europe. Inspiring as that imagery was, the torch relay in 1936 was also choreographed to represent symbolically to all of Europe the link between ancient Greece – the racially homogeneous apogee of ancient civilization – with the Third Reich, to which the torch was now passed as it travelled from Olympia, across European territories that the Nazis would seize within a few years, to Berlin. Within Germany itself, the relay rekindled the visceral experiences Germans felt during the German Storm Troopers' midnight torch parade following Hitler's seizure of power on 30 January 1933. 'By the tens of thousands,' Shirer (1960: 4–5) recalled, the joyous Nazi Storm Troopers 'emerged in disciplined columns from the depths of the Tiergarten, passed under the triumphal arch of the Brandenburg Gate and down the Wilhelmstrasse.' The Sturm Abteilung (SA) filled the night with 'the thunderous beating of the drums' as they sang the 'Horst Wessel Song' and 'other tunes that were as old as Germany'. The SA jack-boots beat 'a mighty rhythm on the pavement, their torches held high forming a ribbon of flame that illuminated the night and kindled the hurrahs of the onlookers massed on the sidewalks.'

Nazi ideology glorified youth, strength, struggle and conquest, emphasizing genetic and racial endowment in the natural, Darwinian struggle for the survival of the fittest. Coubertin's Games also celebrated nature, power and struggle. It was easy for the Nazis to weave into the Olympic aesthetic their ideology of racial supremacy. The intended message – *Ein Volk, ein Führer, ein Reich* (One Racially Pure People, One Leader, One Expansive Empire) – was impossible to escape as Hitler's Germany swept the competition aside en route to a stunning national triumph over the nations that had defeated it in the First World War.

The climax to the 1936 Games replicated Speer's 'cathedral of light' from the 1934 Nazi Party Congress at Nuremberg – the fascists' largest mass demonstration after seizing political power. Anti-aircraft spotlights, placed at forty-metre intervals around the perimeter of the Olympic Stadium, shot powerful beams of light deep into the black of the night. 'At first the columns of light were straight up,' Mandell (1971: 312) wrote, 'but then the infinitely distant tops of the shafts gradually converged to enclose the darkened stadium in a temple composed entirely of glowing spirit' (see also Speer, 1969: 96–7). The spectacular effect symbolized the majesty of the Olympics along with the imperial stature of Nazi Germany. Coubertin affirmed that the Nazis had fully captured the grandeur of the Olympic spectacle as he had intended it (Teichler, 1982). The political legacy of the Berlin Olympics was the permanent fusion of the Games' Promethean symbolic power with the political objectives of various regimes throughout the twentieth century.

In the wake of the 1936 Games, the Olympics would never be the same. The product of athletic labour had become – and would continue to be on an expanding scale – controlled and shaped by the small group in each host country who organized – and owned and controlled – each set of Olympic Games. The Olympics would still centre on athletic labour – without the athletic spectacle, the Games could not exist – but the product was more than the contests between athletes; a dominant text was the competition among, and the ranking of, nations. After the Berlin Olympics, the product of the participating athletes' labour was completely estranged from them as they became the immediate producers of a spectacle that extended well beyond their own personal aspirations.

As ominous as the symbolic power of the Games became after 1936, the human cost of a highly politicized Games became even more apparent in the post-war era. Intent on surpassing the capitalist world in every realm of social life, including sport, Soviet leader Joseph Stalin developed a large-scale, fully coordinated high-performance sport system in the Soviet Union in the immediate post-war period (Riordan, 1977: 161–2). The system included an infrastructure of high-quality facilities, professional coaches, scientific training programmes, and financial incentives for successful athletes (*ibid.*: 162–4). At the same time, Walter Ulbricht, the first General Secretary of the Central Committee of the Socialist Unity Party in the German Democratic Republic (GDR), followed Stalin's lead in using sport as a source of national pride and propaganda. Sport, the Olympic Games and nationalist aspirations would accelerate in importance well beyond the 1936 standard during the Cold War (see Beamish and Ritchie, 2006: 66–104). The increased alienation of the Games took two interrelated forms.

The first was a thoroughgoing intensification of the athletic labour process. The 1952 Games in Helsinki brought the two post-war superpowers head to head for the first time in the Cold War. Although the Americans ultimately won the unofficial points total, it was the USSR's gold, silver and bronze medals in weightlifting that would fundamentally change the conditions of sport labour in the Olympic movement. American weightlifting coach Bob Hoffman charged that the Soviet weightlifters had used testosterone to beat the Americans, and at the 1954 World Championships American team physician John Ziegler confirmed that suspicion (Todd, 1987: 93). With the assistance of the Ciba pharmaceutical company, Ziegler developed methandieone (Dianabol), which he gave to American weightlifters (Goldman, 1984: 94). Steroid use spread rapidly and by the early 1960s athletes in every strength event (weightlifting, shot put, discus, hammer throw and others) were using them (Yesalis and Bahrke, 2002: 53). But it was not steroids that changed the Games but the principles that lay behind their development and use. The 1952 Games ushered in a completely new approach to how high-performance athletes would be produced and developed as well as the actual conditions of their athletic labour.

Following Helsinki, it would no longer suffice for Olympic athletes to rely on raw talent and sporadic training during the competitive season to remain competitive (let alone win). Olympic sport increasingly drew upon science and certain performance-enhancing technologies to pursue personal glory and national honour. Politically motivated by Cold War antagonisms between the USA and the Soviet Union, between the GDR and the Federal Republic of Germany (FRG), and even between the GDR and the USSR, high-performance sport, post-1952, would increasingly draw upon science, technology and secretly funded programmes of performance enhancement in the all-out pursuit of Olympic victory. Centralized state-funded sport systems spread from the East to the West as athletes increasingly toiled in a system that controlled, monitored and shaped as much of their lives as possible (see Beamish and Ritchie, 2006: 85–104; Hoberman, 1992). In the 1950s, there was a dramatic paradigm shift in high-performance sport and from that point on instrumental rationality dominated athletic labour in everything from training and lifestyle to technique and tactical decisions in the heat of Olympic battle (Beamish and Ritchie, 2005).

The East–West conflict between athlete Cold Warriors made excellent television because it allowed spectators around the world to experience the intensity of Olympic combat vicariously as it happened. More important, the nature of the televised product allowed networks to deliver the highly coveted audience of males between eighteen and thirty-five years of age to merchandisers who wanted to sell products to that specific target market. To continue to attract that niche audience, television, through various event organizers, provided athletes with the funds needed to pursue the limits of human athletic performance continually. While Eastern Bloc athletes were fully state supported, those in the West were soon receiving under-the-table funds that would enable them to compete on an increasingly level playing field.

The movement towards the full commercialization and professionalization of high-performance sport – the full subordination of the Olympic Games to the political economy of Western capitalism and Eastern Bloc state capitalism – was the second major force that increasingly alienated Olympic athletes from the product of their labour, the production process and the actualization of their full human potential. The attempt to resist the material forces that were shaping and continue to contour the Games illustrates the extent to which an ideal – no matter how Olympic its proportions – is powerless in its efforts to alter an entrenched, material reality unless it is focused on the material relations that must be altered to bring about real social change.

Coubertin's project had been developed to turn Europe away from the crass materialism of the late nineteenth and early twentieth centuries, and Avery Brundage – the most tenacious supporter of Coubertin's original principles and goals – did all he could to resist the increasing influence of the political economy on the production of the Olympic Games. In the face of the growing professionalization and scientific rationalization of world-class sport, Brundage decided to enshrine 'amateurism' directly into the Olympic Charter in 1964 (see Killanin, 1976). As one might expect, the formal regulation of Olympic athletes had no effect, and following a review of the amateurism question in 1969 and 1970, a joint IOC/National Olympic Committees' report recommended that the IOC replace amateurism with an 'Eligibility Code'. Brundage continued to resist; he permitted the name change to Rule 26 but introduced the most restrictive code the Games had ever employed. Despite his fierce opposition to the full intrusion of the forces of the broader market economy into all aspects of the Olympic Games, he could not change the reality of high-performance sport by bureaucratic fiat and the eligibility question came back almost immediately after he stepped down as IOC President in 1972.

In 1974, the IOC changed Rule 26 so that under its by-laws athletes could receive money and material benefits for their athletic performances. The IOC formally opened the Games to the best eligible athletes who competed for Olympic gold, financial rewards and national prestige. The change decisively shifted the focus of the Games to the scientifically assisted quest for victory and the unrestricted pursuit of the linear record. The 1974 change to the Eligibility Code meant that the labour of athletes was clearly directed to goals, market interests and political objectives that the athletes, themselves, did not set; the system of high-performance sport, which rested on the immediate labour of athletes, required athletic labour to exist but it was owned and controlled by individuals who had very specific objectives in mind (Beamish and Ritchie, 2006).

Conclusion: high-performance sport as alienated labour

Using Marx's conception of alienation to examine the Olympic Games accomplishes three specific outcomes. First, it allows one to understand the central significance Marx saw in material productive activity. From Marx's perspective, all forms of labour, including sport labour, have the potential to fully actualize the species-character of humankind through objectification. However, when labour is conducted under the conditions of private property, it de-actualizes – diminishes – the immediate producers. Losing control over the products of their labour and alienated from the production process, workers within the political economy create a system that opposes them as well as the individuals who confront them as their overseers. The rich creative potential of humankind is torn from it and production meets the 'needs' of the market economy.

Second, on the basis of these insights and the particular objects of analysis that Marx's theory of alienation singles out, there is a general guide one may use to examine specific, historically located forms of sport practice. This chapter has focused on Coubertin's Olympic Games because they were designed to overcome the same conditions of alienation that Marx had identified in his critique of political economy. By using Marx's framework, it is apparent why the Games could never realize Coubertin's goals and ambitions.

Finally, while Marx's theory of alienation establishes a general framework with which one can examine labour in general or the Olympic Games in particular, it does not reach very deeply into the actual mechanisms by which production under conditions of political economy produce and reproduce the conditions of alienation. One can begin, as Marx did, with alienation as a first guide but, like Marx, one is led progressively into a more detailed examination of the product of labour under the private ownership of the means of production – that is, the commodity and its value form and substance – as well as the nature of the labour process under capitalist production. If Marx's draft text for *The Critique of Politics and Political Economy* provides a general framework with which one can begin to assess the labour of high-performance athletes critically, it is the detailed analyses of *Capital* to which one is led in the pursuit of a more detailed critical understanding of how labour is deformed in and through capitalist production. Fortunately, Marx completed enough of his analyses of capital to provide the critical sport scholar with further direction into a more detailed analysis of sport production in capitalist society.

Notes

1   One gets a sense of the volume of work Marx amassed during his lifetime when looking at the plans for Part IV – *Exzerpte und Notizen* [*Excerpts and Notes*] – in the new Marx/Engels complete works project; to date, 10 of the projected 32 volumes have been published. See Marx and Engels (1976–91: Pt. IV, Vols. 1, 2, 3, 4, 6, 7, 8, 9) and Marx and Engels (1999: Pt. IV, Vols. 31, 32).

2   One indication of the scope of Marx's intellectual purview may be seen in his personal library. See Kaiser (1967) and Marx and Engels (1999: Pt. IV, Vol. 32).

3   For Marx's critique of Hegel's *Philosophy of Law*, see Marx and Engels (1982: Pt. I, Vol. 2: 3–137, 170–83).

4   On the contract with Leske, see Marx and Engels (1975: Pt. III, Vol. 1: 492, 516, 851–2). Marx never completed the books and Leske cancelled the contract in 1846. In addition to the notebooks comprising Marx's 'Economic and Philosophic Manuscripts', Marx began an outline of a book on the modern state; see Marx and Engels (1932: 532).

5   On the manuscripts that Marx left relating to volume two of *Capital*, see Marx (1926: xxxii–xxxvi) and Rubel (1968: cxxi–cxxvii, 501–4) and Marx and Engels (2005: Pt. II, Vol. 12).

6   See Friedrich Engels, 'Umrisse zu einer Kritik der Nationalökonomie' [Outlines of a Critique of Political Economy], in Marx and Engels (1985: Pt. I, Vol. 3: 467–94).

7   Marx's draft text draws upon Hegel to examine political economy critically and political economy to examine Hegel's idealism critically. The centrally creative role of labour and its alienated reality are found in both parts of the manuscript. In critically assessing Hegel, Marx (Marx and Engels, 1982: Pt. I, Vol. 3: 404) wrote the following: 'The greatness of the Hegelian *Phenomenology* and its end result the dialectic of negativity as the moving and generating principle is thus first Hegel grasps the self-creation of man as a process, objectification as externalization [*Vergegenständlichung als Entgegenständlichung*], as alienation and transcendence of this alienation; that he thus grasps the essence of *labour* and comprehends objective man, genuine because actual man, as the result of his *own labour*.'

8   The key statement in this tradition is Johan Huizinga (1950). Gruneau's (1980) commentary on the potential of play and sport still remains one of the most important commentaries on this dimension of sport. See also Weiss (1969).

References

Beamish, R. (1992) *Marx, Method and the Division of Labor*, Chicago: University of Illinois Press.

Beamish, R. (1993) 'Labor Relations in Sport: Central Issues in Their Emergence and Structure in High Performance Sport', in A. Ingham and J. Loy (eds) *Sport in Social Development: Traditions, Transitions, and Transformations*, Champaign: Human Kinetics.

Beamish, R. and Ritchie, I. (2004) 'From Chivalrous Brothers-in-Arms to the Eligible Athlete: Changed Principles and the IOC's Banned Substance List', *International Review for the Sociology of Sport* 39, pp. 355–71.

Beamish, R. and Ritchie, I. (2005) 'Performance and Performance-Enhancement in Sport: The Paradigm Shift in the Science Of "Training" and Performance-Enhancing Substances', *Sport in History* 25, pp. 434–51.

Beamish, R. and Ritchie, I. (2006) *Fastest, Highest, Strongest: The Critique of High-Performance Sport*, London: Routledge.

Coubertin, P. (2000) *Olympism: Selected Writings*, Lausanne: International Olympic Committee.

Goldman, B. (1984) *Death in the Locker Room: Steroids and Sports*, South Bend: Icarus Press.

Gruneau, R. (1980) 'Power and Play in Canadian Society', in R. Ossenberg (ed.) *Power and Change in Canada*, Toronto: McClelland and Stewart.

Guttmann, A. (2002) *The Olympics: A History of the Modern Games*, Urbana and Chicago: University of Illinois Press.

Hoberman, J. (1992) *Mortal Engines: The Science of Performance and the Dehumanization of Sport*, New York: The Free Press.

Huizinga, J. (1950) *Homo Ludens: A Study of the Play Element in Culture*, Boston: Beacon Press.

Kaiser, B. (1967) *Ex Libris Karl Marx und Friedrich Engels [From the Library of Karl Marx and Friedrich Engels]*, Berlin: Dietz Verlag.

Killanin, L. (1976) 'Eligibility and Amateurism', in L. Killanin and J. Rodda (eds) *The Olympic Games: 80 Years of People, Events and Records*, Don Mills: Collier-Macmillan.

Krüger, A. and Murray, W. (eds) (2003) *The Nazi Olympics: Sport, Politics and Appeasement in the 1930s*, Champaign: University of Illinois Press.

Mandell, R. (1971) *The Nazi Olympics*, New York: Ballantine Books.

Marx, K. (1926) *Das Kaptial [Capital]*, Vol. 2, ed. F. Engels, Berlin: J.H.W. Dietz.

Marx, K. and Engels, F. (1932) *Gesamtausgabe [Complete Works]*, Berlin: Marx–Engels Verlag.

Marx, K. and Engels, F. (1975–91) *Gesamtausgabe [Complete Works]*, Berlin: Dietz Verlag.

Marx, K. and Engels, F. (1992–2005) *Gesamtausgabe [Complete Works]*, Berlin: Akademie Verlag.

Rentschler, E. (1996) *The Ministry of Illusion: Nazi Cinema and Its Afterlife*, Cambridge, MA: Harvard University Press.

Riordan, J. (1977) *Sport in Soviet Society*, Cambridge: Cambridge University Press.

Rubel, M. (1968) 'Introduction', *Karl Marx Oeuvres Économique [Karl Marx, Economic Works]*, Vol. 2, Paris: Gallimard.

Schmidt, A. (1962) *Der Begriff der Nature in der Lehre von Marx [The Concept of Nature in Marx's Works]*, Frankfurt-am-Main: Europäische Verlagsanstalt.

Shirer, W. (1960) *The Rise and Fall of the Third Reich*, New York: Simon and Schuster.

Speer, A. (1969) *Erinnerungen* [Memoirs], Berlin: Verlag Ullstein.

Teichler, H.-J. (1975) 'Berlin 1936 – ein Sieg der NS-Propaganda?' [Berlin 1936 – A Victory for Nazi Propaganda?], *Stadion* 2, pp. 265–306.

Teichler, H.-J. (1982) 'Coubertin und das Dritte Reich' [Coubertin and the Third Reich], *Sportwissenschaft* 12, pp. 18–55.

Todd, T. (1987) 'Anabolic Steroids: The Gremlins of Sport', *Journal of Sport History* 14(1), pp. 87–107.

Weiss, P. (1969) *Sport: A Philosophic Inquiry*, Carbondale: Southern Illinois University Press.

Welch, D. (1993) *The Third Reich: Politics and Propaganda*, London: Routledge.

Yesalis, C. and Bahrke, M. (2002) 'History of Doping in Sport', *International Sports Studies* 24(1), pp. 42–76.

Part III

The sporting poetics of class, race and gender

7 Post-Marxism, black Marxism and the politics of sport

Brett St Louis

[C]lass interest, class position, and material factors are useful, even necessary, starting points in the analysis of any ideological formation. But they are not sufficient – because they are not sufficiently determinate – to account for the actual empirical disposition and movement of ideas in real historical societies.

Stuart Hall, 'The Toad in the Garden: Thatcherism among the Theorists'

Introduction

As with any social activity, the specific form and function of sport are heavily disputed. This contestation is amplified by the pivotal position that sport occupies, where, as Pierre Bourdieu (1990a: 166) has acknowledged, it presents 'with the maximum acuteness the problem of the relations between theory and practice, and also between language and the body'. Thus, further reflecting one of Bourdieu's (1990b) main sociological concerns, sport is a 'practice', a practically integrated whole of thought, perception and action.

In addition to its complex formation, the meaning of sport has been strenuously assessed. Much social scientific and critical work on sport has asked whether it is an innocent and edifying form of 'play' or instead serves as an instrument of social discipline that is all the more effective because of its ability to pursue this agenda across physical and ideational domains. Put simply, recast within the familiar sociological dichotomy, sport has often been seen empirically as a determining structure reproduced, at least in part, through an ideology of agency.

The question of precisely how this phenomenological account of sport should be analytically developed poses immense challenges as it is at once compatible with and contrary to various analytical frameworks employed within Sport Sociology, including figurational, feminist, post-structuralist and psychoanalytical (see Giulianotti, 2004). And given Bourdieu's ostensibly Marxian framework, there is the further problem of how this perspective might be politically situated: for example, does this holism identify a network of disciplinary regimes or is it a rigid reductionism that is unable to countenance the internal specificity of distinct sporting practices? Viewed from a left perspective, this conundrum reflects a set of methodological, analytical and political disputes within Sport Sociology that reflect the larger intellectual and political chasm between Marxism and post-Marxism.

Taking this tension as a point of departure, this chapter attempts to stage a productive conversation between Marxist and post-Marxist approaches and concerns. Although the differences in terms of method and methodology are so vast as to render rapprochement impossible, the chapter draws on the critique of economic reductionism and engagement with the symbolic register of cultural politics insightfully developed within 'black Marxism' as a 'proto post-Marxism' that is yet resolutely Marxist. The purpose of this framing is twofold: first, to develop a more rounded sociological account of the hegemonic interaction between social actors, relations and structures; and second, to assess whether anything politically valuable can be retrieved from attempting to bridge the separate empirical and discursive registers that the contemporary left and Sport Sociology find themselves pulled between to divisive effect.

By way of an example, the chapter draws on Maurice Clarett's unsuccessful legal case against the NFL's draft policy as 'restraint of trade' to advocate the simple Marxian proposition of analysing 'social relationships'. In arguing that this case offers an important opportunity to move beyond the singular determinism of the economic, the false explanatory salience of the racial, and the pathology of the problem, the chapter draws on Bourdieu's holistic perception of sport mentioned above to frame the complexity and meanings of sporting practice as emergent across its practical and symbolic realms. This tension demands a more nuanced consideration as Marx himself arguably foresaw it, famously recognizing the determining force of materiality over consciousness in *The German Ideology* while later noting in the *Grundrisse* that the concrete is itself the product of a series of prior determinations. Ultimately, this chapter seeks to think through what is at stake in our various commitments – methodological, analytical and political – and articulate the conditions under which sport offers valuable opportunities for incisive critique as well as stimulating elusive political affinities across insular differences.

The post-Marxist problematic

The fragmentation of the 'traditional' proletarian coalition is crucial within accounts of the recent Euro-American trajectory of Marxism. In its conceptual and operational form as a practical unity, the proletariat, so a version of the story goes, was unable to countenance its forms of significant internal differentiation. As such the full extent of professed leftist commitment to various 'Questions' – for example the Woman, Race, Negro and Colonial Questions – was often doubted. Similarly, the implicit or explicit status of gender and racial experiences and issues as either ancillary to the pivotal character of class or grossly inflated for agitprop purpose was also problematic for many who subscribed to Marxism in order to understand and organize against racism and economic exploitation.

In arguing for the autonomy and integrity of the black struggle in the USA, C.L.R. James (1978) would remark as early as 1939 that the absolutist rhetoric of black chauvinism did not represent intrinsic racial essentialist attitudes among black people but was the expression of a class antagonism that lacked the reflexive and political insight of a mature class consciousness. In other words, grassroots black Americans' affinity with separatist black belt doctrine was gestural. For James, black Americans did not want only racial justice and equality but also full US citizenship and rights: they demanded justice against racism and full social participation as citizens. But in reaction to the continued experience of marginality and (suspected) opportunism of various Marxist political organizations, the flight of many subjects of sectional 'Questions' from the institutional left was perhaps inevitable, as was the subsequent ascent of 'identity' and 'interest' politics. This unease with institutional Marxism and critique of party condescension and paternalism is expressed in a voluminous literature across a range of genres, including autobiography, fiction and polemical essays (Césaire, 1957; Ellison, 1965; Wright, 1977, 1987).

This practical fissure is also significant for the analytics of Marxism. A corrective of the economistic, masculinist and ethnocentric overdeterminations of orthodox Marxisms initiated within the emergence of the New Left during the 1950s (Kolakowski, 1978) is profoundly extended and deepened within contemporary post-Marxist critiques (see Fisk, 1993; Jameson, 1997; Sim, 1997). Paradigmatic post-Marxist accounts, such as the loose New Times project – see *Marxism Today* (October 1988) and Hall and Jacques (1989) – or Laclau and Mouffe (1985), are taken as surveying the shifting practical and theoretical terrain of Euro-American political culture and civil society and proffering a radical diagnosis. In a key statement, Stuart Hall and Martin Jacques (1989: 116) suggest that the 'New Times' in question is less an abandoning of Marxism and more about stimulating a left discussion on developing 'new descriptions and analyses of the social conditions it seeks to transcend and transform'. This observation is accompanied by no less of a radical prognosis for oppositional political struggles in their existing form. In their prominent 1985 text, *Hegemony and Socialist Strategy: Towards a Radical Democratic Politics*, Ernesto Laclau and Chantal Mouffe state unambiguously that the previously unquestioned ontological status of modern categories of labour within the capitalist process are now under irresistible pressure from diverse subjective processes and the multiplicity of identities-in-formation.

Viewed from elsewhere within the left, this putative post-Marxist predicament is assessed differently. It is taken as signalling (and indeed producing) a crisis where the original sites and actors of class politics are situated antagonistically against the exaggerated efficacy of proliferating identities and new social movements in a struggle for analytical primacy (Wood, 1986). It is notable here that more strident critics dismiss post-Marxist projects as a modish capitulation to semiotic and discursive analytical frameworks and the esoteric minutiae of identity and representation that evacuates the material battleground of (class) politics (Callinicos, 1989; Wood, 1986; Sivanandan, 1990; Geras, 1990). As such, particular strands of post-Marxism are regarded as only tenuously linked to Marxism and represent a pervasive rightward shift under the paradigmatic social reformation throughout the Western world exemplified by the Thatcher and Reagan administrations in Britain and the United States.

Sport and the identity dilemma

This state of affairs is also recognizable within Sport Studies. Although functionalist approaches have tended to dominate analyses of sport, Marxist or Marxian analytical tools have also been used, as has been the case within much of the social and human sciences. And although these approaches and positions cannot be fully restated here, it is worth noting that they have been usefully characterized broadly as two main varieties: first, a New Left school that advanced a sport-as-work thesis; and second, a hegemony approach, less economistic and more culturalist than the first but still founded in and driven by a general concern with sport-as-discipline (Morgan, 1994). However, more recently, these approaches have largely come to be regarded as rather blunt analytical instruments and their efficacy has been reassessed.

Two important issues of note emerge here. First, the complexity of social situations wherein sport is located is increasingly understood as (re)produced beyond strict materialist and class confines. And second, the very question of the primacy and salience of both class categories and analysis has been subject to intense scrutiny. The result of this is evident within the proliferation of Cultural Studies treatments of sport alongside the more traditional sociological texts (see, for example, Andrews and Jackson, 2001; Rail, 1998; Rowe, 2004; Wenner, 1998). Furthermore, as Cultural Studies texts have arguably supplanted the strictly sociological in terms of profile and demand, a significant shift in content and analysis has taken place: 'non-traditional' sports, sites, questions and actors have been engaged through the insights offered by a set of oppositional critical perspectives, including feminism, queer theory, post-structuralism and post-colonialism. And, without wishing to oversimplify a multifaceted history here, while there are obvious examples that apply sociological approaches to some of the newer issues on the agenda, such as sexuality (e.g., Guttmann, 1996), it is clear that a 'sea change' has taken place.

In his keynote address to the North American Society for the Sociology of Sport (NASSS) 2004 Annual Conference in Tucson, Arizona, Ben Carrington remarked that this shift has developed – and been fought – over the question of 'identity' (Carrington, 2007). In this specific instance, 'identity' is taken in reference to various subject positions arranged around sexuality, gender, ethnicity and so on that have disturbed the positivistic model of the social actor taken as a normative object. Carrington argues that the reactionary defence of Sport Sociology in its meaningful past – 'before identity', so to speak – generates a set of key objections to the 'new' Sport Sociology concern with identity. However, for the discussion at hand two objections to the 'new' Sport Sociology are worth focusing on: first, to its anti-positivist methodologies; and second, to its apolitical repudiation of leftist-materialist concerns.

This sporting struggle over the analytical and political status of identity is symptomatic of a much wider intellectual-scholarly and social-political shift. The breach in the practico-theoretical efficacy of Marxism forced by the growing dissatisfaction with its explanatory capacity in the academic human and social sciences as well as profound political shifts – such as the emergence of the New Right and the fall of Eastern European state communism – has had significant effects. As such the identity-before-identity dispute fought out within Sport Sociology can be contextualized as a battle in a larger conflict between Marxism and post-Marxism: the struggle over the status of issues such as identity and representation as 'proper' analytical and political concerns, disputes over the validity of respective psychoanalytical and empiricist frameworks, as well as a broad disagreement over the form of politics and requisite political practice are all clearly discernible across both fields.

The controversy surrounding identity, sporting and non-sporting alike, is more than simple academic or intellectual formalism and episodically operates within an impassioned register: Norman Geras (1987: 42–3) derides Laclau and Mouffe's, *Hegemony and Socialist Strategy* as 'a product of the very advanced stage of an intellectual malady'; Eric Dunning (1996) dismisses the postmodern turn within some Sports Studies and its non-empirically grounded, overabstracted theoretical jargon; and Jennifer Hargreaves (2004) expresses concern with the problematic influence of postmodernism on sport feminism as further widening the theory/praxis divide and more allied to intellectual posturing and career advancement instead of emancipatory political ends. Within each of these positions a separate accusation is implicit. The seductive pull of the emperor's new clothes – in this case post-Marxism, postmodernism and post-structuralism – becomes manifest through individual compliance. Therefore, the emergence of these critical 'post-s' and their pre-eminence are not simply a random accident, but the direct result of individual responsibility – or lack thereof. In short, the errant postmodernists slavishly follow modish concerns and erroneously eschew a strong analytical-political programme.

Unsurprisingly, the response to this intimation of individual weakness exacerbates the divide. In reply to Geras (1987), Laclau and Mouffe (1987: 81) state they had anticipated 'attacks . . . from the fading epigones of Marxist orthodoxy'. Additionally, Carrington (2007) argues for a progressive form of interventionist scholarship that combines the requirements of sociological understanding with the necessity of political engagement against reactionary nostalgia for the venerable past of Sport Sociology 'before identity'. However, given the broadly stated commitment to progressive politics and social change across this chasm, there are some entirely consistent commonalities that deserve examination. Geras (1987: 82), for example, acknowledges his 'partial agreement' with Laclau and Mouffe's (1985) interest – albeit, for Geras, inconsistent with their larger project – in the fulfilment of individual 'human capacities'. And, for their part, Laclau and Mouffe (1987) reject the charges of self-serving, wilful obscurantism levelled at them and declare their commitment to democratic politics and the (reconstituted) socialist project.

This situation highlights the epistemological and methodological divide between the empirical and discursive basis of, and analytical approach to, politics, and is at the centre of the Marxist/post-Marxist divide. There is, however, a more important point of convergence that emerges out of the dilemma facing radical politics apparent in the work of Sivanandan, one of post-Marxism's most ardent critics. While accepting the potentially dangerous insularity of a radical politics founded solely on self-referential positions, Sivanandan (1990: 32) also expresses an awareness of working-class movements overlooking and rejecting valid experiential political claims based on social identities such as gender, race and sexuality. Sivanandan's perceptive insight usefully recognizes the political validity of particularistic existence as relatively autonomous from class within a Marxist framework; this particular/universal dialectic demonstrates an important substantive commonality (potentially) across the left. As such, Sivanandan can be situated within the tradition of black Marxism that is informative to an assessment of the arguments within Sport Sociology.

Black Marxism and the problem of articulation

The empirical and discursive methodological differences between Marxism and post-Marxism provide the basis for their divergent understandings of the social. Their agreement over the existence of different categories within the social aside, disagreement effectively reigns over whether one can justifiably distinguish between first- and second-order abstractions. As such, 'workers' or 'humans' might be seen as primary categories that represent empirical objects existing within 'society' – another such primary category. Other groupings such as 'ethnicities' and 'homosexuals' might be seen as subsidiary categories that are derived from the primary order – they are subsets of 'workers' and 'humans'. Conversely, all such categories (primary and subsidiary alike) might be approached as reified instead of empirical objects and their meaning or efficacy regarded as discursively emergent within linguistic practice and relationships of power. Within this dichotomy there can be no rapprochement. For proponents of strong versions of the argument on either side, neither the symbolic nor the practical exists prior to being constituted by the other: within this logic the symbolic is constitutive of the material or vice versa.

There are, however, allied analytical problems here: the problem of accounting descriptively for difference, what it is; and the issue of explaining it, establishing how it has come about. But, given the interventionist tenor of Marxism, there is another concern with prescription: what is to be done with and about difference as well as how. In relation to the various differences within the social – racial, sexual, national and so on – evident in the problem of 'identity' facing Sport Sociology, this predicament constitutes a problem of articulation. Simply put, disputes over the proper status of different forms, whether as primary or subsidiary categories or discursive representations, do not obviate the question of establishing precisely how they are interrelated or not related. For example, is mapping the relationship between race, class and gender to be achieved through the method of triangulation, the principle of intersectionality or some other model/ process? The attempt to situate differences of identity within the non-homologous unity of left praxis through the management of difference poses a methodological and substantive 'problem of articulation', as specified within Stuart Hall's (1996) discussion of the unifying connection of two separate elements within certain conditions as the process of articulation. This 'problem' raises some important questions. To what extent, if at all, can such differences be unified within political struggle? And, if possible, within which theoretical and practical conditions is it feasible?

This problematic of countenancing difference and multiplicity within a viable political project can be productively staged through a consideration of the Marxism/post-Marxism dichotomy alongside the insights offered by black Marxism. While unconvinced that the term 'black Marxism' has any unified internal coherence, I refer to it paradigmatically to invoke an instructive preoccupation shared by many black Marxist activist-intellectuals. Put simply, while the competing demands posed by definitive class locations and the fluidity of unstable subject positions might appear to pose a rather contemporary tension, it is far from the case. Indeed, a cursory appreciation of the insights of a series of radical black activist-intellectuals reveals the error of such presentism: C.L.R. James (1980) pondering race as empirically supplemental to class but not ana-lytically incidental, and Aimé Césaire (1957: 15) navigating his way between a 'strait particularism' and 'fleshless universalism' in an attempt to realize 'a universal rich with all that is particular' offer two individual but by no means isolated examples.

There is a crucial point of emphasis here. In the midst of significant variation within the loose tradition that might be identified as black Marxism the attempt to address race-specific or -relevant issues such as apartheid and colonialism as not racially explicable is relatively constant. And if, for many, this initially meant adopting class struggle as the causal explanation par excellence for racism and racial stratification, a subsequent broad dissatisfaction and disillusionment with its limitations can be noted. But this discontent is particularly striking because, although it sometimes led to a repudiation of Marxism, it often formed the basis for rethinking the question of racism and social oppression and relevant analytical tools from within the left. What is most instructive about black Marxism for the purposes of our discussion, therefore, is the attempt to think through the social processes of racism in a way that apprehends both the discursive and practical specificity of racialization while not distorting reified racial categories as valid empirical explanations for what is fundamentally a general social process. It is within this formulation that the now monumental divide between identity as subject-position and class-position is less the insurmountable void it initially appears to be.

Race/class articulation

The political etiology of racism

At the beginning of his magnificent essay *Discourse on Colonialism*, Césaire (2000: 31) explicitly sets out the problem of identifying racism without committing the error of assuming it is founded in a racial metaphysics:

> The fact is that the so-called European civilization – 'Western' civilization – as it has been shaped by two centuries of bourgeois rule, is incapable of solving the two major problems to which its existence has given rise: the problem of the proletariat and the colonial problem; that Europe is unable to justify itself either before the bar of 'reason' or before the bar of 'conscience'; and that, increasingly, it takes refuge in a hypocrisy which is all the more odious because it is less and less likely to deceive.

In the midst of such incendiary prose there are three key points that deserve emphasis: first, the debasement of European/Western civilization is the result of bourgeois rule, not a pathological regional or racial decadence or malignancy; second, this bourgeois civilization has produced the social problems posed by proletarian and colonial exploitation; and third, given the Enlightenment ethos foundational to this bourgeois civilization, neither the proletarian nor the colonial problem can be rationally or morally justified.

Unlike Adorno and Horkheimer (1997), who saw no inconsistency in the gross inequities carried out under the aegis of universal reason and justice but only the manifestation of modernity's instrumental rationality and will to domination, Césaire's faith in modern civilization in the intrinsic sense of enlightenment is clear. There is, arguably, another reason for this. In carefully specifying bourgeois rule as the culprit, Césaire meticulously avoids inflating a racial matrix of colonialism into a causal explanation. He continues in this vein, notably arguing 'colonization works to *decivilize* the colonizer, to *brutalize* him in the true sense of the word' (Césaire, 2000: 35; emphasis in original).

This humanistic magnanimity has been seen as a regrettable gesture, the ideological price of his membership of the Communist Party of France (PCF) (Kelley, 2000). But Césaire does not indemnify the West from ethical critique or release it from political responsibility. That it is the unparalleled 'crime against the white man' and exportation of the practice of genocide previously reserved for the colonies into mainland Europe which attests to the heinousness of Nazism (Césaire, 2000: 36) lays bare the specificity and hierarchies of racial terror. Moreover, this bold assertion is a unifying human instead of a racially solipsistic move; as a reflexive undertaking, it initiates Césaire's attempt to establish the basis for progressive political solidarity across racial lines. To this end, and with customary poetic force, Césaire asserts the need to create 'a new society . . . rich with all the productive power of modern times, warm with the fraternity of olden days' (ibid.: 52).

Ultimately, Césaire seeks to open an important humanistic and affective dimension. Class struggle provides the basis for Western civilization and its violence, and yet a solely structural account of racism is not enough; Césaire develops an account of the existential dimensions of racism in order to encourage intersubjective empathy alongside political understanding. And although this narrative approach and its content are not entirely consistent with an economistic version of Marxism fixated on the determining base, it is not incompatible with Marx. It is reminiscent of the account of species-being and the degradation of the worker separated from their creative and productive human capacity articulated by the 'young Marx' (Marx, 1974).

Racialization, politics and social reproduction

An important methodological issue arises alongside this politically strategic use of a humanistic narrative. The 'hypocrisy' of European civilization identified by Césaire is developed within C.L.R. James's illuminating analysis, *Nkrumah and the Ghana Revolution* (1977). James here discusses 'the myth' of the superiority of the colonizer and inferiority of the colonized as legitimating and justifying colonial benevolence and paternalism. But while the myth helps support the survival of colonialism it is not a static form: instead it is adaptive and transforms, it makes concessions and accommodations – for example, it reinforces self-determination as an ideal but also asserts the principle of 'under correct conditions', conditions that are always just out of reach as well as overseeing piecemeal change such as the nomination of selected locals to legislative councils. And finally, the myth is composed largely of commonsensical, dominant ideas: it is unconscious, logical and illogical thus difficult to critique; the myth 'just is', it is a 'customary pattern of thought' that is deeply embedded within society and proceeds largely unchallenged.

This Jamesian formulation of what is essentially an ideological process is reminiscent of – though not indistinguishable from – the Gramscian concept of hegemony. The 'historical bloc' and 'national popular' in which Gramsci situates hegemonic processes are roughly approximated by James's sketch of an era of expansionist capital and the benign, civilizing self-image at the heart of British imperialism. However, James's use of 'the myth' as a discursive device in order to describe the ideological processes of social reproduction within the Gold Coast is not extended into a form of social explanation. In terms of explaining Crown colony governance and its concomitant racial stratification, James alludes to what we now commonly refer to as 'racialization'. Within this concept there is no such thing as race in a natural, objective state; instead, there is an idea of 'race' that, once naturalized, obscures its social production as a natural fact (Miles, 1989). For James, therefore, there is an ideology of race articulated through the myth. However, 'myth' here does not operate in the normative sense identified by Lévi-Strauss (1968) as salving various existential anxieties and addressing metaphysical questions. Instead, as suggested by another anthropologist, Ashley Montagu (1997: 41), 'the functional role of the [race] myth is to provide a sanction for a course of action'. Thus, for Montagu, racial myths support the building of hierarchical racial taxonomies which in turn form the justificatory basis for war, conquest and genocide among myriad other racist practices.

This is entirely consistent with James's understanding of the sociopolitical function of the myth. However, while Montagu condemns racial myths as 'witchcraft', 'demoniacal' and 'America's Original Sin', James eschews building an assessment of it as irrational and immoral. Conversely, James presents the myth as a racialized narrative that provides the ideological justification for Crown colony government and capitalist profiteering instead of signalling the individual and collective moral turpitude of whites. This much is clear in his magnum opus, *The Black Jacobins* (1980), where he carefully states that the Haitian Revolution must not be misunderstood as a 'race war' but rather as indicative of the internal contradictions within the capitalist-industrial complex that could no longer be suppressed or managed once the slaves gained class (not racial) consciousness of their exploitation and oppression. None the less, their racialized subjectivity and experience as proto-proletarian black Jacobins is pedagogically significant, stimulating the emergence of class consciousness:

> From the start there had been the gap, constantly growing, between the rudimentary conditions of the life of the slave and the language he used. There was therefore in West Indian society an inherent antagonism between the consciousness of the black masses and the reality of their lives, inherent in that it was constantly produced and reproduced not by agitators but by the very conditions of the society itself.
>
> (James, 1980: 407)

In what is sometimes understood as a controversial move, James, like Césaire, uses his analysis of the black Jacobins as a proto-proletariat in order to promote internationalist socialism. For James, the myth is not simply to be exploded for the benefit of black Africa and other colonized peoples, but for the political emancipation of the white metropolitan proletariat that have also been incul-cated with it; 'British people', James (1977: 34) writes, invoking Marx and Engels's hopes in *The Communist Manifesto*, 'as a whole are ready for new relations, human relations, for the first time in four centuries'. This argument, however, is strongly contested. The race/class problematic has been addressed analytically in terms of whether in fact the racism and racial opportunism within Marxist political movements can be understood less as the result of individual and organizational deficiencies but as indicative of the intrinsic defectiveness of Marxist analytical tools (Mills, 2003). In this sense, as a positivistic enter-prise, Marxism is at best woefully unable to apprehend the specificity of racial histories and subjectivities as they become subsumed within the dogma of class struggle. And, at worst, Marxism is an ethnocentric analytical framework based in deracinated categories such as 'labour' and 'worker' and fails to comprehend variable human conditions of social existence within the ideal-type of universal species-being. Thus, instead of being authentically universal, species-being is particularistic in its reinforcement of a normative 'human' that tacitly endorses 'Western' values – scientific, secular, rational and so on – over non-Western, aboriginal peoples' ontological, cosmological and metaphysical specificity (Senghor, 1994).

None the less, in terms of understanding the complexity of sport as a 'practice' in Bourdieu's sense that extends across practical and symbolic realms, and developing a prescriptive political programme that addresses racialization and racism without falling prey to tautological forms of epiphenomenal racial explanation, engaging the problematic of class and racial articulation is unavoidable. The methodological and prescriptive acuity of black Marxism is evident in James's understanding of and struggle with the analytical problem of how racism is (re)produced in articulation with class instead of attempting to identify which one holds analytical primacy over its subordinate other. Indeed, as Frantz Fanon (1967) so incisively recognized, racialization is *both* social process *and* existential habitus. Therefore, empiricism, class analysis and materialist politics are not necessarily analytically placed in an antagonistic and mutually exclusive zero-sum game with subjectivism, humanistic concerns, the affective dimension, and discursive and representational methodological approaches. What is essentially at stake here is the form of social mapping and political project within which racialization and economic exploitation are to be located. It is at this practico-theoretical conjuncture – the Marxist/post-Marxist impasse and disputes over the efficacy of identity outlined above – that an analysis of sport and racism drawing on the insights offered by black Marxists such as James and Césaire is particularly instructive.

The shamateur ethic and the capitalist-athletic complex

I shall illustrate this necessarily abstract overview by introducing an example that, when approached through the insights of black Marxism, demonstrates expanded political possibilities. In 2004, Maurice Clarett, a twenty-year-old African American football player at Ohio State University (OSU), brought a legal action against the National Football League (NFL), challenging their rule that a player is eligible for the NFL draft only if they are at least three years out of high school.[1] Clarett contested this rule as restraint of trade while the NFL countered that, as it was established through the collective bargaining agreement in consultation with the players' union, it was valid.

As existing NFL players' support for this rule is significantly influenced by self-interest, framing the league/labour consultative process as justification for a restraint of trade exemption is at best disingenuous. In sympathy with this perspective, the initial ruling in a lower court went in Clarett's favour. It was found that the NFL was unable to demonstrate that the rule enhanced competition and effectively breached federal antitrust laws by excluding him – and all players in the same situation – from attempting to enter the only feasible employment market for his skills.[2] This judgement was subsequently overturned by a three-judge panel of the US Court of Appeals for the Second Circuit that found in favour of the NFL: players entering the league 'prematurely' was found to be not in the best interests of the players, the league or the wider game.[3] This story generated a great deal of attention as Clarett had been a star performer for one year in the National Championship football team at OSU, then surrounded by controversy concerning his acceptance of preferential academic treatment as well as gifts and money – illegal under National Collegiate Athletic Association (NCAA) regulations. Clarett was subsequently suspended by OSU for the entire 2004 season, hence his appeal to enter the NFL draft.

Perhaps the most notable aspect of this unfolding story was the attention that it drew to issues of structural power beneath the courtroom drama and salacious revelations of various academic transgressions and financial impropriety. For many commentators, the basis of the NFL's concern was transparent: the erosion of the free and effective 'farm system' provided by college football (see Eitzen, 2003; Sperber, 2001; Zimbalist, 2001). Other critics of the NFL have advocated the 'pay for play' principle, notably supported by the Nebraska Senator Ernie Chambers. During his tenure in the state legislature, Chambers introduced a series of bills that would – against the NCAA's wishes – pay college athletes instead of 'exploiting' them.

None the less, the restriction of rights and legal contradiction that 'pay for play' brings to the fore has broader economic, social and political implications. Indeed, despite NCAA claims to the contrary, college sport is a financially lucrative enterprise at the elite Division IA level. Some institutions' athletic departments and merchandising operations have multi-million-dollar yearly turnovers and the NCAA's total operating revenue for 2005–6 was $521.1 million;[4] the association also has an eleven-year television broadcast rights contract with CBS for $6.2 billion, terminating in 2013.[5] This puts the NCAA in an incongruous position: it is charged with upholding 'amateurism and academic integrity' and rigidly enforces a series of restrictions on institutions and athletes to this end while itself operating within and benefiting from the free market (Parent, 2004).

The question then arises of why the NCAA resolutely avoids even discussing the issue of financially rewarding those athletes who contribute to consumer interest and financial income. This disinclination is easily justified through the assertion that students are simply that, students, and not paid employees of their universities as well as platitudes citing the intrinsic benefits of varsity sports that reflect Olympian ideals of participation over winning – let alone the vulgar pursuit of financial gain (Brand, 2006). This argument works when the student athlete is primarily a student who competes for purely recreational purposes. However, when the student athlete is primarily a high-performance athlete, and recruited into the academic institution on that basis, then the platitudes ring hollow. One might instead ask: who or what profits financially and what are the prevalent relations of production? The former president of the University of Washington, William Gerberding, is critically reflective regarding this: 'I have become increasingly uncomfortable about having a largely white establishment maintaining an elaborate system of rules that deprives student-athletes, many of whom are non-white, of adequate financial support in the name of "the ideals of amateurism'" (cited in Parent, 2004: 243). Or, as Senator Chambers remarks, athletic scholarships are akin to 'contracts of indenture' (*ibid.*).

The relations of athletic production and the 'public interest'

Utilizing antitrust legislation and its foundational premise of protecting market freedoms does not, at face value, appear to be an appropriate method of advancing a progressive leftist political project. Were the initial judgement in Clarett's favour upheld at appeal the 'victory' would have secured him 'only' the opportunity to attempt to sell his labour in a precarious market. Similarly, the success of 'pay for play' campaigns would in effect institute a semi-professional stratum within the academy where the already lower and slower graduation rates of (male) student athletes would possibly increase further as their contractual status as athletes and economic value became the primary basis of their institutional existence. Indeed, given the minute possibility for NCAA Division IA student athletes progressing into the professional sporting ranks, their receipt of a meaningful education that enhances their non-athletic career opportunities and life chances remains a paramount objective. But in both of these 'success' scenarios, the structures of the capitalist-athletic complex remain intact and a select and still small number of individuals have won the right only to insert themselves into a system of uncertainty as, on average, professional careers within the NFL and National Basketball Association (NBA), for example, are of a short duration. What is necessary here, therefore, is a thorough reconsideration of the internal contradictions of the capitalist-athletic complex and the constitutive function that racial ideologies play in its reproduction.

Bearing in mind the inherent contradictions of capitalism, it is important to recognize that professional sports leagues – and ironically especially North American sports leagues such as the NFL, Major League Baseball (MLB) and NBA – often operate through capitalist oligarchical arrangements. Individual teams operating as franchises licensed and regulated by the league; draft selections where the least successful teams pick first from the new talent available from the farm system; and the imposition of a salary cap to ensure a degree of parity in teams' expenditure on athletic personnel: all contradict free market ideology. But to note this is not to reject this corporatist ethos in favour of an unrestricted free market. Instead it is useful as a means of illustrating such inconsistencies as entirely consistent with a specific process of capitalist accumulation as opposed to a random, aberrant occurrence. As a functional oligarchy, the league develops policies in order to maintain (as far as possible) a stable product able to keep if not expand audience share in a burgeoning entertainment market. Within this context, the relationship between the professional leagues and the NCAA as its farm system must function effectively as a cartel. I want to suggest that the focus on and analysis of this consistent contradiction of the capitalist-athletic complex as a 'practice' in Bourdieu's sense and through a *specific* reference to antitrust legislation has an important role to perform in a progressive leftist political project.

The basis of this possibility lies in the twin pillars of antitrust law that are supposed to offer protection against the development of monopolies: first, the preservation of market freedom; and second, the – suitably vague – notion of the 'public interest'. In relation to American sports, Stephen F. Ross (2003: 318) argues that the NFL and MLB have fought to secure exemptions from antitrust law on the basis that sports leagues are 'single entities with owners akin to divisional heads within a corporation not subject to the prohibition on conspiracies in restraint of trade contained in the Sherman Act and that any agreements involving players' unions were exempt under judicially created labor exemptions'.

Initially, this legal sophistry prevents the recognition of sports leagues as markets without positively appealing to the public interest, as discrete 'corporate entities' leagues are ipso facto *not* markets. However, when the 'public interest' is strategically invoked, for example – as in Clarett's case – in relation to the ban on professional teams drafting players with remaining college eligibility, the argument is tenuous. For Ross, pious concerns over addressing the situation where many student athletes do not complete their studies despite remaining in college for the duration of their competitive eligibility[6] are disingenuous. By 'redshirting'[7] freshmen and offering those leaving with remaining eligibility the option to return later to complete their degrees, universities are simply acting in their own interests by attempting to maximize the collegiate competitive eligibility of their student athletes. Why else is it, Ross asks, that the 'public interest' worth assiduously defending in this vein is largely reserved for male football and basketball players who leave college with remaining eligibility?

A simple remedy is available, although, unsurprisingly, the NCAA and universities reject it out of hand. Ross argues that contractual arrangements could be developed within the framework of amateurism that would require student athletes to remain in the institution for the duration of their eligibility. However, colleges do not pursue this mainly due to their fear of being legally bound to bear the – for them prohibitive – financial costs of their liability to workers' compensation payments in the event of serious injury for those under extended contracts (Ross, 2003: 321–2). For Ross, then, the professional leagues' rationale for maintaining these rules that periodically come under antitrust scrutiny is twofold: first, it averts bearing the cost of identifying and developing young players currently borne by the colleges; and second, it helps maintain good relations with NCAA college programmes (*ibid.*: 322). If this appears rather close to, if not synonymous with, the definition of a cartel, Ross's conclusion that 'Neither purpose justifies an authorization of this rule as being in the public interest' (*ibid.*) is indeed apposite.

'Black Marxism' in practice: articulating sport, identity and the political

The inadequacies of these appeals leave open the issue of what properly constitutes the public interest beyond preserving market freedoms. As such, we might begin to think about the constraints on opportunity and access through the related principles of justice and equity in relation to a wider notion of social goods and the public interest instead of one narrowly focused on market considerations. And furthermore, it might help us to formulate the 'public interest' in relation to our own political projects and concerns. Building on Nancy Fraser's (1995) formulation of the left as ensnared within a divisive stand-off between the 'politics of recognition' and the 'politics of redistribution', John Beverley (1997: 45–6; emphasis in original) asks a pertinent question:

> is there a way of raising the ante, in terms of recognition demands, that pushes them into contradiction with the perceived needs of capital or of its ideological superstructure? If this could be done, then it might be possible to produce out of the demands of heterogeneous social movements the people/power bloc contradiction, precisely because these movements come to understand that the possibility of realizing *their* specific demands depends on entering into an alliance with others.

In relation to our discussion this demands urgent consideration because the processes of racialization that constitute race as both a scientific and a legal concept (Guillaumin, 1995b) are operationalized within recognition and redistributive arenas. As much work within critical race theory (CRT) argues, the assiduous cultivation of the 'colour-blind' basis of law has worked historically to protect and promote (white) privilege. By extension, this colour-blind ideology is used to frame disputes over the organizational operation of sports oligarchies as cartels solely – and unfavourably – in relation to redistributive agendas where all actors are equal before the law. Senator Chambers' argument that 'big-time college football players are subjected to treatment, restrictions and conditions that would never be tolerated if applied across the board to all students' (cited in Parent, 2004: 227) begs the question of whether the social – read class and racial, for example – status of student athletes deems their individual and collective interests as less worthy of legal protection or support. In support of this assessment, it is crucial to note the processes of racialization through various discourses that naturalize the predominance of physical and intellectual propensities as racially distributed.

Certain contemporary strands within sport and popular science have detailed the natural and racial basis of athletic ability. As I have argued elsewhere, some of these arguments demonstrate a degree of rhetorical sophistication, attempting to forestall charges of racism and biological reductionism by articulating a biocultural form of explanation. This perspective gestures to environmental and cultural factors as informing athletic propensity – but unsurprisingly reify and naturalize culture while asserting the primacy of the biological within this process of articulation (St Louis, 2003). The biocultural explanation is also constituted as 'commonsense' through a combination of naïve inductive methodology coupled with an expedient appropriation of liberal multicultural vocabulary that, ironically, justifies this project as conversant with the benign recognition of human biodiversity and celebration of 'difference' (St Louis, 2004). In addition to these scientific explanations of natural racial athletic propensity, more qualitative racialized discourses referring to the zero-sum relationship between physical and intellectual capacity further entrench the commonsense basis for understanding racial stratification as reflective of natural states (St Louis, 2005). Read alongside conservative criticisms of interventionist social programmes to raise levels of educational attainment within racialized and poor communities, the implication is clear: despite their 'obvious' and 'intrinsic' intellectual short-comings student athletes are in college because of and to develop their physical capacities.

It is, however, crucial to situate these racial discourses socially instead of mis-understanding them as the pathological or misguided interpretation of intrinsic racial difference. In this sense I refer above to the racial *and* class status of student athletes for a specific reason. In charting the emergence of race as a legal concept, Guillaumin (1995b) carefully specifies the *legal production* of racial categories – for example, to legitimate racial segregation and the uneven distribution of resources in apartheid South Africa – in order to foreground the social conditions of this constitutive process. The acuity of this is evident when, for example, CRT is presented as an interventionist tool to 'shape the discourses of minds closed to "race" *centred* perspectives' (Hylton, 2005: 92; emphasis added) and challenge 'white privilege and power . . . [and] the hegemonic influence of the white establishment' (*ibid.*: 91).

Two things are dangerously unclear within this formulation. First, why does race have to be 'centred'? And second, what descriptive and explanatory function does 'race' perform? While, as Hylton (*ibid.*) notes, sport, like law, is presented as a 'level playing field' and yet works as a 'key tool in the subjugation of black people', the reference to a *white* establishment, privilege and power does not specify whether this establishment, privilege and power are intrinsically racial or refer to racialized political and economic elites. This is precisely the trap that Guillaumin (1995a: 143; emphasis in original) wishes to avoid, which is worth restating at length:

> The crux of the question really is: A *social relationship*, here a relationship of domination, of power, of exploitation, which secretes the idea of nature, is regarded as the product of traits internal to the object which endures the relationship, traits which are expressed and revealed in specific practices. To speak of a specificity of races or of sexes, to speak of a natural specificity of social groups is to say in a sophisticated way that a particular 'nature' is *directly productive* of a social practice and to bypass the *social relationship* that this practice brings into being. In short, it is a pseudo-materialism.

Certain reservations over the limitations of CRT are prescient for the discussion here, including its 'uncompromising emphasis on "race" . . . the conspicuous absence of a systematic discussion of class and, more importantly, a substantive critique of capitalism' (Darder and Torres, 2004: 98–9). A grave political irony and error are signalled here: by myopically focusing on race, its autonomous status as a naturalized concept is further reinforced and the false causality that explains or implies racism as the result of racial differences disengages its constitutive complexity and the social, political and economic interests that (re)produce it. The imperative, therefore, is to decouple the analysis of racism from being fixed within a simplistic recognition agenda that determines analyses must be 'race-centred'. Instead, guided by the spirit of Césaire and James, we can also eschew the alternate polarity of becoming over-reliant on distributive agendas and instead forge a critical space capable of moving between the two. However, where Césaire's and James's internationalism and articulation of recognition and redistributive agendas foundered as abstractions, the pervasiveness of sport throughout social and cultural life offers valuable political opportunities.

Conclusion

The denouement of the Maurice Clarett saga is deeply significant, given the arguments raised throughout this chapter. After his failed civil suit against the NFL, Clarett went a year without competition, unable to return to OSU. He entered the subsequent 2005 draft having performed poorly in the 'combine' – the pre-draft workout – and was eventually selected in the third round as the 101st pick by the Denver Broncos. Although this was far from the high-value first-round pick his earlier exploits may have merited, many commentators felt that, given his poor physical condition, he was fortunate to have been picked so 'early' by the Broncos. Now suitably contrite, Clarett offered all the set-piece utterances about 'wanting to leave the past behind' and 'just wanting to play football'; at the behest of the Broncos, he even signed a contract without a signing bonus of approximately $400,000, agreeing instead to an incentive-related package worth up to $7 million over four years.[8] However, after sustaining injuries that limited his ability to practise during pre-season training – as well as muted complaints within the organization from fellow players and officials alike about his diligence to the injury rehabilitation programme – he was released by the team in August 2005. He then failed to gain a contract with another NFL team.

As if this isn't enough, the story gets worse. On New Year's Day 2006, the police department in Columbus, Ohio, announced that they were looking for Clarett in relation to an alleged armed robbery. On reporting to the police the following day, Clarett was charged with two counts of aggravated robbery, and he was later indicted on these and five other counts. Eight months later the now familiar image of a handcuffed and crestfallen Clarett was once again splashed liberally across media outlets, graphically depicting his latest reversal of fortune. Clarett, wearing a bullet-proof vest and in the possession of three handguns and an AK47 assault rifle, was arrested following a high-speed chase after being subdued with pepper spray. With these additional charges, including carrying a concealed weapon without a permit, Clarett faced a prison sentence of up to thirty-four years. Entering an arranged guilty plea, he received a seven-and-a-half-year sentence with the possibility of release after three and a half.

In a sense this is a tragic story of one man's demise. However, it can also be taken as an indictment of an, at best, unfair system. His personal failings aside, Clarett has been well and truly defeated by the capitalist-athletic complex, from his failure to gain a meaningful education at OSU (despite helping them win a national championship with its concomitant financial rewards) through to his failed civil action against the NFL and the 'lost year' that ensued and perhaps precipitated his unravelling. The expansive reach of this complex is manifest within Bourdieu's insistence on making 'connections after connections, so that sport practices and their meanings are understood as part of the social and cultural totality' (Tomlinson, 2004: 165). And, more importantly, this understanding of sporting practice through the analytical articulation of cultural process and social formation 'demonstrates the deeply entrenched relation between social class and sport, *but without ossifying this dynamic*' (*ibid.*: 166; emphasis added). It is, perhaps, this appreciation of practice as not ossifying the empirical and discursive realms that might mediate the divergent epistemological and methodological concerns that have driven the Marxist/post-Marxist cleavage.

We would also do well to remember and learn from the long-standing attempt at such a reconciliatory project for the race/class problematic as an enduring feature of black Marxism. In what is probably the most famous passage in his entire corpus, C.L.R. James, with great acuity, framed this problematic and the response it demands as long ago as 1938 in *The Black Jacobins*: 'The race question is subsidiary to the class question in politics, and to think of imperialism in terms of race is disastrous. But to neglect the racial factor as merely incidental [i]s an error only less grave than to make it fundamental' (James, 1980: 283). As disputed and controversial as this passage is, James's point is simple and remains deeply instructive. While race is incapable of explaining itself and its effects and is actually formed through objective class struggles, it is not insignificant and the failure to recognize this delicate proposition is politically damaging. James formulates what we might consider a proto post-Marxist dilemma here, asserting the articulation of objective empirical conditions and subjective existence where neither enjoys an unassailable analytical primacy.

To me, the wider efficacy of this commitment is striking. As a sociologist who has taught both general survey and sport courses (among others) in the UK and US, I find the comparative ease with which students are able to grasp issues of power, agency, discipline, politics and so on within the study of sport is markedly apparent. Just as students may be unsure of the detail and depth of their political understanding in the broad, formal sense, sport is a known social and cultural entity. And while this sometimes informs a resistance to engage in analysis and critique, sport is also an efficacious device for the translation of political ideas and practices into an accessible register. Part of our task is to continue this pedagogical project and extend it into the wider social and political sphere, drawing attention to the complex and opaque formation and operation of sport as a practice that reproduces dominant social relations and structures but also makes envisioning progressive alternatives possible.

Notes

1 *Clarett v. National Football League*, S.D.N.Y. No. 03-CV-7441.
2 *Clarett v. National Football League*, S.D.N.Y., No. 03 Civ. 7441 (SAS), 5 February 2004.
3 *Clarett v. National Football League*, U.S.C.A., 04-0943, 24 May 2004.
4 http://www1.ncaa.org/finance/2005-06_budget.pdf.
5 http://www1.ncaa.org/eprise/main/Public/CBA/BrdcstMan/Sect6/Internet.
6 In response to such concerns over institutions overemphasizing student athletes' sporting contributions at the expense of their formal academic education, the NCAA now monitors the academic progression rate of student athletes within colleges and athletic programmes with the power to levy penalties, including the loss of athletic scholarships. This was formally adopted into the NCAA Constitution as the following article in 2004: '3.2.5.5 Failure to Satisfy the Academic Performance Program. A Member institution may be placed in a restricted and/or corresponding membership category if the institution or its sports team(s) has failed to comply with the established requirements of the academic performance program' (NCAA, 2005: 12).
7 A 'redshirt' is a student athlete who does not compete for an entire academic year and thus retains eligibility for a year of competition within a maximum of four years. A 'redshirted' freshman at a four-year university having completed a year of study, therefore, still has four years of competitive eligibility remaining.
8 http://www.nbc4i.com/sports/4909305/detail.html.

References

Adorno, T. and Horkheimer, M. (1997) *Dialectic of Enlightenment*, London: Verso.
Andrews, D.L. and Jackson, S.J. (eds) (2001) *Sports Stars: The Cultural Politics of Sporting Celebrity*, London: Routledge.
Beverley, J. (1997) 'Does the Project of the Left Have a Future', *Boundary 2* 24(1), pp. 35–57.
Bourdieu, P. (1990a) 'Programme for a Sociology of Sport', in *idem, In Other Words: Essays towards a Reflexive Sociology*, Cambridge: Polity.
Bourdieu, P. (1990b) *The Logic of Practice*, Cambridge: Polity.
Brand, M. (2006) 2006 NCAA State of the Association Address: 'The Principles of Intercollegiate Athletics', at http://www2.ncaa.org/portal/media_and_events/press_room/2006/january/200601 07_soa.html.
Callinicos, A. (1989) *Against Postmodernism: A Marxist Critique*, Cambridge: Polity.
Carrington, B. (2007) 'Merely Identity: Cultural Identity and the Politics of Sport', *Sociology of Sport Journal* 24(1), pp. 49–66.
Césaire, A. (1957) *Letter to Maurice Thorez*, Paris: Présence Africaine.
Césaire, A. (2000) *Discourse on Colonialism*, trans. Joan Pinkham, New York: Monthly Review Press.
Darder, A. and Torres, R.D. (2004) *After Race: Racism after Multiculturalism*, New York: New York University Press.
Dunning, E. (1996) 'On Problems of the Emotions in Sport and Leisure: Critical and Counter-Critical Comments on the Conventional and Figurational Sociologies of Sport and Leisure', *Leisure Studies* 15(3), pp. 185–207.
Eitzen, D.S. (2003) *Fair and Foul: Beyond the Myths and Paradoxes of Sport*, 2nd edn, Lanham: Rowman and Littlefield.
Ellison, R. (1965) *Invisible Man*, London: Penguin.

Fanon, F. (1967) *Black Skin, White Masks*, trans. Charles Lam Markmann, New York: Grove Press.

Fisk, M. (1993) 'Post-Marxism: Laclau and Mouffe on Essentialism', in R.S. Gottlieb (ed.) *Radical Philosophy: Tradition, Counter-Tradition, Politics*, Philadelphia: Temple University Press.

Fraser, N. (1995) 'From Redistribution to Recognition: Dilemmas of Justice in a "Post-Socialist" Age', *New Left Review* 212, pp. 68–93.

Geras, N. (1987) 'Post-Marxism?', *New Left Review* 163, pp. 40–82.

Geras, N. (1990) *Discourses of Extremity: Radical Ethics and Post-Marxist Extravagances*, London: Verso.

Giulianotti, R. (ed.) (2004) *Sport and Modern Social Theorists*, Basingstoke: Palgrave.

Guillaumin, C. (1995a) 'Race and Nature: The System of Marks', in *idem, Racism, Sexism, Power and Ideology*, London: Routledge.

Guillaumin, C. (1995b) 'The Idea of Race and Its Elevation to Autonomous Scientific and Legal Status', in *idem, Racism, Sexism, Power and Ideology*, London: Routledge.

Guttmann, A. (1996) *The Erotic in Sports*, New York: Columbia University Press.

Hall, S. (1988) 'The Toad in the Garden: Thatcherism among the Theorists', in C. Nelson and L. Grossberg (eds) *Marxism and the Interpretation of Culture*, Urbana and Chicago: University of Illinois Press.

Hall, S. (1996) 'On Postmodernism and Articulation: An Interview with Stuart Hall', ed. L. Grossberg, in D. Morley and K.-H. Chen (eds) *Stuart Hall: Critical Dialogues in Cultural Studies*, London: Routledge.

Hall, S. and Jacques, M. (eds) (1989) *New Times: The Changing Face of Politics in the 1990s*, London: Lawrence and Wishart.

Hargreaves, J. (2004) 'Querying Sport Feminism: Personal or Political?', in R. Giulianotti (ed.) *Sport and Modern Social Theorists*, Basingstoke: Palgrave.

Hylton, K. (2005) '"Race", Sport and Leisure: Lessons from Critical Race Theory', *Leisure Studies* 24(1), pp. 81–98.

James, C.L.R. (1977) *Nkrumah and the Ghana Revolution*, London: Allison and Busby.

James, C.L.R. (1978) 'The Discussions in Coyoacán', 'Self-Determination for the American Negroes' and 'Plans for the Negro Organization', in George Breitman (ed.) *Leon Trotsky on Black Nationalism and Self-Determination*, 2nd edn, New York: Pathfinder.

James, C.L.R. (1980) *The Black Jacobins: Toussaint L'Ouverture and the San Domingo Revolution*, London: Allison and Busby.

Jameson, F. (1997) 'Five Theses on Actually Existing Marxism', in E. Meiksins Wood and J. Bellamy Foster (eds) *In Defense of History: Marxism and the Postmodern Agenda*, New York: Monthly Review Press.

Kelley, R.D.G. (2000) 'Introduction: A Poetics of Anticolonialism', in A. Césaire, *Discourse on Colonialism*, trans. Joan Pinkham, New York: Monthly Review Press.

Kolakowski, L. (1978) *Main Currents in Marxism: Its Rise, Growth and Dissolution, Volume 2: The Golden Age*, trans. P.S. Falla, Oxford: Clarendon.

Laclau, E. and Mouffe, C. (1985) *Hegemony and Socialist Strategy: Towards a Radical Democratic Politics*, London: Verso.

Laclau, E. and Mouffe, C. (1987) 'Post-Marxism without Apologies', *New Left Review* 166, pp. 79–106.

Lévi-Strauss, C. (1968) *Structural Anthropology*, trans. Claire Jacobson and Brooke Grundfest Schoepf, London: Allen Lane/Penguin Press.

Marx, K. (1973) *Grundrisse: Foundations of the Critique of Political Economy*, Harmondsworth/London: Penguin/New Left Review.

Marx, K. (1974) 'Economic and Philosophical Manuscripts', trans. Gregor Benton, in *Karl Marx: Early Writings*, Harmondsworth: Penguin.

Marx, K. and Engels, F. (1970) *The German Ideology*, London: Lawrence and Wishart.

Miles, R. (1989) *Racism*, London: Routledge.

Mills, C.W. (2003) 'Under Class under Standings', in *idem, From Class to Race: Essays in White Marxism and Black Radicalism*, Lanham: Rowman and Littlefield.

Montagu, A. (1997) *Man's Most Dangerous Myth: The Fallacy of Race*, 6th edn, Walnut Creek: AltaMira Press.

Morgan, W.J. (1994) *Leftist Theories of Sport: A Critique and Reconstruction*, Urbana and Chicago: University of Illinois Press.

NCAA (2005) *2005–06 NCAA Division 1 Manual: Constitution, Operating Bylaws, Administrative Bylaws*, Indianapolis: NCAA.

Parent, C.M. (2004) 'Forward Progress? An Analysis of Whether Student-Athletes Should Be Paid', *Virginia Sports and Entertainment Law Journal* 3(2), pp. 226–56.

Rail, G. (ed.) (1998) *Sport and Postmodern Times*, Albany: SUNY Press.

Ross, S.F. (2003) 'Antitrust, Professional Sports, and the Public Interest', *Journal of Sports Economics* 4(4), pp. 318–31.

Rowe, D. (ed.) (2004) *Critical Readings: Sport, Culture and the Media*, Buckingham: Open University Press.

Senghor, L. (1994) 'Negritude: A Humanism for the Twentieth Century', in P. Williams and L. Chrisman (eds) *Colonial Discourse and Post-Colonial Theory: A Reader*, New York: Columbia University Press.

Sim, S. (ed.) (1997) *Post-Marxism: A Reader*, Edinburgh: Edinburgh University Press.

Sivanandan, A. (1990) 'All That Melts into Air Is Solid: The Hokum of New Times', in *idem, Communities of Resistance: Writings on Black Struggles for Socialism*, London: Verso.

Sperber, M. (2001) *Beer and Circus: How Big-Time College Sports Is Crippling Undergraduate Education*, New York: Henry Holt.

St Louis, B. (2003) 'Sport, Genetics and the "Natural athlete": The Resurgence of Racial Science', *Body and Society* 9(2), pp. 75–95.

St Louis, B. (2004) 'Sport and Common-sense Racial Science', *Leisure Studies* 23(1), pp. 31–46.

St Louis, B. (2005) 'Brilliant Bodies, Fragile Minds: Race, Sport and the Mind/Body Split', in C. Alexander and C. Knowles (eds) *Making Race Matter: Bodies, Space and Identity*, Basingstoke: Palgrave Macmillan.

Tomlinson, A. (2004) 'Pierre Bourdieu and the Sociological Study of Sport: Habitus, Capital and Field', in R. Giulianotti (ed.) *Sport and Modern Social Theorists*, Basingstoke: Palgrave.

Wenner, L.M. (ed.) (1998) *MediaSport*, London: Routledge.

Wood, E.M. (1986) *The Retreat from Class: A New 'True' Socialism*, London: Verso.

Wright, R. (1977) *American Hunger*, New York: HarperCollins.

Wright, R. (1987) *Native Son*, New York: Harper Perennial.

Zimbalist, A. (2001) *Unpaid Professionals: Commercialism and Conflict in Big-Time College Sports*, Princeton: Princeton University Press.

8 Venus and Serena are 'doing it' for themselves

Theorizing sporting celebrity, class and Black feminism for the Hip-Hop generation

Jayne O. Ifekwunigwe

The one thing that most of the Black women of the Hip-Hop generation have in common is that they all came of age in the post-Black power era . . . The head start made by earlier Black women has made claiming a space from which to speak somewhat easier; however, Black women today are still plagued with some of the same issues.

Gwendolyn D. Pough, *Check It While I Wreck It: Black Womanhood, Hip-Hop Culture and the Public Sphere*

Pro sports play two primary roles in our society: on the one hand, they are critical for the reinforcement of 'values' like discipline, hard work, and patriotic obeisance. On the other, they represent one of the United States' biggest global cash cows. Players like Michael Jordan [and the Williams Sisters] . . . have brought corporate values and profits together in one smiling red, white and blue package.

Dave Zirin, *What's My Name Fool?: Sports and Resistance in the United States*

Introduction

Do you know where you were on 13 September 1996 and 9 March 1997? According to Kitwana (2002), these two dates, which respectively mark the gun-related deaths of former best friends turned rival West Coast/East Coast gangsta rappers Tupac Shakur and Biggie Smalls, were defining socio-political moments for Black constituents of the American Hip-Hop generation[1] (HHG), which he earmarks as those born between 1965 and 1984. In fact, Kitwana suggests that the untimely demises of Shakur and Smalls are etched on the memories of the post-Civil Rights generation in much the same way as the assassinations of Malcolm X and Martin Luther King, Jr resonate for their Civil Rights generation (CRG) forebears. Although both cohorts have their fallen male heroes, there is a perceived disjunction between the actual political achievements of the CRG and the imagined apolitical aspirations of the HHG.

Persistent academic and media emphases (Boyd, 2003; Chang, 2005; Lan 2000) on this generational rift obscure three significant resonances. The first is that not all Black youth of the HHG have reaped the social, economic and political rewards of these earlier liberation struggles (Green, 2001; Kinshasa, 1997). Both the over-representation of young Black men in penal institutions rather than institutions of higher learning (Kitwana, 2002) and the increased criminalization of young Black women (Sudbury, 2002) point to the triumph of the prison industrial complex over affirmative action. The second is that, like polymorphous 'on-the ground' Hip-Hop culture as opposed to its monolith 'gangsta' popular/corporate renderings, grassroots HHG activism is not a contradiction in terms but rather manifests itself in myriad shapes and forms. In an interview with author/journalist Chang, long-standing HHG activist Angela Brown situates the 'lunch counter'[2] political strategies of the HHG in this current post-industrial, neo-liberal, digital age:

> 'The way in which they built their movement was around the "lunch counter" – SNCC [Student Non-violent Coordinating Committee] and others coming down to the South to challenge segregation on the "lunch counter" . . . We didn't have a single "lunch counter". We had many "lunch counters". Our fight has been a constant barrage of struggles.' [Chang adds:] No longer was there a single Movement, but dozens of movements – civil rights, education, environmental justice, AIDS, prisons, the list went on.
>
> (Chang, 2005: 451)

Finally, the hyper-visible yet still marginalized status of Black women and our counter-hegemonic resistance strategies are the sturdy bridges connecting the gendered contradictions of Hip-Hop politics to those inherent in earlier social movements (Collins, 2006). These links extend from the Civil Rights and Black Power movements of the 1950s, 1960s and 1970s back to the cultural nationalist campaigns of the early twentieth century and beyond to the abolitionist and suffrage political projects of the nineteenth century:

> Black women have always embodied, if only in their physical manifestation, an adversary stance to white male rule and have actively resisted its inroads upon them . . . and their communities in both dramatic and subtle ways. There have always been Black women activists – some known, like Sojourner Truth, Harriet Tubman, Frances E.W. Harper, Ida B. Wells Barnett, and Mary Church Terrell, and thousands upon thousands unknown – who had a shared awareness of how their sexual identity combined with their racial identity to make their whole life situation and the focus of their political struggles unique. Contemporary Black feminism is the outgrowth of countless generations of personal sacrifice, militancy, and work by our mothers and sisters.
>
> (Combahee River Collective, 1977/2000: 262)

Though the transformative potential of Black feminisms, celebrated by the Combahee River Collective over thirty years ago, has been sustained, Black feminisms' ideological limitations as they pertain to the construction of a unitary Black female political subject also persist (James, 1999).

In the American society within which the HHG evolves, the polarization of the 'Black community' along class, gender and sexuality fault-lines has only intensified (Cole and Guy-Sheftall, 2003; Neal, 2005; McBride, 2005; hooks, 2000; Pattillo-McCoy, 1999; Kelley, 1997). These fissures widen in part as a result of proliferating multimedia technologies that manufacture, promote and export the ideologies of predatory capitalism by any patriarchal, imperial, heteronormative means necessary (Collins, 2004; Sharpley-Whiting, 2006). With generational undertones, the inclining presence of a Black middle/upper-middle class without the declining existence of a Black 'under-class' has reproduced what Dyson (2005: xiii–xiv) characterizes as an 'Afristocracy' and a 'ghettocracy', respectively. In the same breath, Dyson reminds us that 'class in black America has never been viewed in strictly literal economic terms; the black definition of class embraces style and behavior as well' (*ibid.*: xv).

Firmly situated within the specific socio-political milieu of Black America (as opposed to, for example, the United Kingdom, where there are different and perhaps less subtle class registers), it is these negotiated and contested meanings of class as both an economic and a symbolic (but always already gendered and racialized) category that my discussion will explore (Lawler, 2005; Aronowitz, 2003). Within such dialectical parameters, tennis super-star sisters Venus and Serena Williams (and other Black (women) celebrity performers) can and do simultaneously signify 'the ghetto' and 'the suburb' as two intersectional symbolic spaces where differential discourses on class and 'race' are (re)produced (Dyson, 2005; hooks, 2000). As such, any twenty-first-century conceptualization of Black feminisms must move beyond a totalizing narrative towards a more dynamic reconfiguration, which is heterogeneous in process and contradictory in nature (Phillips *et al.*, 2005). No cohort of Black women embodies these antagonisms and ambivalences more than the HHG (Collins, 2006; Pough, 2004; Morgan, 2005).

Against a political economic backdrop that highlights the differential structural positions of young Black women in the United States, the following discussion explores what has been retained from 'older' Black feminist praxis and traces the contours of a 'new' Hip-Hop Black feminist theory and practice. By analysing specific media constructions and representations of the tennis super-star sisters Venus and Serena Williams,[3] I illustrate the ways in which these sporting Black females both embody a new Hip-Hop Black feminist world-view and reproduce a gendered and racialized hegemonic social order predicated on the 'just do it' liberal political rhetoric of meritocracy and inclusion, which has been appropriated by (conservative) Republicans in the US. Utilizing fused Marxist, Cultural Studies and Black feminist analyses, this chapter situates these representational 'race', gender, generational and class politics beyond and within the arena of high-performance professional sport studies (Scraton, 2001; Birrell, 2000).[4]

While a deliberate reflection of my disciplinary moorings outside Sport Studies, this conceptual approach also facilitates my engagement with three entangled problematics, which in turn highlight the complexities and contradictions of global capitalism as a dual process of de-territorialized but racialized global commodification and territorialized local signification of specific historically situated, engendered and racialized power dynamics. Rather than questions in search of definitive answers, they (and the chapter in general) are intentionally polemical: first, what constitutes protest and complicity for the post-Civil Rights Hip-Hop feminist generation (Morgan, 1999; Springer, 2002; Chambers, 2003)? Second, invoking Priti Ramamurthy's (2003) theoretical formulation, what are the 'perplexities'[5] of the symbiotic relationship between transnational corporate patronage and global Black female sporting celebrity? Third, is the burden of talent and entitlement heavier for young, Black American and female sporting celebrities such as Venus and Serena Williams (Douglas, 2005; Schultz, 2005; Spencer, 2001)? That is, do they have an ethical as opposed to a charitable responsibility[6] to the economically disadvantaged and the politically disempowered, which include both working-class young African American women and the predominantly young female workforces in Caribbean and South East Asian sweatshops who produce the sporting commodities they endorse (Ross, 2004; Hapke, 2004)?

In addition to my critical engagement with literature across multiple (inter-) disciplinary fields, the raw materials for this chapter include a wide range of newspaper and magazine articles spanning the breadth of this sister-act's relatively brief sporting career, which I critically read as discursive texts. Interwoven with textual analyses are three theoretical threads, which collectively contribute to the shaping of a new Hip-Hop Black feminist praxis on the dialectics of young Black American female sporting celebrity. First, situating 'on the court' representations of Venus and Serena Williams as 'ghetto Cinderellas' within a Black feminist frame uncovers continuities in the 'changing same' depictions of resisting Black women as representations of deviant sexuality located outside the scope of Eurocentric standards of beauty and femininity (Ifekwunigwe, 2004b). Second, assessing the class politics of 'Black American Princesses' (BAPs), the 'off-the-court' (post-Civil Rights) persona I have fashioned for Venus and Serena, uncovers a shift towards an individual bourgeois (Chambers, 2003) rather than a collective socialist (Davis, 1989/2000) Black (American) female politics of empowerment. Third, by illustrating how high-performance Black sporting celebrities, such as the Williams sisters, collude with their transnational corporate patrons in the marketing of 'The American Dream' in both its Horatio Algier and Martin Luther King, Jr manifestations, I expose the very limited and overdetermined ways in which Blackness is personified in the public sphere (Jackson, 2005). In other words, this chapter will interrogate the interface between 'real' Blackness and the 'authentic'/'sincere' (*ibid.*: 28) dimensions of athleticism, class consciousness and ethical responsibility, or what in colloquial terms is known as 'giving back'.

Black Venus strikes back: athleticism and 'changing same' representations of Black womanhood

There are different gendered, racialized, ethnic, class-based and cultural conceptions of sporting female bodies, which are the discursive products of specific knowledge systems and particular historical circumstances, such as plantation slavery (Douglas, 2002). In particular, sports journalism plays an important role in the manufacture of a racialized and sexualized sporting female aesthetic (Spencer, 2001; Rowe, 2004). In the tennis world, the differential media discourses on the 'super-feminine' Anna Kournikova and the 'transmasculine/she-male' Williams sisters presuppose a heterosexual White male gaze and erase the possibility of lesbian sport spectatorship while also paradoxically constructing muscular female athletes as the popular stereotype of a lesbian (Griffin, 2002; Collins, 2004). For example:

> no player has ever had Kournikova's impact, and the X-factor to supplement her abundant natural beauty. Exceptionally photo- and telegenic . . . her slight accent, her icy demeanor, the persistent whispers of alleged ties to the Russian Mafia, the bizarre love triangles, and the conga line of revolving suitors imbue her with a sense of mystery and a lightning bolt of eroticism . . . Kournikova knows how to play the crowd and enflame the boys.
>
> (Wertheim, 2002: 149)

Wertheim's depiction of Kournikova reinscribes a particular version of White European beauty which then becomes the yardstick for the measurement of Venus and Serena's heterosexual attractiveness (McDonald, 2005; Douglas, 2002; Scraton, 2001). For example:

> REHIRED: Radio reporter Sid Rosenberg, who was fired two weeks ago after saying on Don Imus' syndicated show that Venus Williams was an animal and that she and sister Serena had a better shot at posing nude for *National Geographic* than *Playboy*. He apologized and showed he understood he was wrong, says program director Mark Chernoff of Imus' flagship station, WFAN, in New York City. Rosenberg also sent a written apology to the Williamses.
>
> (*Sports Illustrated*, 2001: 34)

Sharpley-Whiting (1999) provides the historical context for Rosenberg's outburst. Though primarily engaging with nineteenth- and twentieth-century French representations of Black women from Hottentot Venus to Josephine Baker, throughout the text and explicitly in the epilogue, Sharpley-Whiting (*ibid.*: 6) argues that the Black Venus master-narrative is reasserted in other milieux and in contemporary historical moments: 'black women, embodying the dynamics of racial/sexual alterity, historically invoking primal fears and desire in . . . men, represent ultimate difference (the sexualized savage) and inspire repulsion, attraction, and anxiety, which gave rise to the collective . . . male imaginations of Black Venus (primitive narratives)'.

Regarding the ways in which this master-narrative is reproduced in contemporary tennis journalism, I was surprised to discover the number of times the sisters were described or referred to as 'delicious', revealing the ambivalent semiotics of 'inter-racial' desire: 'The notion of the Williams sisters battling in Grand Slam finals, their hair beads and gargantuan groundstrokes whipping through the wind, is beyond the delicious fantasy stage' (Silver *et al.*, 1999: 39). That said, Ms. magazine's rationale for including Venus and Serena Williams among the 2001 recipients for 'Ms. Women of the Year' offers an alternative but still racialized and therefore relational feminist characterization, which claims to celebrate the very attributes which rendered the sisters undesirable to a heterosexual male market: 'For serving up a discomfiting mix of sinew, grit, coal black kink and 'tude – and daring to call it woman' (Ms. Online, 2001). Hence, these four media examples confirm that what it means to be an embodied Black sporting female is already and always oppositional (Zirin, 2005; Hoberman, 1997). With both their ever-changing hairstyles and dress codes, on the court Venus and Serena actively challenge these same prevailing representations of the Black embodied female aesthetic while also defying the conventional etiquette of the lily-White elite tennis world. In doing so, they strategically subvert their contradictory positioning as hyper-sexual Black women and hyper-masculine female athletes (Schultz, 2005).

Mindful of the dangers of racial essentializing shaped by authenticity claims, I also suggest that both sisters exploit an 'authentic ghetto Blackness' in both its embodied symbolic and its commodified expressive forms: 'to say it is a "black" thing doesn't mean it is made up entirely of black things' (Kelley, 1997: 42). Constituent parts of a racially transcendent reinvention process that produces the American origin myth of the 'rags-to-riches' self-made (wo)man (Grewal, 2005), I argue that *on the court* they position themselves and are indeed constructed as 'ghetto Cinderellas'. This performative role was fashioned for them by their father Richard Williams, who joins a long line of 'tennis-fathers' (Spencer, 2001). As a 'present Black father', Williams has also been instrumental in challenging the stereotype of the 'Black father' whose absence is said to have such a deleterious social impact on burgeoning Black womanhood (Wertheim, 2002). Journalist Allison Samuels (2001: 46) refers to him as 'part huckster, part stage dad, part ambassador, part entrepreneur'. Despite the fact that by ages eleven and ten, respectively, Venus and Serena had left 'the 'hood' and were living in suburban Florida, where they attended private school and had a professional coach, in a 1998 interview, Papa Williams (as he is known on the circuit) perpetuates the myth of his daughters' *exclusively* 'ghetto' origins and artfully intertwines their embryonic development as athletes with the emergent West Coast Hip-Hop scene:

> Richard began taking Venus regularly to the courts, and a year later, Serena began coming along. Among the locals who strolled through the park, he says

were future rap stars Eazy-E and Snoop Doggy Dogg. There was also the neighborhood crack dealer with his AK-47 . . . Gradually Richard befriended the local gang members, and the three Williamses became fixtures on the Compton courts.

(Jenkins, 1998: 103)

Regarding Papa Williams' conjuring of Compton, sadly life imitated art, when, in 2003, Venus and Serena's half-sister Yetunde Price was murdered in their old neighbourhood. Two years later, as part of a larger media assault on 'knuckle-heads' in the 'Black community', entertainer, educator and activist Bill Cosby led a one-man crusade to repatriate Venus and Williams symbolically and reclaim them for Compton:

'How difficult is it for Compton to have a parade so that parents can bring the children and hold them up and say: "They're from here?"' he asked the hundreds of residents who came to talk about turning things around in their violence-plagued city . . . 'You're known for a lot of things, Compton – not many of them good ones. Why don't you bring them out?'

(Garvey, 2005)

Ironically, the 'ghetto' dimensions of their Compton beginnings are parts of a past neither Venus nor Serena could strategically afford to disavow (Kelley, 1994). It is both these 'authentic' origins and their indisputable talent which also make them ready-made role models for many Black fans on the other side of the Atlantic:

The sisters' singular achievement has been to bring to tennis a black culture that previously was almost entirely missing: in their style, their sense of fashion, their physique, their self-confidence and their flamboyance . . . Venus and Serena are wonderful role models not only, and most obviously, for young black women, but for us all. Long may they reign.

(Jacques, 2005: 20)

By focusing on the Williams family's calculated deployment of authentic 'ghetto Blackness', I am not thereby discounting the political and historical significance of the sisters' athletic achievements and prowess nor how their dominance of the game has transformed the social landscape of tennis and exposed the racism at its core (Douglas, 2005). Yet, racism and caricature notwithstanding, one can never underestimate the power nor the expectations Black female sporting celebrity status yields (Zirin, 2005; Andrews and Jackson, 2001; Spencer, 2001).

Suburban Cinderella and her fairy god-mammies: Black bourgeois feminism and the politics of entitlement

Black feminist standpoint theories, like other (post)modern paradigm shifts, including feminist standpoint epistemology, clear space and make textual room for multiple subjectivities and bestow agency upon the formerly silenced (Hull *et al.*, 1982; hooks, 1984; Collins, 1990). In doing so, (post)modern Black feminisms contest the limited Enlightenment definition of 'the reasoning subject', challenge all claims to truth and objectivity, and acknowledge the historically situated, socially/culturally specific and strategic nature of knowledge production as it is integral to the dynamics of all power relations (Hammonds, 1997; Kaplan and Grewal, 2002). Yet, such an anti-essentialist stance does not erase the existence and persistence of structural inequalities (Alexander and Mohanty, 1997). That said, institutional marginalization on gender, 'race' or disciplinary grounds aside, those of us who do strive to reconcile the materialist and post-structuralist war(s) of position(s) cannot evade suspicion as self-appointed mouthpieces for 'the weak' while simultaneously producing these knowledges within the confines of relative ivory-tower privilege and prestige (Adair, 2005; hooks, 2000; Mohanty, 2003; Grewal, 2005). Nevertheless, I write from a critical space that is mindful of the ideological and epistemological pitfalls of a Black feminist critique of class, however it is reconfigured: 'In the absence of ideologies and activism for economic justice and human rights, conventional feminisms displace radicalism, reducing radical and revolutionary black feminisms to a shadow's shadow; a poor reflection of black bourgeois feminism' (James, 1999: 182). Taking James's lead, I am staging an encounter between 'the shadow' and 'its shadow'. Put another way, I trace the contours of a post-Civil Rights/post-'race' class consciousness in an era of what Mohanty (2003: 6) describes as 'free-market feminism'.

While the figure of 'ghetto Cinderella' functions as a potent symbol of Black working-class female transgression within the exclusive and exclusionary, predominantly White tennis world, the BAP (not to be confused with 'Ghetto Fabulous') facilitates readings of Venus and Serena's *off the court* complex and contradictory identity performances. Defined by the authors of *The BAP Handbook: The Official Guide to the Black American Princess*, a BAP is: 'An African-American female whose life experiences give her a "sense of entitlement"' (Johnson *et al.*, 2001: 1). Tongue firmly in cheek, Gates (2001: 11) elaborates:

> Oprah's one. Halle's one, too. Venus and Serena round out the list . . . Like JAPs (Jewish American Princesses) and preppies who came before them, BAPs are sophisticated shopaholics who put Sarah Jessica Parker and her Manolo Blahniks to shame. But it takes a lot more than a Fendi baguette full of MAC cosmetics and a Neiman Marcus charge card to qualify as a BAP. She should attend the correct school: exclusive Spelman College in Atlanta. And a respectable BAP must give back to her community, supporting such causes as the United Negro College Fund and sickle-cell anemia research. Some may be offended by the handbook's suggestion that women with the names beginning with 'la' and 'sh' and ending with 'isha' and 'ika' can't be BAPs.

As the epitome of the bourgeois Black feminism that James (1999) criticizes, BAPs symbolize both the partial victories of the Civil Rights and Women's movements and the complete reign of free-market capitalism (Pough, 2004; Springer, 2002; Chambers, 2003). While mindful of Serena and Venus's inclusion in *The BAP Handbook*'s role-call of famous BAPs (curiously both Rosa Parks and Angela Davis are also mentioned!), my relegating them to BAP status is inspired by two particularly illuminating texts. The first is their self-help book entitled *Venus and Serena: Serving from the Hip: 10 Rules for Living, Loving and Winning* (Williams *et al.*, 2005). The second is their appearance on *Oprah* to promote this new book, which coincidentally aired on 30 March 2005, the day after they played each other in the quarter-finals of the Nasdaq-100 Tennis Open. Their book appeals to 'raceless' suburban female adolescent constituents, whose everyday realities are a far cry from the authentic 'ghetto Blackness' to which they make coded references, signifying they are 'hip sistuhs' (*ibid.*). 'Got your back', 'back in the day', 'crib', 'bling bling', as well as both the title of the book – *Serving from the Hip* – and the 'Sister Rules' framework are all linguistic plays on authenticating Black signifiers (*ibid.*). At the same time, there is only one explicit reference to 'race', and this was to mention an 'inspiring' poem, 'Dreams' by Black artist of the Harlem Renaissance Langston Hughes. Deference to expressive Blackness without a broader reference to embodied Blackness is also evident in the pumping Hip-Hop soundtrack that accompanies the 'dream-making' segment on *Oprah*. In fact, Oprah has become a billionaire by cooking up a digestible Black feminist politics of acceptability and serving it to 'ordinary' Americans (Collins, 2004; Marshall, 1997). This mainstreaming is exemplified by the show on 'The Secret Life of Girls', featuring Venus and Serena Williams, the actress Jada Pinkett Smith and a Black woman psychologist as emotional 'wet-nurses', and 'troubled teens' as guests, but not the lived experience of even one young Black woman. The stories *Oprah* showcases include those of a sixteen-year-old who is 'notorious' for having had sex with eight boys, a seventeen-year-old who seeks plastic surgery to correct her 'hideous' nose, and a sixteen-year-old emotionally 'empty' overeater. The powerful 2002 series 'The War on Girls' in the Black women's magazine *Essence* paints a more inclusive and complete picture of this 'crisis' wherein:

> Black girls are twice as likely as White girls to be overweight (Centers for Disease Control and Prevention's Youth Risk Behavior Surveillance System).
>
> Black teen girls are almost twice as likely as White girls and in 1999 were 22 percent more likely than Black boys to be victims of crime (Bureau of Justice Statistics). Black girls are nearly 3 times as likely as White girls and more than twice as likely as Hispanic girls to have had intercourse by age 13 (Centers for Disease Control and Prevention's Youth Risk Behavior Surveillance System).
>
> Delinquency cases involving all girls rose 83 percent from 1988 to 1997, with a 106 percent hike among Black girls compared with a 74 percent rise among White girls (American Bar Association/National Bar Association).
>
> (Villarosa, 2002: 95)

In spite of earlier feminist struggles to uncouple these dichotomous public/private associations, *Oprah*'s 'Secret Life of Girls' episode and to a lesser extent *Essence* magazine's 'War on Girls' reproduce a differentially gendered youth discourse on loci of social control (Pilkington and Johnson, 2003; Valentine *et al.*, 1998; Wulff, 1995; Amit-Talai, 1995). That is, in post-industrial urban Western societies, young women are primarily relegated to the private sphere, where their practices are individualized, sexualized and medicalized: that is, promiscuity, body image and eating disorders (Griffin, 1997). While by implicit comparison, young men are predominantly situated in the public sphere, where their actions are collective, criminalized and legislated: that is, gang behaviour (Kinshasa, 1997). That said, the cited *Essence* statistics, contemporary incidences of anorexia among young men and the rise in female gangs defy this binary logic.

Thanks to Title IX legislation, competitive sport is a public sphere activity that can vanquish the body image anxieties that plague so many teen women (Birrell, 2000; Dworkin and Messner, 2002). For example, among the teen tales recounted on the aforementioned episode of *Oprah* is that of Kelly, a suburban White blonde teenager in the eighth grade who is 'truly disadvantaged' because she is six feet tall and wears a size 12 shoe at age thirteen. Her only refuge from the 'fe fi fo fum' taunts of her schoolmates is the tennis court, where she has competed successfully in many tournaments. Not surprisingly, her chosen role models are Venus and Serena, whom Oprah recruits to help stage 'Operation Surprise Kelly'. This unsuspecting suburban Cinderella is picked up in a white stretch limousine and whisked away to the Nasdaq-100 Tennis Open's Center Court in Miami, where Venus and Serena, her fairy god-mammies, await. Before 'the ball', Nike, Serena Williams' transnational corporate patron, dresses Kelly from head to toe. Prior to their coaching Kelly on the finer points of 'achieving the dream', including 'leaving the negative people behind', Venus and Serena play her in a two-on-one match – their figurative dance at the ball. However, the climax of this suburban fairytale is yet to explode back at Harpo Studios in Chicago. After publicly extolling the virtues of Kelly's 'inner and outer beauty', Serena draws the magical tale to a close by presenting Kelly with a custom-made size 12 tennis 'slipper' – courtesy of Nike.

Collins (2004: 138–9) offers a useful analysis of the BAP syndrome promulgated by Oprah and promoted by Venus and Serena:

> the controlling images associated with poor and working-class Black women become texts of what not to be . . . Oprah Winfrey reinforces an individualistic ideology of social change that counsels her audience to rely solely on themselves . . . Yet Winfrey's message stops far short of linking such individual changes to the actual resources and opportunities that are needed to escape from poverty.

At the heart of a rose-tinted BAP outlook is an amnesia that deliberately downplays the lived repercussions of persistent social inequalities. These structures make 'dreams' affordable for the few rather than the many. When this

bourgeois feminism is harnessed to the predatory capitalist interests of transnational corporations, as was the case with the multi-million-dollar endorsement
deal Venus and Serena forged with McDonald's, the outcome is particularly
compelling:

> McDonald's created a campaign for Venus and Serena about an 'African
> American History Year' in response to a national 'African American History
> Month': 'My ancestors have opened far too many doors for me to only walk
> through one' . . . It is hard to imagine what an earlier black winner of a
> women's grand slam title, Althea Gibson, would have thought of such
> comments made so lucratively on behalf of a multinational company such
> as McDonald's. When Gibson was at the same stage as Venus and Serena in
> 1955, after 10 years of tennis and as the reigning French Open champion, her
> life had scarcely changed: 'I am still a poor Negress, as poor as when I was
> picked up off the back streets of Harlem and given a chance to work my way
> up to stardom,' she said.
>
> (Adams, 2005: 19–21)

The multi-million-dollar endorsement deals with multiple multinationals
garnered by Black super-star sporting celebrities such as Venus and Serena
Williams, golfer Tiger Woods, basketball greats Michael Jordan before and
LeBron James since are frequently wheeled out as evidence of how far the winds
of social change have blown since the segregationist era of Althea Gibson or even
Arthur Ashe (Zirin, 2005). Three shifts in the political economy are closer to fact.
One is that, in the twenty-first century, sport in all its myriad forms is a colossal
and lucrative business (Schaaf, 2004; Zirin, 2005). The second is that Madison
Avenue advertising executives now shamelessly embrace and in fact pander to the
buying power represented by the 'Black dollar' (*Brandweek*, 2005; Chin, 2001).
Third, these same corporate image-makers consistently exploit the abilities of
certain Black celebrity athletes (and entertainers) to convert the symbolic social
and cultural capital encoded in commodified and fetishized urban Black cool into
hard-cash profits (Dyson, 2001; Carter, 2003).

'All about the money, honey': transnational corporate patronage and the 'perplexities' of 'giving back'

There is a memorable scene in Cameron Crowe's 1996 hit film *Jerry Maguire*
where the Black wife of a professional Black football player is negotiating with her
husband's agent for a more lucrative contract, which would include what she
refers to as 'the Four Big Jewels of Celebrity Endorsement' – the shoe, the car, the
clothing line and the soft drink. This comical exchange between the characters
played by Regina King and Tom Cruise highlights the significant ways in which
the economic destinies of professional sport, transnational corporate enterprise
and the multimedia are entwined. Corporations produce commodities, and then

deploy advertising executives to market their products to willing c
In this global age of overexposed celebrity worship, the super-star athle
also a performer, is frequently hired to accomplish this marketing fe
2004; Marshall, 1997). As Andrews and Jackson (2001: 7) suggest, '
facturing of sporting celebrities has become a highly systematized, almost
McDonaldized . . . process . . . the sport celebrity is effectively a multi-textual and
multi-platform promotional entity'. With the globalization and commodification
by corporate America of caricatured urban Black culture as the pinnacle of cool,
it is increasingly Black celebrity athletes who are 'shown the money' (Carrington
et al., 2001; Dyson, 2001; Ross, 2004).

As suggested earlier, the most famous Black celebrity athlete turned commodity
endorser and one who is said to have paved the sponsorship way for other twenty-
something Black super-star athlete-performers such as Tiger Woods and the
Williams sisters is former Chicago Bulls basketball player Michael Jordan (Schaaf,
2004; Kellner, 2001). Yet, to invoke an old adage: to whom much is given, from
whom much is expected. In the 1990s, when the media trained its spotlight on
both Nike's exploitative labour practices in subcontracted Asian sweatshops and
the spate of alleged Air-Jordan related crimes in 'inner-city' American communities, Jordan was criticized for neither taking a political stance nor uttering a
condemning statement (hooks, 2000; LaFeber, 1999; Hapke, 2004).

Sport, commerce and media represent an 'unholy trinity' (Schaaf, 2004) and
Black super-star celebrities are the lubricant greasing the wheels of this global
capitalist machinery (LaFeber, 1999). Before I focus on the entangled fortunes of
Serena Williams and Nike as they represent the tainted bountiful fruits of what
I conceptualize as transnational corporate patronage, it is worth pointing out
what I refer to as 'the eclipse of Venus'. That is, while Serena seems to court
celebrity assertively (on and off the court), as much as is possible when one's every
move is chronicled in the press, her more introspective and shy older sister Venus
appears more comfortable beyond the glare of the limelight (Spencer, 2001;
Wertheim, 2002). By signing her as a global icon and 'trademarked Nike Goddess'
(Adams, 2005: 19), Nike has been instrumental in the multimedia cultivation of Serena Williams' celebrity image. However, by capitalist design on Nike's
part and by strategic decision on Serena's, the moment that deal was sealed, for
both, the possibility of any real political engagement with social and economic
injustice is foreclosed. Thus, any acts of 'corporate responsibility' orchestrated by
Nike, which usually bear the public face of celebrity-athlete-performers such as
Williams, are in reality 'perplexing' manifestations of what I call ethical charity
as opposed to responsible social action. Put simply, ethical charity is a form of
reputation management for multinational corporations, like Nike, whose labour
practices are deemed not only unethical but exploitative (Hapke, 2004).

As an illustration of the political-economic dynamics of transnational
corporate patronage, the cover story for the March 2005 edition of the business
magazine *Black Enterprise* was 'The 50 Most Powerful African Americans in
Sport'. This feature showcased the accomplishments of Black men and a few Black
women, who as agents/promoters, coaches/managers, executives or athletes had

managed to transcend the colour barrier in professional or collegiate sports. Only three athletes made the cut – the 'old timer' Michael Jordan and two 'newcomers', Serena Williams and Tiger Woods. The rationale for their being chosen was:

> [These] big-name athletes . . . represent a new generation of athletes who are able to garner millions of dollars in endorsement deals while changing the face of sports and the type of athletes who play. Both Woods and Williams made the lily-white sports of tennis and golf accessible and attractive to young black children across the country. They also made white players step up their game in an effort to dethrone them from their No.1 spots.
>
> (Hughes, 2005: 12)

The three 'big-name' athletes in this line-up all have multi-million-dollar contracts with Nike. Two of the corporate executives on the list also work for Nike. The first is Trevor Edwards, corporate vice-president of global brand management and the individual responsible for Serena Williams' $55-million endorsement deal (BBC News, 2003). The second is Larry Miller, president of Nike Jordan Brand, which achieved sales of $500 million, or an increase of 288 per cent, after he took over in 2001 (Hughes, 2005). In 2004, Nike sales were up 15 per cent to $12.3 billion (Holmes, 2004), but it spends a record $56.6 million a year on magazine advertising alone (*Brandweek*, 2005). Writing about the inequities in Nike's production practices as opposed to its consumption strategies, Hoechsmann (2001: 274) observes:

> Jordan and other celebrity endorsers stand on the cusp between production and consumption . . . Given that Nike has a number of celebrity endorsers at any given time, and the princely sums paid to them do not include the costs of high-end television and magazine ads in which they appear, it appears that Nike spends more money on promoting the consumption of their products than on producing them.

By literally and figuratively harnessing 'authentic ghetto Blackness' to Nike commodities so that its signification conveys as much brand recognition as 'the Swoosh', Edwards and Miller use the 'master's tools' not to build – in the words of Audre Lorde (1984) – a 'master's house' but rather to erect a palatial mansion. For example, a few clicks of the mouse will take the Hip-Hop or 'wannabe' hip consumer to nike.com, and for a mere eighty-five dollars she can purchase an 'SW Iconic Nike Sphere Hoody' from Serena Williams' Early Winter 2005 Collection. For the tennis player who is more concerned about 'the swoosh in her swing' than 'the sexy swish' of her 'SW Iconic Skirt', there is the utilitarian 'Statement Skirt II' for forty-five dollars. With women accounting for more than 80 per cent of all sporting goods purchases, this is niche marketing at its best (Schaaf, 2004).

For celebrity super-star athletes such as Williams, there is a different dynamic at work: the seduction of transnational corporate patronage. I prefer to describe

Figure 8.1 Serena and Venus Williams pose during a photo call to promote the WTA's 'Get in Touch with Your Feminine Side' ad campaign at Wimbledon, London, June 2004 © Getty Images

this as a patron–performer rather than a master–slave relationship since the former recognizes the free will of both actors and the potential for mutual capital gain, which is lacking in conditions of enslavement. Nike and Serena Williams collaborate to accomplish two goals: cultivate a recognizable global brand and thereby move more merchandise. At the press conference to announce the sponsorship agreement, Williams declared:

> I am extremely happy to be a part of the Nike family. The company's innovation, creativity and worldwide marketing and retail expertise will be valuable assets for me. I will be working closely with Nike's team of experts to design and create my tennis shoe and apparel, and will also be given creative input in its sports and leisure wear lines for the female consumer. I can't think of a better company to be affiliated with, particularly with my strong interest in design and my involvement in the fashion industry. This will be a great partnership. I want to thank Mr Phil Knight and all of the people at Nike, who worked so hard to make this agreement a reality. They won't be sorry.
>
> (Nikebiz.com, 12 December 2003)

As mentioned earlier, the merchandizing strategy underpinning this partnership is the perpetuation of her now iconic status as a Black siren with a powerful

Figure 8.2 Serena Williams takes to the court during the US Open in New York City, September 2004 © Getty Images

forehand, which was confirmed when she wore 'that catsuit' in the 2002 US Open (Schultz, 2005). In an interview for the Black magazine *Upscale* just prior to signing with Nike, she recalled: 'The catsuit really took it to a whole new level ... but I think it's great. Even though I don't consider myself a sex symbol, I am' (Ashton, 2004).

Connecting the dots, with so much potential profit to be made, trailblazing in the corporate sports sphere aside, for both Nike's Black marketing executives and their celebrity-performer-endorsers, 'Just Doing It' for Nike will always be more important than 'Doing the Right Thing'. This 'Just Do It' philosophy is echoed in the sisters' aforementioned book for young girls (Williams *et al.*, 2005). In fact, Serena's self-fashioned motto is 'Do You'. She and her sister are collectively worth $100 million, yet in the social class-inflected '"Sister Rule 8": All About the Money, Honey: Bling-Bling Isn't Everything, When it Comes to Cash it's Better to Stash than Flash', Serena advises:

> You can create a fun and exciting future whether or not you're loaded. Of course, you have to work hard and squirrel away your funds instead of spending them all at the mall. But when you save some money every week from your allowance, babysitting or job, you're preparing for life and you can really feel proud of that. By stashing your fund for things that are meaningful – like music lessons or an instrument, basketball camp or a trip to France with your French class – you can learn things and have experiences that will stay with you forever. These types of expenses are 'investments', the type of spending that builds you up and benefits you for a long period of time.
>
> (*Ibid.*: 103)

Such advice is predicated on a specific set of assumptions about access to material wealth and social capital (Green, 2001; Pattillo-McCoy, 1999). Collectively, these suburban realities are emblematic of a Black bourgeois feminist politics of entitlement made manifest by the political struggles of the Civil Rights and Women's movements (Cole and Guy-Sheftall, 2003; Pough, 2004; Springer, 2002). In her feminist manifesto for the Hip-Hop generation, Morgan (1999: 59) declares:

> We are the daughters of feminist privilege. The gains of the Feminist Movement (the efforts of black, white, Latina, Asian, and Native American women) had a tremendous impact on our lives – so much we often take it for granted. We walk through the world with a sense of entitlement that women of our mother's generation could not begin to fathom. Most of us can't imagine our lives without access to birth control, legalized abortions, the right to vote, or many of the same educational opportunities available to men. Sexism may be a very real part of my life but so is the unwavering belief that there is no dream I can't pursue and achieve simply because I'm a woman.

These dreams may no longer be deferred for Williams, Morgan or the women featured in Chambers' controversial book, who, in Chambers' (2003: 86) words, are in search of 'empowerment without the expectation . . . that [they] would carry the mantle of the race'. However, Hurricane Katrina, which struck the Gulf Coast of the United States in August 2005, brought to the consciousness of the nation the number of young Black women living the American nightmare. Serena Williams' very public response to this tragedy – pledging $100 per ace for the remainder of the year and then subsequently donating a pair of borrowed diamond earrings with a retail value of $40,000 to be auctioned off on TennisKatrina.com – generated media controversy regarding the true extent of her ethical and charitable inclinations:

> As the rest of the country shudders about Hurricane Katrina, the Williams Sisters fed nearly every bad stereotype about rich, spoiled, self-absorbed athletes there is. You'd never know their father, Richard, hails from a Louisiana family of sharecroppers, a personal connection that you'd think might make the disaster more deeply felt . . . The reason Venus and Serena deserve to be singled out is no one has preened more about their nouveau riche status or called attention to their conspicuous consumption like the Williamses have at this year's Open or in their vapid reality show before that. The sight of Serena – a regular on *Forbes* magazine's list of top-paid athletes in recent years – hailing herself as a 'philanthropist' for her underwhelming hundred bucks-an-ace pledge while she was using her fingers to play with her diamond necklace was just too much to take. Especially when she suddenly noticed her reflection on the desk in front of her and began turning her head this way and that to admire the light exploding off the diamonds
>
> (Johnette Howard of *Newsday* quoted in Tandon, 2005)

To make matters worse, when USA Network broadcaster Michael Barkann informed Serena Williams that the infamous diamond earrings had a retail value which surpassed the $21,700 career earnings of her US Open opponent Jung-Jan Chan, her response was: 'You gotta have the bling' (Rovell, 2005).

Conclusion

Under such charged complex social, political and economic conditions, what will become of Serena and Venus Williams and their 'philanthropic' endeavours is a sideline story yet to unfold. However, deploying the popular cultural figures of the 'ghetto Cinderella' and the 'Black American Princess', who represent the extremes of social deprivation and entitlement respectively, this chapter sheds light on the nuanced complexities of political progress and stasis as they are played out in a post-Civil Rights Hip-Hop generation moment in African American history. The seemingly contradictory on-the-court/off-the-court performances executed by tennis super-star celebrity sisters Venus and Serena Williams provide the ideal context for the critical exploration of upwardly mobile young Black women's strategic impression management (Goffman, 1959). Moreover, in a twenty-first-century refashioning of a Duboisian double-consciousness (though Du Bois (1903) is never directly cited), the research findings of Jones and Shorter-Gooden (2003: 6–7) 'prove' that the Williams sisters' ghetto/bourgeois code-switching is far from an aberration:

> Black women in our country have had to perfect what we call 'shifting', a sort of subterfuge that African Americans have long practiced to ensure their survival in our society. They shift to accommodate differences in class as well as gender and ethnicity . . . From one moment to the next, they change their outward behavior, attitude or tone, shifting 'White', then shifting 'Black' again, shifting 'corporate', shifting 'cool'.

As instructive as this concept of 'shifting' is, what I find more captivating are both the apparent dominance of 'the one-drop rule' as an explanatory model for defining racial differences, and more explicitly Blackness, in the United States (Ifekwunigwe, 2004a) as well as the ways in which social status is configured in specific racialized ways. This 'racial' hegemony is evident in my 'ghetto Cinderella' and 'Black American Princess' appropriations, wherein 'race' and class are also conflated.

By focusing on two of America's major obsessions, sport and celebrity, I have argued that mediated by corporate America and its shameless appropriation, commodification, and manufacture of a prescribed 'authentic ghetto Blackness' while keeping the heterogeneous Black populace at bay, celebrity-sport-performance like popular Hip-Hop culture in all its gendered political economic manifestations selectively and individually empowers but collectively and strategically disempowers African American young women and men, who cannot translate ghetto cultural capital into 'bling-bling' economic capital (hooks, 2000; Edwards, 2000; Carter, 2003; Kelley, 1997). In particular, I suggest that for the post-Civil Rights Hip-Hop feminist generation, protest and complicity take on multiple, contradictory and complex forms. These 'perplexing' contradictions are exemplified by the Black super-star sporting celebrity sisters Venus and Serena Williams, whose athletic achievements signal the triumph of talent over adversity but whose lucrative sponsorship deals also highlight the seductive double-bind of transnational corporate patronage.

Acknowledgements

This chapter has been enhanced by stimulating exchanges with colleagues at several conferences in the United States and Brazil, and I am thankful to all who provided insightful feedback and engaged so enthusiastically with my work. Special thanks to Ben Carrington and Ian McDonald for shrewd editorial assistance and collegiality as well as for inviting me to participate in the 'Politics of Sport' symposium and conference, which provided the impetus for this exciting and important collection. An extra-special thank you to my husband and self-professed 'sports junkie' Chris (Felix) Nwoko, for the invaluable and frequently impromptu 'vibeing' sessions, which facilitated the birthing of this chapter. Finally, a joyful 'shout-out' to Isaiah Uchenna, our beautiful son, who was born during the production process.

Notes

1 As I have argued elsewhere (Ifekwunigwe, 2004a), conceptions of 'race' are histori- cally, geographically and culturally specific and thus do not travel easily. Throughout this chapter, when I use the term 'Black' it is in reference to the American 'one-drop rule', which subsumes anyone with at least one known African ancestor under this heading (irrespective of whether they also have European and/or Native American ancestry). Similarly, like Kitwana (2002), when I discuss the 'Hip-Hop generation', I am specifically referring to Black youth. This does not discount the fact that as a social movement, Hip-Hop has always been multiracial and multi-ethnic. For excellent histories of Hip-Hop and its generation, see Chang (2005) and Watkins (2005).

2 The 'lunch counter' is in specific reference to four Black college students, who in 1960 staged a sit-in at an all-White Woolworth's lunch counter in Greensboro, North Carolina. This non-violent protest of apartheid conditions in the Southern United States inspired others to participate in additional sit-ins over a period of months. These sit-ins were also replicated by activists in other parts of the South. This direct action eventually led to the desegregation of Woolworth's and other chains.

3 Venus Ebone Starr Williams was born on 17 June 1980 in Lynwood, California. She turned professional in 1994. Since then, her athletic achievements have been many and significant, including winning two Gold Medals at the Sydney summer Olympics in 2000 (the singles and the doubles with her sister as partner), the 1999 French Open doubles with her sister Serena, and five other doubles and two mixed-doubles grand slams. In 2000, she won the singles tournaments at both Wimbledon and the US Open and successfully defended both titles in 2001. In 2002 and 2003, Venus was the finalist at five major finals, all of which she lost to her sister Serena. Although ranked only 14 at the time, in 2005 Venus made a turnaround and competed in the longest women's Wimbledon final in history, in which she beat Lindsay Davenport and garnered her third Wimbledon title in six years. After this dramatic victory, she was plagued by wrist injuries, which contributed to a considerable drop in her ranking. However, in 2007, she won the WTA Cellular South Cup in Memphis, Tennessee, and astounded all when she also clinched her fourth Wimbledon title in eight years. This final was significant for three reasons. First, her opponent, Frenchwoman Marion Bartoli, had made history the day before by beating the number 1 seed Justine Henin. Second, the final was contested by two of the lowest-ranked players: Bartoli was seeded 18 and Williams 23. Finally, this was the first time the playing field was level in terms of the prize money garnered by female and male athletes at Wimbledon. Tennis legend Billie Jean King had fought tirelessly for pay equity and happened to be in the stands watching this historic match. In her victory speech, Williams thanked King for spear- heading the equal-pay campaign as well as for all she had done to advance women's tennis. In 2008, Venus retained the Wimbledon singles title by defeating her sister in the final. In 2005, *Tennis* had named Venus number 25 in its list of the 40 greatest players during the magazine's existence. This multi-talented tennis star is also an aspiring interior designer, with her own company, Venus Starr Interiors. For more on Venus Williams, see www.venuswilliams.com. Serena Jameka Williams was born on 26 September 1981 in Saginaw, Michigan. She turned professional in 1995, and has accomplished as much in the athletic arena as her sister. In 1999, with her US Open

victory, she became the first African American woman since Althea Gibson in 1958 to win a grand slam tournament. That year, she and her sister also won the doubles at the US Open. She won the US Open singles again in 2002, the French Open in 2002, Wimbledon in 2002 and 2003, and the Australian Open in 2003 and 2005. Unfortunately, her tennis career has also been interrupted by injuries, particularly to her knee. Many doubted her staying power until she made an astounding comeback at the Australian Open in January 2007. She was the lowest-ranked woman (81) to win a grand slam singles trophy in three decades. She dedicated this triumphant win to her murdered sister Yetunde Price. That same year, she went on to win the Sony Ericsson Open in Miami, Florida. In 2008 Serena won the US Open, and with Venus won the doubles at both Wimbledon and the Gold Medal at the Beijing Summer Olympic Games. Both sisters have reached number 1 in the WTA (Women's Tennis Association) standings. Like her older sister, Serena's talents and interests extend beyond the tennis court. She is an emerging fashion designer with her own clothing line, Aneres, and aspires to be an actress, having appeared on several television shows and in films. In April 2005, ABCFamily aired a reality television show, *Venus and Serena: For Real*, a behind-the-scenes look at their lives. For more on Serena Williams, see www.serenawilliams.com.

4 Although there are feminist scholars of sport who do engage with 'race' and gender politics (Birrell, 2000; Scraton, 2001, Spencer, 2001), I was approached by Ben Carrington, the co-editor of this anthology, to contribute a piece as a corrective to the under-representation of Black feminist voices in Sport Studies.

5 'I focus on how identities are embodied through consumption, and how consumption constitutes women as gendered subjects through language, through market and cultural interactions, and through class and labor in multiple modes of social becoming. As subjects operating within economic constraints and interpellated in multiple discourses, perplexity reveals the excess of subjects – how they are more than just their bodies' (Ramamurthy, 2003: 543).

6 This distinction was influenced by co-contributor Grant Farred's chapter, which is partly a philosophical treatise on the proprietary relationship between the 'overwaged' professional soccer player and the 'underwaged' fan.

References

Adair, V.C. (2005) 'US Working-Class/Poverty-Class Divides', *Sociology* 39(5), pp. 817–34.

Adams, T. (2005) 'Selling the Sisters', *Observer Sport Monthly* 59, January, pp. 14–21.

Alexander, M.J. and Mohanty, C.T. (1997) 'Introduction: Genealogies, Legacies and Movements', in *idem* (eds) *Feminist Genealogies, Colonial Legacies and Democratic Futures*, New York/London: Routledge, pp. xiii–xlii.

Amit-Talai, V. (1995) 'Conclusion: The "Multi" Cultural of Youth,' in H. Wulff and V. Amit-Talai (eds) *Youth Cultures: A Cross-Cultural Perspective*, London/New York: Routledge, pp. 223–33.

Andrews, D. (2001a) 'Michael Jordan Matters', in *idem* (ed.) *Michael Jordan, Inc: Corporate Sport, Media Culture and Late Modern America*, Albany: State University of New York Press, pp. xiii–xx.

Andrews, D. (2001b) 'The Fact(s) of Michael Jordan's Blackness: Excavating a Floating Racial Signifier', in *idem* (ed.) *Michael Jordan, Inc: Corporate Sport, Media Culture and Late Modern America*. Albany: State University of New York Press, pp. 107–52.

Andrews, D. and Jackson. S. (2001) 'Introduction: Sport Celebrities, Public Culture and Private Experience', in *idem* (eds) *Sport Stars: The Cultural Politics of Sporting Celebrity*, New York/London: Routledge, pp. 1–19.

Aronowitz, S. (2003) *How Class Works: Power and Social Movements*, New Haven: Yale University Press.

Ashton, N. (2004) 'The Baddest Chick', *Upscale* December/January, pp. 56–60.

BBC News (2003) 'Nike Confirms Serena Deal', http://news.bbc.co.uk/go/pr/fr/-/sport1/hi/tennis/3312119.stm.

Birrell, S. (2000) 'Feminist Theories for Sport', in J. Coakley and E. Dunning (eds) *Handbook of Sport Studies*, London/Thousand Oaks: Sage, pp. 61–76.

Boyd, T. (2003) *The New H.N.I.C.: The Death of Civil Rights and the Reign of Hip Hop*, New York/London: New York University Press.

Brandweek (2005) 'Apparel and Accessories', *Brandweek* 26(37), p. SR19.

Carrington, B., Andrews, D., Jackson, S. and Mazur. Z. (2001) 'The Global Jordanscape', in D. Andrews (ed.) *Michael Jordan, Inc: Corporate Sport, Media Culture and Late Modern America*, Albany: State University of New York Press, pp. 177–216.

Carter, P. (2003) '"Black" Cultural Capital, Status Positioning, and Schooling Conflicts for Low-Income African American Youth', *Social Problems* 50(1), pp. 136–55.

Chambers, V. (2003) *Having It All?: Black Women and Success*, New York: Harlem Moon/Broadway Books.

Chang, J. (2005) *Can't Stop Won't Stop: A History of the Hip-Hop Generation*, New York: St Martin's Press.

Chin, E. (2001) *Purchasing Power: Black Kids and American Consumer Culture*, Minneapolis/London: University of Minnesota Press.

Cole, J. and Guy-Sheftall, B. (2003) *Gender Talk: The Struggle for Women's Equality in African American Communities*, New York: One World/Ballantine Books.

Collins, P.H. (1990) *Black Feminist Thought: Knowledge, Consciousness and the Politics of Empowerment*, Boston: Unwin Hyman.

Collins, P.H. (2004) *Black Sexual Politics: African Americans, Gender and the New Racism*, New York/London: Routledge.

Collins, P.H. (2006) *From Black Power to Hip Hop: Racism, Nationalism and Feminism*, Philadelphia: Temple University Press.

Combahee River Collective (1977/2000) 'A Black Feminist Statement', in J. James and T.D. Sharpley-Whiting (eds) *The Black Feminist Reader*, Malden, MA/Oxford: Blackwell, pp. 261–70.

Davis, A. (1989/2000) 'Women and Capitalism: Dialectics of Oppression and Liberation', in J. James and T.D. Sharpley-Whiting (eds) *The Black Feminist Reader*, Malden, MA/Oxford: Blackwell, pp. 146–82.

Douglas, D. (2002) 'To Be Young, Gifted, Black and Female: A Meditation on the Cultural Politics at Play in Representations of Venus and Serena Williams', *Sociology of Sport Online* 5(2), http://physed.otago.ac.nz/sosol/v5i2/v5i2_3.html.

Douglas, D. (2005) 'Venus, Serena and the Women's Tennis Association: When and Where "Race" Enters', *Sociology of Sport Journal* 22, pp. 256–82.

DuBois, W.E.B. (1903) *The Souls of Black Folk*, Chicago: A.C. Mc Clurg and Co.

Dworkin, S. and Messner, M. (2002) 'Just Do . . . What?: Sport, Bodies and Gender', in S. Scraton and A. Flintoff (eds) *Gender and Sport: A Reader*, London/New York: Routledge, pp. 17–29.

Dyson, E. (2001) 'Be Like Mike?: Michael Jordan and the Pedagogy of Desire', in D. Andrews (ed.) *Michael Jordan, Inc: Corporate Sport, Media Culture and Late Modern America*, Albany: State University of New York Press, pp. 259–68.

Dyson, E. (2005) *Is Bill Cosby Right? (Or Has the Black Middle Class Lost its Mind?)*, New York: Basic Civitas Books.

Edwards, H. (2000) 'Crisis of Black Athletes on the Eve of the 21st Century', *Society* 37(3), pp. 9–13.

Garvey, M. (2005) 'Cosby Takes a Stand in Compton', *Los Angeles Times*, 20 October.

Gates, D. (2001) 'The Royal Treatment', *Newsweek* 138(2), p. 11.

Goffman, E. (1959) *The Presentation of Self in Everyday Life*, Garden City: Doubleday.

Green, C. (2001) *Manufacturing Powerlessness in the Black Diaspora: Inner City Youth and the New Global Frontier*, Lanham: AltaMira Press.

Grewal, I. (2005) *Transnational America: Feminisms, Diasporas, Neoliberalisms*, Durham, NC/London: Duke University Press.

Griffin, C. (1997) 'Troubled Teens: Managing Disorders of Transition and Consumption', *Feminist Review* 55, pp. 4–21.

Griffin, P. (2002) 'Changing the Game: Homophobia, Sexism and Lesbians in Sport', in S. Scraton and A. Flintoff (eds) *Gender and Sport: A Reader*, London/New York: Routledge, pp. 193–208.

Hammonds, E.M. (1997) 'Toward a Genealogy of Black Female Sexuality', in M.J. Alexander and C.T. Mohantey (eds) *Feminist Genealogies, Colonial Legacies and Democratic Futures*, New York/London: Routledge, pp. 170–82.

Hapke, L. (2004) *Sweatshop: The History of an American Idea*, New Brunswick/London: Rutgers University Press.

Hoberman, J. (1997) *Darwin's Athletes: How Sport Has Damaged Black America and Preserved the Myth of Race*, Boston: Houghton Mifflin.

Hoechsmann, M. (2001) 'Just Do It: What Michael Jordan Has to Teach Us', in D. Andrews (ed.) *Michael Jordan, Inc: Corporate Sport, Media Culture and Late Modern America*. Albany: State University of New York Press, pp. 269–76.

Holmes, S. (2004) 'Nike: Can Perez Fill Knight's Shoes?' *Business Week Online*, 22 November.

hooks, b. (1984) *Feminist Theory: From Margin to Center*, Boston: South End Press.

hooks, b. (2000) *Where We Stand: Class Matters*, New York/London: Routledge.

Hughes, A. (2005) 'The 50 Most Powerful African Americans in Sports', *Black Enterprise* March, pp. 88–108.

Hull, G.T., Scott, P.B. and Smith, B. (eds) (1982) *All the Women Are White, All the Blacks are Men, but Some of Us Are Brave: Black Women's Studies*, Old Westbury: Feminist Press.

Ifekwunigwe, J. (2004a) 'Introduction: Rethinking "Mixed Race" Studies', in *idem* (ed.) *'Mixed Race' Studies: A Reader*, London/New York: Routledge, pp. 1–29.

Ifekwunigwe, J. (2004b) 'Recasting "Black Venus" in the New African Diaspora', *Women's Studies International Forum* 27, pp. 397–412.

Jackson, J. (2005) *Real Black: Adventures in Racial Sincerity*, Chicago/London: University of Chicago Press.

Jacques, M. (2005) 'The Sisters Expose Tennis's Racist Heart', *Observer Sport Monthly* 59, p. 20.

James, J. (1999) *ShadowBoxing: Representations of Black Feminist Politics*, New York: St Martin's Press.

Jenkins, S. (1998) 'Double Trouble', *Women's Sport and Fitness* 2(1), pp. 102–6.

Johnson, K., Lewis, T., Lightfoot, K. and Wilson, G. (2001) *The BAP Handbook: The Official Guide to the Black American Princess*, New York: Broadway Books.

Jones, C. and Shorter-Gooden, K. (2003) *Shifting: The Double Lives of Black Women in America*, New York: HarperCollins.

Kaplan, C. and Grewal, I. (2002) 'Transnational Practices and Interdisciplinary Feminist Scholarship: Refiguring Women's and Gender Studies', in R. Wiegman (ed.) *Women's Studies on Its Own*. Durham, NC/London: Duke University Press, pp. 66–81.

Kelley, R.D.G. (1994) *Race Rebels: Culture, Politics and the Black Working Class*, New York/London: The Free Press.

Kelley, R.D.G. (1997) *Yo' Mama's DisFUNKtional: Fighting the Culture Wars in Urban America*, Boston: Beacon Press.

Kellner, D. (2001) 'The Sports Spectacle, Michael Jordan, and Nike: Unholy Alliance?', in D. Andrews (ed.) *Michael Jordan, Inc: Corporate Sport, Media Culture and Late Modern America*, Albany: State University of New York Press, pp. 37–63.

Kinshasa, K. (1997) 'Crisis and Lifestyles of Inner City Bloods: Youth Culture as a Response to Urban Environment', in C. Green (ed.) *Globalization and Survival in the Black Diaspora: The New Urban Challenge*, Albany: State University of New York Press, pp. 289–305.

Kitwana, B. (2002) *The Hip Hop Generation: Young Blacks and the Crisis in African American Culture*, New York: Basic Civitas Books.

LaFeber, W. (1999) *Michael Jordan and the New Global Capitalism*, New York/London: W.W. Norton and Company.

Lang, C. (2000) 'The New Global and Urban Order: Legacies for the "Hip-Hop Generation"', *Race and Society* 3, pp. 111–42.

Lawler, S. (2005) 'Introduction: Class, Culture and Identity', *Sociology* 39(5), pp. 797–806.

Lorde, A. (1984) *Sister, Outsider*, Trumansburg: Crossing Press.

McBride, D.A. (2005) *Why I Hate Abercrombie & Fitch: Essays on Race and Sexuality*, New York/London: New York University Press.

McDonald, M. (2005) 'Mapping Whiteness and Sport: An Introduction', *Sociology of Sport Journal* 22, pp. 245–55.

Marshall, P.D. (1997) *Celebrity and Power: Fame in Contemporary Culture*, Minneapolis/London: University of Minnesota Press.

Moghadem, V.M. (2005) *Globalizing Women: Transnational Feminist Networks*, Baltimore/London: Johns Hopkins University Press.

Mohanty, C.T. (2003) *Feminism without Borders: Decolonizing Theory, Practicing Solidarity*, Durham, NC/London: Duke University Press.

Morgan, J. (1999) *When Chickenheads Come Home to Roost: My Life as a Hip-Hop Feminist*, New York: Simon and Schuster.

Morgan, M. (2005) 'Hip-Hop Women Shredding the Veil: Race and Class in Popular Feminist Identity', *South Atlantic Quarterly*, Special Issue on 'Racial Americana', 104(3), pp. 425–44.

Ms. Magazine Online (2001) 'Ms. Women of the Year', http://www.msmagazine.com/dec01/woty.asp.

Neal, M.A. (2005) *New Black Man*, New York/London: Routledge.

Pattillo-McCoy, M. (1999) *Black Picket Fences: Privilege and Peril among the Black Middle Class*, Chicago/London: University of Chicago Press.

Phillips, L., Reddick-Morgan, K. and Stephens, D.P. (2005) 'Oppositional Consciousness within an Oppositional Realm: The Case of Feminism and Womanism in Rap and Hip-Hop, 1976-2004', *Journal of African American History* 90(3), pp. 253–77.

Pilkington, H. and Johnson, R. (2003) 'Peripheral Youth: Relations of Identity and Power in Global/Local Context', *European Journal of Cultural Studies* 6(3), pp. 259–83.

Pough, G.D. (2004) *Check It While I Wreck It: Black Womanhood, Hip-Hop Culture and the Public Sphere*, Boston: Northeastern University Press.

Ramamurthy, P. (2003) 'Material Consumers, Fabricating Subjects: Perplexity, Global Connectivity Discourses, and Transnational Feminist Research', *Cultural Anthropology* 18(4), pp. 524–50.

Ross, R.J.S. (2004) *Slaves to Fashion: Poverty and Abuse in the New Sweatshops*, Ann Arbor: University of Michigan Press.

Rovell, D. (2005) 'Serena Jewels Raise $21.100 for Charity', Espn.com, 25 September.

Rowe, D. (2004) *Sport, Culture and the Media*, 2nd edn, Maidenhead: Open University Press/McGraw-Hill Education.

Samuels, A. (2001) 'Life With Father', *Newsweek* 138(1), p. 46.

Schaaf, P. (2004) *Sports, Inc.: 100 Years of Sports Business*, Amherst: Prometheus Books.

Schultz, J. (2005) 'Serena Williams and the Production of Blackness at the 2002 US Open', *Journal of Sport and Social Issues* 29(3), pp. 338–57.

Scraton, S. (2001) 'Reconceptualizing Race, Gender and Sport: The Contribution of Black Feminism', in B. Carrington and I. McDonald (eds) *'Race', Sport and British Society*, London/New York: Routledge, pp. 170–87.

Sharpley-Whiting, T.D. (1999) *Black Venus: Sexualized Savages, Primal Fears and Primitive Narratives in French*, Durham, NC/London: Duke University Press.

Sharpley-Whiting, T. D. (2006) *Pimps up, Ho's Down: Young Black Women, Hip-Hop, and the New Gender Politics*, New York/London: New York University Press.

Silver, M., Cook, K. and Mravic, M. (1999) 'Serena's at Peace with Herself', *Sports Illustrated* 90(12), p. 38.

Spencer, N.E. (2001) 'From "Child's Play" to "Party Crasher": Venus Williams, Racism and Professional Women's Tennis', in D. Andrews and S. Jackson (eds) *Sport Stars: The Cultural Politics of Sporting Celebrity*, New York/London: Routledge, pp. 87–101.

Sports Illustrated (2001) 'Blotter', *Sports Illustrated* 94(26), p. 34.

Springer, K. (2002) 'Third Wave Black Feminism?', *Signs* 27(4), pp. 1059–82.

Sudbury, J. (2002) 'Celling Black Bodies: Black Women in the Global Prison Industrial Complex', *Feminist Review* 70(1), pp. 57–74.

Tandon, K. (2005) 'The Williams Match-up Goes Dud', *Tennis Reporter.Net Newsletter* 146, 23 September.

Valentine, G., Skelton, T. and Chambers, D. (1998) 'Cool Places: An Introduction to Youth and Youth Cultures', in T. Skelton and G. Valentine (eds) *Cool Places: Geographies of Youth Cultures*, London/New York: Routledge, pp. 1–34.

Villarosa, L. (2002) 'Our Girls in Crisis', *Essence*, January, pp. 92–5 and 119–21.

Watkins, C. (2005) *Hip-Hop Matters: Politics, Popular Culture and the Struggle for the Soul of a Movement*, Boston: Beacon Press.

Wertheim, J.L. (2002) *Venus Envy: Power Games, Teenage Vixens and Million-Dollar Egos on the Women's Tennis Tour*, New York: Perennial.

Williams, V., Williams, S. and Beard, H. (2005) *Venus and Serena Serving from the Hip: 10 Rules for Living, Loving and Winning*, Boston: Houghton Mifflin.

Wulff, H. (1995) 'Introducing Youth Culture in Its Own Right: The State of the Art and New Possibilities', in H. Wulff and V. Amit-Talai (eds) *Youth Cultures: A Cross-Cultural Perspective*, London/New York: Routledge, pp. 1–18.

Zirin, D. (2005) *What's My Name Fool?: Sports and Resistance in the United States*, Chicago: Haymarket.

9   Socratic solitude

The Scouser two-as-one

Grant Farred

For now we see through a glass, darkly; but then face to face: now I know in part; but then I shall know even as also I am known.

I Corinthians 13:12

If there is a problem any city could have, this city has it.

Dan Georgakas and Marvin Surkin, *Detroit, I Do Mind Dying*

Introduction

It strikes the visitor as an untenable relationship. It is difficult to reconcile the imposing, well-resourced and -maintained building with the literally crumbling and boarded-up community that surrounds it. House after dilapidated house, street after garbage-filled street, there is seemingly no end to the devastation. This is a community that has long since, even before it became vulnerable to the antipathies of Maggie Thatcher's Tories in the 1980s, been battered by economic decline. With its historic dependence on the 'docks and its ancillary industries' (Williams *et al.*, 2001: 5), themselves susceptible to the vagaries of the maritime business, Liverpool has always been a 'city apart,' a northern English city renowned for its culture – from the music of the Beatles to Echo and the Bunnymen to the fandom of Elvis Costello – and its football, yet seemingly in a perpetual economic downturn: 'Even in the late 1940s, unemployment in Liverpool rose to two-and-a-half times the national average and it has been some way above the national average ever since, catastrophically so in the 1980s' (*ibid.*; see also Lane, 1997). In other words, not even when the docks were more or less fully functional did Liverpool thrive as a city.

Today Liverpudlians' lives, to the outside observer, the casual passer-by, appear to have been shattered many times over since the turn of the twentieth century. To name the visitor a '*flâneur*', after the strollers of Walter Benjamin's *Arcades Project* (2002), would surely be too grand and unfitting a term. Maybe this view of the post-industrial city is what T.S. Eliot anticipated in his famous denunciation of the psychic isolation and the bleak industrialized landscapes produced by modernity: 'the burnt out ends of smoky days' goes that memorable line from Eliot's poem 'Preludes' (Eliot, 1930: 21). Cities from the American Midwest, of which Dan Georgakas and Marvin Sarvin write so memorably in *Detroit: I Do Mind Dying*, to German port cities such as Hamburg, all bear their own scars, inscribe in their own tragic visages the histories of other moments, of different, better, economic times, now indisputably gone by. Times when there were jobs to be had, when families could be sustained, when the unions were strong, and when the future did not hint so determinedly of an inexorably bad end. In Benjamin's terms, whose concept of the *flâneur* might be useful after all, what the visitor is encountering is evidence of a 'vanished time' (Benjamin, 2002: 416).

These aporetic representations, the act of outside observers – the 'daytrippers', as the locals so disparagingly call them – narrating a history is, however, more than the product of a speculative imagining. It is demanding cultural and intellectual work, the critical labour of reconciling the disjunctive sights, the building and community; it is work undertaken because of the visual, visceral incongruity that is forced upon the passer-through, the visitor who has lost her or his way to or from the imposing building or the football fan from afar curious to locate the building in relation to its neighbours. It is an affectively demanding task to link the towering physical structure with the decay that is everywhere (else). While devastation may be the post-industrial norm in too many 'burnt out' cities, it remains conceptually and affectively difficult to think poverty and plenty in such proximity.

The disjuncture between rich and poor is, however, more than visually disconcerting. This disconnect is foundational in the Platonic sense of producing 'wonder': according to Plato, 'wonder is what the philosopher endures most; for there is no other beginning of philosophy than wonder' (Arendt, 2005: 32). To wonder is to be unsettled; it is to recognize the material discrepancies at hand and to ponder their beginnings. To wonder as the non-resident, or even as the native fan (though perhaps only occasionally in the latter's case), is to identify in the visual problematic a historicity. To *wander* is not only to spatialize inequity; it is to wonder about its temporality. The devastated history of the present provokes enquiries not only about the moment itself and the moment that came before but about the uncertainty of future destruction.

It is easy to experience this sense of wonder in a city such as Liverpool, particularly about the towering football stadium, the building that is named Anfield Road. This stadium is home to Liverpool Football Club (FC), historically Britain's greatest club. Founded in 1892, Liverpool FC have won a record eighteen League Championship titles and the most coveted club trophy in world football, previously called the 'European Cup' and now known as the 'Champions League', a competition in which only the best clubs in Europe participate, five times. Liverpool most recently won the Champions League in a memorable match against Italy's AC Milan in Istanbul in 2005. Few English clubs even come close to matching these achievements. So renowned is the club, especially in its most successful era, the mid-1960s through to 1990, that its style has been dubbed the 'Liverpool Way'. Rooted in simplicity, creativity, organized defending, slick passing and, most importantly, a deep commitment to the team, this was pioneered by the club's legendary managers: the Scotsman Bill Shankly, and his successor, the avuncular Geordie (from Newcastle in the northeast of England) Bob Paisley. The Liverpool Way represents an unmatched football blend: the primacy of the communal and the capacity to accommodate the individual, a club in a working-class city that has, generation after generation, bred its own aristocrats of football, aristocrats who became increasingly wealthier as the decades passed, and especially so from the early 1990s onwards.

And so, how could the wealth of 'Anfield', as the stadium is known internationally, be autochthonously, intimately, related to the relative poverty of the surrounding community? How is Liverpool FC related not only to the community of Liverpool 4 (L4), which surrounds the ground, but to the entire city of Liverpool, this northwest English city that has for most of the twentieth century been acclaimed for its working-class militancy?[1] From the historic transport workers' strike of 1911 through to the 1980s, Liverpool has been 'synonymous with "militancy"' (Taaffe and Mulhearn, 1988: 13). The first recorded strike in the city, however, goes back to 1756, when Liverpool's shoemakers downed their tools. Following in this tradition more than two hundred years later, the city's people made nationally (and internationally) known their profound revulsion for the Thatcher government. In the stirring leftist terms of Peter Taaffe and Tony Mulhearn, 'here is a city of half a million, formerly the major seaport of the mighty "British Empire", which witnessed a convulsive movement of the working class and compelled the "Iron Lady" to beat a retreat in 1984. No other section of the British working class, apart from the miners in 1981, humbled the government in such a fashion' (*ibid.*). This is the radical northern culture in which Liverpool, and their close neighbours Everton, play their football. The bond of radical communalism between regional politics and football was accentuated when Liverpool were managed by the Scottish socialist Shankly, the ex-miner from the village of Glenbuck who never lost his commitment to the cause of the British working poor. 'Train the right way. Help each other. It's a form of socialism without the politics,' Shankly is reputed to have said. Here is about as apt a summation of radical politics, both football and ideological, as there is, one might venture.

There are few other communities in the world with a great football club where there is such a strong link between the club and its city's residents. There are, arguably, only three clubs that, in their distinct ways, approximate Liverpool FC's relationship with Liverpool. In terms of the rootedness within the community, the club that comes closest is Boca Juniors of Argentina, where the honour roll of players runs, in the recent past, from Diego Maradona to Carlos Tevez. Boca play at the world-famous La Bombanera, 'The Chocolate (or Bonbon) Box' (so named because of the tiered shape of the ground), a 60,000-plus-seater stadium that is situated in the heart of La Boca neighbourhood, one of the poorer sections of Buenos Aires. This is in contrast to their arch-rivals, River Plate, who make their home in a richer, outlying 'suburban' area of Buenos Aires (although Boca itself has a sizable middle-class following).

Like Anfield, the breathtaking La Bombanera on Brandsen Road is surrounded by a working-class community – although the residents of La Boca are decidedly not as impoverished as those who live in L4. Furthermore, both Liverpool and Buenos Aires are port cities (the residents of Buenos Aires are called 'Porteños'). Both the British and the Latin American city thrived during the eighteenth and nineteenth centuries as key sites of global trade (albeit one more notoriously than the other): Buenos was a bustling merchant port and Liverpool, with its nefarious role in slavery, was vital to the British economy's trade in human cargo.

In terms of the ideological patina of working-class militancy, Liverpool FC shares a great deal with Glasgow Celtic, Scotland's pre-eminent 'Catholic' club. Founded by Brother Walfrid, a Catholic priest, as a charitable institution which served to centralize the religious and social lives of immigrant Irish Catholics during the years of the Great Famine (1845–51) and long after, Celtic went on to become the political symbol of cultural difference in and resistance to histori-cally Presbyterian Scotland.[2] The 'Bhoys' of Celtic, like Liverpool, have always been, in FC Barcelona's Catalan expression, *'mes que un club'* – 'more than a club.' To be, as the phrase goes, 'Celtic-minded' is to enunciate a particular way of being – either literally or symbolically – Irish Catholic in the diaspora, be that nineteenth-century Scotland or twenty-first-century Australia. Little wonder, then, that there is such a close relationship between Liverpool and Celtic, clubs that understand – and, indeed, proudly wear – their status as anti-hegemonic institutions. Liverpool and Glasgow are both 'Celtic' cities in that in the nine-teenth century they experienced substantial waves of Irish immigrants. Although Liverpool is not as sectarian a city as Glasgow, where the Protestant–Catholic divide retains much of its historic ideological force, the clubs are linked by the Scottish players who moved south to join both Merseyside teams and by a shared sense of alienation from the mainstream of British political life. For Liverpool, the Scottish bond runs deep – from Ian St John and Ron Yeats in the 1960s to the mercurial, much-loved (Protestant) Celtic icon Kenny Dalglish, who both played for and managed Liverpool after coming to the city from the Bhoys in 1977. So closely tied are the clubs that Celtic fans adopted the Liverpool anthem 'You'll Never Walk Alone'. The clubs also 'share', uniquely in football, a scarf: half Liverpool, half Celtic (in addition, of course, to their own scarves).[3]

In the case of all these clubs, their footballing success is only metonymic in relation to their exceptionality. Liverpool, Celtic, Boca and Barcelona's success on the field – their various league championships and European Cup (or Copa Libertadores, in Boca's case) trophies – stands as only a part of the reason for their greater socio-political importance. These clubs, especially in relation to their fiercest rivals (Liverpool–Everton; Celtic–Rangers; Boca–River; and Barcelona–Real Madrid), represent more than football. They constitute the *raison d'être* for their fans; they are an ideology – they are an entire way of Shanklean (political) life.

Within the football lexicon, 'Anfield' is, like La Bombanera or Barcelona's Camp Nou, a name that inspires romance. Liverpool FC's ground has a name steeped in local history, a name burnished and gilded by the club's magnificent triumphs on the field (with its five European Cup victories, it ranks alongside Real Madrid and AC Milan in a trio of greats of the European game). Anfield is a name that vivifies and animates the relationship between community and club. Anfield is the very incarnation, not simply the symbol, of the city and Liverpool FC's exceptionality. The stadium is exceptional not only because of what it stands for, but because it is at the very core of a collapsing community. Anfield's representations are signal both within England and in Europe. On those Wednesday night games in the European Cup against the Continent's best, not so much Shankly but his managerial successor Paisley made Anfield impregnable, a daunting venue for any opposition. Still, it was Shankly who dubbed the ground 'Fortress Anfield', and as the club acquired silverware in Europe the moniker stuck, the legend grew, and the great clubs from Italy, Spain and Germany dreaded travelling to the city.

All teams that visit Anfield, as they walk up the tunnel that leads on to the pitch, have to pass under a simple sign that has gained mythic status since those magnificent Shankly/Paisley years. 'This Is Anfield', the sign reads. But that sign is more than a mere geographical marker. It is meant to instil, in the Liverpool players, respect for the club and its traditions, respect for the Liverpool Way. Over the years it has also created, in sides visiting Anfield (there is no other sign like it in the football world), a mixture of awe, fear and respect, in equal measure. A Scotsman of great hubris, Shankly did not intend, but was always pleased by, the intimidating power of that sign. Liverpool's opponents, lowly English teams or elite European sides, could be under no illusions about where they were: at Anfield, home of a British and European great. Imbued as Anfield is with this glorious sense of history, it is simultaneously paradoxical and apropos that it is the relationship of the stadium to the surrounding squalor that makes starkly evident the inequity of capital. Anfield Stadium, on Anfield Road, is what divides the rich from the poor, the Kop End fans from the players, the Scousers (native-born Liverpudlians) from the wealthy players and the upper echelons of the club's administration.

Liverpool FC is exceptional not only in football terms but in starkly material ones, within its local setting because of how capital 'materializes' itself in the physical structure: in the articulation of capital, the stadium, as at once organic to L4 and ideologically 'superior' to it. Such is the contradiction of capital, even in so 'benign' a cultural form as a football stadium: there is always an unequal relationship between the materially resourced cultural site and the populace for whom it 'articulates': those who claim a powerful, affective, psychic and, for many, life-defining relationship to the 'place of culture' are markedly less wealthy than those who own the site – the majority shareholders who literally own it, the managers and coaches who administer the team, and, most importantly, the players who are the stadium's symbolic proprietors.

It is precisely the discrepancy in resources that makes apparent how, at the edge of the exceptional, there resides a cultural, political and economic darkness. It is not only the victories, the memorable moments and proud cultural associations that constitute the exceptional but the traumas, the ignoble defeats, the partial silences about matters of social import, the refusals to own those failures. Or, as the material consequences to the local community around Anfield demonstrate, the costs of slow redress. In writing about the club's uneven respect for community values, David Conn (2005: 70) comments on how the club had to be cajoled, years late, into doing the right thing:

> Liverpool FC were also deeply resented for having bought dozens of houses around the ground and leaving them empty, blighting an area already in severe decline. Since then the club has consulted painstakingly with local residents' groups, and recently refurbished several of their properties on Skerries Road.

The exceptional, following Conn's critique, can be understood as an arithmetical formulation: the exceptional is the sum total of its accomplishments plus, not minus, its failures. The houses bought, neglected and then refurbished reveal how the complex socio-economic constitution of the (Liverpool FC) exceptional emerges out of the dialectic between social neglect and social responsibility, out of the occasionally tense relations between the wealthy institution and the poor residents who double as fans.

'The aristocrats of labour': the rich from/in our ranks

This chapter is concerned with the exceptionality of Liverpool's football club only as it articulates the complicated ethical relationship of the (Scouser) Self to the Other. The focus here is on the relationship of the native Scouser fan of Liverpool FC turned player, the working-class youth turned multi-millionaire in a few short years, to those fans whose ranks he has now transcended – or, abandoned, in a more pejorative rendering – and from whom he has (too quickly) become alienated. The player in question here is Steven Gerrard, the current captain of Liverpool FC, a Scouser raised on the Bluebell Estate in Huyton, which, along with Toxteth and Bootle, is one of the poorest neighbourhoods in the city of Liverpool. (In the 1960s and 1970s, Prime Minister Harold Wilson's constituency included the estate.) In 'The other "S": space' section of this chapter Gerrard is set alongside another former (and briefly returned) Liverpool player and native Scouser, Robbie Fowler, who grew up in Toxteth, Liverpool 8, a racially mixed neighbourhood. After his short but successful return, Fowler signed in July 2007 for Championship (lower-division) side Cardiff. Like Gerrard now does, Fowler once captained Liverpool FC. Both men inhabit, in very different ways, the position Friedrich Engels named the 'aristocrats of labour'.

Engels coined this phrase in his critique of the ways in which trade union leaders, the 'labour elite', were susceptible to being 'bought off' by capital. Engels' wariness about how certain sections of the working class could be co-opted by capital resonates, in the moment of highly paid working-class footballers, with the material and psychic chasm that opens up between players from L4 and L8 and those communities from which they originate. So skilful are Gerrard and Fowler that theirs is, we might say, an 'aristocratic labour'. But they also constitute, in Engels' terms, the aristocrats of (Liverpool) labour: those sons of the working

Figure 9.1 Bill Shankly statue outside Anfield Stadium, Liverpool, August 2005
© Julie Baldwin

Figure 9.2 Steven Gerrard, Liverpool FC captain © Getty Images

class who have been elevated far out of the social confines of Huyton and Toxteth.

So pronounced and widely known is Fowler's wealth that the fans sing, with deadpan humour, in honour of his riches. To the tune of the Beatles' 'Yellow Submarine', they – working-class Liverpudlian 'Scallies' and Mancunians from the council estates the leading among them – lustily bellow, 'We all live in a Robbie Fowler house, a Robbie Fowler house,' in an acknowledgement of how lucratively Fowler has invested his money in property. This working-class lad from Toxteth, this tenant turned landlord, the worker turned (landed) aristocrat, now owns more property than any player in the English Premier League. Despite his ambivalence about his new wealth and status, Fowler has remained decidedly unaristocratic in his demeanour and symbolically rooted within the Scouser working class. It is for precisely this reason that he is so massively beloved by the Kop, who, in January 2006, enthusiastically welcomed his return to Anfield like that of a prodigal son. After his time in the footballing 'wilderness' at Leeds United and Manchester City, this striker whom they nicknamed, with no sense of sacrilege, 'God', because of his ability to score goals, was accepted back to thunderous applause. 'God', sometimes easily confused with God, could now definitively be said to live in L4. Born in Toxteth, baptized in the holy water of the Mersey, resurrected at Anfield.

This chapter turns on a single, and singular, moment in Steven Gerrard's career: the event of solitude that pre-empted his decision to remain at Liverpool FC on 6 July 2005, just a day after he had publicly declared his intention to join London's Chelsea FC. A critical significance is read off this moment, in itself a hermeneutically risky approach. However, I offer this critique because the Gerrardian moment of decision is so instructive for thinking philosophically about the ethics of sport and capital. The Gerrardian instance is so philosophically suggestive because it does not allow for the easy invocation of the ethical. Rather, it demands that the ethical be engaged as a philosophical complex: that phenomenon this essay names 'Socratic solitude'.

The critical imperative of this chapter within the context of this collection is to think a philosophy of sport in philosophical terms. A mode of thinking sport philosophically that, while mindful of the work of critics such as William J. Morgan, Graham McFee, Jim Parry and Mike McNamee,[4] is inflected by a 'literary–Cultural Studies' approach rather than Sport Studies or the philosophy of human movement. In producing this Socratic theory of the communal, reflective quality of solitude, the philosophical modality here is inflected by a spatial theory of the affective in order to explicate the emotionally impacted relationship between fan and player, between the idol and the idolized. This broadly Socratic construct is intended to account for the affective complications in such a way as to explicate how the materiality of space inflects the moment, and the ethical modality, of solitude. (Any use of Socrates is, of course, dependent upon Plato since almost everything that is known about Socrates' life and work comes via Plato. Socrates' thought was never formally written but mediated by Plato's interpretation, so that Plato as well as his successor Aristotle are integral to the deployment of Socratic in this essay.) The psychic space – that space where Gerrard, along with his current and former teammates Fowler, Jamie Carragher and Stephen Warnock,[5] local lads all (the latter a lifetime Koppite, unlike the Evertonian-raised Fowler and Carragher), Liverpudlians who made that epic journey from fan to player, negotiate their intimate relationship to the fans – is deeply materialized in the Gerrardian experience of solitude. In that moment, the psychic and conceptual proximity of Anfield to Liverpool 4 – and Huyton, Toxteth and Bootle, all the rough, impoverished communities – is revealed.

It is worth invoking here, in contradistinction to Plato, an alternate conception of the origins of philosophy. In his signature work on statecraft, *Leviathan*, Thomas Hobbes, with his sententious scepticism, suggests that 'leisure is the mother of philosophy'. Hobbes's pronouncement is provocative here not only because of its reference to 'leisure', a socio-political category into which sport is routinely put. Rather, his declamation could be read as less an instance of the dismissive, though it could easily be construed as such, than as an invitation that has potential relevance for this philosophical project. Following Hobbes, it might now be possible to think the 'time (and form) of sport' – the time needed to participate in it, its marketing as a form of relaxation, the construction of (temporary or permanent) community and material consumption – by delineating the conceptual space in which serious critical reflection, of the 'wondrous' Platonic variety, might be conducted. Moreover, and more to the ethical point, Hobbes reminds us that the 'leisure' status – the gifted, overwaged athlete of the new millennium – obtained by 'Stevie G' (as Gerrard is known to Liverpool fans) is precisely what now distinguishes him from the Scouser fans who chant his name as he once chanted those of his idols – John Barnes, Ian Rush, Alan Hansen and Steve McMahon, Kop heroes of Gerrard's youth. How does the player from the exceptional place, where traditions of labour, community organization and a strong sense of a local working-class identity hold, reconcile his aristocratic status to those of the fans? Does the aristocratic Self recognize itself in the labouring, or non-labouring (because unemployed or unemployable) Other? Or, in Hobbes's terms, is the Self figuratively at 'warre' with itself in the struggle to understand its dislocation from its previous Self, the fan who is now in the position of Other?

The three 'S's: Socrates, solitude and Stevie G

> Nor will a generous man take from the wrong source; that kind of taking is not characteristic of a man who holds material goods in low esteem.
>
> (Aristotle, 1962: 85)

It was Stevie G's adoption of Socratic solitude that saved the Liverpool skipper for his hometown club in the summer of 2005, when, for a second consecutive off-season, he flirted with the millions of pounds on offer from Chelsea FC.[6] After leading Liverpool to victory in the 2005 Champions League final in Istanbul over the much-fancied AC Milan (Gerrard was instrumental in orchestrating a historic comeback win after Liverpool were 3–0 down at the interval), he returned eager to work out a long-term contract with the club. Contract talks stalled, and in the first week of July 2005 Chelsea moved in to make their offer, reputedly in the region of £32 million, with Gerrard collecting wages of £120,000 per week, making him one of the highest-paid players in world football. The Liverpool hierarchy countered, but Gerrard still seemed poised to sign for Chelsea, to leave the club he had joined as a schoolboy, the club he had skippered to a glorious, memorable victory in Istanbul.

Then, the moment of Socratic solitude to counter the tumult surrounding his proposed move to Chelsea. Faced with the prospect of terminating his relationship to Liverpool FC, Gerrard turned – as Thomas Hardy might have it – away from the 'madding crowd'. Gerrard 'changed his mind', he said, 'when he sat down at home . . . with his girlfriend [Alex Curran] and agent Struan Marshall. "I was just thinking, how have we got into this mess and what is the best way out of it."'[7] In a television interview that evening, he added that he had to 'be alone' in order to negotiate his way out of the 'mess'.[8] A key part of that 'mess' required that Gerrard forswear the Kop End fans, the Scousers he had grown up with in Huyton and neighbouring Bootle (home to Carragher). Could he make himself irredeemably alien to the city of his birth by joining Chelsea, a club hated by all Liverpudlians, Liverpool and Everton fans alike, because of the Londoners' massive wealth, their almost infinite capacity to buy players from all over the globe?

According to Socrates, human beings live in a condition of radical singularity. Human beings are never alone, even when they are completely on their own, because then they are in the company of themselves; moments of solitude make the solitary individual a discursive being and, therefore, incapable of solitude. All human beings understand the principles of social interaction not because they learn them through engagement with others but because they are in a dialogic relationship with themselves. Because human beings think through talking with themselves, they possess a singular 'plurality' that enables them to grasp the discursive demands of public life. In Arendt's (2005: 21) reading, 'What Socrates was driving at (and what Aristotle's theory of friendship explains more fully) is that living together with others begins with living together with oneself.' (It is, of course, possible to amend Arendt's non-dialectical formulation. Her location of the origin of the dialogic in the individual is problematic because it is equally likely that the notion of the two-in-one emerges from the social rather than the individual. The very notion of an origin undermines the ways in which the dialogic socializes, in a relentlessly productive dialectic, the individual subject in solitude. Or, in Gerrard's case, most especially in solitude.)

The Self does not constitute a singular one but a 'two-in-one': the dialogic two. The dialogic is that moment when the one engages itself and recognizes itself as sufficiently different to be able to confront itself about its role, how it acts, what it should do, in the public sphere. It is through the dialogic that the Pauline philosophy (as articulated in St Paul's Letters to the Corinthians) of self-recognition can be understood – 'I know even as also I am known.'[9] Gerrard comes to see himself dialogically in a moment of 'darkness'. The dialogic is the only modality in which thinking, of both the philosophical and vernacular variety, takes place. The Self must become a singular plurality in order to grasp the functioning of the polis. However, while it is critical that the Socratic two is folded into the one, it is equally crucial that the two, in the appropriate moment, 'reconstitutes' and represents itself as a critically self-conscious one.

By situating himself within the solitude of his home, surrounded by only his confidants, more alone with his thoughts than he had been for the six weeks since Istanbul, Gerrard was able fully to apprehend the deeply communal politics of Socratic 'Solitude, or the thinking dialogue of the two-in-one' (Arendt, 2005: 36). It is through solitude that Gerrard's singular plurality can enunciate itself: that he can think dialogically about himself as footballer and Liverpool resident, as Liverpool FC skipper and potential Chelsea player, as ex-working-class Scouser-turned-aristocrat and Huyton native-about-to-abandon his hometown team. In his solitude Gerrard is compelled to, in a Platonic sense, 'endure wonder'. He has to think critically about where he, as cultural subject, begins, and he has to wonder if he is embarking upon a trajectory that is, as Liverpool FC player and as Scouser, tenable. In Engels' terms, it is in the moment of Socratic solitude that the working-class footballer determines the magnitude of his 'aristocracy': will he, at the very least, remain true, if not (entirely) to his class, then to his geographical place? It is only through creating the possibility for a radical plurality, an 'internal class conflict', a dialogic that is simultaneously a dialectic of/between the 'two selves', that Gerrard can understand why Chelsea represents the unethical proposition.

It is precisely the lack of privacy within solitude that suggests, even as Gerrard retreats far away from the public (only to confront it again fully, like the return of the Freudian repressed, within the imagined privacy of his home), that the moment of Socratic solitude can easily take place within public space, such is the intimate link of the two-in-one. However, it is within the confines of the putatively private that the full dialogic force of the two-in-one is encountered. There can be no experience of the two-in-one as disconcerting – or illuminating – as the unexpected irruption of the public into the private: to imagine the Self as being in private, and then to confront in that moment how 'invasive', how dialogically present, the public is. For this reason there is a significant experiential difference between the encounter of the dialogic in public and in private. The 'private' encounter with the public is expected to be 'public', while the 'intrusion' of the public into the private is disruptive because it is not anticipated. Hence the power of the two-in-one derives from its capacity to disarticulate the private, to articulate the public into the private.

In Aristotle's cryptic judgement, 'Nor will a generous man', or a man who thinks himself rooted in the cultural and ideological generosity of his native community, 'take from the wrong source' (Aristotle, 1962: 85). To do so would be an affront both to the man himself and to the community with whom he sees himself in closest proximity. Generosity is, for Aristotle, about ethical discrimination, about assigning ethical weight – and a name, 'wrong' – to every important choice. Socrates creates the terms in and conditions under which to think;

Aristotle requires the appropriate act – the ethical wherewithal to identify the source as wrong, and to reject it as a means of enhancing personal wealth. Chelsea were reputedly offering Gerrard up to £32,000 more, per week, than Liverpool, which was willing to – and eventually did – make him their highest-paid player at £100,000 per week.[10]

Confronted with the lucrative possibility of leaving Liverpool, compelled to reason with himself, made to explain himself – his *raison d'être* – to himself, there was no Aristotelian alternative for Gerrard: Chelsea is the inconceivable, anti-Socratic and anti-Aristotelian prospect. 'The last thing I wanted to do', Gerrard said, 'was leave, I just could not do it.'[11] It is in this way that solitude constitutes political immersion in the public sphere, in the life of the city (Athenian or Liverpudlian). Solitude does not mark the withdrawal from the political into the personal. Conceptually speaking, solitude is the most intensely public form of political self-reflection because it demonstrates the extent to which the concerns of the polis are at the core of the dialogic between the two-in-one. In the time of and for decision, the ethical moment, the power of the two is at its most profound. In creating the space in which to be by himself, Gerrard was most viscerally in the company of others: the working class, the poverty of Huyton and L4 could not be excised from Gerrard's aristocratic (private) space. To phrase this most reductively, both Gerrard's public and private selves understood the ethical enormity of what was at stake when faced with the recognition that leaving Liverpool was not an ethical possibility; he understood that the Liverpool fans (the polis) wanted, and why they wanted him, their captain and local hero, to remain among them. Not coincidentally, the very claims that the public was making on him were the claims that 'private' Gerrard made of himself. The two, the Liverpool public and the Liverpool player, were, in this instance, inextricably one; the latter in the singular plurality of solitude, the former unabashedly in public – on radio call-in shows, in the newspapers, on the streets of Liverpool, in their painful act pre-emptively disowning him in public. (Liverpool fans burned their replica Gerrard jerseys, their Liverpool FC number 8s and 17s of seasons gone by, in bitterness at his, so they thought, betrayal of them and his imminent departure. Or one, at the very least, did so outside Anfield.)

This 'aggregation' of the two into a greater One could not, however, have been achieved without solitude. It was solitude that allowed Gerrard once again to become, if only for that moment (which is not to deny how significant a moment it was), the Huyton-bred Scouser that he once was, for the symbolic working-class sensibility to triumph over his aristocratic Self. So much so that he not only apologized to the fans for what he had put them through, sadness and anger in equal measure, but promised that he would never again repeat his equivocations.

In Gerrard's decision-making process, the most important of his career, the moment of solitude constitutes the act of ethical political judgement. Gerrard's solitude demonstrates how it is within the space of the domestic that solitude is most acutely active; it is in the domestic, not in the press conference or playing in a stadium in front of thousands of Scouser fans, that the political is most, not least, immanent.

However, to configure the domestic as the space of solitude is to gender it specifically male. As feminists since at least Virginia Woolf's call for a 'room of one's own' (within the space of the household) have argued, it is the very public and commercial nature of the home that has deprived women of the kind of opportunity for privacy and reflection that Gerrard has such ready access to in his solitude. It is for this reason that one of the greatest gains Woolf can imagine for her figurative novelist Mary Carmichael is Platonic philosophy: the 'freedom to think of things in themselves' (Woolf, 1989: 39). For women the home as domestic space is not an enclave but a site of almost ceaseless activity; for women there is no retreat from the bustle of public life, only its transmutation into a more contained and, therefore, more intensely demanding space. What is for many women (and some men) the primary site of (primary and secondary) labour is, because of elevated class position, for Gerrard the only place of respite.[12] In philosophical terms, Gerrard is the figure of Platonic contemplation. The Scouser footballer is metaphorically the philosopher who values, like Plato, the opportunity to 'wonder' about his relationship to the polis in symbolic privacy. Not for the Liverpool FC captain the Socratic act of wandering among the polis. What is clear, however, is that he heard the polis in his domestic space as surely as Socrates canvassed political opinion about the state of Athens among its citizens. In that Socratic way, the domestic becomes a potentially feminist space: the home as a further confrontation with the demands of public life, the home as a further irruption of the polis within the ostensibly non-public sphere. In his solitude, the domestic articulates itself as a space permeable to and shaped by the public.

Rendered as a spatial logic, the Socratic notion of two-in-one makes it possible to suggest an equally significant reconciliation. In the solitude of his masculinized domestic space, an expensive neighbourhood far removed from the Bluebell Estate where he was raised, it is not simply that Gerrard figuratively puts himself in dialogue with his fellow Scousers. It is, as importantly, that he establishes the centrality of spatiality in thinking domestic solitude. The entire dilemma about staying or going, and the psychic consequences of that deracination from Liverpool to London, is deeply rooted in the materiality of place – the costs of dislocation not only to Gerrard but to the Liverpool FC fans. In the solitary dialogic with the Self, Gerrard has to think Anfield Stadium, L4, together with its relation to his upper-class new home; reflecting upon his own upward class trajectory requires that Gerrard recognize these various material inequities. He has to understand the material distance he has travelled from the Bluebell Estate and its relation to the psychic lives he affects on Skerries Road and other blighted parts of L4 by flirting with Chelsea. He could not take Huyton, L4 and the 'Scally' culture of Liverpool with him. In London he would be, Socratically speaking, forced to live in a solitude that could never sustain him. There, perhaps, in London, he would be compelled to live with the 'solitary', ghostly presence of the L4 he (thought) he had left behind.

The ethical Gerrardian moment reveals another dimension of Liverpool FC's exceptionality. In contrast to Gerrard's decision to remain at Anfield in the summer of 2005, there is the previous summer's decision by Everton's star Wayne

Rooney to bolt from the Liverpool club to Manchester United, an Everton enemy of long standing. There was nothing in Everton's history, its traditions or its status as a club (it is too unsuccessful to bear comparison to Liverpool FC) to persuade Rooney to act, as Gerrard did, ethically. By leaving Everton for United, Rooney revealed that Liverpool FC's exceptionality had more to do with the specific football institution than the city of Liverpool itself. The very act that Rooney could commit was, in the final instance, thinkable but not doable for Gerrard. (In contrast to both these Scousers stands Jamie Carragher. Not for him the dilemma of contracts. There is, for 'Carra', no club outside of Liverpool FC. He is the true scion of the city. So, while the fans sing of Fowler's wealth to the tune of 'Yellow Submarine', they have another version of that song reserved for Carragher: 'We all dream of a team of Carraghers.' Loyalty has its melodic privileges.)

The other 'S': space

> When know that, in the course of the flânerie, far-off times and places interpenetrate the landscape and the present moment.
>
> (Benjamin, 2002: 419)

In his solitude, Gerrard has to negotiate, as a peculiar native informant, his own deeply historicized relationship to the streets around Anfield. He has to decide how he understands the relationship between Anfield Road and L4; he is, in this moment, compelled to recognize both his own alienation, as massively entitled occupant of Anfield Road Stadium, from L4 and how his personal history – his familiarity with the two spaces – enables him to mediate the resourced building to the community. Growing up a Scouser fan of Liverpool FC, Gerrard cannot but grasp the ethico-political dimensions that attend to the domestication of public space. Like all fans in all sports, Scousers have a domesticated relationship to the building, most obviously and affectionately contained in their naming Anfield or Celtic Park or La Bombanera their 'home ground', an affective bond encouraged by both the club and its fans. What this domestication produces is the affect of a putative, symbolic ownership by the fans of the stadium, an ownership upon which the players, coaches and club administration rely.

The club officials depend, at the most basic level, upon the hometown fans to support 'their' club; the club expects the local fans to domesticate the space so that it provides Liverpool FC or Celtic FC or FC Barcelona with an advantage. The club, quite literally, relies upon the local fans to make the 'local' players feel 'at home' in their own stadium. The players have a familiarity with the field and the fans are familiar with the players on their team – the fans are, preferably, psychically bonded through excessive attachment with several players on their team. More than the players, it is the fans who make the stadium home to the local team and unfriendly, if not downright hostile, to the opposition. It is the fans who make the crucial difference between home and away fixtures. Apart from the fans, the material conditions of the game are pretty much the same – the dimensions of the field, the number of players on each side, the rules of the game.

It is the fans, as the club officials and players all too willingly recognize (except when they are barracked by the home fans), who domesticate the local space for the players; it is they who make (the) home (stadium) home.

There is an unrecognized reciprocity in the process of domesticating the local space. As much as the fans participate in the commodification of local affect, through the purchase of replica jerseys and other club paraphernalia (all of which swells the club's coffers), so the players depend upon the fans affectively identifying with them. In this strangely circular affective economy, as much as the fans want to be like the players, so the players want the fans to want to be like them so that they, the players, can feel truly at home when they are at home. In domesticating the space, the club inadvertently – and simultaneously – masculinizes and feminizes the fans. Club players and administrators not only rely on the boisterous (masculine) support of the fans but expect those fans to nurture the players in difficult moments. The fans are expected to be sympathetic to the players in times of difficulty – managers often ask the fans for support in their press conferences, especially during losing streaks, the elimination from prestigious competitions, or losses to supposedly inferior teams. Fans are relied upon to create a haven for the team during away games; for those games they are expected to blunt the hostility of the opposing fans (who are at home) and to protect the players from and offset the numerical superiority of the other team's fans.

The American businessmen Tom Hicks and George Gillett now own Liverpool FC, and the new brass understand the affective, political and symbolic value of the club's Anfield history. The proposed new stadium, formidable and beautiful in equal measure (at least in the planning stages), will try to recreate the famed Kop in the as-yet-unbuilt venue. It is doubtful that such a re-creation will be possible, but the very gesture speaks of a respect for the club and the community's past. The Gerrardian moment, we might suggest, represents a watershed event: the imperative to reflect upon a Liverpool FC about to dislocate itself, relocate itself and understand itself – its Two-some (Anfield/post-Anfield) Self – in relation to its past, but never passed (into forgotten history) into the past, Self. Whatever its physical structure, whatever its capacity to call upon the spirit of the Kop, the new stadium will always stand in relation to Anfield. It will, as the Koppites might say, 'never stand alone'.

The fans are, then, relied upon for both their (re)collective and 'maternal' skills. This evokes, suggestively rather than directly, that well-known terrace phrasing of infidelity, no doubt in part derived from the experience accrued by both players and (male) fans on their travels away from their home stadium: 'playing away' or 'playing away from home'. It is the responsibility of the fans to demand, as the incarnation of 'domesticity' and felicity in hostile territory, that the players be 'faithful' to the cause. Fans remind the players of their club that 'promiscuity', the possibility of succumbing to the 'temptation' of under-performance away from home, will not be tolerated. In a profoundly symbolic way, the club and its players are 'married' to the fans, sworn – because of the fans' commitment, their travelling to hostile away stadiums – to fidelity or, at the very least, maximum effort away from home. Little wonder, then, that Robbie Fowler, in his final home game for Liverpool in 2007, was publicly appreciative of manager Rafa Benítez for giving him, like a departing lover, the chance to say 'goodbye' to his soon-to-be 'ex'. Benítez's dour predecessor, Gerrard Houllier, never afforded the Toxteth local that clearly desired opportunity for a proper parting of the ways – a bond, of course, that could never be fully severed.

The long history of making Anfield home for Liverpool players creates the kind of cultural and ideological exchange system that enunciates itself, in moments of crisis, as an ethical opening; and, in moments of intense player identification, as the memorable event of player–fan–city solidarity, a rare and powerful nexus, to be sure. On rare occasions, there is, for the fans, the expectation of reciprocity. The fans have acquired the historic right to make demands of the players they have supported so loyally over the years, often decades. In Liverpool's case the crisis of Hillsborough Stadium on 15 April 1989, when ninety-six Liverpool fans died before the start of the FA Cup semi-final against Nottingham Forest, marks arguably the key ethical moment in the club's history. (While the disaster of Heysel, Brussels, 1985, was truly a horrific moment in the club's history, Hillsborough signifies differently, primarily because it was Liverpool fans who died. At Heysel, more than thirty Juventus fans died after skirmishes with British fans before the European Cup final.) In the aftermath of Hillsborough, the grieving fans did not have to ask for the players' support because the Liverpool players and their manager, Kenny Dalglish, recognized their ethical responsibility to the fans. According to Phil Hammond, chairperson of the Hillsborough Family Support Group, 'Kenny Dalglish and his wife Marina made themselves available 24 hours a day after the disaster' (Conn, 2005: 70). The Dalglishes' public accessibility was borne out of the recognition that this tragedy was a domestic one.

In the moment of Hillsborough, the symbolic relationship among fans, players and club officials was substantiated into a genuinely familial one. The grief constituted a singularity out of the plurality (fans–players–city) that attached itself to, and identified itself with, Liverpool FC. This was, moreover, not the solitary one talking with itself, but the constitutive One talking – impromptu counselling through the sheer physical presence of the Dalglishes and Liverpool players – its collective Self through grief, pain and loss. The Liverpool players and manager's response to Hillsborough was an act of Aristotelian generosity: 'He will not give to anybody and everybody, so that he may have [something] to give the right people at the right time and when it is noble to do so' (Aristotle, 1962: 85). What distinguishes Aristotle's notion of generosity is his insistence upon discrimination: the 'right people at the right time and when it is noble to do so'. Hillsborough undoubtedly meets these Aristotelian criteria so that Kenny and Marina Dalglish's selfless acts in the wake of familial death added considerably to more than the already widely held perception of Liverpool FC's exceptionality; its capacity to care in response to a terrible trauma.

The tragedy of 1989 revealed the Liverpool FC ethical as a conjunctural practice. The appropriate response in the moment of crisis extends Aristotelian generosity in that the Liverpool FC ethical requires that the 'right people' do not have to ask. The act of pre-empting the Other's request for assistance is not motivated by the 'nobility' of the generous (which would reduce it to little more than *noblesse oblige*). The Other, in this instance, is also the Self. Rather, the very act of making demands for the injured, traumatized Self in a moment of crisis suggests that the 'generous' man or woman – those not physically hurt or psychologically injured – has already failed to grasp the direness of the situation.

In recent Liverpool FC history, there has been no instance of a footballer's identification with the city's working class greater than that of Robbie Fowler. Working-class Toxteth and a fierce champion of the city's working poor, Fowler used the occasion of scoring a goal against SK Brann (of Bergen, Norway) to hoist his number 9 jersey over his head to reveal a red T-shirt that read: 'Support 500 Sacked Liverpool Dockers'. Fowler's gesture, in that March 1997 game in the UEFA Cup Winners' Cup, was a clear instance of One-ness that emerges out of Two-ness. The Toxteth player, symbiotically linked to the fans, the city and in support of the striking dockers' cause, made public his identification in the most visceral way: on the pitch, in front of the fans, in solidarity with a cause the fans understood as their own. The dialogic Two presented itself as Socratic One: Robbie Fowler – of the Scousers, for the Scousers, as a Scouser on the hallowed Anfield pitch. Fowler's declaration of support constitutes a demonstration of, in contradistinction to the privacy of Gerrard, solitude in public. It was a remarkable moment not only in Liverpool FC history but in the history of contemporary English football: the native son going native, the public extension of the dialogic into a spectacular solitude.

Fowler's act of Scouser solidarity stands in sharp distinction to Gerrard's 'redemption' into Scouserdom. (In January 2006, of course, Fowler experienced his own Liverpool 'resurrection' when he returned to the club.) Whereas Gerrard's solitude demonstrates the complexities of political loyalty to the local, Fowler's constitutes an act of planned, contingent spontaneity – what would he have done if he had not scored that goal? Fowler was fined £900 for his public demonstration, not by Liverpool FC officials but by the European governing body (UEFA). His was a powerful political statement, a unique moment that symbolically brought the fans' politics on to the pitch, made it – for a key instant, the celebration of a goal that was also a political critique – a part of the game itself. It is a moment distinct from Gerrrad's, free from Gerrardian equivocation. Fowler was sold because he underperformed, because he did not conform to the discipline required of him by his manager, Houllier; he was in fact made captain by Houllier, so the story goes, in an attempt to make him more responsible. Fowler's moment was the product of a long Socratic dialogue between the player and the community, uniting, in a memorable instant, Anfield Stadium to Liverpool 4 to L8, all of which was connected, in that moment, to the most pressing political issue for Liverpool's workers. In the contemporary moment of overwaged footballers, such a display of political commitment seems inconceivable – who among them would be prepared to risk endorsements, fines or admonition from their club officials to support a political cause? It is hard to imagine that the Fowler display will be repeated unless under very extreme circumstances. In our conjuncture, it is in Gerrardian solitude that the complexities of the ethical will reside, itself at best an entangled, ambivalent statement of political One-ness – never to be confused with Fowlerian commitment – that is always contingent upon the intervention of the dialogic Two-ness. And even Gerrard's about-face with Chelsea is attributable to Liverpool FC's exceptionality.

The solitary process by which Gerrard arrived at his decision is, of course, in no way analogous to either Fowler's proud political brandishing or the Hillsborough tragedy. However, all these events share, in their distinct ways, the Liverpool FC ethical. Because of the ways in which the two symbolic spaces, Anfield and L4 (as well as Huyton and Toxteth), infuse each other, because of how they construct the psychic architecture of Fowler's bold display of public solitude or Gerrard's solitude as a powerful singularity, it is not conceptually necessary for the fans – in the latter's case – to interrogate their skipper directly about his loyalty to them. The 'interpenetration' of other times and other spaces, as Benjamin reminds us, makes such an enquiry redundant. The moment of decision or demonstration (Fowler) is already informed by the political interpenetration of the dialogic. The ways in which these two spaces conjoin to form one in Gerrard's solitude mean that those questions are pre-emptively present in, if not constitutive of, his solitude. (It is clear, of course, in Fowler's case that he was never in the position of Socratic solitude, that condition through which Gerrard redeems himself into Liverpool FC. Despite his reputation as a wayward personality, his penchant for getting into fights (a description the player firmly and repeatedly denies in his autobiography), Fowler – who will acknowledge that he is a 'Scally' with a propensity for mischief – was never in the kind of 'mess' that Gerrard created for himself in July 2005. See Fowler, 2005).

This is what Gerrard means when he describes his solitude as a contemplation on 'this mess'. The flirtation with Chelsea and his request for a transfer generates a series of 'messy' questions that demand accountability: Why am I leaving? What am I leaving? Whom am I leaving behind? Who am I if I leave? Existential questions to be sure, the foundational kind of enquiries that emerge from the Self's understanding of itself as a one in constant dialogue with other ones who greatly resemble each other. Gerrard's rejection of Chelsea represents the process of accounting for the self that enabled that self to emerge from a messy situation, some of which was of his own making, with its radical singularity reanimated. 'The last thing I wanted to do was leave.' What that Gerrardian formulation excludes is the interrogative: not *why* did Gerrard not leave, but how is it that he *could* not, rather than *did* not, leave? In order not to leave, the One had to confront the Two so that it could explain itself to Itself and to (the several) Other(s).

In topophilic conclusion

Like all cultural space, Anfield Road is imbued with topophilia. For the fans, the players and the club officials, there is a love for the physical place that is in excess of its materiality. The space is infused with a history and a symbolic value that cannot be measured in material terms; which is to say, either in terms of property value or even in the number of trophies and honours that the club has accrued.

The space, as affective site, as repository of memory (those European Anfield nights or games against special foes or the event of witnessing a great game, a game-breaking move, or the debut or final game of a great player), acquires a singular symbolic import. The place is always more than just a space. Anfield is never merely the physical construct on Anfield Road in L4. It is the place where Shankly and Paisley managed, where Toshack and Keegan struck fear into the hearts of opposing defenses, where Dalglish hip-shimmied and Souness strode with imperious dominance, where Barnes broke the racist barrier with his sublime skill, where Rush scored hundreds of goals, and . . . where topophilia rules.

Within the calculus of contemporary capital, Gerrard's decision to remain at Liverpool demonstrates that it was, in the critical instance, not about the money. That is, if – an unimaginably big 'if' – one is willing simultaneously to applaud Gerrard for turning down an extra £80–100,000 per month and (which might be more difficult to justify) to suspend judgement about the mind-boggling sums of money that footballers take home every week. Saliently, the Liverpool FC fans in general do not seem to begrudge the players their exorbitant salaries and their 'flash' lifestyles. A few fans, however, did accuse Gerrard of greed when he quibbled about his wages in his new contract. One of them pointed out that he was still trying to pay off his debt racked up by the trip to Istanbul while Gerrard was haggling about an extra £20,000 per week: the price, as it were, that the fan was happy to pay – until Gerrard's dissatisfaction became public, that is – to make the Atatürk Olympic Stadium in Istanbul 'home' to Gerrard and his teammates for the Champions League final. Gerrard's decision to stay was not even about the fame or the glory. Chelsea, with its Russian oil billions, courtesy of owner Roman Abramovich, have been able to buy any player they want, sometimes at extravagant – inflated, say their critics – prices. Any player, that is, except Steven Gerrard. Liverpool's 2005 Champions League victory was a footballing miracle,[13] but even the club's most pathologically loyal fans – among whom I most certainly number – wonder, even with the newly minted North American capital, whether the Scousers have the financial clout to compete with the likes of Chelsea or even, God forbid, Manchester United and Arsenal. Even in the blissful aftermath of Istanbul, and the achievement of a second Champions League final two years later (in which AC Milan gained revenge for their defeat in 2005), we wonder about Liverpool winning the domestic league in the next few years. We Liverpool fans would like to be surprised, but we're not banking on anything, if you'll excuse the pun on Roman's roubles. With the club's magnificent history, Liverpool fans expect trophies even as we recognize the slight grandiosity of our dreams. (Sometimes winning in Istanbul can be bad for your psyche.)

Stevie G's choice was, for this precise reason, about something else, grounded in something different. It was not even about Liverpool's exceptionality, grasped quickly by David Conn as he compares the Scousers to the Manchester Uniteds and Chelseas of the English Premier League. It is only of the Liverpool players that he can say: 'you see a link between today's millionaires' dressing room and Liverpool's sense of itself as a club, and the greatness and grief of its history' (Conn, 2005: 70). That unique combination of greatness, history, tradition and exceptionality produced, in its different ways, both Fowler and Gerrard. In truth, no other club could have done this – not corporate-minded Manchester United, certainly not rouble-rich Chelsea; and, as Rooney's transfer makes evident, there in nothing in Everton to bind player to club. It was in and through his dialogic solitude, through his recognition of what his leaving would mean, both to himself and to the club's fans, that Gerrard understood: the ethical decision can be achieved only when the One recognizes that it is not only Two in relation to itself, but that its Two-ness demands the psychic dislocation of the Self into the space of the Other that is a powerful articulation of the Self. This complicated narration of the ethical self is what Hannah Arendt, one of the finest historians of the philosophy of ideas (in addition to her own original contributions to philosophy), means when she delineates Plato's severe response to Socrates' belief in Athenian equality and Aristotle's sharp retreat from the affairs of the polis.

Angry at Socrates' death by the polis, even more angry at the treatment of philosophers, first Plato and then his heir Aristotle forswore equality or any easy faith in Athenian democracy. Unlike Socrates, 'Aristotle explains that a community is not made out of equals, but on the contrary of people who are different and unequal' (Arendt, 2005: 17). Gerrard cannot but understand that he has a different, which is to say privileged, relationship to Liverpool FC and that the Scouser fans are not his material equals. It is, however, through Socratic solitude that he confronts how these differences and inequalities are negotiated in the public domain that is his masculinized domestic space. Gerrard cannot leave Liverpool FC because that would mean not only his rejection of his native community but his ex-communication from it. It would make manifest his outsiderness in much more visceral a way than his short physical trek, but massive class elevation, from the Bluebell Estate to his fancy house in a gated community. It is because of his own topophilia, his own symbolic attachment to the city of Liverpool and its working-class Scousers, it was because of his fear of his cultural and ideological disenfranchisement by his own people, that he would not leave Liverpool FC. Not only would playing for Chelsea make him 'different' from the Anfield fans (where he would now, upon visiting the stadium, experience not its domestic supportiveness but its virulent hostility, subjected to a derisive Othering that the Self reserves for those selves who betray the polis), it would make him a footballing Other – in the lesser than Orientalist sense of the term – to the fans who sing at the Kop End. While he did not leave Liverpool FC, his differences were tenable because they were based only (?) on class; if he did depart Liverpool FC, he would be making himself 'unequal' to the Scousers. His huge weekly salary already made him different from the fans, but playing for Chelsea would make him something far worse: less than them, less than what he had been in a red Liverpool jersey. In order to retain any notion of himself as a Scouser, Gerrard had to blend Socratic equality – the belief that the polis can be engaged dialectically, in its entirety – with amended Aristotelian scepticism – the anticipation that different relations to the institution vitiate inequality.

This Gerrard did. Out of this Athenian Two, Gerrard fashioned a Liverpudlian One. In his solitude he dialogued symbolically with the fans, admitting the affective power of history, ideology and Liverpool FC exceptionality, without pretending material equity. Such are the historic valences of the Liverpool FC ethical that in this city (even) the aristocrats of labour (or possibly because they are the aristocrats of labour) are compelled, by their own autobiographies, to dialogue with themselves in public. The aristocrats are made to account for themselves to themselves in full view of others, because those others are always doubly present: through the Other's symbolic occupation of both the public and the Self's private space, and through the presence of the Other in the Self. The aristocrats of labour occasionally, and in moments of crisis especially, have to negotiate the ideological tensions with/in themselves that are analogous to the material disjuncture they encounter. How could they not be aware of it? The inequities are so stark.

It is in solitude that Anfield cannot be thought apart from L4 or Huyton or Bootle. In Socratic solitude they press against each other in a relentless dialogic and they may confound not only the daytripper but the native son who, because of his privileged access, has become an ideological transient in his own symbolic home. Will the drive in to Anfield Stadium from his expensive house through the decrepit streets of L4 ever look the same again to Steven Gerrard?

The experience of Socratic solitude demonstrates how the articulation of class consciousness is both disguised (lost, we might even suggest) and forcefully present in the solitary moment. While it may seem that class consciousness will recede in the time and space of 'bourgeois reflection', especially in relation to so manifestly working class a cultural practice as football, it is precisely in Socratic solitude that the disjunctures, difficulties and ambivalences of class elevation through sport articulate a complex self-awareness of class origins. It is not only that Gerrard knows, however imperfectly, what he might be leaving if he signed for Chelsea; he dreads the complete breaking off from the Liverpool working class to which he is now only symbolically, and therefore precariously, connected.

The identity of the working-class hero made ('aristocratic') good is, it might be argued, never more powerfully in affective and political play than when that identity – so deeply rooted in the place of origin – faces the threat of being liquidated. Especially when it is the Socratic Self that is itself responsible for severing the symbolic relationship of the (singular) Self to the (plural, Huyton, L4) Self. Even aristocrats need to be from somewhere, linked to some place. For aristocrats of labour, especially for aristocrats of labour, because they are so awkwardly, tangentially linked to their Socratic Selves, the possibility of not being rooted in 'their' class is the most devastating political and affective threat of all. It is because the consciousness about being working class is never completely dislocated or unlearned – permanently residual, as Raymond Williams might have it – by the aristocrats of labour that that consciousness returns so emphatically, disruptively and constitutively in the moment of Socratic solitude.

Notes

1 See, for example, Taaffe and Mulhearn (1988), who not only provide a history of the city's militancy but give an account of Liverpool's resistance to the Thatcher regime during the 1980s.
2 See Bradley (2004), a collection of essays on the club that is wide ranging in terms of its critique of the 'Celtic mystique'. Of special significance, for a sense of the origins of the club, is Mark Burke's essay, 'Case for Brother Walfrid'. See Murray (1998, 2003).
3 See Raymond Boyle's essay, 'Football and Religion: Merseyside and Glasgow', on this issue in Williams *et al.* (2001).
4 See McNamee and Parry (1998), a collection in which all four have essays.
5 In early 2007 Warnock was sold to Blackburn Rovers, who also signed Fowler in September 2008.
6 See Williams and Hopkins (2005) for a critical account of what Gerrard's 'flirtations' with Chelsea meant to die-hard Liverpool fans, a constituency among which both authors number.
7 'Gerrard to sign Liverpool contract on Friday', 6 July 2005, http://www.rte.ie/sport/2005/0706/gerrards.html.
8 In the USA that interview was carried on the Fox Soccer Channel on 6 July 2005.
9 I Corinthians 13:12.
10 Gerrard renegotiated his contract in 2007 so that he is now even more handsomely rewarded for his labour.
11 'Gerrard to sign Liverpool contract on Friday', 6 July 2005, http://www.rte.ie/sport/2005/0706/gerrards.html.
12 Woolf is especially clear about how recent the notion is that women can access the space Gerrard so easily does: 'In the first place, to have a room of her own, let alone a quiet room, was out of the question, unless her parents were exceptionally rich or very noble, even up to the beginning of the nineteenth century' (Woolf, 1989: 52).
13 See Williams and Hopkins (2005).

References

Arendt, H. (2005) *The Promise of Politics*, New York: Schocken Books.

Aristotle (1962) *Nicomachean Ethics*, trans. Martin Ostwald, New York: Macmillan.

Benjamin, W. (2002) *The Arcades Project*, trans. Howard Eiland and Kevin McLaughlin, Cambridge, MA: Harvard University Press.

Bradley, J. (2004) *Celtic Minded: Essays on Religion, Politics, Society, Identity . . . and Football*, Argyll: Glendaruel.

Conn, D. (2005) 'Liverpool's Respect for Values rather than Raw Commercialism Appeals to Neutrals', *Independent*, 30 April, p. 70.

Eliot, T.S. (1930) 'Preludes' [1917], in *idem*, *Poems 1909–1925*, London: Faber and Faber, pp. 21–3.

Farred, G. (2006) 'God's Team: The Painful Miracle on the Bosphorus', *South Atlantic Quarterly* 105(2), pp. 303–19.

Fowler, R., with David Maddock (2005) *My Autobiography*, London: Macmillan.

Georgakas, D. and Surkin, M. (1998) *Detroit, I Do Mind Dying: A Study in Urban Revolution*, Cambridge, MA: South End Press.

Lane, T. (1997) *Liverpool: City of the Sea*, Liverpool: Liverpool University Press.

McNamee, M. and Parry, J. (eds) (1998) *Ethics and Sport*, London: Routledge.

Murray, B. (1998) *The Old Firm in the New Age: Celtic and Rangers since the Souness Revolution*, Edingburgh: Mainstream Press.

Murray, B. (2003) *Bhoys, Bears and Bigotry: The Old Firm in the New Age*, Edingburgh: Mainstream Press.

Taaffe, P. and Mulhearn, T. (1988) *Liverpool: A City that Dared to Fight*, London: Fortress Books.

Williams, J. and Hopkins, S. (2005) *The Miracle of Istanbul: Liverpool FC from Paisley to Benítez*, Edinburgh: Mainstream Press.

Williams, J., Hopkins, S. and Long, C. (eds) (2001) *Passing Rhythms: Liverpool FC and the Transformation of Football*, Oxford: Berg Press.

Woolf, V. (1989) *A Room of One's Own*, Orlando: Harcourt, Brace and Company.

Part IV

Key concepts, critical theorists

10 Michel Foucault and the critique of sport

Toby Miller

Introduction

Michel Foucault is an emblem of post-structuralism and postmodernism, theoretical and artistic movements that are often seen as reactions, *inter alia*, to a supposedly mechanistic Marxism. It is easy to see why. Foucault did not write a great deal about class, class struggle or imperialism; he did not refer to technology and value as motors of economic and hence social transformations; and he was not a historical determinist measuring change via successive modes of production. And where Marxism locates power in the ruling class and the state, Foucault looks for power on the periphery as well as at the centre. Renowned for criticizing Western Marxism's investment in ideology critique, which presupposes an idealist subject imbued with a consciousness ready to be worked on, he substitutes discourse for ideology, extending the concept of relative autonomy beyond what most political economists can endure. His concern with discourse is seen as opposed to the notion of material interests, while his account of power as a productive force is at odds with both utopic and *dys*topic aspects of Marxism. Foucault hauls us away from the conventional split between base and superstructure in Marxist accounts of the person 'under' a given mode of production and the romantic or liberal-humanist aesthetic of the creative soul. He argues that the raw stuff of human beings is not individuals: people *become* individuals through discourses and institutions of culture, via a 'mode of subjection [*mode d'assujettissement*], that is, the way in which people are invited or incited to recognize their moral obligations' (Foucault, 1983: 66–7). This constitutes a simultaneous internalization and externalization, individuation and collectivization.

Foucault's non-*a priori* account of the person does not deny the significance of the category, or its utility. Rather, he interrogates the discourse of the human and the conditions of its emergence. It may well be that subjection derives from forces connected to production, class conflict, or ideology. But Foucault maintains that the *loci* and logic of governance over the past five hundred years are not merely to be found among the interests or persuasions of the class that controls it, because government operates at a micro level as well as through and because of general economic forces. This micro level relies on the formation of public subjects. The determining logics of those subjects do not necessarily provide intelligible accounts of action if they are always led back to the economic. In short, Foucault's account of the social redisposes dialectical reasoning away from the grand stage of history and towards an analysis of conjunctures.

Despite these differences, it will be my contention that an opposition between Foucault and Marxism is misplaced; that these formations can be fruitfully combined. Support for this position can be found both in Foucault's writings and their uptake at the intersection of Cultural Studies and sport, where he has latterly joined the pantheon of approved parents of social and cultural theory in the canon of Anglo writings. The chapter takes us successively through his relations to Marxism and to sport, including the uptake of his work by Cultural Studies and Sociology.[1]

. . . And Marx

Foucault's principal quibble with Marx and his true believers lay in their focus on class, to the comparative exclusion of struggle.[2] He complained that the second half of the grand dialectical couplet received less than equal treatment, specifically the precise materialities of power that were not simply about accreting *bourgeois* dominance or state authority – hence his close archival readings and engaged political actions, re prisons, hospitals and asylums. This research and activism revealed the micropolitics of forming and controlling subjects in ways that cannot be read off from macroeconomic blocs, a micropolitics that is as much to do with dispensing power as accumulating or exercising it (Foucault, 1982: 782 and 1980: 58). But Foucault drew extensively on Marx to construct homologies between civil and military training via 'docile bodies', comparing the division of labour to the organization of infantry. *Discipline and Punish* (Foucault, 1979a) has many Marxist features in its model of the development of disciplinary power inside capitalism, demonstrating how élites addressed the interrelated problems of sustaining a productive and compliant labour force and social order.

Foucault's studies and public-intellectual contributions have been important examples and inspirations to leftists living under authoritarian regimes, such as the Argentine *junta* (Abraham *et al.*, 2004). And he was forever engaging Marxism as embodied in two particularly influential French intellectual formations of his era – the humanism of Jean-Paul Sartre and the structuralism of Louis Althusser (who taught Foucault). The many political actions and interviews Foucault participated in were either shared with Sartre or inspired by his example, for all that the reasoning subject at the heart of existentialism was as foreign to Foucault's projects as its equivalent in bourgeois Anglo-Yanqui liberalism. It is worth recalling Foucault's recommendation to 'open Althusser's books', and the latter's contention that 'something from my writings has passed into his' (Foucault, 1989: 14 and Althusser, 1969: 256). As Foucault (1991b: 55) said of their relationship, 'I followed'. There is a significant link between the two men's views on the relations between subjects, objects, representation and interpretation. The accusation of functionalist Marxism sometimes levelled at Althusser, because of his totalizing view of ideological apparatuses, is similar to certain critics' lament for the absence of an outside to power in Foucault's account of discipline. Of course, there are major methodological differences as well as similarities. Althusser investigates problematics and their underpinning ideology in the context of the real. Conversely, Foucault looks at statements, their preconditions, and their settings in discursive formations, then moves on to research a related archive. Only Althusser privileges science, however veiled it may be by class (Miller, 1994).

Perhaps the most subtle and complex engagement between Foucault and Marxism emerged over the state. Roland Barthes (1973: 130) coined the term 'governmentality' during the high point of his own Marxism to describe market variations and the state's attempt to claim responsibility for them (when the outcome was positive). It was an ironic neologism, one that Foucault (1991b: 4) developed to account for 'the way in which the modern state began to worry about individuals' by asking: 'How to govern oneself, how to be governed, how to govern others, by whom the people will accept being governed, how to become the best possible governor.' These issues arose as twin processes: the displacement of feudalism by the sovereign state, and the similarly conflictual Reformation and its counters. Daily economic and spiritual government came up for redefinition. While the state emerged as a centralizing tendency that sought to normalize itself and others, a devolved religious authority was producing a void, via ecclesiastical conflicts and debates about divine right. The doctrine of transcendence fell into crisis, with royalty now representing managerial rather than immanent rule (Foucault, 1991a: 87–90).

With the upheavals of the seventeenth century, such as the Thirty Years War and rural and urban revolt, the conditions for implementing new modes of social organization arose. In eighteenth-century Europe, the government of territory became secondary to the government of things and social relations. Government was conceived and actualized in terms of climate, disease, industry, finance, custom and disaster – literally, a concern with life and death, and what could be calculated and managed between them. Wealth and health became goals to be attained through the disposition of capacities across the population once 'biological existence was reflected in political existence' through 'bio-power'. Bio-power brought 'life and its mechanisms into the realm of explicit calculations' and made 'knowledge-power an agent of transformation of human life'. Bodies were identified with politics, because managing them was part of running the country, with 'the life of the species . . . wagered on its own political strategies' (Foucault, 1991a: 97, 92–5 and 1984: 143).

The arts of government were freed from the strictures imposed by sovereign and household *motifs*. Not only did the population displace the prince as a site for accumulating power, but the home was displaced by the economy as a newly anthropomorphized and international dynamic of social intervention and achievement. The populace became the province of statistics, bounded not by the direct exertion of juridical influence or domestic authority, but by forms of knowledge that granted 'the people' a life that could not be divined from the model of the family. City, country and empire substituted for home, with all the hierarchical dislocation that implies. The epidemic and the map displaced the kitchen and the church (Foucault, 1991a: 98–9).

Governing people came to mean, most centrally and critically, obeying the 'imperative of health: at once the duty of each and the objective of all'. So even as revolutionary France was embarking on a regime of slaughter, public-health campaigns were under way. The state constructed an ongoing Janus-faced 'game between death and life' (Foucault, 1991b: 277, 4). Clearly, the emergence of modern capitalism connected to the rise of the state, which was concerned to deliver a docile and healthy labour force to business; but not only to business, and not merely in a way that showed the lineage of that desire. Cholera, sanitation and prostitution were figured as problems for governments to address in the modern era, through 'the emergence of the health and physical well-being of the population in general as one of the essential objectives of political power'. The entire 'social body' was assayed and treated for its insufficiencies. In shifting its tasks from naked, controlling power to generative, productive power, government in general increasingly aimed to '"make live and 'let' die", as well as "take life or let live"' (Foucault, 2003: 241).

The critical shift here was away from an accumulation of power by the sovereign, and towards the dispersal of power into the population. The centre invested people with the capacity to produce and consume things, insisting on freedom in some compartments of life, and obedience in others (Foucault, 1994: 125). Out of that came the following prospect: 'Maybe what is really important for our modernity – that is, for our present – is not so much the étatisation of society, as the governmentalization of the state' (Foucault, 1991a: 103). The 'problem of the central soul' of the state was immanent in 'multiple peripheral bodies' and the messy labour of controlling them. Such a move allowed for 'transformation not at the level of political theory, but rather at the level of the mechanisms, techniques, and technologies of power' (Foucault, 2003: 37, 29, 241). So Foucault sought to uncover the history of how mental conditions were identified as problems in need of treatment, with the aim of explaining how these forms of demographic problematization functioned as techniques, economies, social relations and knowledges, such that 'some real existent in the world' became 'the target of social regulation at a given moment' (1994: 123 and 2001: 171). He was careful to avoid arguing that madness did not exist, or was a product of medicine: 'people are suffering . . . people make trouble in society or in their families, that is a reality'. But he contended that when psychiatry intervened in the legal field of Western societies, it established the right to define individuals as sane or otherwise, and claimed a role in justice and punishment – two key forms of demographic management (Foucault, 2000: 176–200).

Foucault proposed a threefold concept of governmentality to explain life today. The first utilizes economics to mould the population into efficient and effective producers. The second is an array of apparatuses designed to create conditions for this productivity, via bodily interventions and the promotion of fealty and individuality (bio-power). And the third is the translation of methods between education and penology that modifies justice into human 'improvement'. Put another way, we might understand this as the indoctrination of the state by the social – and the infestation of sovereignty with demography (Foucault, 1991a: 102–3). Governmentality centres the population as desiring, producing and committed subjects with manifest contradictions. But this does not imply an ever-increasing state sector. In Foucault's words, the market has latterly become 'a "test", a locus of privileged experience where one . . . [can] identify the effects of excessive governmentality' (Foucault, 1997: 76). This is a way of resituating management of the social squarely within civil society – a transformation in governmentality. As he argued, 'civil society is the concrete ensemble within which these abstract points, economic men, need to be positioned in order to be made adequately manageable' (Foucault, 1979b). For Foucault, technologies of governance organize the public by having it organize itself, through the material inscription of discourse into policies and programmes of the state and capital. He defines a technology as 'a matrix of popular reason'. It has four categories: 'technologies of production' make for the physical transformation of material objects; 'technologies of sign systems' are semiotic; 'technologies of power' form subjects as a means of dominating individuals and encouraging them to define themselves in particular ways; and 'technologies of the self' are applied by individuals to make themselves autotelically happy (Foucault, 1988b: 18). Is this so far from Marxism?

. . . And sport

The articulations between Foucault and sport start with his own direct address of the topic, in the context of an ethics of the self and advertisements for fitness to rule others. He undertook this analysis by examining Western philosophy's origins. In ancient Greece and Rome, the body was the *locus* for an ethics of the self, a combat with pleasure and pain that enabled people to find the truth about themselves and master their drives (Foucault, 1986: 66–9). Austerity and hedonism could be combined through training:

> The metaphor of the match, of athletic competition and battle, did not serve merely to designate the nature of the relationship one had with desires and pleasures, with their force that was always liable to turn seditious or rebellious; it also related to the preparation that enabled one to withstand such a confrontation.
>
> (*Ibid.*: 72)

Xenophon, Socrates and Diogenes held that sexual excess and decadence came from the equivalent of sporting success. In sex and sport, triumph could lead to failure, unless accompanied by regular examination of the conscience, and physical training. Carefully modulated desire in both spheres became a sign of the ability to govern. Aristotle and Plato favoured regular, ongoing flirtations with excess, as tests as well as pleasures. This ethos was distinctly gendered: the capacity of young men to move into positions of social responsibility was judged by charioteering and man-management. Their ability to win 'the little sports drama' was akin to dealing with sexually predatory older males (Foucault, 1986: 72–7, 104, 120, 197–8, 212).

Five hundred years later, Roman sexual ethics attached anxieties to the body and sport. Spirituality had emerged to complicate exercises of the self as a means of training for governance:

> The increased medical involvement in the cultivation of the self appears to have been expressed through a particular and intense form of attention to the body. This attention is very different from that manifested by the positive valuation of physical vigour during an epoch when gymnastics and athletic and military training were an integral part of the education of a free man. Moreover, it has something paradoxical about it since it is inscribed, at least in part, within an ethics that posits that death, disease, or even physical suffering do not constitute true ills and that it is better to take pains over one's soul than to devote one's care to the maintenance of the body. But in fact the focus of attention in these practices of the self is the point where the ills of the body and those of the soul can communicate with one another and exchange their distresses; where the bad habits of the soul can entail physical miseries, while the excesses of the body manifest and maintain the failings of the soul . . . The body the adult has to care for, when he is concerned about himself, is no longer the young body that needed shaping by gymnastics; it is a fragile, threatened body, undermined by petty miseries.
>
> (Foucault, 1988b: 56–7)

In place of personal excesses, which had preoccupied fourth-century BC Athens, first-century AD Rome was principally concerned with frailty – the finitude of fitness and life itself. Arguments were imbued with 'nature and reason', and exercises of the self joined this more elevated search for truth (Foucault, 1988b: 238–9). Foucault's studies indicate how sex has been central to social control, in two senses. On the one hand, it is subject to individual control methods for managing desire. On the other, it is subject to collective methods for managing procreation (Foucault, 2003: 251).

So what has the Cultural Studies of Sport done with this example, and other directions suggested by his contributions?[3] It is still possible to publish a (very good) progressive sociology-of-sport textbook without mentioning Foucault and his legacy (Horne *et al.*, 1999) but even here there is some discussion of discipline, so encrusted in contemporary social theory is this Foucauldian contribution (*ibid.*: 10–11). Other fine texts are more overt in their debt (Rowe, 1999: 33). In addition to proposals to write a genealogy of sport (de la Vega, 1999), there have been some excellent meta-introductions for the normal scientists of functionalism and kinesiology (Andrews, 1993 and Cole *et al.*, 2004, for instance). Dave Andrews and C.L. Cole, both collectively and individually, have shown that Foucault's work can be providential for political economy, feminism and critical race theory as applied to sport, through their investigations of topics from basketball to advertising, celebrity feminism to journal gatekeeping. They manage to maintain the non-humanist base to Foucault, and his commitment to discourse and power, without losing the significance of social movements and the political economy, unlike many celebrants and critics.

But numerous sports scholars are ambivalent about Foucault's legacy, or condemnatory of it. Some of this concern comes from structural-functionalists, who once owned the field and are stuck on the margins with sociobiologists; some from their fellow travellers in kinesiology who want to measure the angle at which feet come down to strike balls; and some from the left – the ones that concern me, since the others are unlikely to read what I have to say in a forum such as this.

Feminist critiques and Gramscian-inflected ideas of hegemony have provided vital means of attacking the prior dominance of reactionary celebrations and instrumentalizations of sport. Gramsci offers a model of power located in specific agents. A frustration for many of his followers is that Foucault is seen as endowing power with an agency of its own, at the same time as subjects of history are eviscerated (see Gruneau, 1993, 1999). Ruing his own marginality in French academic life, the Trotskyite Jean-Marie Brohm scorns any eclecticism that assumes Foucault can be mixed and matched with Marxist methods, because of the primacy that 'must' be given to means and modes of production and class struggle (Brohm and Bui-Xuan, 2005). Before his latter-day descent into lapsed leftism, John Hargreaves (1986: 135) alerted readers to 'the danger of a Foucaultian analysis of consumer culture', which apparently lies in 'the implication that control programmes actually achieve their desired effects'. Ian Henry (2001: 3) bizarrely argues that there has been virtually no Foucauldian influence on studies of leisure policy. Garry Robson's attempted recuperation of Millwall Football Club fans from the dustbin of racist proletarian masculinism (Robson, 2000: 71–2, 77) is critical of the supposed 'passivity' inscribed on people by Foucault. And Valda Burstyn (1999: 33) thinks that gendered sporting power is solidly tied to the expression of interests, rather than being multifaceted, as per Foucauldian feminism.

I think these critiques are wrong. Subjects are very present in Foucault – the mad, the ill, the deviant, the incarcerated – and ever present in his political actions with those same groups, as are immigrants, with race and nation key categories in his work that are often ignored by critics (Foucault, 2003). So when a rather unfortunate metaphor is chosen to argue against 'swallowing Foucault whole' (Gruneau, 1993: 103) because of a supposed denial of agency, this is as inaccurate as it is unfortunate. As we have seen, the subject is neither a point of origin in Foucault nor a destination, because subjects vary with time and space. This is an affront to conceptions of consciousness that posit the reasoning person at the heart of social activity. But it does not in any way preclude politics, choice, or social-movement activism. If there were no room for agency, why have so many feminists, queers, medical professionals, prison activists and post-colonial critics found things of value here for their political practice?

We are also sometimes told, by both protagonists and antagonists, that Foucault's legacy stands opposed to grand narratives. As a consequence his influence is deemed either baleful or useful, based on the analyst's views of power and discourse (Wiggins and Mason, 2005: 48; Markula and Denison, 2005: 166; Morgan, 1995). Sometimes Foucault is valorized for decentring traditional norms of writing and agents of history. At others, he is derided for encouraging sectarian social movements and irrationality. This idealist version of Foucault says he discounts the real in favour of a focus on language, licensing a kind of Barthesian or Derridoidal free play of the signifier. Again, it seems misleading, given what I have outlined. Foucault was attracted by philosophy at the limit, but he was equally concerned with the manufacture and governance of rules – and their inevitability.

It is clear to most critical scholars that industrialized and post-industrialized societies subject people to bodily and ethical regimes that equate body and mind: a visual economy of public and private sites. With the body a 'site of condensation for a whole range of social anxieties' in the neo-liberal era of self-responsibility, moral panics and calculations of risk became diurnal forms of social control and calculation, rendering the disciplined body a key analytic tool (King, 2005: 25–6). This Foucauldian insight has proven especially fruitful in engaging the impact of masculinity on sport, and sporting masculinity on society (Mangan, 1999: 12 and Pringle, 2005). A trend towards ruling-class control of male sport is structurally homologous with, and historically connected to, state monopolies on legitimate violence. The work of governments in normalizing sport has been crucial: policing holidays to standardize vacations and regularize recreation as play and spectatorship, securing the conditions of existence for a partial commodification that makes sport governed rather than classically competitive, and allocating resources to sport as a diplomatic symbol and domestic training mechanism. The state is also concerned about sport as a route to improved urban public health, military fitness, and the diversion of rebellious politics. From Chancellor Hitler and Marshal Pétain to President Carter, modern heads of state have initiated physical-fitness tests to invigorate and ideologize the young.

Scholars have found much of value in Foucault's work to help analyse these developments. Numerous investigations have been made of school sports, marching, military drills, gymnastics and physical education (PE). David Kirk (1998) has demonstrated how gendered regimes of corporeal regulation, individualization and differentiation underpinned PE in colonial and post-colonial Australia, intersecting with eugenics, racism and national efficiency and fitness. Beyond white-settler histories, Foucault's work has also stimulated enquiry into the South Asian body disciplined through sport (Mills and Dimeo, 2003). Despite misgivings, John Hargreaves (1986) argues that the cardinal values of contemporary school sport and PE programmes are disciplinary, and Burstyn (1999: 78–9, 99) uses Foucault's history of the body. Jean Harvey and Robert Sparks (1991) show how PE and gymnastics in the late nineteenth century dovetailed with bio-power, Susan Brownell (2000) looks at China disciplining its citizenry through sport, and Helena Wulff (2003) examines the nationalist rhetoric of Irish dance as social control.

Beyond PE, consider these sites of Foucauldian influence: investigations of football[4] 'hooligans' that reject both their romantic annunciation as working-class scions and their criminalization via moral panics (Armstrong and Young, 1997 and Armstrong, 1998); evaluations of the panoptic design of contemporary football stadiums (Giulianotti, 1999: 80–2); studies of masculinist domination and feminist resistance and critique (Jennifer Hargreaves, 1994; Duncan, 1994; Montez de Oca, 2005; Rahilly, 2005; Pringle, 2005; Chisholm, 1999, 2002); interrogations of women's football and cultural citizenship (Giardina and Metz, 2005); and analyses of racism (Ismond, 2003; King and Springwood, 2001; Gardiner and Welch, 2001).

Cole (1998) notes that sporting bodies are powerful symbols because they appear to embody free will, self-control, health, productivity and transcendence (also see MacNeill, 1998). Patricia Vertinsky (1998) highlights the medical-ization of women's bodies in the Victorian era, which still permeates health-and-fitness-promotion campaigns. Since the Second World War, additional factors have made bio-power crucial. The contest for international sporting supremacy between the former protagonists in the Cold War, developments in pharmaceu-tical research, increasing commodification, and the dominance of instrumental rationality have seen biomedical science applied to enhance performance and identify deviance. Shari Lee Dworkin and Faye Linda Wachs (2000) make effective use of Foucault to investigate HIV panics and athletes (also see Pronger, 1998). Samantha King (2001) questions the corporate social responsibility ethos of companies that use fitness to elevate their public standing. Why should these accounts be regarded as incommensurate with studies of the labour process or ideology (Giulianotti, 1999: 108–9)?

. . . And Miller

And me? I'm a wee bit tentative writing about my own formation in these matters, but we've been asked to address this topic by the editors. 'Worried' not because I am concerned about self-disclosure – who cares? – but because I inhabit the *land* of self-disclosure. The first country in world history with the majority of its population living in suburbia, the United States compensates for this low-density retreat into sameness by fetishizing the self in a way that I find rather banal. And it has a corollary in US culturalist academics' fascination with revealing their really rather dull selves and psyches in public. That said, I've blended Marxism and Foucault throughout my work on sport over the last two decades, both collaboratively and alone. The most recent examples are *Globalization and Sport* and *SportSex* (Miller *et al.*, 2001 and Miller, 2001). They had earlier lives in conference papers, journal articles and book chapters from the late 1980s. And I frequently sit astounded as I confront oppositions drawn by many scholars between Marxism and Foucault. For me, it is the most obvious thing in the world to look at the materiality of discourse, to grant it the status of social relations, to consider it in terms of institutions and power, to disavow the notion of a super-structure that reflects a substructure, to think of Foucault as a post-industrial

Marx, to look at them in a way that says 'and' rather than 'or' – and not to worry about the bad readings of Foucault that license anti-Marxism or ludic silliness. While Foucault does not outline how to undertake a political economy of institutions based on ownership, he does encourage and guide analysis of their control; while he does not address class issues in great detail or as the motor of history, he looks at the implications of power as expressed over the bodies of the weak, the impoverished and the disenfranchised; and while he is not arguing for the economy as the centre of research and action, he is mindful of it.

Sport is a key site of pleasure and domination, via a complex dialectic that does not always produce a clear synthesis from the clash of opposing camps. It involves both the imposition of authority from above and the joy of autonomy from below. It exemplifies the exploitation of the labour process, even as it delivers autotelic pleasures. And these dualities, the tensions they embody, are nowhere better analysed than with the tools provided by Marx and Foucault. What does this mean in political terms? It means being strategic and tactical – allowing for the temper of the times, while taking certain precepts as non-negotiable. Market socialism is fine with me, as is a notion of power as polyvalent and polymorphous. Sectarianism that practises exploitative and domineering politics, such as nationalism or hierarchical control of the labour process, is not. Ideas of freedom and choice that operate from the notion of a pre-existent, ratiocinative subject are naïve. The elevation of sport as a transcendent form of life, beyond the social or embodying its best aspects, is ridiculous. Conversely, the notion of sport as a technique of the self that is equally a technique of domination makes sense. It suggests a search for the political technology *and* the political economy of popular subjectivity. That looks like a good agenda for the Cultural Studies of Sport.

Notes

1 Thanks to the editors for their work on an earlier draft. I have sought to incorporate as many of their changes as I could without becoming as polite as they are, and while acknowledging that I am, as they say in sport, too old, too fat and too slow to enter on 'a crazed bibliographic gallop' (Downing and Husband, 2005: 25). This chapter does not refer to every usage of Foucault and/versus Marxism within Sport Studies.
2 For a useful primer on Marxism within the social sciences, in which several essays take various positions on Foucault, see Gamble *et al.* (1999).
3 Not all the scholars used here would identify themselves as Marxist, or as working within Cultural Studies, but they generally adopt a critical rather than celebratory or neutral outlook on professional sport, and address questions of power and inequality.
4 I refer here to real football, not the sixty-minute stroll sixteen times a year that laughably claims the name in the Yanqui lexicon.

References

Abraham, T., G. García, L. Chitarroni, E. Díaz, L. Gusman and E. Castro (2004) 'Aquel filósofo que escribía cajas llenas de herramientas', *Página 12*, 25 June, at http://www.pagina12.com.ar/diario/cultura/7-37176-2004-06-25.html.

Althusser, L. (1969) *For Marx*, trans. B. Brewster, Harmondsworth: Penguin.

Andrews, D. (1993) 'Desperately Seeking Michel: Foucault's Genealogy, the Body, and Critical Sport Sociology', *Sociology of Sport Journal* 10(2), pp. 148–67.

Armstrong, G. (1998) *Football Hooligans: Knowing the Score*, Oxford: Berg.

Armstrong, G. and M. Young (1997) 'Legislators and Interpreters: The Law and "Football Hooligans"', in G. Armstrong and R. Giulianotti (eds) *Entering the Field: New Perspectives on World Football*, Oxford: Berg, pp. 175–91.

Barthes, R. (1973) *Mythologies*, trans. A. Lavers, London: Paladin.

Brohm, J.-M. and G. Bui-Xuan (2005) 'Nouveau millénaire, Défis libertaires', at http://1libertaire.free.fr/Brohm05.html.

Brownell, S. (2000) 'Why Should an Anthropologist Study Sports in China?', in N. Dyck (ed.) *Games, Sports and Cultures*, Oxford: Berg, pp. 43–63.

Burstyn, V. (1999) *The Rites of Men: Manhood, Politics, and the Culture of Sport*, Toronto: University of Toronto Press.

Chisholm, A. (1999) 'Defending the Nation: National Bodies, US Borders, and the 1996 US Olympic Women's Gymnastic Team', *Journal of Sport and Social Issues* 23(2), pp. 126–39.

Chisholm, A. (2002) 'Acrobats, Contortionists, and Cute Children: The Promise and Perversity of US Women's Gymnastics', *Signs* 27(2), pp. 415–50.

Cole, C.L. (1998) 'Addiction, Exercise, and Cyborgs: Technologies of Deviant Bodies', in G. Rail (ed.) *Sport and Postmodern Times*, Albany: State University of New York Press, pp. 261–75.

Cole, C.L., M.D. Giardina and D.L. Andrews (2004) 'Michel Foucault: Studies of Power and Sport', in R. Giulanotti (ed.) *Sport and Modern Social Theorists*, Houndsmills: Palgrave, pp. 207–23.

de la Vega, E. (1999) 'La función política del deporte: Notas para una genealogía', *EF y deportes* 4(17), at http://www.efdeportes.com/efd17/edelav.htm.

Downing, J. and C. Husband (2005) *Representing 'Race': Racisms, Ethnicities and Media*, London: Sage.

Duncan, M.C. (1994) 'Sports Photographs and Sexual Difference: Images of Women and Men in the 1984 and 1988 Olympic Games', *Sociology of Sport Journal* 7(1), pp. 22–43.

Dworkin, S.L. and F.L. Wachs (2000) '"Disciplining the Body": HIV-Positive Male Athletes, Media Surveillance, and the Policing of Sexuality', in S. Birrell and M.G. McDonald (eds) *Reading Sport: Critical Essays on Power and Representation*, Boston: Northeastern University Press, pp. 251–78.

Foucault, M. (1979a) *Discipline and Punish: The Birth of the Prison*, trans. A. Sheridan, New York: Vintage.

Foucault, M. (1979b) Lecture, Collège de France, 4 April.

Foucault, M. (1980) 'Body/Power', in *idem*, *Power-Knowledge: Selected Interviews and Other Writings 1972–77*, ed. C. Gordon, New York: Pantheon, pp. 55–62.

Foucault, M. (1982) 'The Subject and Power', trans. L. Sawyer, *Critical Inquiry* 8(4), pp. 777–95.

Foucault, M. (1983) 'How We Behave', *Vanity Fair* November, pp. 66–7.

Foucault, M. (1984) *The History of Sexuality: An Introduction*, trans. R. Hurley, Harmondsworth: Penguin.

Foucault, M. (1986) *The Use of Pleasure: The History of Sexuality Volume Two*, trans. R. Hurley, New York: Vintage.

Foucault, M. (1988a) *Technologies of the Self: A Seminar with Michel Foucault*, ed. L.H. Martin, P.H. Hutton and H. Gutman, London: Tavistock.

Foucault, M. (1988b) *The Care of the Self: Volume 3 of The History of Sexuality*, trans. R. Hurley, New York: Vintage.

Foucault, M. (1989) 'The Discourse of History', trans. J. Johnston, in *idem*, *Foucault Live: (Interviews, 1966–84)*, ed. S. Lotringer, New York: Semiotext(e), pp. 11–34.

Foucault, M. (1991a) 'Governmentality', trans. P. Pasquino, in G. Burchell, C. Gordon and P. Miller (eds) *The Foucault Effect: Studies in Governmentality*, London: Harvester Wheatsheaf, pp. 87–104.

Foucault, M. (1991b) *Remarks on Marx: Conversations with Duccio Trombadori*, trans. R.J. Goldstein and J. Cascaito, New York: Semiotext(e).

Foucault, M. (1994) 'Problematics: Excerpts from Conversations', in R. Reynolds and T. Zummer (eds) *Crash: Nostalgia for the Absence of Cyberspace*, New York: Third Waxing Space, pp. 121–7.

Foucault, M. (1997) *Ethics: Subjectivity and Truth: The Essential Works of Foucault 1954–1984 Volume One*, ed. P. Rabinow, trans. R. Hurley *et al.*, New York: Free Press.

Foucault, M. (2000) *Power: Essential Works of Foucault 1954–1984 Volume Three*, ed. J.D. Faubion, New York: New Press.

Foucault, M. (2001) *Fearless Speech*, ed. J. Pearson, Los Angeles: Semiotext(e).

Foucault, M. (2003) *'Society Must Be Defended': Lectures at the Collège de France 1975–1976*, trans. D. Macey, ed. M. Bertani and A. Fontana, New York: Picador.

Gamble, A., D. Marsh, and T. Tant (eds) (1999) *Marxism and Social Science*, Urbana: University of Illinois Press.

Gardiner, S. and R. Welch (2001) 'Sport, Racism and the Limits of "Colour Blind" Law', in B. Carrington and I. McDonald (eds) *'Race', Sport and British Society*, London: Routledge, pp. 133–49.

Giardina, M.D. and J.L. Metz (2005) 'All-American Girls? Corporatizing National Identity and Cultural Citizenship with/in the WUSA', in M.L. Silk, D.L. Andrews and C.L. Cole (eds) *Sport and Corporate Nationalisms*, Oxford: Berg, pp. 109–26.

Giulianotti, R. (1999) *Football: A Sociology of the Global Game*, Cambridge: Polity.

Gruneau, R. (1993) 'The Critique of Sport in Modernity: Theorizing Power, Culture, and the Politics of the Body', in E. Dunning, J.A. Maguire and R.E. Pearton (eds) *The Sports Process: A Comparative and Developmental Approach*, Champaign: Human Kinetics, pp. 85–109.

Gruneau, R. (1999) *Class, Sports and Social Development*, rev. edn, Champaign: Human Kinetics.

Hargreaves, Jennifer (1994) *Sporting Females: Critical Issues in the History and Sociology of Women's Sports*, London: Routledge.

Hargreaves, John (1986) *Sport, Power and Culture: A Social and Historical Analysis of Popular Sports in Britain*, Oxford: Polity Press.

Harvey, J. and R. Sparks (1991) 'The Politics of the Body in the Context of Modernity', *Quest* 43(2), pp. 164–89.

Henry, I. (2001) *The Politics of Leisure Policy*, 2nd edn, Houndsmills: Palgrave.

Horne, J., A. Tomlinson and G. Whannel (1999) *Understanding Sport: An Introduction to the Sociological and Cultural Analysis of Sport*, London: E & FN Spon.

Ismond, P. (2003) *Black and Asian Athletes in British Sport and Society: A Sporting Chance?*, Houndsmills: Palgrave.

King, C.R. and C.F. Springwood (2001) *Beyond the Cheers: Race as Spectacle in College Sport*, Albany: State University of New York Press.

King, S. (2001). 'An All-Consuming Cause: Breast Cancer, Corporate Philanthropy, and the Market for Generosity', *Social Text* 69, pp. 115–43.

King, S. (2005) 'Methodological Contingencies in Sports Studies', in D.L. Andrews, D.S. Mason and M.L. Silk (eds) *Qualitative Methods in Sports Studies*, Oxford: Berg, pp. 21–38.

Kirk, D. (1998) *Schooling Bodies: School Practice and Public Discourse*, London: Leicester University Press.

MacNeill, M. (1998) 'Sex, Lies, and Videotape: The Political and Cultural Economies of Celebrity Fitness Videos', in G. Rail (ed.) *Sport and Postmodern Times*, Albany: State University of New York Press, pp. 163–84.

Mangan, J.A. (1999) 'The Potent Image and the Permanent Prometheus', in J.A. Mangan (ed.) *Shaping the Superman: Fascist Body as Political Icon of Aryan Fascism*, London: Frank Cass, pp. 11–22.

Markula, P. and J. Denison (2005) 'Sport and the Personal Narrative', in D.L. Andrews, D.S. Mason and M.L. Silk (eds) *Qualitative Methods in Sports Studies*, Oxford: Berg, pp. 165–84.

Miller, T. (1994) 'Althusser, Foucault and the Subject of Civility', *Studies in Twentieth Century Literature* 18(1), pp. 97–117.

Miller, T. (2001) *SportSex*, Philadelphia: Temple University Press.

Miller, T., G. Lawrence, J. McKay and D. Rowe (2001) *Globalization and Sport: Playing the World*, London: Sage.

Mills, J. and P. Dimeo (2003) '"When Gold is Fired it Shines": Sport, the Imagination and the Body in Colonial and Postcolonial India', in J. Bale and M. Cronin (eds) *Sport and Postcolonialism*, Oxford: Berg, pp. 107–22.

Montez de Oca, J. (2005) '"As Our Muscles Get Softer, Our Missile Race Becomes Harder": Cultural Citizenship and the "Muscle Gap"', *Journal of Historical Sociology* 18(3), pp. 145–72.

Morgan, W.W. (1995) '"Incredulity Toward Metanarratives" and Normative Suicide: A Critique of Postmodernist Drift in Critical Sport Theory', *International Review for the Sociology of Sport* 30(1), pp. 25–45.

Pringle, R. (2005) 'Masculinities, Sport, and Power: A Critical Comparison of Gramscian and Foucauldian Inspired Theoretical Tools', *Journal of Sport and Social Issues* 29(3), pp. 256–78.

Pronger, B. (1998) 'Post-Sport: Transgressing Boundaries in Physical Culture', in G. Rail (ed.) *Sport and Postmodern Times*, Albany: State University of New York Press, pp. 277–98.

Rahilly, L. (2005) 'Is *RAW* War?: Professional Wrestling as Popular S/M Narrative', in N. Sammond (ed.) *Steel Chair to the Head: The Pleasure and Pain of Professional Wrestling*, Durham, NC: Duke University Press, pp. 213–31.

Robson, G. (2000) *'No One Likes Us, We Don't Care': The Myth and Reality of Millwall Fandom*, New York: Berg.

Rowe, D. (1999) *Sport, Culture and the Media: The Unruly Trinity*, Buckingham: Open University Press.

Vertinsky, P. (1998) '"Run, Jane, Run": Central Tensions in the Current Debate about Enhancing Women's Health Through Exercise', *Women and Health* 27(4), pp. 81–111.

Wiggins, D.K. and D.S. Mason (2005) 'The Socio-Historical Process in Sport Studies', in D.L. Andrews, D.S. Mason and M.L. Silk (eds) *Qualitative Methods in Sports Studies*, Oxford: Berg, pp. 39–64.

Wulff, H. (2003) 'The Irish Body in Motion: Moral Politics, National Identity and Dance', in N. Dyck and E.P. Archetti (eds) *Sport, Dance and Embodied Identities*, Oxford: Berg, pp. 179–96.

11 Re-appropriating Gramsci
Marxism, hegemony and sport

Alan Bairner

I have often been asked why do Labour leaders show such hatred towards the Communists? Why do so many of them betray the movement? The answer to this is simple. It is because their social relations and social life is in such sharp contradiction to the impulse of the movement of which they have become leaders. Always, members of the middle class have seen the advantage of using the working class in order to force concessions from the big bourgeoisie. But always they have been afraid of the working class getting out of hand. A well-behaved working class, responsive to the guiding hand of the 'better educated' middle class is the ideal for which they aim. So periodically these well-disposed gentlemen will speak at a public meeting and identify themselves with the aims and desires of the workers; that is essential if they are to get the support of the workers for their aims and desires. Being so much better fitted for the job, on account of their greater experience and higher education, they will graciously agree to represent the workers in Parliament. But all the time, between periodic meetings, their social life is something entirely apart from the workers and the movement which the workers with so much sacrifice have sought to build. This social life of theirs, so pleasant, so interesting and in many ways so indolent, must on no account be disturbed by wild, uncontrolled action on the part of the working class. On the other hand, if the big bourgeoisie becomes too rapacious, a clash is almost sure to follow. They have a double task, therefore, to persuade the big bourgeoisie to moderate their exploitation and to keep the workers under control while their persuasive powers are operating.

William Gallacher, The Rolling of the Thunder

Introduction

These words were written in 1948 by William Gallacher, the British Communist Party Member of Parliament for the West Fife constituency. They make very clear the differences between reformist socialists and Marxists. Today, however, that distinction is increasingly blurred, if not entirely obliterated, not least by the false friends of certain Marxist thinkers, one of them being Antonio Gramsci, a founding member of the Communist Party of Italy, a committed Marxist who died at the age of forty-six having spent more than nine years in the hands of his Fascist captors. This chapter represents part of an ongoing project aimed at the re-appropriation of Antonio Gramsci (Bairner, 2007). This involves re-appropriating Gramsci and his work *for* Marxism and also *from* scholars in the sociology of sport and beyond who have consciously or unconsciously used Gramsci's ideas in ways that have inevitably meant that his own Marxist orientation has become conveniently forgotten.

The idea of re-appropriating Gramsci was prompted by a growing concern that students of the sociology of sport have little knowledge of the intellectual origins and political objectives of Gramsci's thought, despite their regular reference to his work. This in turn is linked to a more general concern that Gramsci has been appropriated by scholars whose primary interest is in the politics of identity as opposed to the politics of class struggle. It is certainly undeniable that many sociologists of sport together with many other social scientists have been inspired by Gramsci's ideas and have sought to apply them for their own theoretical purposes. The consequence of much of this, however, might best be described as a re-making of Gramsci. The Gramsci with whom students of sports sociology become familiar is not so much the historical figure as a partially invented or imagined one. Re-appropriating Gramsci for Marxism specifically involves ensuring that his appreciation of the ultimate primacy of material conditions is properly understood and that his concept of hegemony is recognized as involving a dialectical relationship between force and consent as opposed to the substitution of the former by the latter. Understanding the reasons for his appeal represents the first stage in this re-appropriation project.

Gramsci's appeal

With the possible exceptions of Norbert Elias, Michel Foucault and Pierre Bourdieu, Antonio Gramsci has arguably become the most frequently cited theorist in literature on the social and political significance of sport. This is in keeping with a more general trend in the social sciences whereby Gramsci became the favourite author of scholars who had lost faith in orthodox Marxism and were looking for theoretical insights that would allow them to retain a radical impulse while simultaneously rejecting both deterministic analysis and Stalinist politics. Gramsci was particularly useful in the latter respect for the simple reason that, having died in 1937, he had not been forced to address the failings of Soviet-style communism, a recognition of which was largely responsible for a widespread rejection of Marxist ideas in general. Inspired by a perceived need to replace official Marxism–Leninism, many on the political left sought out versions of Marxism that embraced the concept of democracy as understood in liberal political debate and that did not espouse dogmatic economic determinism. For this reason, the work of Gramsci and other supposedly unorthodox Western Marxists was seized upon. Increasingly, however, what is Marxist in the writings of such thinkers has been pushed to one side or, if this could not be successfully achieved, as in the case of Karl Korsch, their work has been ignored almost completely.

In the case of Gramsci, it was on the basis of perceptions of his understanding of the relationship between base and superstructure that his contribution was so enthusiastically seized upon by neo-Marxist Sociology and by Cultural Studies. It became widely accepted that Gramsci offers more scope for human agency than is permitted by orthodox Marxist theory. What is conveniently forgotten here is that Marx (1972: 10) himself wrote that 'Men make their own history', although he added, in words that are not inconsistent with anything that Gramsci appears to have believed, that 'they do not make it just as they please; they do not make it under circumstances chosen by themselves, but under circumstances directly encountered, given and transmitted from the past'. In addition, it was argued that Gramsci's concept of hegemony, while offering a subtle explanation of how ruling élites govern in Western societies, points to the very real possibility of resistance not only in relation to the politics of class but within the context of race, gender, nationalism and so on. Furthermore, and of specific relevance to this chapter, by apparently according special importance to superstructural phenomena, Gramsci's ideas allowed for the possibility that Marxist and socialist intellectuals could begin to take seriously all forms of culture, sport included.

Of course, not all socialists prior to the upsurge of interest in Gramsci's thought had adopted an élitist perspective towards sport. From the last decades of the nineteenth century, sport's allure could be viewed with a certain degree of disdain and also disquiet. But it was nevertheless a reality and one that, especially given the amount of working-class interest, could not simply be dismissed by socialists. Realizing this was the first stage in a process that culminated in the setting up of workers' sports clubs and the hosting of separate competitions for workers (Nitsch, 1996). Worker sport, as Riordan (1996: vii) writes, was intended to provide 'a socialist alternative to bourgeois competitive sport, to commercialism, chauvinism, and the obsession with stars and records'. There was, of course, also a strategic purpose to all of this. If workers would not leave the sports fields to attend socialist meetings, then the socialists were obliged to enter the field of sport and thereby establish contact with the workers. However, this also meant that socialists and communists were taking the first steps towards treating sport as worthy of intellectual examination. If workers were not to become merely passive consumers of the sports product and of capital more generally, then it was essential that they become involved in the construction of an alternative, counter-hegemonic sports culture (Jones, 1988). Indeed, the critical study of sport owes much to the dashed hopes of those élitist socialists who had overestimated their own ability to point workers in the true, non-sporting direction. Gramsci's contribution in this respect was to stress the importance of popular culture of which sport is an implied, but never stated, constituent part.

Many of Gramsci's contemporaries sought to explain the failure of communist revolution to materialize in Western Europe in the wake of events in Russia in 1917 by blaming themselves and each other – hence the proliferation of internecine disputes and schisms – or by complacently asserting that material conditions had simply not been ripe for revolution. Gramsci, on the other hand, turned his attention to the nature of the opposition and even faced the possibility that victory is in no way guaranteed. It can be secured only once the strengths of opponents are fully understood and strategies have been developed to counteract these. For Gramsci, the opposition's greatest strength was the fact that it did not rely solely on coercion for its continued position of pre-eminence. Indeed, the capacity of bourgeois democracies to generate consent, particularly through the institutions of civil society, enabled it to use force relatively sparingly. Thus he advocated a tactical switch for Marxists that would involve them in a war of position aimed at undermining the hegemonic power upon which bourgeois rule rested. For this counter-hegemonic struggle to be a strategic success, it had to be underpinned by a proper understanding of how consciousness is mediated by various elements of civil society. That meant taking seriously many aspects of people's lives which earlier Marxists had dismissed as being at best mere reflections of economic relations and at worst diversions which should simply be railed against rather than subjected to proper analysis. However, as will be argued later in this chapter, the war of movement remained a key element in the revolutionary strategy and with it the requirement for political, economic and industrial struggle. But before considering the implications of this, it is worth thinking briefly in relatively general terms about the validity of applying ideas to social circumstances that differ markedly from those in which they originated.

Using Gramsci

There is, of course, a long-standing debate within the history of political and social thought concerning the universality of ideas. Berki (1977), among others, argued strongly that the study of past ideas alerts us to the universal and timeless qualities of political affairs. Against this, however, an influential revisionist school, inspired in particular by the work of Quentin Skinner (1978a, 1978b) asserted that the study of the history of political thought can permit us only to understand the context out of which these ideas emerged. It cannot offer us opportunities to apply these ideas to our own situation.

This debate is particularly relevant in the case of Gramsci because of his own attachment to historicism. The latter may be understood in a variety of ways within the context of Gramsci's work, but central to one version of his historicism is the belief that 'truth is relative to its historical conditions' (Morera, 1990: 2). According to Gramsci (1971: 404), 'that the philosophy of praxis thinks of itself in a historicist manner, that is, as a transitory phase of philosophical thought, is not only implicit in its entire system, but is made quite explicit in the well-known thesis that historical development will at a certain point be characterised by the passage from the reign of necessity to the reign of freedom'. As Crehan (2002: 28) notes, 'what he had no time for was theory that had become detached from the concrete reality of actual history'. Thus, taking Gramsci's thought and applying it to contexts other than his own is potentially problematic not least in the light of his own reservations concerning this type of practice. As Jarvie and Maguire (1994: 112) caution, 'perhaps the first lesson to be learned from Gramsci's own writings is that if one wants to adapt Gramscian insights and concepts to relatively new fields of enquiry then one has to carry out more specifically theoretically integral and historically concrete accounts of sport and leisure'.

One should add, however, that using Gramsci's ideas specifically to further our understanding of the social significance of sport in our own historical conditions is additionally problematic for the simple reason that Gramsci himself wrote nothing about sport and our use of his concepts in this area of study is inevitably based on inference and speculation. It is not inconceivable, given his own physical frailties, that Gramsci himself never managed to empathize with the sporting enthusiasms of others. In fact, despite his genuine sensitivity to many aspects of working-class life in his native Italy, he fails to mention football in his *Prison Notebooks* (1971) even though these were written during a period when the Italian national team twice became world champions. The fact that the team was representing a nation that had succumbed to the political and physical might of Fascism cannot really explain the omission, since the game's popularity was as strong among socialists and communists as it was among their Fascist enemies. Perhaps physical activity simply failed to excite the physically disabled young Sardinian. Or maybe he had succumbed to an élitist understanding, still widely held on the left at the time, of sport's ultimately frivolous character. It is ironic, therefore, that Gramsci's version of Marxist political theory was to prove crucial to the development of a new and more open intellectual climate regarding sport and other forms of popular culture – albeit largely through a lens fashioned by scholars such as Raymond Williams and Stuart Hall rather than as a direct result of reading and engaging with Gramsci.

Marxism, Gramsci and the sociology of sport

At the academic level Gramsci's influence has been felt most directly in the development of an entirely new discipline – Cultural Studies. It is undeniable, however, that his insistence on taking all cultural forms seriously has also had an impact on sociologists and historians, among others. As regards the study of sport, Gramsci's influence became particularly apparent in the widespread use of hegemony theory (Clarke and Critcher, 1985; Donnelly, 1988; Gruneau, 1999; Hargreaves, 1986; Ingham and Hardy, 1993; Sugden and Bairner, 1993). In common with the founders of Cultural Studies in Britain, the first generation of hegemony theorists of sport maintained the connection between sport and the material conditions of society. Indeed, as Morgan (1994b: 66) claims, for hegemonists, 'sport is a material, productive activity'. It is only later that the link becomes increasingly dissolved.

Two works in particular are widely believed to have pioneered the use of Gramsci's ideas in the sociology of sport. As Rowe (2004: 105) reminds us:

one influential early study is Richard Gruneau's (1983) *Class, Sports and Social Development*, which addresses sport at the abstract level and in the specific Canadian context in a manner heavily influenced by the Gramscian perspective as interpreted by Raymond Williams (1977), supplemented by

Williams's model of co-existent cultural forms that are (currently) dominant, residual (formerly dominant) and emergent (potentially dominant).

This is a fair overview not least because it indicates the primacy given to Williams rather than Gramsci in Gruneau's study. Indeed, Gruneau's (1999: 140) only direct reference to Gramsci is in a footnote where his role in the development of the concept of hegemony is acknowledged but it is made apparent that Gruneau's particular use of the concept owes more to Williams and to Stuart Hall. Interestingly, neither Gramsci's *Prison Notebooks* nor any of his other writings appear in the book's bibliography.

To be fair to Gruneau, in his postscript to the revised edition of his work (1999: 117), he comments that the claim that his is a Marxist book 'is debatable, to say the least, because of the pervasive influence in the analysis of non-Marxist writers, such as Veblen, C. Wright Mills, and Giddens'. That said, Gruneau (*ibid.*) expresses a debt to Western Marxism (without mentioning Gramsci by name) and acknowledges that 'in the years since the book was originally published, Western capitalism has tightened its grip on social and cultural life around the world' – a statement that implies the continuing relevance of theoretical approaches that acknowledge the central importance of economics to social development.

The other work that is regarded as pioneering as regards the application of Gramsci's ideas to sport is John Hargreaves's *Sport, Power and Culture* (1986), 'one of the most cited sociological works deploying Gramsci', according to Rowe (2004: 106). While it is true that Hargreaves is frequently cited in this context, his work contains little direct reference to Gramsci. He discusses the relationship between civil society and the state in a way that is consistent with at least one reading of Gramsci's presentation of that relationship (Anderson, 1976). Moreover, his definition of hegemony is much closer to Gramsci's understanding of the concept than is the case in much subsequent hegemony theory work. Thus, hegemony 'is a power relation in which the balance between the use of force and coercion on the one hand, and voluntary compliance with the exercise of power on the other, is shifted so that power relations function largely in terms of the latter mode' (Hargreaves, 1986: 7). The important point to note is that the balance is 'shifted' but there is no suggestion that coercion becomes redundant.

Those who have adopted this Gramscian approach have sought to distance themselves from sport's more implacable left-wing critics by arguing that, far from simply reproducing existing power relations, sport can be an arena for social contestation. Some of their critics, however, are not wholly convinced that they have achieved this. Morgan (1994b: 83), for example, argues that 'the undifferentiated way in which hegemonists depict the social constitution of sport glosses over the variegated and complex nature of its actual social constitution'. Thus, they ignore how its own constitutive rules drive a wedge between sport and its social context and produce inevitable constraints in relation to human agency. A debate on these issues and others relating to the whole question of how best to theorize sport was conducted in the pages of the *Sociology of Sport Journal* over a number of years. Suffice to say that as this discussion has progressed, sport itself has been increasingly relegated to the sidelines (Hargreaves and Tomlinson, 1992; Ingham and Beamish, 1997; MacAloon, 1992; Morgan, 1994a, 1997).

However, hegemony theory can also be critiqued from a different direction from that taken by Morgan, MacAloon and others – whose comments, like those of their adversaries, suggest to me that the differences of opinion which have been voiced owe more to the distinctive intellectual and political climates of the United States, on one hand, and Britain and Canada, on the other, with reference to Marxist thinking as a whole and specifically as regards the importance of social class. As Jarvie and Maguire (1994: 124–5) express it, 'we might even be tempted to say that all roads lead back to Gramsci but unfortunately much of the Cultural Studies research into sport and leisure has been extremely selective when considering Gramsci's praxis'. Of course, this is part of a more general problem which has affected most post-Gramscian social theory – namely, the tendency to attribute *too much* autonomy to superstructural institutions and activities.

This is not to suggest that we should simply return to crude economistic interpretations, although, as Greaves (2004: 2) has argued, Gramsci's 'residual economism' is in reality 'the intellectual anchorage of such concepts as hegemony, intellectuals and historical bloc, and these are rendered incoherent without it'. Thus it is highly appropriate that John Hargreaves (1986: 209) should himself acknowledge that sports are 'more determined . . . than determining'. In contrast to the New Left critics of sport such as Paul Hoch (1972), Jean-Marie Brohm (1978) and Bero Rigauer (1981), however, it is important to recognize that the fact that sport reflects economic power relations is no excuse for ignoring its social significance or its potential as an arena for cultural struggle. In any case, the material circumstances which sport currently reflects are substantially different from those which confronted the New Left and, indeed, Marx and the orthodox Marxists before them. A political reading of sport can be proposed that is clearly influenced by Gramsci. However, the Gramsci in question does not ignore the continuing impact of political economy on popular culture. As Greaves (2004: 2) notes, 'Gramsci did not seek to liberate himself from "objective reality"; merely to liberate Marxism from too much dependency on transcendentalism outside of the experience of the mass of historical actors involved in demonstrating reality as life'. Thus, the re-appropriation of Gramsci that is called for here involves reminding people that Gramsci lived and died a Marxist, a revolutionary communist, and while it may be permissible to make use of his ideas for purposes other than his own, it is important to remember that these are Marxist ideas and not the ideas of a democratic élitist (Finocchiaro, 1999), a social democrat (Tamburrano, 1963) or, worse still, a prophet of postmodernity (Holub, 1992).

In countless books on the sociology of sport, however, Gramsci is detached from Marxism. For example, in Jay Coakley and Eric Dunning's *Handbook of Sports Studies* (2000), Gramsci warrants only a brief mention in Bero Rigauer's chapter on Marxist theories (Rigauer, 2000) but figures much more prominently in the chapter that follows, written by Jennifer Hargreaves and Ian McDonald and concerned with Cultural Studies and the sociology of sport (Hargreaves and McDonald, 2000). Jarvie and Maguire (1994) devote an entire chapter to

Gramsci in addition to one titled 'Classical Marxism, Political Economy and beyond'. A similar approach is taken by Giulianotti (2004, 2005). At one level all of this simply reflects the disproportionately large influence that Gramsci has had on the study of sport and leisure when compared with other Marxists. Nevertheless, one is fearful of the consequences of students being given the impression that Gramsci does not fit into either of the categories of 'classical Marxism' or 'beyond classical Marxism'. It is in the light of such concerns that Kate Crehan's work on Gramsci becomes particularly worthy of consideration.

Gramsci the Marxist

Crehan (2002: 5) notes that Gramsci 'was first and foremost a political activist'. She adds, 'it is important to stress that Gramsci saw his intellectual project in the *Prison Notebooks* as rooted in Marxism, just as his political activity prior to his arrest had been' (*ibid.*: 21). She recognizes that there has emerged an 'overtly idealist Gramsci' within her own discipline (Anthropology) which she attributes to a reading of Raymond Williams rather than of Gramsci, whose intellectual project, she repeats, 'is framed within an unambiguously Marxist problematic' (*ibid.*: 176); 'from first to last', she contends, 'Gramsci remains a Marxist – albeit an extraordinarily open and flexible one – for whom the fundamental actors in history are classes' (*ibid.*: 72).

As his interest in what he regarded as the quasi-autonomous superstructural realm indicates, he was not an economic reductionist. 'What', Gramsci (1971: 242) asks, however, 'is the point of reference of the new world in gestation?' 'The world of production', he replies, 'work'. Thus, 'the level of development of the material forces of production provides a basis for the emergence of various social classes, each one of which represents a function and has a specific position within production itself' (*ibid.*: 180–1). Nor did he ignore in his own work matters relating to economics and to the need for industrial struggle. His work on Taylorism (and scientific management) and Fordism highlights the former; his personal involvement in the factory council movement and in the occupation of the factories in post-First World War Italy is a clear indication of the latter (Clark, 1977; Fiori, 1973). Korsch's (1970) defence of his own theoretical perspective could apply equally to Gramsci. It was, he writes (*ibid.*: 102), 'a conception of Marxism that was quite undogmatic and anti-dogmatic, historical and critical, and which was therefore materialist in the strictest sense of the word'. It is for this reason that Gramsci (1971: 407) argues that 'the claim, presented as an essential postulate of historical materialism, that every fluctuation of politics and ideology can be presented and expounded as an immediate expression of the structure, must be contested in theory as primitive infantilism, and combated in practice with the authentic testimony of Marx, the author of concrete political and historical works'.

As Jarvie and Maguire (1994: 116) remind us, 'because of the complex nature of state power Gramsci saw it necessary to wage a political battle on a broad terrain encompassing every area in which capitalist power was exerted'. For many, however, the idea of 'a broad terrain' upon which struggle should be based has led inexorably towards an emphasis on cultural struggle and identity politics and away from economic and industrial struggle, thereby neglecting a central element of Gramsci's revolutionary theory. It is easy to understand why this narrow reading has had great appeal for intellectuals, since it appears to open the way for a revolution that takes place largely in the realm of ideas. For Gramsci, however, this type of cultural struggle was only one aspect of a broader revolutionary strategy – a war of position which would be followed by more traditional methods that are consistent with a war of movement.

In addition to ignoring the need for more traditional revolutionary activities, harnessing Gramsci for the cause of cultural struggle has been bound up with a large degree of optimism as to the eventual outcome of the intellectual battles that lie ahead. By exaggerating the extent to which Gramsci regarded the possibility of resistance as the key feature of conditions in which hegemonic power is exerted, hegemony theory has been guilty of ignoring the pessimism of Gramsci's intelligence or what Morgan would regard as the constraints placed upon human agency. Although, according to Gramsci's analysis, hegemony undeniably allows for campaigns of resistance at the cultural as well as the industrial and political levels, the concept itself indicates how difficult it is to challenge bourgeois power in advanced capitalist societies successfully. Furthermore, it is complemented by a number of other concepts, such as passive revolution and Caesarism, which underline the difficulties that face any revolutionary project.

For Gramsci (1971: 59), passive revolution is '"revolution" without a "revolution"' – 'a process of modernization presided over by the established elites, who used the "revolutionary" changes to maintain their supremacy and consolidate the extant order' (Femia, 1981: 48). Caesarism involves the intervention of a third party in 'a situation in which the forces in conflict balance each other in such a way that a continuation of the conflict can only terminate in their reciprocal destruction' (Gramsci, 1971: 219). It can be progressive. In its reactionary form, however, it leads to the restoration of the old order. With such concepts in mind, it is scarcely surprising that Gramsci (*ibid.*: 175) chose as a guiding principle the maxim 'Pessimism of the intelligence, optimism of the will'. Despite its inherent call for political action, the phrase simultaneously underlines why it is so dangerous to underestimate the breadth of Gramsci's theory of revolution and to ignore his pessimism when one turns one's attention to examples from the world of sport that have been subjected to analysis from a hegemony theory perspective.

Uses and abuses of Gramsci's concept of hegemony

This final section of the chapter offers a necessarily brief discussion of some of the ways in which distorted readings of Gramsci and in particular of his concept of hegemony can and have been applied to sport with what are often naïve and utopian results. In most cases, those who have sought to use Gramsci's ideas have done so in good faith. What is of concern, however, is how readers, and specifically students of the sociology of sport, are likely to interpret this body of work.

The themes discussed here are the counter-hegemonic potential of sports fans, campaigns to end the use of Native American names and mascots in North American sport, extreme and lifestyle sports as forms of cultural resistance and, finally, gender and social transformation.

In addition to underestimating the extent to which Gramsci continued to accord primacy to material conditions, sociologists of sport, as has been suggested earlier, have also modified the concept of hegemony while continuing to refer specifically to Gramsci's development of the term. For example, Jennifer Hargreaves (1994: 22) suggests that 'hegemony describes a form of control that is persuasive rather than coercive'. This is certainly what most sociologists of sport with an interest in Gramsci's work appear to believe he was arguing. However, as two of his English translators, Quintin Hoare and Geoffrey Nowell-Smith (Gramsci, 1971) point out, Gramsci commonly refers to hegemony as constituted by both direction and domination or, to express it slightly differently, by persuasion *and* coercion. This is in line with the 'dual perspective' with which Gramsci viewed the relationship between political and civil society, which form an organic and mutually dependent totality.

The study of association football's historical development is replete with indirect references to the ideas of hegemony and counter-hegemony as they have come to be (mis)understood. Orthodox Marxists tend to be characterized as seeing the emergence of popular team sports such as football as little more than mechanisms whereby ruling élites would be able to control an increasingly restless urban proletariat. Hegemony theory, on the other hand, suggests that activities such as football became contested sites upon which the working class could seek to establish its own authority and values. This approach persists in debates about the contemporary world of football with fanzines and unofficial and even semi-official supporters' organizations being considered as potentially counter-hegemonic and fans' representatives being portrayed, by implication, as organic intellectuals in the Gramscian sense (Armstrong and Giulianotti, 1997; Brown, 1998; Crawford, 2004).

Writing with specific reference to Gramsci, Rowe (2004: 103) notes the counter-hegemonic possibilities involved in popular resistance to 'the closure of a football club, the relocation of a sports franchise to another part of the country, or the takeover of a sports club by a media company'. In Gramscian terms, however, it would be more accurate to describe such developments and indeed the entire colonization of football by working-class people, particularly men, as nothing more threatening to the economic relations that underpin professional sport than a 'passive revolution'. Giving fans a voice may create an impression of change but the fundamental principles of ownership remain largely intact. At the risk of appearing to be simply repeating New Left arguments (although arguably a Gramscian perspective has at least as much in common with that critique as with the positions adopted by the more cultural wing of Cultural Studies), it is usually only when clubs are facing economic collapse and capital investment is denied to them that supporters and their representatives are permitted to exercise any degree of control. Furthermore, these representatives themselves may also undergo personal passive revolutions as they make the transition from grass roots to boardroom. In this respect nothing was more pitiful than the sight of Manchester United's lesser shareholders and the representatives of the club's supporters making the bold but ultimately untenable claim during 2005 that their club was 'not for sale'. First, it was not and is not their club, at least in terms of actual ownership. Second, it is an undeniable fact that Manchester United Football Club, like most other commodities in a capitalist system, is permanently for sale (Andrews, 2004). The idea that new owner Malcolm Glazer is a rapacious robber baron who will bleed the club dry whereas previous owners J.P. McManus and John Magnier, or indeed the Edwards family who preceded them, are paternalistic guardians of the club's soul is not only ludicrous in itself but serves to illustrate the hopeless idealism that has come to be associated with counter-hegemonic strategies that are neglectful of economic realities. This is by no means the only example.

Numerous monographs, articles and book chapters in the sociology of sport and beyond have been devoted to a debate on the prevalence in American sport of Native American names – Braves, Blackhawks, Redskins and so on – and symbols – headdresses, the tomahawk chop and the notorious Chief Wahoo, mascot of the Cleveland Indians. Of necessity, the struggle to force franchises to abandon the use of such offensive symbolism has been conducted on the cultural terrain, often by academics and/or what might be regarded, in Gramscian terms, as organic intellectuals of the Native American population. The moral force of the arguments presented is undoubted. Those who have sought to claim that such caricatures as Chief Wahoo are intended to honour Native American people would not even contemplate 'honouring' other ethnic minorities with similar iconography. There could be no place in American sport, as Ward Churchill (1993) satirically proposes, for the 'San Diego Spics', the 'Kansas City Kikes' or the 'St Louis Sluts'. Yet, for owners of franchises such as the Indians, the name and the symbolism are part of the package into which they have bought. In capitalism, everything has its price – even at the expense of the feelings and aspirations of already marginalized peoples.

This is not to argue that cultural struggle around an issue of this sort should simply be abandoned. According to Gramsci's own revolutionary theory, it is right and proper that radical intellectuals should write about such subjects and seek to influence public opinion, thereby to bring some degree of pressure to bear on owners and sponsors. The fact remains, though, that many of those who are most vociferous about this kind of issue create the impression that the material context within which decisions are taken or more commonly not taken can be largely ignored. Arguably some of them may also fail to understand the mindset of fans who spend hard-earned cash to support franchises and clubs, who do not like change and who are largely disinclined to withdraw their financial backing to promote undeniably good causes. This is not something that is likely to change in response to well-reasoned ethical arguments, for, as Crawford (2004: 78) argues, 'though modern professional sport has always involved . . . associated acts of consumption, it is evident that in recent decades contemporary sport venues have become increasingly commodified and commercialized environments'. Changing the name of a college sports team is a much easier task than altering the identity of a long-established and financially lucrative professional franchise. As Sigelman (1998: 323) notes in relation to the Washington Redskins, 'not only has the general public failed to rally to this cause, but even those segments of the general public that are most positively disposed remain overwhelmingly unconvinced of the necessity for change'.

Nevertheless, there is a sense in which some of the theorists who promote this particular cause are reluctant to face some uncomfortable truths about sport and consumer capitalism for fear of falling into the clutches of economic determinism. But economics is precisely what this is all about. Try telling the Native American young men with their Washington Redskins and Atlanta Braves baseball caps who spend the day playing pool and drinking Bud that their plight can be bettered by cultural struggle alone. According to Staurowsky (2000: 325), 'as long as there is "Wahoo", racism built on the advantages to be derived from the misappropriation of American Indian culture and the price American Indians pay for that misappropriation (cultural genocide, significantly greater challenges in every respect because of race) will continue to exist, as will the possessive investment in ignorance that is required to sustain it'. True. But without a redistribution of economic power throughout American society, there is no profit to be made from change. Meanwhile, although many native peoples are simply absorbed by the modern North American sports systems, others do demonstrate consistent resistance, for example through the Northern Games (Paraschak, 1997).

Another area in which cultural struggle through physical activity has been identified is that of extreme and lifestyle sports. As Wheaton (2004: 3) observes, 'despite differences in nomenclature, many commentators are agreed in seeing such activities as having presented an "alternative", and potential challenge to traditional ways of "seeing", "doing" and understanding sport'. In this, however, there are echoes of Marcuse's (1964) claims for the Great Refusal consisting of those people who, in a one-dimensional society without apparent opposition, operate outside the system. Like Marcuse's *refuseniks*, moreover, exponents of various lifestyle sports frequently become incorporated, through the commodification and co-option of their activities, within that system to which putatively they are opposed (Wheaton, 2005).

Similar comments could be made in relation to nationalism as a potentially progressive, counter-hegemonic force in specific contexts. Thus, Silk *et al.* (2005: 7) argue, 'simply put, and prefigured on the operations and machinations of multi-, trans- and supra-national entities, the politico-cultural nation of the nineteenth century has been replaced by the corporate-cultural nation of the twenty-first century'. National identities, like replica football shirts, Native American mascots and equipment and clothing for lifestyle sports, are marketable and, as such, all of them in their different ways underline the hegemonic power of late capitalism – a type of power that is based in large part on the capacity to provide consumers with what they want – and the limited potential of counter-hegemonic strategies located solely, or even predominantly, in the cultural realm.

In general terms, as has already been argued, the concept of hegemony has been increasingly utilized by scholars concerned with the relationship between sport and the politics of identity. Whereas class has virtually disappeared from much of the sociological writing on sport, there is no shortage of references to gender, sexuality, 'race', ethnicity, national identity, disability and so on. This is not to imply that identity politics should be ignored but rather to stress that, for example, the politics of national identities in relation to sport can best be explained, *in the final analysis*, with reference to material realities, broadly defined (Bairner, 2005). Following Gramsci, or perhaps one should say a reading of Gramsci that is true to his own Marxist project, it can be argued that the same claim applies to other issues that have attracted the attention of radical sociologists of sport.

Arguably nowhere is the concept of hegemony more widely used these days than in the study of gender power relations. In particular, following Connell (1987, 1995), the idea of hegemonic masculinity has become omnipresent. Commenting on Gramscian attempts to understand the struggles for power between dominant and subordinate groups, Jennifer Hargreaves (1994: 23) bemoans the fact that 'antagonistic class relations have provided the focus for such accounts, and although reference has been made to the relationship between class and gender, and even to the way that class and gender divisions are constructed together, there have been no specific attempts to explore this relationship rigorously or to look at specific complexities of male hegemony'. According to Hargreaves (*ibid.*: 24), 'the crux of feminist criticisms of all varieties of Marxism is that sexual categories are not intrinsic to Marxists concepts, but have only been appended to them'. This is undeniably true. The danger, however, albeit not one to which Hargreaves succumbs, is that much discussion of sexual categories takes place without references to key ideas in Marxism, not least social class. Inevitably this leads to essentialist interpretations of gender.

For her part, Hargreaves (2004: 187; emphasis added) recognizes 'the production of hegemonic *and* subordinated sporting masculinities', with social class as one of the characteristics of subordinated masculinity. For many feminist social theorists, however, the use of the concept of hegemony in this context becomes the basis for an assumption that most men exercise hegemonic power and that they do so consistently over time and space. In fact, it is important to draw a distinction between hegemonic masculinity and the power that is exerted by hegemonic men. Thus the tattooed skinhead football fan and the male chief executive of a multinational corporation both contribute to hegemonic masculinity in specific ways. The 'hard men' in the stands at soccer matches impose themselves on football culture, for example by denigrating women and also those men who fail to pass their rudimentary tests of masculinity. The real hegemonic males, however, are in the directors' boxes and the executive suites, secure in the knowledge that they can ultimately exercise control even over the 'hard men'. Ironically it may well have been the latter, in the guise of football hooligans, who have posed the greatest threat in modern times to the development of Football plc. But there are very few hegemony theorists who would wish to recognize football-related violence as a form of counter-hegemonic struggle (although, in this respect, the early work of Ian Taylor (1969, 1970) is arguably well worth revisiting). Indeed, there is consistently something very selective about which arguments and forms of behaviour are recognized as resistant and/or transgressive by those proponents of identity politics who have taken the concept of hegemony and detached it from class politics and the war of movement.

None of this is intended to suggest that, while developing the concept of hegemonic masculinity, Connell (1987, 1995) or indeed other writers in this area such as Michael Messner (1997) and Toby Miller (2001) ignore the very real distinctions between different sorts of men. There is a danger, nevertheless, that the concept of hegemonic masculinity can be abstracted from material conditions and used in the interests of essentialist readings of gender.

In the words of Gruneau (1999: 125), 'no single narrative can address every form of oppression, identity, or political aspiration'. Thus, there is undeniably scope for a multiplicity of approaches that are concerned with different forms of oppression. An analysis based directly on Gramsci's work, however, must be primarily concerned with the economic exploitation of one social class by another and with the ways in which, in commoditized sport, as in other areas of popular culture, this exploitative relationship is successfully reproduced.

Conclusion

Perhaps the supreme irony of the foregoing discussion is the fact that Gramsci and sport are so often mentioned in the same breath. It is also ironic that Gramsci has come to be associated with sociology which he described as 'an attempt to create a method of historical and political science in a form dependent on a pre-elaborated philosophical system, that of evolutionist positivism, against which sociology reacted, but only partially' (Gramsci, 1971: 426). It was sociology rather than Marxism that was rooted in 'vulgar evolutionism'. Once one has come to terms with the fact that Gramsci was not a sociologist and certainly not a sociologist of sport, the next consideration concerns the applicability of sociological concepts over extended periods of time. What needs to be considered is whether we can use these concepts as we see fit regardless of how their author originally employed them. If so, we must be prepared to argue that by so doing, we are thinking for ourselves but with a little help from ideas that have legitimately been taken out of their historic context and have acquired new resonance at a different conjuncture. Despite attempts to re-imagine his work, Gramsci's Marxism is surely in no doubt. Thus the challenge that faces most hegemony theorists is to demonstrate that Gramsci's ideas make sense when removed from their Marxist setting. It can be argued, however, that their next challenge is to show that an understanding of capitalist society and specifically of sport in a capitalist setting can do without Marxist ideas, including those of Antonio Gramsci.

According to Rowe (2004: 107), the 'Gramscian moment' appears to have passed. He claims that its passing 'has registered in the displacement of class relations as the central problematic by a range of other sites of conflict – gender, race, sexuality, and so on'. The central contention of this chapter, however, is that, to a considerable extent, it was the misuse of Gramsci's thought which led to that very marginalization of class and of political economy in relation to social conflict. Rowe (*ibid.*: 108) contends that Gramsci's ideas 'have influenced much of the best social theory of sport in the last two decades, and continue to inform new work in the field'. It is a matter of concern, however, what is actually being taken from Gramsci and, at least as importantly, what is being discarded.

Those who genuinely wish to use Gramsci's ideas in the same spirit as he formulated them are advised to heed Willie Gallacher's words and to concentrate on what distinguishes social democrats together with those who practise various forms of identity politics from communists who continue to believe in the need for a radical economic transformation of society. As Gramsci intimated, this will be no easy task and will involve struggle at the cultural level but also in other spheres of human activity. It cannot be achieved at all, however, if we assume that the concept of hegemony automatically implies resistance and if we content ourselves with resistance on behalf of specific group interests as opposed to resistance in the interests of all humankind. Gramsci's concept of hegemony explains how power is maintained by economically dominant social groups. His work underlines the need for ever more sophisticated political interventions in order to facilitate change. Nothing is guaranteed. As Gramsci (1975: 121) wrote of his imprisonment, 'For me, it represents one episode in a political battle that was being fought and will continue to be fought, not only in Italy but in the whole world, for who knows how long a time.'

Acknowledgements

Earlier versions of this chapter were presented at a research seminar at the Department of Sports Studies in the University of Stirling, March 2005, and at the 'Marxism, Cultural Studies and Sport' symposium held at the University of Texas at Austin, April 2005. The author is grateful to Joe Bradley, Grant Jarvie and Wray Vamplew at Stirling for their general observations, and to Irene Reid for her comments on the relationship between hegemonic masculinity and hegemonic men. The author also wishes to acknowledge the support and advice provided by the editors of this collection and by all of the contributors to the University of Texas symposium.

References

Anderson, P. (1976) 'The Antinomies of Antonio Gramsci', *New Left Review* 100, pp. 5–78.
Andrews, D.L. (ed.) (2004) *Manchester United: A Thematic Study*, London: Routledge.
Armstrong, G. and Giulianotti, R. (eds) (1997) *Entering the Field: New Perspectives on World Football*, Oxford: Berg.
Bairner, A. (2005) 'Sport and Nation in a Global Era', in L. Allison (ed.) *The Global Politics of Sport: The Role of Global Institutions in Sport*, London: Routledge, pp. 87–100.

Bairner, A. (2007) 'Back to Basics: Class, Social Theory, and Sport', *Sociology of Sport Journal* 24(1), pp. 20–36.

Berki, R.N. (1977) *The History of Political Thought: A Short Introduction*, London: Dent.

Brohm, J.-M. (1978) *Sport: A Prison of Measured Time*, London: Ink Links.

Brown, A. (ed.) (1998) *Fanatics! Power, Identity and Fandom in Football*, London: Routledge.

Churchill, W. (1993) *Indians Are Us? Culture and Genocide in Native North America*, Monroe: Common Courage Press.

Clark, M. (1977) *Antonio Gramsci and the Revolution that Failed*, New Haven: Yale University Press.

Clarke, J. and Critcher, C. (1985) *The Devil Makes Work: Leisure in Capitalist Britain*, Basingstoke: Macmillan.

Coakley, J. and Dunning, E. (eds) (2000) *Handbook of Sports Studies*, London: Sage.

Connell, R.W. (1987) *Gender and Power*, Berkeley: University of California Press.

Connell, R.W. (1995) *Masculinities*, Berkeley: University of California Press.

Crawford, G. (2004) *Consuming Sport: Fans, Sport and Culture*, London: Routledge.

Crehan, K. (2002) *Gramsci, Culture and Anthropology*, Berkeley: University of California Press.

Donnelly, P. (1988) 'Sport as a Site for "Popular" Resistance', in R. Gruneau (ed.) *Popular Cultures and Political Practices*, Toronto: Garamond Press, pp. 68–82.

Femia, J.V. (1981) *Gramsci's Political Thought: Hegemony, Consciousness, and the Revolutionary Process*, Oxford: Clarendon Press.

Finocchiaro, M.A. (1999) *Beyond Right and Left: Democratic Elitism in Mosca and Gramsci*. New Haven: Yale University Press.

Fiori, G. (1973) *Antonio Gramsci: Life of a Revolutionary*, New York: Schocken Books.

Gallacher, W. (1948) *The Rolling of the Thunder*, London: Lawrence and Wishart.

Giulianotti, R. (2005) *Sport: A Critical Sociology*, Cambridge: Polity Press.

Giulianotti, R. (ed.) (2004) *Sport and Modern Social Theorists*, Basingstoke: Palgrave Macmillan.

Gramsci, A. (1971) *Selections from the Prison Notebooks*, ed. Quintin Hoare and Geoffrey Nowell Smith, London: Lawrence and Wishart.

Gramsci, A. (1975) *Letters from Prison*, selected, trans. and introduced by Lyne Lawner, London: Jonathan Cape. (Letter written to his sister, Teresina, 20 February 1928, Milan.)

Greaves, N. (2004) 'Why Gramsci Rolls in his Grave: An Attempt at a Rescue from Laclau and Mouffe', paper presented at the annual conference of the Political Studies Association, University of Lincoln, April.

Gruneau, R. (1983) *Class, Sports, and Social Development*, 1st edn, Amherst: University of Massachusetts Press.

Gruneau, R. (1999) *Class, Sports, and Social Development*, rev. edn, Champaign: Human Kinetics.

Hargreaves, J.A. (1994) *Sporting Females: Critical Issues in the History and Sociology of Women's Sports*, London: Routledge.

Hargreaves, J.A. (2004) 'Querying Sport Feminism: Personal or Political?', in R. Giulianotti (ed.) *Sport and Modern Social Theorists*, Basingstoke: Palgrave Macmillan, pp. 187–205.

Hargreaves, J.A. and McDonald, I. (2000) 'Cultural Studies and the Sociology of Sport', in J. Coakley and E. Dunning (eds) *Handbook of Sports Studies*, London: Sage, pp. 48–60.

Hargreaves, J.E. (1986) *Sport, Power and Culture: A Social and Historical Analysis of Popular Sports in Britain*, Oxford: Polity Press.

Hargreaves, J.E. and Tomlinson, A. (1992) 'Getting There: Cultural Theory and the Sociological Analysis of Sport in Britain', *Sociology of Sport Journal* 9(2), pp. 207–19.

Hoch, P. (1972) *Rip off the Big Game*, New York: Doubleday.

Holub, R. (1992) *Antonio Gramsci: Beyond Marxism and Postmodernism*, London: Routledge.

Ingham. A. and Beamish, R. (1997) 'Didn't Cyclops Lose His Vision? An Exercise in Sociological Optometry', *Sociology of Sport Journal* 14(2), pp. 160–86.

Ingham, A. and Hardy, S. (1993) 'Sports Studies through the Lens of Raymond Williams', in A. Ingham and J. Loy (eds) *Sport in Social Development*, Champaign: Human Kinetics, pp. 1–19.

Jarvie, G. and Maguire, J. (1994) *Sport and Leisure in Social Thought*, London: Routledge.

Jones, S.G. (1988) *Sport, Politics and the Working Class*, Manchester: Manchester University Press.

Korsch, K. (1970 [1930]) 'The Present State of the Problem of "Marxism and Philosophy" – an Anti-Critique', in *idem, Marxism and Philosophy*, New York: Monthly Review Press.

MacAloon, J. (1992) 'The Ethnographic Imperative in Comparative Olympic Research', *Sociology of Sport Journal* 9(2), pp. 104–30.

Marcuse, H. (1964) *One Dimensional Man*, London: Routledge and Kegan Paul.

Marx, K. (1972 [1852]) *The Eighteenth Brumaire of Louis Bonaparte*, Moscow: Progress Publishers.

Messner, M. (1997) *Politics of Masculinities: Men in Movements*, London: Sage.

Miller. T. (2001) *Sportsex*, Philadelphia: Temple University Press.

Morera, E. (1990) *Gramsci's Historicism: A Realist Interpretation*, London: Routledge.

Morgan, W. (1994a) 'Hegemony Theory, Social Domination and Sport: The MacAloon and Hargreaves–Tomlinson Debate Revisited', *Sociology of Sport Journal* 11(3), pp. 309–29.

Morgan, W. (1994b) *Leftist Theories of Sport: A Critique and Reconstruction*, Champaign: University of Illinois Press.

Morgan, W. (1997) 'Yet Another Critical Look at Hegemony Theory: A Response to Ingham and Beamish', *Sociology of Sport Journal* 14(2), pp. 187–95.

Nitsch, F. (1996) 'The Two International Worker Sport Organisations: Socialist Worker Sports International and Red Sport International', in A. Krüger and J. Riordan (eds) *The Story of Worker Sport*, Champaign: Human Kinetics.

Paraschak, V. (1997) 'Variations in Race Relations: Sporting Events for Native Peoples in Canada', *Sociology of Sport Journal* 14(1), pp. 1–21.

Rigauer, B. (1981) *Sport and Work*, New York: Columbia University Press.

Rigauer, B. (2000) 'Marxist Theories', in J. Coakley and E. Dunning (eds) *Handbook of Sports Studies*, London: Sage, pp. 28–47.

Riordan, J. (1996) 'Introduction', in A. Krüger and J. Riordan (eds) *The Story of Worker Sport*, Champaign: Human Kinetics.

Rowe, D. (2004) 'Antonio Gramsci: Sport, Hegemony and the National-Popular', in R. Giulianotti (ed.) *Sport and Modern Social Theorists*, Basingstoke: Palgrave Macmillan, pp. 97–110.

Sigelman, L. (1998) 'Hail to the Redskins? Public Reactions to a Racially Insensitive Team Name', *Sociology of Sport Journal* 15(4), pp. 317–25.

Silk, M.L., Andrews, D.L. and Cole, C.L. (2005) 'Corporate Nationalism(s)? The Spatial

Dimensions of Sporting Capital', in *idem* (eds), *Sport and Corporate Nationalisms*, Oxford, Berg, pp. 1–12.

Skinner, Q. (1978a) *The Foundations of Modern Political Thought, Volume I: The Renaissance*, Cambridge: Cambridge University Press.

Skinner, Q. (1978b) *The Foundations of Modern Political Thought, Volume II: The Reformation*, Cambridge: Cambridge University Press.

Staurowsky, E. (2000) 'The Cleveland "Indians": A Case Study in American Indian Cultural Dispossession', *Sociology of Sport Journal* 17(4), pp. 307–30.

Sugden, J. and Bairner, A. (1993) *Sport, Sectarianism and Society in a Divided Ireland*, Leicester: Leicester University Press.

Tamburrano, G. (1963) *Antonio Gramsci: La vita, il pensiero, l'azione*, Manduria: Lacaita.

Taylor, I. (1969) 'Hooligans: Soccer's Resistance Movement', *New Society*, 7 August, pp. 204–6.

Taylor, I. (1970) 'Football Mad: A Speculative Sociology of Soccer Hooliganism', in E. Dunning (ed.) *The Sociology of Sport*, London: Frank Cass, pp. 352–77.

Wheaton, B. (ed.) (2004) *Understanding Lifestyle Sports: Consumption, Identity and Difference*, London: Routledge.

Wheaton, B. (2005) 'Selling out? The Commercialisation and Globalisation of Lifestyle Sport', in L. Allison (ed.) *The Global Politics of Sport: The Role of Global Institutions in Sport*, London: Routledge, pp. 140–61.

Williams, R. (1977) *Marxism and Literature*, Oxford: Oxford University Press.

12 Sport, culture and late capitalism

David L. Andrews

What 'late' generally conveys is rather the sense that something has changed, that things are different, that we have gone through a transformation of the life world which is somehow decisive but incomparable with the older convulsions of modernization and industrialization, less perceptible and dramatic, somehow, but more permanent precisely because more thoroughgoing and all-pervasive.

Frederic Jameson, *Postmodernism: Or, The Cultural Logic of Late Capitalism*

Introduction

Frederic Jameson's influential characterization of the late capitalist condition – most intensively enunciated within *Postmodernism: Or, The Cultural Logic of Late Capitalism*, and developed within various explorations of consumer society over the past two decades (see Jameson, 1983, 1991, 1996, 1998) – represents an important contribution towards the process of propelling Marxist analysis beyond the productive confines of the factory gates, and into the complex consumptive realm of everyday life. This chapter is premised on the assumption that there is much to gain from an explication of Jameson's late capitalist cosmology, particularly as it pertains to sport's complex relationship with the new superstructural relations and dynamics operating as the locus of this 'third stage of capitalism' (Jameson, 1991: xxi).

In the second half of the twentieth century, the global sport landscape (at the international and national levels) became systematically colonized (initially in the United States and Canada, subsequently in Western Europe, Japan, Australasia and beyond) by this emergent strain of late capitalism prefigured on the aggressive exploitation of culture as a pivotal source, and process, of capital accumulation. As a result, virtually all aspects of the global sport infrastructure (governing bodies, leagues, tournaments, teams and individual athletes) are now driven and defined by the interrelated processes of: commercialization (the exploitation of an object or practice for capital gain); corporatization (the rational structuring and management of sporting entities according to profit motives); and spectacularization (the production of entertainment-driven experiences). Evidently, contemporary sport culture represents a vivid exemplar of late capitalism's decisive break with the modern industrial order, through it being an incontrovertible demonstration of how 'culture has come to play a more important role in the life of capital' and how 'capital correspondingly has become ever more deeply rooted in the domain of culture' (Hardt and Weeks, 2000: 5). Thus, Jameson's suggestive cultural Marxism represents an important (yet largely overlooked or, at best, superficially engaged) point of theoretical engagement and embarkation: a crucial starting point for critically dissecting the complex cultural economy of late capitalist sport.

So, within this chapter, the aim is to: invoke Jameson's conceptual precursor, Ernest Mandel, as a means of understanding sport's conclusive capitalization in the broadest sense; utilize Jameson more specifically in identifying the centrality of culture to the workings of late capitalism, hence providing an interpretive framework for engaging the corporate sport schema; provide a focused analysis of the late capitalist convergence of fields (cultural, political, economic, technological, etc.) as expressed in, and through, the complexities of the contemporary sport spectacle; and, lastly, encourage the extension and expansion of the dialogue pertaining to Jameson's relevance for the analysis of contemporary sport culture.

Industrializing the sporting superstructure

Any examination of Jameson's work and influence is compelled to engage the figure of Ernest Mandel, the Marxist economist, whose characterization of the late capitalist condition both 'inspired and confirmed' Jameson's (1991: 36) contextual reasoning. All too frequently, however, the specificities of Mandel's work are glossed over in the rush to Jameson's postmodern cultural logics. Since Jameson (*ibid.*) explicitly stated that his cultural periodization is 'both inspired and confirmed' by Mandel, it is perhaps only fitting to ponder, however selectively, his intellectual legacy. First published in 1972 (originally in German), Mandel's *Late Capitalism* represents a prophetic vision of contemporary consumer culture. Mandel sought to account for the development of capitalism in the second half of the twentieth century; the adjective 'late' used to connote not a new stage of capitalist development but rather an extension of the 'imperialist, monopoly-capitalist' order which dominated and defined the Western economies of the late nineteenth and early twentieth centuries (Mandel, 1999: 9). As the apogee of capitalism's search for perpetual growth – itself a mechanism for the avoidance of potentially debilitating crises of overproduction (and, by inference, underconsumption) – late capitalism constituted a *'generalized, universal industrialization* for the first time in history' (*ibid.*: 387). This saw the penetration of capital investment into, and hence the capitalization (the investment of capital as a means of accumulating surplus value, and hence profit) of, an ever-broader swath of social existence. As he stated, late capitalism became organized around the 'industrialization of superstructural activities' (be they leisure, education, art, health or, indeed, sport related) that are increasingly produced 'for the market and aim at maximization of profit' (*ibid.*: 502). In addition to identifying capital's expansion into previously underexploited realms, Mandel crucially provided a coherent rationale for this occurrence based in his particular understanding of Marxist economics.

At the most fundamental level, Mandel (*ibid.*) argued that capitalist economies are primarily concerned with securing the continual, and indeed accelerating, transformation of surplus value into further accumulated capital: their aim being to invest productively, as opposed to consume unproductively, accumulated capital. However, with the emergence of an economy characterized by monopolistic surplus-profits, a condition of overaccumulation results, in which capital becomes *relatively* non-productive due to the impossibility of perpetually realizing exponentially growing rates of return on capital investment. Differently put, a state of relative economic inertia (in terms of the rate of growth of surplus value) is the virtually unavoidable corollary of capitalism's monopolistic tendencies, and ultimately encourages capitalists to invest their accumulated capital speculatively in areas identified as possessing the best prospects for capital growth. This subsequently prompts a 'frantic search for new fields of capital investment' in either new geographic or sectoral terms (*ibid.*: 595). Although the former is not the focus herein, it has to be noted that the late capitalist rise of 'big capital' (*ibid.*: 379) is characterized by a concentration (monopolistic colonization) of capital on a global scale: it is, fundamentally, an 'international capitalist economy . . . with the multinational corporation as the main phenomenal form of capital' (*ibid.*: 7, 9).

However, the focus here is the process of centralization (sectoral expansion) through which 'big capital' has been able to utilize its reserves of non-productive capital in the most fiscally remunerative manner. This phenomenon of 'overcapitalization', and the attendant sectoral investment and expansion, became the 'hallmark' (*ibid.*: 378) of late capitalism during the second half of the twentieth century. During this time – and as a means of avoiding the risks associated with over-specialized investment, of securing returns on the largest possible volume of capital, and of benefiting from any savings derived from potential rationalization initiatives – multinationals 'indiscriminately' expanded to incorporate, quite literally, seemingly disparate elements into their conglomerated wholes. Thus, Mandel (*ibid.*: 389) spoke of the seemingly curious combination of 'steel production, electric machine construction, insurance companies, land speculation and large department stores'.

The very availability of capital that could not be 'valorized in industry proper' (*ibid.*) proved a precondition for the identification and exploitation of new realms of capital investment. This was certainly nothing new, as the maturation of industrial capitalism in the second half of the nineteenth century had encouraged many capitalists to explore 'enclaves of simple commodity production and production of pure use-values' (*ibid.*: 378) – the commercially under-exploited remnants of pre-capitalist existence – with their non-invested, hence non-productive, surplus capital. However, as monopoly capitalism threatened to be undermined by its own stagnation-inducing mastery of industry proper, so investment capital extended its reach into less accustomed realms, ultimately leading to a situation in which all sectors of society become prey to the commercially rationalizing prescriptions of industrialization and capitalization. Or, as Mandel (*ibid.*: 387) described it, 'the 'profitability' of universities, music academies and museums starts to be calculated in the same way as that of brick works or screw factories'. In general terms, he referred to this extension of commercial exchange and relations as a capitalization of the service sector (a precondition for which, it should be noted, was the emergence of a sufficiently sizeable consumer class able, and indeed willing, to partake in such exchanges), leading to the further realization of surplus value within the capitalist economy.

Mandel considered carefully the economic and cultural aspects of late capitalism, and the necessary relation between the two. However, in addition to identifying the industrial economies' intensified capitalization of the cultural realm, he underscored the intensive cultural work required for the successful assimilation of the industrial populace into capitalism's maturing productive-consumptive order; or what he described as the 'social prison' of consumer capitalism realized through the subordination of human existence to the 'laws of the market' (*ibid.*: 502). The exigencies of a consumer capitalist economy demanded both the presence of a sufficiently affluent consumer class able to substantiate viable markets (economic regulation), and a directive nurturing of normative attitudes towards the very practice of consumption (cultural regulation). Increases in the scale and scope of consumption can be linked to the elevated levels of relative affluence attained by the mass industrial work-force through their ability to sell their productive labour more consistently. Nevertheless, the breadth of their consumptive options, and the depth of their consumption experiences, is contingent on the successful penetration of invest-ment capital in capitalizing individual needs, desires and aspirations, through the production of specific goods, services and experiences (Pine and Gilmore, 1998). In other words, both sides of the consumer capitalist equation need to reach a level of symbiosis: the consuming populace needs to be sufficiently affluent, and sufficiently motivated, to consume the yield of consumer capitalist production; whereas the capitalist producers need to manufacture both the appropriate panoply of goods, services and experiences sought by the consuming throng, and, indeed, the very consumer desires driving such commodified expectations and aspirations. Mandel (1999: 393, 394) referred to this latter process as the fabrication of 'indirect socially manipulative compulsions', realized through the circulation of the '*social* pressure' embedded within advertising discourse. He thus indicated how the ceaseless cultivation of ever more elaborate and non-essential consumer desires, and hence the ongoing constitution of consuming publics, represented as vital a productive element of late capitalism as the manufacture of the perpetually changing array of goods, services and experiences intended for their consumption.

In crafting a suggestive framework for conceptualizing the economy's multi-faceted turn to the cultural sector (as both a relatively under-exploited realm of capital investment, and an important driver of the capitalist economy in general), Mandel provided a basis for understanding how sport and recreation became 'just as industrialized as the organization of work' (*ibid.*: 387). While making few references to sport *per se*, he briefly discussed the example of German sport organizations during the period 1890–1933. He thus illustrated how the non-work existence of the urban industrial proletariat, including its sport and recreation, became incorporated into processes of capitalist commodity production and circulation, and led to the '*reprivatization of the recreational sphere* of the working class' (*ibid.*: 393). Throughout Western Europe and North America at this time, national sporting cultures were certainly becoming institutionalized. However, the advancement of sport as a vehicle for capital investment, and thereby a generator of surplus value, was a welcome derivative, rather than a primary objective, of capitalists' early forays into the organized sport realm. Through rationalizing and codifying popular sporting practice (through regulating participation), and sanctioning mass spectacle forms of cathartic release (through the sponsorship of teams and contests), the patrician-industrialist power bloc appropriated sport as a mechanism for constraining the bodies of the labour force to the demands and discipline of the industrial workplace. This was achieved while advancing their own position of sociopolitical authority, and, lest it not be forgotten, stimulating the capitalization of urban leisure culture (Braverman, 1998; Butsch, 1990). Thus, within the modern industrial era, institutionalized sport became an emergent site of 'surveillance, spectacle, and profit' within the newly defined realm of 'free' time (Miller and McHoul, 1998: 61). That having been said, and perhaps compelled by some residues of Corinthian idealism, many sport organizations and institutions outwardly continued to resist the lure of capitalist incorporation well into the twentieth century. However, the intensifying *crisis* of 'over-capitalization' (Mandel, 1999: 378) experienced by maturing industrial economies in the second half of the twentieth century (admittedly in a staggered sequence, with the USA being the first to experience the trend in the economic boom years of the 1950s) created a vast surplus of investment capital looking for productive use which, coupled with the rising levels of affluence among the general populace, heralded the ascension of an economy and culture driven and defined by commodity and service consumption.

Within this burgeoning 'consumer society' (Lee, 2000), sport's position at the periphery of commercial processes and relations was simply untenable: it was only a matter of time before sport (and particularly mass spectator sport) was intensively, and seemingly irreversibly, industrialized, such that it 'emerged as the correlative to a society that is replacing manual labor with automation and machines, and requires consumption and appropriation of spectacles to reproduce consumer society' (Kellner, 2002: 66). Due to the rampant capitalization of the sport system, its very structure, delivery and experience have come to exude the 'profit-making' focus and 'rationalized organizational procedures' exhibited by the more readily accepted forms of industrialized mass culture (Negus, 1997: 77). Despite Hesmondhalgh's (2002) reluctance to identify it as such, sport's considerable popularity, and hence significant capital-generating capacity, renders it a legitimate culture industry (Adorno, 2001): it represents a lucrative site for the accumulation of capital via the rationalized manufacture of popular practices, products and pleasures for mass audiences. Thus sport, arguably the culture industry of the contemporary moment, has progressed through pre-commercial and commercial to its current (borrowing form Walsh and Giulianotti, 2001) hyper-commercial phase (see also Alt, 1983; Brewer, 2002; Brookes, 2002; Cole and Hribar, 1995; Donnelly, 1996; Goldman and Papson, 1998; McKay and Miller, 1991; Miller and McHoul, 1998; Miller *et al.*, 2001; Parry and Malcolm, 2004; Real, 1998; Rowe, 1995; Sage, 1996; Silk, 2004; Slack, 2004) in which all aspects of the sport sector (goods, services, experiences *et al.*) are now transformed into commodities to be hawked within the commercial market place. Thus, in Adorno's own words (when drawing Walter Benjamin's attention to the commercially corrupted nature of both high and mass culture), contemporary sport culture bears the indelible 'stigmata of [*late*] capitalism' (quoted in Jameson, 1983: 123).

The corporatist logics of late sporting capital

Mandel provided a considered explanation for the expansion, in scale and scope, of the economy associated with the shift to the late capitalist order. In faithful homage to Mandel's epochal understanding, Jameson identified the capitalist penetration and colonization of both Nature (through the advent of the so-called Green Revolution in agriculture) and the Unconscious (through the expanding influence of the media and advertising industries), as exemplars of how pre-capitalist enclaves become absorbed by late capitalism's covetous impulses. To be sure, the quest for surplus value and capital valorization remain capitalism's *raison d'être*; however, Mandel (1999) identified the intensively mobilized and extensively manifest *cultural* energy source that now powers the profit motor of the late capitalist economy. Evidently, it was the economy's turn to culture with which Jameson was primarily preoccupied, and through which he exemplified the 'prodigious expansion of capital into hitherto uncommodified areas' that accompanied, and indeed facilitated, the ascension of this 'purist form of capital' (Jameson, 1991: 36). At the heart of Jameson's understanding is the manner in which the logic of late capitalism has undermined the relative, or semi-, autonomy previously experienced by the cultural realm in relation to the forces and relations of economic production. This has not led to the 'disappearance' or evisceration of culture; rather, it has resulted in an 'expansion of culture throughout the social realm, to the point at which everything in our social life – from economic value and state power to practices and to the very structure of the psyche itself – can be said to have become "cultural"' (*ibid.*: 48).

As a Marxist literary critic seeking to interpret the aesthetic workings and orientation of contemporary capitalism, Jameson's broader aim was thus to contribute to an understanding of changes in the mode of production – what he described as 'the specific logic of the cultural production' – associated with the third (late, multinational, consumer) stage in the evolution of capital. Within this moment, the cultural sphere occupies a 'special functional place' (*ibid.*: 406) in realizing the accumulated capital through which the late capitalist order is able to reproduce itself: culture simultaneously acts both as a core product (through the commodification of superstructural elements) and a core process (through the symbolic manipulation of commercial consumption) through which late capitalism becomes instantiated and experienced. In terms of the latter, the accumulation of capital within industrial economies keyed on accentuating the surplus values derived from the transformation of raw materials into mass manufactured products, and their subsequent exchange for capital in the wider market place. Within the contemporary 'mode of information' (Poster, 1990) associated with late capitalism's regimes of accumulation, surplus capital is generated from the manufacturing of a product's symbolic values, which in turn help substantiate their use and ultimately exchange values. This, in essence, is the centrifugal cultural process undermining the brand (Klein, 1999), promotional (Wernick, 1991) or commodity sign (Goldman and Papson, 1996) culture propelling late, multinational or consumer capitalism. Through the creative outpourings of the 'cultural intermediaries' (Bourdieu, 1984) working within the advertising, marketing, public relations and media industries, commodities often produced within low-wage industrializing economies are symbolically constituted to the consuming publics within the developed world. However, it should not be overlooked that much of the cultural productivity within late capitalist economies is centred on the manufacturing of consuming lifestyles, through attempts to both stimulate and regulate consumer consciousness and desire. In Firat and Venkatesh's (1995: 248) terms, 'it is not goods and services that are produced, as a superficial analysis would imply, but the culture of consumption itself, in which goods and services are embedded and consumed'.

As McRobbie (2005: 154, 155) noted, Jameson outlined a 'new political economy of culture' within First World economies (the Third World becoming spaces of exploited manual labour) in which culture has become the defining feature of the contemporary 'mode of production', meaning late capitalism has to be understood as a mode of *cultural* production. Jameson thus intimated a condition within which distinctions between economic and cultural realms have conclusively dissipated. This observation was subsequently developed within his reflective elaboration upon the cultural logic of the postmodern conjuncture in which 'economics has come to overlap with culture' (Jameson, 1998: 73). As McRobbie (2005: 155) notes: 'In the most recent stage of capitalist development culture is integral to the economy; it provides the economy with a new dynamic, a new source of growth, a new world of possibilities for profit and for control.' This has particular implications for the understanding of contemporary sport. Within earlier capitalist epochs, namely market and monopoly phases, US culture in general, and sport culture in particular, represented a 'semiautonomous sphere' (Jameson, 1991: 48), somewhat removed from the practices and pressures of economic reproduction. This despite the fact that numerous sporting entities (not least Major League Baseball (MLB), the National Basketball Association (NBA), the National Football League (NFL) and the National Hockey League (NHL)) originated as putative professional entities. However, the extensity and intensity of sport's commercialization was attenuated, primarily due to the broader economy's preoccupation with the capitalization of the flourishing industrial sector (Mandel, 1999). In the post-war era, as the industrial economy matured to the point of saturation and both the demand and supply sides of the American consumer economy evolved accordingly, so sporting culture, and particularly mass spectator sport entities, became ever more subject to the impulses of the mutating industrial order. In very general terms, 'Sport was thereafter effectively and efficiently reorganized in accordance with corporate commercial structures and logics which routinely placed economic (profit maximization) ahead of sporting (utility maximization) imperatives: sport, to invoke an oft cited cliché, became *big business*' (Andrews, 2006: 5–6). Clichéd it may be, but such thinking is rooted in the empirical: corporate sport entities (franchises, leagues, events, etc.) may not rival the corporate leviathans of contemporary capitalism in terms of revenue generation (Wal-Mart, Exxon Mobil, Citigroup, IBM *et al.*); however, their multifaceted commercial interconnectedness, overdetermined economic rationale and considerable popular presence render them emblematic features of late capitalism's *new* cultural economy. Thus, and in the terms of Jameson's dualism, the aggressive commercialization of US sport in the second half of the twentieth century has meant within the late capitalist conjuncture, 'everything, including commodity production and high and speculative finance', has looked to sport as a vehicle for capital accumulation, while sport has 'equally become economic or commodity oriented' (Jameson, 1998: 73).

Jameson consciously acknowledged the impossibility of late capitalism as a universal phenomenon; there being, instead, local iterations of the various processes and relationships that constitute the immediate structure and experience of the late capitalist condition. Nevertheless, he also conceded the American focus of his analysis, which to some insinuated a totalizing aspect to his project. Jameson justified this Americocentric orientation through recourse to the influence of the USA as the 'hothouse' (Jameson, 1991: xx) of capitalist reformation during the period 1945–73. As the proving ground for the late capitalist economic and cultural order, his work is based on the assumption that the USA represents an instructive window into the perils and possibilities of this 'strange new landscape' (*ibid.*: xxi). If one accepts this assumption, then postmodernism (according to Jameson, the cultural logics and expressions of the late capitalist condition) can be considered the 'first specifically North American global style' (*ibid.*: xx), and late capitalism the first truly North American economic–political–cultural order. Given the advent of a *pax Americana* around the mid-point of the twentieth century, it is far from surprising that the rapidly developing cultural economy of American sport should have had such an influence around the world. Whereas Britain proved to be the socio-spatial nucleus of modern sport forms in their early phases of development (Elias and Dunning, 1986; Holt, 1989), later phases in the sportization process (the shift from a multiplicity of localized sports and pastimes to a relatively narrow global economy of commercially rationalized sport forms) were most definitively American in derivation and orientation (Maguire *et al.*, 2002; Maguire, 1999, 2000). Indeed, the status and influence of America as the *hothouse* of late capitalist sport provides the rationale for the tacit Americocentrism of this chapter. According to Jameson, 'this whole global, yet American, postmodern culture is the internal and superstructural expression of a whole new wave of American military and economic domination through the world' (Jameson, 1991: 5): sporting domination also, not perhaps in the sense of an overarching global homogeneity in prevailing sport forms, events or athletes, but definitely in the uniform manner through which local sport cultures have been corporatized.

The spectre of the profit-driven corporation has proved to be the structural and ideological conduit for the 'infiltration' (Habermas, 1979) of capital into previously under-exploited realms of social existence. According to the ensuing 'social hegemony' of corporatization (Alt, 1983: 98), the commercial corporation is the naturalized, and largely unquestioned, blueprint for all domains of societal experience and organization. Alt (*ibid.*) argues:

> The history of modern capitalism is the corporatization of social life worlds once under communal and normative control. Education, health, leisure and sport, marriage, child-rearing, work, community life, welfare (the traditional infrastructures of publics) lose their relative cultural autonomy to a formal dependency upon bureaucratic organizations, professional experts, and the imperial decisions of invisible executives.

The corporatization of US sport has been realized through the pervasive adoption of 'modern forms of domination, such as "business administration", and techniques of manipulation, such as market research and advertising' (Bourdieu, 1998: 35). However, it should not be overlooked that the forces responsible for the congealing corporate sport hegemon came from both internal and external points of origin. In terms of the former, many sport administrators simply acquiesced to what was perceived to be an unrelenting late capitalist tide, as a corporatizing wave spread across the sporting landscape, vanguarded by a new generation of profit-driven executives (Butsch, 1990; McKay and Miller, 1991). The reorganization of sport in accordance to the strictures of economic rationality was also informed by externally grounded influences. Sport's latent, and largely under-exploited, commercial potential was clearly vulnerable to corporate colonization. Within an ostensibly consumption-based economy, ownership of a commercial enterprise invoking a level of popularity and loyalty exceeding far 'beyond most other experiences' (Miller *et al.*, 2001: 1) made sport an attractive proposition for institutional and individual investors alike. So, through a series of takeovers by various corporate interests (from traditional manufacturing and, more recently, from the burgeoning financial, mass media and high-technology sectors), outmoded sporting structures and sensibilities have largely been replaced by the profit-driven architectures and rationalities of corporate managerialism.

Sport's corporatization, and the comparatively resigned response to its widespread instantiation, illustrates the degree to which the late capitalist order is not only responsible for, and indeed realized through, the collapsing of the economic into the cultural and *vice versa*. The very triumph of sporting corporatism also suggests the manner in which politics – in the form of dominant ideologies of sociopolitical order and governance – now similarly help substantiate, and are substantiated by, the economic and the cultural. Interestingly, this vindicates Jameson's (1992) understanding of the necessary relationality of cultural objects, which exist, and have to be understood in coexistence, with various interrelated historical, sociopolitical and economic dimensions. Within the late capitalist moment, the tyrannical individualistic rhetoric of neo-liberalism has created a political culture, organized around the 'modalities of privatization, deregulation, and commercialization' (Giroux, 2004: xv), within which the very concept of the *free* market offers a compelling model of societal existence (hence the historically contingent linkage between sociopolitical and economic dimensions). As Jameson (1991: 273) noted:

> Market ideology assures us that human beings make a mess of it when they try to control their destinies ('socialism is impossible') and that we are fortunate in possessing an interpersonal mechanism – the market – which can substitute for human hubris and planning and replace human decisions altogether. We only need to keep it clean and oiled, and it now – like the monarch so many centuries ago – will see to us and keep us in line.

As the facilitator of the neo-liberal, free market system, the profit-driven corporation became the expected, nay demanded, institutional model through which American life (from cradle to grave, through medical, educational and religious sectors, to name but three) was moulded to the demands of a kind of unfettered 'radical capitalism, with no other laws than that of maximum profit' (Bourdieu, 1998: 35). Thus, sociopolitical and economic dimensions combine to inform the cultural landscape.

Within the US sport context, the process of corporatization has had wide-ranging effects, as indicated by the emergence of the 'corporate sport' schema: the now accepted structural and ideological blueprint for commercial sport organizations (McKay and Miller, 1991; Walsh and Giulianotti, 2001). In seeking to follow the corporate sport hegemon (through developing a highly regulated, controlled and predictable mass entertainment product, designed to generate maximum profit across numerous revenue streams), administrators and executives routinely adopt the following, seemingly *de rigueur*, commercial strategies: the cultural management of the sport entity as a network of merchandizable brands and embodied sub-brands; the differentiation of sport-related revenue streams and consumption opportunities; profit-driven executive control and management hierarchies; cartelized ownership and franchized organizational structures; rational (re)location of teams and venues; the entertainment-driven mass mediation of sporting spectacles; the reconfiguring of sport spectacles and spaces as sponsorship vehicles for advancing corporate visibility; and the advancement of marketing and promotional strategies aimed at both consolidating core and expanding new sport consumer constituencies. Indeed, while there may be alternatives (pre-meditated or otherwise) to this corporate sport modality, these are few and far between, and do not challenge its global hegemony. Thus, currently there would appear to be no sustainable, viable or, indeed, even imaginable alternatives to the late capitalist, corporatist iteration of sport (Andrews, 2006).

The integrated sport spectacle

Implied in the very nomenclature, corporate sport encompasses a complex inter-relationship between capital and sport: between the economy and culture. As Rowe (1995: 115) identified, 'sport industry is imbricated with a series of inter-dependent economic and cultural institutions, and so is further cemented into a leisure complex in which the constituent parts appear increasingly naturalized and indispensable'. Arguably, the rampant commercial corporatization of sport represents the quintessential illustration of the 'new kind of dynamic' linking the economic base with the social superstructure within the 'third stage' of capitalism (Jameson, 1991: xxi). For, with the advent of late capitalism, events unfolding in the empirical world brought into sharp relief the inadequacies of the functionalist reductionism that plagued much Marxist thought for much of the twentieth century (which posited the various components of the social superstructure as being rigidly determined by the economic base of the society). Differently put, late capitalism's commercial colonization of the cultural, and concomitant cultural colonization of the commercial – the cultural evolution of the capitalist mode of production – challenged the interpretive capacity of conventional Marxist thought:

> No longer, then, is the Marxist cultural critic restrained by the fact that 'in the last instance' it is the economy which dictates what occurs in the cultural superstructure; no longer is the world of literature, the arts, images and representations somehow secondary or reflective of the real world of economy and 'base'.
>
> (McRobbie, 2005: 155)

The 'new dynamic' of the late capitalist mode of production involved the collapsing 'back into one another' of the economic and the cultural, which now 'say the same thing in an eclipse of the distinction between base and super-structure' (Jameson, 1991: xxi). Interestingly, Hardt and Weeks (2000: 9) argue that while Jameson's acknowledgement of the reciprocal lines of determination causality linking the economic with the superstructure is an important (if hardly novel) insight, of considerably more significance is the manner in which he engages 'the base–superstructure metaphor as a problematic that will force us continually to ask the question of how culture relates to other fields'. Jameson's response to this conundrum is plain: 'I have consistently argued, over the last few years, that that conjuncture is marked by a dedifferentiation of fields' (Jameson, 1998: 73), such that the structures and associated spheres of influence of such sectors as culture, politics, the judiciary, military, religion, the media, technology and, indeed, the economy are now liable to converge to form complex amalgams, displaying culturally and historically contingent sectoral inflections. As Jameson

(2000: 120) noted, 'My own position has always been that everything changes when you grasp the base-and-superstructure not as a full-fledged theory in its own right, but rather as the name for a problem, whose solution is always a unique, ad hoc invention.' Hence, the mode of production through which capitalism reproduces itself is never a purely economic, cultural, political, social and/or technological entity; rather, it incorporates all, some or indeed none of these, according to the specificities of time and space (Hardt and Weeks, 2000).

Jameson's understanding of the late capitalism moment, and hence mode of production, was prefigured on one pivotal point of convergence: namely that between the economy, culture and the mass media. For, in many respects, Jameson offered a model of the social totality within which the mass media (and particularly commercial television) occupy an unprecedented position and influence at the heart of social, cultural, political and economic life. This media-oriented conceptual schema represented an antidote to traditional Marxist economics' inability to understand the 'gradual and seemingly natural mediatization of North American society in the 1960s', which was followed by the precipitous mediatization of Western Europe in subsequent decades: 'Lenin on imperialism did not quite seem to equal Lenin on the media' (Jameson, 1991: 400). Of course, in their groundbreaking critiques of the culture industries, Horkheimer and Adorno (1999) famously dissected the mass media's constitutive relation to the workings of monopoly capitalism within the 1930s and early 1940s. In doing so, they played an important role in exposing the pervasive industrial structures, processes and relations underlying mass mediated cultural production in the modern era:

> for culture now impresses the same stamp on everything. Films, radio and magazines make up a system which is uniform as a whole and in every part . . . Under monopoly all mass culture is identical, and the lines of its artificial framework begin to show through . . . Movies and radio need no longer pretend to be art. The truth that they are just business is made into an ideology in order to justify the rubbish they deliberately produce.
> (Horkheimer and Adorno, 1999: 120, 121)

Nevertheless, the hypercommercialism of late capitalism represents such an exaggerated elaboration of the processes identified by Horkheimer and Adorno, Jameson (1991: x) declared: 'any sophisticated theory of the post-modern ought to bear something of the same relation to Horkheimer and Adorno's old "Culture Industry" concept as MTV or fractal ads bear to fifties television series'. He thus updated Horkheimer and Adorno's understanding of the 'culture industry' by highlighting the 'gradual disappearance of the physical marketplace', and thereby indicating the manner in which the media and the market become indivisible within the late capitalist moment (*ibid.*: 275)

The late capitalist mode of (cultural) production both relies upon and accentuates the 'intimate symbiosis between the market and the media' (*ibid.*:). This results from the market being realized through mass mediated products (the manufacturing of mediated experiences as commodities), mass mediating processes (the constituting of commodity signs on and through the mass media), and the mass media's incorporation into the broader economy (the intensive capitalization of mass media industries). Given the primacy of the mass media to contemporary economic forces and relations, compounded by the aggressive commercial mobilization of sport as a form of potentially lucrative popular culture, the current 'institutional alignment of sports and media' would appear to be an unavoidable corollary of the late capitalist condition (Real, 1998: 15). Contemporary sport has become subject to the logics of a society, and indeed a high-technology capitalist economy, propelled by commercially mediated spectacles and circuitry (Dyer-Witheford, 1999). American sport culture has been characterized as the 'sports/media complex' (Jhally, 1989), the corollary of which is 'mediasport' (Wenner, 1998). Underpinning such assertions are the mass mediated sport entertainment spectacles that represent the primary motor of sport's cultural economy, and a significant element of the broader cultural economy too. According to Kellner (2003: 65), 'the extent to which sports have become commercialized and transformed into a spectacle' is one of the characteristic features of contemporary society.

Such allusions to Debord's conceptualizing are wholly appropriate when seeking to forge a Jameson-inflected understanding of late capitalist sport, since he explicitly acknowledged a debt owed to the French Situationist (Jameson, 1991). Jameson was, like many others, particularly interested in Debord's theorizing on the society of the spectacle (Debord, 1994). However, unlike many others (e.g.Tomlinson, 2002), Jameson recognized, and sought to benefit from, the complexity of Debord's understanding of the spectacle. Debord illustrated the multidimensionality of the spectacle, and its dualistic function within spectacular society: 'The spectacle appears at once as society itself, as a part of society and as a means of unification' (Debord, 1994: 12). Confirming this observation, Debord identified two, necessarily interdependent, orders of the spectacle: the upper-case Spectacle (the mass mediated mega-event) and the lower-case spectacle (the relentless outpourings of corroborating and/or parasitic culture forms). These, respectively, provided the monumental and vernacular architecture of a society within which – as late capitalist product and process – the spectacle 'is both the outcome and the goal of the dominant mode of production' (*ibid.*: 13).

Corporate sport evokes Debord's dualistic conceptualizing by incorporating both the monumental (the production of sport media mega-events) and vernacular (the ancilliary commercial texts, products and services) orders of the spectacle. According to league commissioner David Stern, the NBA is less a traditional sporting organization than it is a 'major entertainment and consumer goods company' (quoted in Lombardo, 2004: 1). Such an evaluation – equally applicable to other high-profile sport ventures in the US – exemplifies the degree to which contemporary sport entities exist and operate at the intersection of the monumental and the vernacular. In terms of the latter, over the past three decades or so, the major professional sports in the US have transformed themselves into multifaceted consumer entertainment complexes, with mass mediated

Spectacles (largely in the form of live network television game coverage) acting as their integrative and generative core. Hence, in order to secure a place in the American popular consciousness, and nurture interest in the league, its franchises and players, sport organizations such as MLB, the NBA, NFL, NHL and latterly NASCAR have recognized the primacy of televisualization (Miller *et al.*, 2001). This has led to a convergence of interests between sporting and mass media concerns, each reliant on the other for providing, on the one hand, popular media content, and, on the other, mass distribution platforms. The ensuing 'seductively consumerist union of commerce, sport and television' (Rowe, 1996: 566) – an efficient merging of sport and entertainment (Hall, 2002) – has prompted the operation and realization of sport as monumental Spectacle. As one commentator opined in relation to NBC's coverage of the 2006 Turin winter Olympic Games:

> These are NBC's games, and by now we should know how they're played. The network sees the Olympics less as sports than as spectacle, at least in prime time, and it packages them accordingly into a sort of athletic variety show. Events are delayed, results are hidden, and while bad news is not ignored, it's not stressed, either. This is not *Monday Night Football*. The game is not the thing.
>
> (Bianco, 2006: 1D)

Clinging desperately to the last vestiges of its perceived semi-autonomous relation to other societal sectors (particularly the economic and political), sport, or more correctly the highly commercialized, entertainment-driven image of the sport Spectacle, represents the 'final form of commodity reification' (Jameson, 1991: 18). The vernacularity of the corporate sport spectacle is evident in the intensive theming and merchandising that expanded that which constitutes the sport experience, while cultivating the aura of the sport Spectacle (Bryman, 1999). This has resulted in the circulation of a 'panoply of pop-cultural offerings' (Holbrook, 2001: 142) through which leagues, franchises and players can be consumed, and thereby experienced, in multifarious commodified forms. Thus, the cultural economy of corporate sport vindicates Debord's (1994: 29) assertion that we are ensconced within the 'historical moment at which the commodity completes its colonization of social life . . . commodities are now all there is to see; the world we see is the world of the commodity'.

Within *Comments on the Society of the Spectacle*, Debord (1990) identified a new, heightened stage in the evolution of the society of the spectacle, announced by the emergence of the 'integrated spectacle'. This concept represented the synthesized extension of Debord's earlier notion of the 'diffuse' (characterized by neo-liberal freedom) and 'concentrated' (marked by command economy alienation) spectacles, and is manifest in the seeming contradiction of increased governance of the market place (in terms of the commercial direction of social practices and subjectivities). Through the integrated spectacle, the 'autocratic reign of the market economy' reached a new level of rational efficiency, such that the 'spectacle has never before put its mark to such a degree on almost the full range of socially produced behavior and objects' (*ibid.*: 2, 9). In this vein, the integrated spectacle that is corporate sport contributes to the covert governance of the consumer market place, through the advancement of an interdependent economy of commodity signs (i.e., licensed apparel and merchandise, videos/ DVDs, computer games and even themed restaurants), designed to stimulate positive sensory experiences with the core brands (the league and its franchises) and their constitutive embodied sub-brands (players). Spectacularized sports can thus be considered to be emotive autocracies, since, in addition to generating capital, their ancilliary products (the vernacular spectacle) seek to control and direct consumer emotions in a manner that enhances the aura of the sport event (the monumental Spectacle), and thereby further stimulates desires for its myriad commodified forms. In Debord's (1994: 15) terms, spectacular sport 'is essentially tautological, for the simple reason that its means and its ends are identical. It is the sun that never sets on the empire of modern passivity [while] basking in the perpetual warmth of its own glory'.

Considering late capitalism

Readers of this chapter may have been anticipating something quite different from that which they encountered. At the beginning of this project, there was what could be considered an understandable compulsion to interpret contemporary sport culture through Jameson's readily identified cultural logics of late capitalism: his vividly observed expressions of postmodernism, such as cultural depthlessness, schizophrenia, pastiche, simulation, the waning of affect and the attendant crisis of historicity (Jameson, 1991). Certainly, the contemporary sporting landscape abounds with instructive examples of Jameson's understanding of postmodernism's expressive forms (Andrews, 1999). However, approaching late capitalism from the vantage point of its aesthetic sensibilities and incarnations, and their particular relation to sport, intimated the worst kind of abstract and reductionist theoreticism (Tomlinson, 2002). So, rather than examine the cultural logics (plural) of late capitalism, it appeared considerably more productive to attempt to develop a broader understanding of Jameson's cultural logic (singular) through which he theorized the late capitalist order, particularly in terms of associated transformations in the mode of production. For, arguably, it is when Jameson is at his most totalizing (something which he readily identified *sans* demur – Jameson (1991, 1998)), that it is possible to discern his considerable contribution towards furthering Marxist analyses of the radical transformations in the nature and workings of both capital and capitalism, many of which Marx himself did not (and nor could he have been expected to) foresee. Jameson clearly enunciated such grand ambitions when referring to his attitude towards the very term 'postmodernism': it 'is not just another word for the description of a particular style'; rather, he viewed it as a 'periodizing concept', a 'new moment' in the evolution of capitalism that correlates to 'new formal features in culture with the emergence of a new type of social life and a new economic order' (Jameson, 1998: 3). So, this chapter has attempted to excavate, from Jameson's challenging prose, an understanding of the mechanisms and machinations of late capitalism, while simultaneously forging a more nuanced comprehension of its complex relationship with an interrelatedly evolving cultural economy of sport.

According to Jameson, late, multination or consumer capitalism is dialectically linked to particular historical, political and socioeconomic contingencies, from which emerge the cultural forms, forces and relations through which this new order becomes identified, experienced and understood. Over the past five decades, sport has evolved in concert with the epochally characteristic 'indifferentiation' of distinctions between base and superstructure, between the economic and cultural, between the market and media, and between the commodity and sign (Jameson, 1991). Thus, as sport has been aggressively, and seemingly irreversibly, commercialized, corporatized and spectacularized, it has transformed into a domain most evocative of the late capitalist condition, yet one whose multidimensional relationality (particularly with regard to economic and political spheres) is regularly overlooked by the consuming masses in a manner which suggests the sporting 'image has become the final form of commodity reification' (*ibid.*: 18). This final point may be somewhat overstated; however, even if it is grudgingly acknowledged, the conclusive and mutually productive insertion of sport into the late/multinational/consumer capitalist formation has – with a few notable exceptions (see Alt, 1983; Brewer, 2002; Brookes, 2002; Cole and Hribar, 1995; Donnelly, 1996; Goldman and Papson, 1998; McKay and Miller, 1991; Miller and McHoul, 1998; Miller *et al.*, 2001; Parry and Malcolm, 2004; Real, 1998; Rowe, 1995; Sage, 1996; Silk, 2004; Slack, 2004; Walsh and Giulianotti, 2001) – yet to generate the type of theoretically informed dialogue that one would expect.

There is an interesting, and unquestionably significant, line of research focused on identifying and encouraging strategies of resistance against corporate capitalist incursions into popular sport cultures (see Hughson and Free, 2006; Free and Hughson, 2006; Walsh and Giulianotti, 2001). Much of the resistance identified in this research – while both material and symbolic in nature – incorporates practices of creative appropriation from within the context of corporate sport. It remains to be seen whether these are anything more than superficial acts of cultural opposition, destined to be (re)incorporated into late capitalist sport's dynamically acquisitive cultural economy, or whether the tautologous circuitry of corporate sport can, in fact, be meaningfully interrupted. From the vantage point of Jameson's late capitalist cosmology, there would seem to be little grounds for optimism, yet perhaps illuminating the workings of a social and cultural system represents the initial step towards intervening into it (Grossberg, 1997). Hence, this chapter could be seen as an attempt to stimulate such a project. At the very least, hopefully it illustrates the general relevance of Jameson's position, and thereby stimulates further – and probably more critical and precise – engagements with his cultural Marxism as a vehicle for understanding the contemporary sporting landscape. Far from exhaustive or definitive, this admittedly selective reading will hopefully be viewed as a mildly provocative invitation to get the Jameson ball rolling, and thereby further the cultural Marxist debate pertaining to the corporate sport juggernaut.

References

Adorno, T. (2001) *The Culture Industry*, London: Routledge.

Alt, J. (1983) 'Sport and Cultural Reification: From Ritual to Mass Consumption', *Theory, Culture and Society* 1(3), pp. 93–107.

Andrews, D.L. (1999) 'Dead or Alive?: Sports History in the Late Capitalist Moment', *Sporting Traditions: Journal of the Australian Society for Sports History* 16(1), pp. 73–85.

Andrews, D.L. (2006) *Sport–Commerce–Culture: Essays on Sport in Late Capitalist America*, New York: Peter Lang.

Bianco, R. (2006) 'Prime-time Olympics: A Variety Show', *USA Today*, 13 February, p. 1D.

Bourdieu, P. (1984) *Distinction: A Social Critique of the Judgement of Taste*, Cambridge, MA: Harvard University Press.

Bourdieu, P. (1998) *Acts of Resistance: Against the Tyranny of the Market*, New York: The New Press.

Braverman, H. (1998) *Labor and Monopoly Capital: The Degradation of Work in the Twentieth Century*, 25th edn, New York: Monthly Review Press.

Brewer, B.D. (2002) 'Commercialization in Professional Cycling 1950–2001: Institutional Transformations and the Rationalization of "doping"', *Sociology of Sport Journal* 19(3), pp. 276–301.

Brookes, R. (2002) *Representing Sport*, London: Arnold.

Bryman, A. (1999) 'The Disneyization of Society', *Sociological Review* 47(1), pp. 25–47.

Butsch, R. (ed.) (1990) *For Fun and Profit: The Transformation of Leisure into Consumption*, Philadelphia: Temple University Press.

Cole, C.L. and Hribar, A.S. (1995) 'Celebrity Feminism: Nike Style – Post-fordism, Transcendence, and Consumer Power', *Sociology of Sport Journal* 12(4), pp. 347–69.

Debord, G. (1990 [1988]) *Comments on the Society of the Spectacle*, trans. M. Imrie, London: Verso.

Debord, G. (1994 [1967]) *The Society of the Spectacle*, trans. D. Nicholson-Smith, New York: Zone Books.

Donnelly, P. (1996) 'Prolympism: Sport Monoculture as Crisis and Opportunity', *Quest* 48, pp.25–42.

Dyer-Witheford, N. (1999) *Cyber-Marx: Cycles and Circuits of Struggles in High-technology Capitalism*, Urbana: University of Illinois Press.

Elias, N. and Dunning, E. (1986) *Quest for Excitement: Sport and Leisure in the Civilizing Process*, Oxford: Basil Blackwell.

Free, M. and Hughson, J. (2006) 'Common Culture, Commodity Fetishism and the Cultural Contradictions of Sport', *International Journal of Cultural Studies* 9(1), pp. 83–104.

Firat, A.F. and Venkatesh, A. (1995) 'Postmodern Perspectives on Consumption', in R.W. Belk, N. Dholakia and A. Venkatesh (eds) *Consumption and Marketing: Macro Dimensions*, Cincinnati: South-Western College, pp. 234–65.

Giroux, H.A. (2004) *The Terror of Neoliberalism: Authoritarianism and the Eclipse of Democracy*, Boulder: Paradigm.

Goldman, R. and Papson, S. (1996) *Sign Wars: The Cluttered Landscape of Advertising*, Boulder: Westview Press.

Goldman, R. and Papson, S. (1998) *Nike Culture*, London: Sage.

Grossberg, L. (1997) *Bringing it All Back Home: Essays on Cultural Studies*, Durham, NC: Duke University Press.

Habermas, J. (1979) 'Conservatism and Capitalist Crisis', *New Left Review* 115, pp. 73–84.

Hall, M. (2002) 'Taking the Sport Out of Sports', *Street and Smith's Sports Business Journal*, 19 August, p. 23.

Hardt, M. and Weeks, K. (2000) 'Introduction', in M. Hardt and K. Weeks (eds) *The Jameson Reader*, Oxford: Blackwell, pp. 1–29.

Hesmondhalgh, D. (2002) *The Cultural Industries*, London: Sage.

Holbrook, M.B. (2001) 'Times Square, Disneyphobia, and HegeMickey: The Ricky Principle, and the Downside of the Entertainment Economy – It's Fun-dumb-mental', *Marketing Theory* 1(2), pp. 139–63.

Holt, R.J. (1989) *Sport and the British: A Modern History*, Oxford: Clarendon Press.

Horkheimer, M. and Adorno, T.W. (1999) 'The Culture Industry: Enlightenment as Mass Deception', in *idem, Dialectic of enlightenment*, New York: Continuum, pp. 120–67.

Hughson, J. and Free, M. (2006) 'Paul Willis, Cultural Commodities, and Collective Sport Fandom', *Sociology of Sport Journal* 23(1), pp. 72–85.

Jameson, F. (1983) 'Postmodernism and Consumer Society', in H. Foster (ed.) *The Anti-aesthetic: Essays on Postmodern Culture*, Seattle: Bay Press, pp. 111–25.

Jameson, F. (1991) *Postmodernism: Or, the Cultural Logic of Late Capitalism*, Durham, NC: Duke University Press.

Jameson, F. (1992) *The Geopolitical Aesthetic*, Bloomington: Indiana University Press.

Jameson, F. (1996) *Late Marxism: Adorno, or, the Persistence of the Dialectic*, London: Verso.

Jameson, F. (1998) *The Cultural Turn: Selected Writings on the Postmodern 1983–1998*, London and New York: Verso.

Jameson, F. (2000) 'Base and Superstructure', in M. Hardt and K. Weeks (eds) *The Jameson Reader*, Oxford: Blackwell, pp. 119–22.

Jhally, S. (1989) 'Cultural Studies and the Sports/Media Complex', in L.A. Wenner (ed.) *Media, Sports, and Society*, Newbury Park: Sage, pp. 70–93.

Kellner, D. (2003) *Media Spectacle*, London: Routledge.

Klein, N. (1999) *No Logo: Taking Aim at Brand Bullies*, New York: Picador.

Lee, M.J. (ed.) (2000) *The Consumer Society Reader*, Oxford: Blackwell.

Lombardo, J. (2004) 'Stern: NBA in Talks to Put More Playoffs on ABC', *Street and Smith's Sports Business Journal*, 20 September, p. 1.

Maguire, J., Jarvie, G., Mansfield, L. and Bradley, J. (2002) *Sport Worlds: A Sociological Perspective*, Champaign: Human Kinetics.

Maguire, J.A. (1999) *Global Sport: Identities, Societies, Civilization*, Cambridge: Polity Press.

Maguire, J.A. (2000) 'Sport and Globalization', in J. Coakley and E. Dunning (eds) *Handbook of Sports Studies*, London: Sage, pp. 356–69.

Mandel, E. (1999) *Late Capitalism*, 6th impression edn, London: Verso Classics.

McKay, J. and Miller, T. (1991) 'From Old Boys to Men and Women of the Corporation: The Americanization and Commodification of Australian Sport', *Sociology of Sport Journal* 8(1), pp. 86–94.

McRobbie, A. (2005) *The Uses of Cultural Studies*, London: Routledge.

Miller, T., Lawrence, G., McKay, J. and Rowe, D. (2001) *Globalization and Sport: Playing the World*, London: Sage.

Miller, T. and McHoul, A. (1998) *Popular Culture and Everyday Life*, London: Sage.

Negus, K. (1997) 'The Production of Culture', in P.D. Gay (ed.) *Production of Culture/Cultures of Production*, London: The Open University, pp. 67–118.

Parry, M. and Malcolm, D. (2004) 'England's Barmy Army: Commercialization,

Masculinity and Nationalism', *International Review for the Sociology of Sport* 39(1), pp. 75–94.

Pine, B.J. and Gilmore, J.H. (1998) 'Welcome to the Experience Economy', *Harvard Business Review* July/August, pp. 97–105.

Poster, M. (1990) *The Mode of Information: Poststructuralism and Social Context*, Chicago: University of Chicago Press.

Real, M.R. (1998) 'MediaSport: Technology and the Commodification of Postmodern Sport', in L.A. Wenner (ed.) *Mediasport*, London: Routledge, pp. 14–26.

Rowe, D. (1995) *Popular Cultures: Rock Music, Sport and the Politics of Pleasure*, London: Sage.

Rowe, D. (1996) 'The Global Love-match: Sport and Television', *Media, Culture and Society* 18(4), pp. 565–82.

Sage, G.H. (1996) 'Patriotic Images and Capitalist Profit: Contradictions of Professional Team Sports Licensed Merchandise', *Sociology of Sport Journal* 13(1), pp. 1–11.

Silk, M.L. (2004) 'A Tale of Two Cities: The Social Production of Sterile Sporting Space', *Journal of Sport and Social Issues* 28(4), pp. 349–78.

Slack, T. (ed.) (2004) *The Commercialisation of Sport*, London: Routledge.

Tomlinson, A. (2002) 'Theorising Spectacle: Beyond Debord', in J. Sugden and A. Tomlinson (eds) *Power Games: A Critical Sociology of Sport*, London: Routledge, pp. 44–60.

Walsh, A.J. and Giulianotti, R. (2001) 'This Sporting Mammon: A Normative Critique of the Commodification of Sport', *Journal of the Philosophy of Sport* 28, pp. 53–77.

Wenner, L.A. (ed.) (1998) *Mediasport*, London: Routledge.

Wernick, A. (1991) *Promotional Culture: Advertising, Ideology and Symbolic Expression*, London: Sage.

Afterword

High-definition sports capitalism

Michael Bérubé

I read the essays in this volume during the National Hockey League playoffs of April–June 2008 – which featured not only a scintillating six-game final between the Pittsburgh Penguins (the youngest team in the league) and the Detroit Red Wings (one of the oldest, but the most talented), but also a Pennsylvania showdown in the Eastern Conference finals between the Penguins and the Philadelphia Flyers. The very fact of my watching the series is a story in itself, because in order to catch the games on television I had to contact Dish Network and upgrade to the 'Top 250' channel package; the 'Top 200', alas, does not include 'Versus', the third- or fourth-tier cable station with which the NHL signed its television contract after spurning what was apparently an unacceptably low offer from ESPN. Formerly known as OLN, the 'Outdoor Living Network', Versus carries the NHL and the Tour de France, as well as a motley assortment of kickboxers, cage-fighters, bull-riders and hunting/fishing shows. This is, perhaps, the outer limit of televised sport in the United States, the ultima thule to which the NHL has been consigned upon being told by ESPN that its perennially low ratings and its disastrous, year-long lockout in 2003–4 did not justify the price it was asking for television rights. (Additionally, in response to the league's decision to sign with Versus, ESPN has cut its hockey coverage back to the barest of mentions.) Foolishly, I thought I had solved the Versus problem by buying a separate 'NHL Center Ice' package from the Dish Network, at a cost of US$140; but alas, that package does not include the later rounds of playoffs, which are televised exclusively on Versus. The final games of the final series were televised on NBC, which (a) is a real (i.e., global) network and (b) is therefore available in places like bars and hotels. Still, for over a month, if I wanted to follow the sport I play and love, it was Versus or nothing.

But if the Eastern Conference finals took place in my home state, why didn't I simply attend one of the games? It's just under three hours to Pittsburgh from Penn State; just over three hours to Philadelphia. I make it a point to try to see at least one game in Pittsburgh every year, though the team's recent success – cultivating spectacularly talented teenagers and early twenty-somethings like Sidney Crosby, Evgeni Malkin, Jordan Staal and goaltender Marc-André Fleury – has made it considerably more difficult to pick up a ticket unless one plans months in advance. (The Penguins were doormats just two years ago, but sold out every home game this year.) But the cost of attending a playoff game, with one or two children in tow (mine are twenty-two and sixteen), is prohibitive: for the conference finals, Penguins tickets sold out within ten minutes, and the *lowest* asking price at the online Penguins ticket exchange was $300. Need I add the further complication that one of my children – Jamie, the sixteen-year-old – has a fear of heights, requiring him to sit in the lower tiers of a stadium?

I did manage to see one game in Pittsburgh this year, a bracing mid-season match-up with my beloved New York Rangers in January. There were no affordable seats available for that one, so I bought an unaffordable one – near centre ice, twenty rows up, $175. Ordinarily, I'll settle for anything in the middle tier of seats, which tend to run $60 to $90. But, as Garry Whannel notes in his contribution to this volume, 'there is not one simple "commodity" here but rather a set of overlapping commodities, embedded in a diverse but linked set of economic relations'. Wherever I have attended a hockey game, from Chicago to St Louis, from Madison Square Garden to the swamps of New Jersey, I have been surrounded by people – not exclusively men – wearing customized team jerseys. Let me explain these commodities briefly, because they are not your casual soccer shirts. As with the other major US sports – basketball, football, baseball – there are two kinds of jersey: authentic and replica. On NHL.com, a *replica* Montreal Canadiens jersey goes for $115; customized with a player's name and number, it is $170. An *authentic* New York Rangers jersey costs $250; customized, $330. The people sitting around me, wearing hundreds of dollars of licensing fees on their backs, are not rich; they are not corporate suits in '87 Crosby' jerseys. They are quite clearly ordinary, middle-class folk who have spent $80 on a ticket, $200 or more on a jersey, and $7 on each beer. And even though I know commodities are mystified and mystifying, I am still mystified. Where does all this money come from? And where does it go?

Hockey, like cricket, is a game of high and difficult technique, and I would love it regardless of who televises it or who manages it or who works out the deal for Pittsburgh's new stadium. But then, Cultural Studies is a game of high and difficult technique as well: it is one (relatively simple) thing to note the costs of sports spectatorship, quite another (more complex) thing to track the cultural formations to which those costs, and the discourse about those costs, are articulated. In the lingo of professional fandom, the fact that a pair of good seats can cost more than a pair of business suits often serves as a basis for complaints about wealthy players or greedy owners. When it is contrasted with the sports economics of a generation ago (when, for example, my father and I had season tickets to home Rangers games that cost just over $200 apiece *for the season*, in the 'green seats' just below Madison Square Garden's upper tier), it almost always serves as licence for nostalgia, for evocations of a simpler time before the advent of free agency, luxury boxes, Nike and bling. Why, I'm so old I can remember when every seat in the blue or green, yellow or red sections of Madison Square Garden was the same price, regardless of whether it was behind the net or on the red line; no one had yet hit upon the idea of charging more for individual sections of good seats nearer centre ice, just as no one had yet hit upon the idea of using the boards for advertising space. Indeed, I'm so old I can remember when sports stadiums were named 'Madison Square Garden' or 'Boston Garden' rather than 'FedEx Field', 'ScottTrade Center' or 'QualComm Stadium', because no one had yet hit upon the idea of licensing the *stadium name itself* to the highest bidder.

But this nostalgia, like so many forms of nostalgia, is partial and pernicious; it overlooks the fact that in that simpler time, players really *were* exploited, in the classic sense, and (with very rare exceptions) the only people who saw any real money were owners. In American baseball, thanks largely to the 'reserve clause' that gave teams the right to re-sign players at the end of each season (thus preventing them from seeking employment elsewhere), players' salaries remained level (relative to the general population) for nearly a century, even into the era of television – and television revenue. The day that Curt Flood challenged the reserve clause (16 January 1970, to be precise) is rightly seen as a turning point in baseball's labour relations; even though Flood ultimately lost his case, free agency was instituted five years later, and certainly no one speaks any longer of 'exploited' players. The average salary in MLB in 1970 was just under $30,000; in 2008, it exceeded $3 million. And what is a leftist to make of this, regardless of whether s/he thinks that Cultural Studies has strayed from the true Marxist path?

Brett St Louis's essay in this volume suggests just how unsettlingly complex, and how complexly unsettling, this question can be:

> Bearing in mind the inherent contradictions of capitalism, it is important to recognize that professional sports leagues – and ironically especially North American sports leagues such as the NFL, Major League Baseball (MLB) and NBA – often operate through capitalist oligarchical arrangements. Individual teams operating as franchises licensed and regulated by the league; draft selections where the least successful teams pick first from the new talent available from the farm system; and the imposition of a salary cap to ensure a degree of parity in teams' expenditure on athletic personnel: all contradict free market ideology. But to note this is not to reject this corporatist ethos in favour of an unrestricted free market.

In fact, the NFL, often considered (with good reason) the most corporate of leagues, is also the most socialist in one sense: every year, the sixteen-game schedule is recalibrated so as to give the previous year's weakest teams the weakest schedules, and the strongest teams the stiffest test. From each according to his abilities, to each according to his needs. But to note this is not to suggest that the NFL is a workers' paradise, any more than golf's handicapping system represents a viable model for social justice. In his black-Marxist analysis of the trials of Maurice Clarett, however, St Louis (relying partly on an analysis elaborated by Steven Ross) comes close to arguing that the ranks of college football – which serve as a farm system for the NFL – *should* be a less restricted market, since the NFL's rule that a player can be eligible for the draft only if he is at least three years out of high school is not justified (or justifiable) in the NFL's terms. As St Louis notes, the lower court that found in Clarett's favour determined that 'the NFL was unable to demonstrate that the rule enhanced competition and effectively breached federal antitrust laws by excluding him – and all players in the same situation – from attempting to enter the only feasible employment market for his skills'. And yet, as St Louis remarks not long thereafter, 'utilizing antitrust legislation and its foundational premise of protecting market freedoms does not, at face value, appear to be an appropriate method of advancing a progressive leftist political project'. And even if Clarett had won his case, 'the structures of the capitalist-athletic complex remain intact and a select and still small number of individuals have only won the right to insert themselves into a system of uncertainty as, on average, professional careers within the NFL and National Basketball Association (NBA), for example, are of a short duration'.

St Louis raises the possibility that college athletes in revenue-generating sports (i.e., football and basketball) might be paid some of the revenue they generate – and mentions Ross's suggestion that 'contractual arrangements could be developed within the framework of amateurism that would require student athletes to remain in the institution for the duration of their eligibility'. But colleges will not hear of it, 'due to their fear of being legally bound to bear the – for them prohibitive – financial costs of their liability to workers' compensation payments in the event of serious injury for those under extended contracts'.[1] So proposals to free up the college-football market have no real chance of succeeding – and if they did succeed, would very likely accelerate the commercialization of collegiate athletics. And yet from a black-Marxist perspective, the present arrangement seems manifestly unjust. What, then, to dust off the perennial question, is to be done?

It is easy enough – though always necessary, all the same – to decry arrangements whereby sports stadiums are built with public funds and the profits therefrom are realized entirely by the private interests who persuaded city managers to institute the stadium tax in the first place. (Of course, the right decries these arrangements as well, seeing them as unnecessary tax initiatives imposed by big government.) But it is harder to determine whether, when faced with harsh and glaring inequities in the capitalist-athletic complex, the left should be arguing for freer markets. 'At most,' Ian McDonald writes, 'it seems that all we can and must do is engage in rearguard and defensive strategies: such as exposing relations of power, engaging in campaigns for equality, formulating critiques.' But what counts as a 'campaign for equality'? I notice that Augusta National Golf Club, the home of the Masters tournament, does not admit women as members. Or I note that, despite the interventions of former NFL defensive tackle Esera Tuaolo and former NBA centre John Amaechi, no gay man in a team sport has yet 'come out' while still a member of an active roster. If sport is, as Ben Carrington's evocation of E.P. Thompson has it, a whole way of struggle, are sexism and homophobia in élite, high-performance sport worth fighting? Or are these merely struggles over 'identity'? And why should struggles over identity, in sport or elsewhere, be 'mere'?[2] From the penultimate paragraph of his essay, I get the sense that McDonald is after other game:

> Based on the notion of critique set with a revolutionary Marxist politics, I suggest that a properly dialectical approach involves denouncing sport while continuing to perpetuate it. It is the idea that sport must be simultaneously preserved and overcome: preserved because its paradoxical nature contains within it an inherent criticality that we can articulate as the utopian dimension of sport; overcome because sport contributes to the legitimacy of extant social relations of power, and serves to incorporate us into a system that causes immense human suffering.

But I do not get a sense here of why sport would be worth preserving at all. Surely it contains within it an inherent criticality and a utopian dimension; nearly every form of human activity does. Why, then, bother to preserve such an egregiously commercial, spectacle-driven, commodity-fetishizing, celebrity-obsessed activity as sport? What about it is worth preserving?

The volume's various critiques of 'high-performance' sport usefully remind me of all the things I can't stand about big-time sports – the hype, the celebrities, the tantrum-throwing coaches, the performance-enhancing drugs, the glorification (among players, coaches and owners alike) of goons, and, of course, the droning of thousands of analysts, chattering ceaselessly about all of the above. There is a word for all this, and – in the US, at least – that word is ESPNization. Yes, sports had its hype and its tantrums and its goons long before ESPN debuted in 1980. But ESPN has, I think, kicked North America's big-time sports culture into media overdrive, initiating a new kind of *high-definition sports capitalism*.

Thirty years ago, no one believed that a cable channel could possibly run sports 24/7, and I remember fondly the early days of the network, when it would televise Australian Rules Football just to fill the airtime. Now, of course, ESPN has metastasized into six channels – I believe I get ESPN SportsCenter, ESPN News, ESPN-2, ESPN Classic, but not ESPN-U or ESPN-Alternate – and has given rise to the joke, in the film *Dodgeball*, that the national championship of the American Dodgeball Association of America will be televised on ESPN's eighth channel, 'The Ocho', on which the tournament is touted as 'bigger than the World Cup, World Series and World War Two combined'. (Apparently, the channel also televises 'seldom-seen sports', such as riding-mower racing, water-skiing for squirrels, and competitive flogging, which would seem to put it in direct competition with the programming on Versus.) Even in the US, we may still be a few years away from The Ocho, but we are quite clearly in the era when everything about the NFL, right down to the annual combine and player draft, is televised. Some years ago, I actually forbade my older son from watching the draft 'live' on ESPN. 'Unless you are an owner, a prospect, or an agent,' I said to him, 'you have no business actually *watching* the draft. I know you're following the fate of the 49ers, but you can read about the draft when it's all over. You may watch bowling, dirt-bike racing, and strongman competitions where guys pull locomotives. That represents the very bottom of what I will tolerate in this house when it comes to sports spectatorship.' Thirty years ago, who could have imagined that there would be people – men, for the most part – who would watch a draft on television? But then, back in 1980, nobody imagined that there would be six ESPNs and a host of cable-channel competitors.

ESPN appears, to me, to be at once cause and symptom of high-definition sports capitalism. It has, as Grant Farred pointed out some years ago, revolutionized sports discourse, promoting a new generation of commentators and (for a while) a savvy, smart, intertextual form of sports talk that is cooler than the other side of the pillow.[3] (Reportedly, one of its competitors, *The Best Damn Sports Show Period*, was created precisely because ESPN's form of commentary had become too savvy, smart and intertextual for some of the mouth-breathing North American sports fans among us.) But at the same time, it has fuelled the behemoth sports machine and ushered us into a world in which college football coaches can be offered multi-million-dollar contracts – only to break them and jump schools in a year or two.[4] And yet here I am, hoping against hope that the wayward NHL will someday return to the network, thoroughly convinced that any sports commissioner who doesn't understand the centrality of ESPN to sports programming in North America doesn't deserve to have a job.

ESPN, I suggest, vividly makes David L. Andrews' point about the relatively slow 'corporatization of US sport'– namely, that it is quite remarkable that it didn't occur until fairly recently. As Andrews writes of the post-war era, 'sport's latent, *and largely under-exploited*, commercial potential was clearly vulnerable to corporate colonization' (my emphasis). When one contemplates the kind of monies now produced by revenue-generating sports, it is impossible not to agree that the commercial potential of sports had gone under-exploited for quite some time, even through the 1960s and 1970s. And yet Andrews' essay leads me to wonder if we can say that our current form of sports commercialism was always already available, waiting for canny entrepreneurs from Pete Rozelle to Michael Jordan to come along and realize it. Perhaps high-definition sports capitalism allows us to see fine-grained details in the social fabric we never saw before; then again, perhaps it creates new spectacles altogether. One does not want (if one is me) to issue glassy-eyed pronouncements about how ESPN Has Changed Everything. On the other hand, one does not want to imagine that the commercial possibility of televising the NFL draft was latent all along, ever since the days of leather helmets and two-way players. I do not yet know what I think about the way the hyper-commercialized sports present has emerged from the under-exploited sports past; I know only that it is critical to understand just how recent and how rapid the metastatization of sports capitalism has been. For, as Andrews argues, sports are 'arguably the culture industry of the contemporary moment' and their corporatization 'illustrates the degree to which the late capitalist order is . . . responsible for, and indeed realized through, the collapsing of the economic into the cultural and *vice versa*'. Regardless of whether one believes that Cultural Studies represents an abandonment of Marxist verities, or whether one believes that Cultural Studies did well to offer a Marxism without verities, we should be able to agree on the importance of historicizing sports capitalism, and on the importance of understanding emergent formations in sports capitalism precisely *as* emergent formulations.

I'll conclude with two general observations about this volume. One is that it offers a quite wonderful tonal range, from McDonald's denounce-and-preserve to Farred's evocations of the world-historical significance of Anfield, its environs and its inhabitants (fans and players alike). It is an especial delight to note that Marx was right after all these years – that Socrates was indeed offside in the Greeks' late goal, as Carrington notes at the outset. Sometimes, though, it seems as if the Marxism–Cultural Studies disputes tend to eclipse the analysis of sport: or, to put that another way, there are moments in some of the essays when the major sport in question seems to be replaying the great Althusser–Gramsci cup finals of the 1970s and 1980s. Not that I have any objection to that for its own sake; the Althusserians–Gramscians rivalry is one for the ages, right up there with Lakers–Celtics, Canadiens–Maple Leafs, Yankees–Red Sox and Liverpool–Manchester United, and it produced some of the most spirited competition in the history of the Marxist League. Besides, it now seems clear that in writing *Hegemony and Socialist Strategy*, Laclau and Mouffe were clearly offside, a few steps ahead of the play. But I am not sure how this critical dispute in Marxist theory can be adjudicated solely by reference to sport. (It is possible, of course, to argue that if one side or the other is right in theory, it is therefore right about every last cultural and economic phenomenon on the planet, but I don't find that argument convincing.)

For that matter, the 'class politics/identity politics' divide remains a conundrum for sports (and critical sport studies), for even as big-time, high-performance sport continues to show us the money, who can deny that sport is a primary venue for the performance of masculinity, and that there have been distinctive tensions between athletes and intellectuals since the first teenaged Greek athlete deposited the first teenaged Greek philosopher in a wastebasket? As I noted in my review of Toby Miller's *SportSex*, the entry of large numbers of women into US sports, thanks chiefly to Title IX of the Education Amendments of 1972, has changed the face of American sport, such that I now find myself playing in a 'men's' hockey league along with a handful of women.[5] Then again, the rise of women's sports has led to a weird rebiologization of gender, as kinesthesiologists (and doctors, and parents, and players) wonder why young women athletes suffer more anterior cruciate ligament (ACL) injuries than their male counterparts.[6]

Likewise, the expansion of sports to people with disabilities seems, on one hand, to be an unambiguous good: there are more venues for wheel-chair sport than ever before, the Special Olympics are global, and athletes like Oscar Pistorius are challenging the very meaning of 'disability'. And yet, on the other hand, disabled athletes tend to become the subjects of the worst kind of 'overcoming' narratives, serving as exemplary 'supercrips'. And when the 'supercrip' phenomenon overlaps with sport as the performance of (disabled) masculinity, you get *Murderball* – a film whose tag line could be 'Show me the testosterone'. With regard to bodies and identities, it seems, there are precious few developments in sport about which it is impossible to be ambivalent.

And although the analyses of urban sports spectacles, Olympic politics and assorted superstars are exceptionally well done here, I'd like to add a brief postscript about the less visible arenas of sports, the arenas in which ordinary people try to participate in sports themselves. For if left intellectuals want to understand The People where they live, then it seems worth the effort to learn where – and, more to the point, why – they play. In youth sports, for example, one will find varieties of instrumentalization and discipline, just as one always suspected: there are the brutal, deluded coaches, acting out their Bobby Knight and Knute Rockne fantasies by screaming at ten-year-olds; there are the crazed stage parents, hoping that little Timmy or Ashleigh will be their meal ticket in a decade or two; there are the innumerable leagues, from baseball's Little League and its pledges to God and country to my own youth league, the New York City Ice Hockey League, whose rather more secular credo was that 'a kid on the ice cannot be in hot water'. But one will also find, from youth sports on upward, people who genuinely love the aesthetic and kinesthetic challenge they can find nowhere else but in sport; people who appreciate high and difficult technique, and the intellectual (not merely physical) challenges posed by practices – from golf to cricket to swimming to basketball – in which the possibility of improvement is infinite, and the ideal of the 'personal best' ever recedes before one on the horizon. Or, as Toby Miller puts it in his essay here:

> Sport is a key site of pleasure and domination, via a complex dialectic that does not always produce a clear synthesis from the clash of opposing camps. It involves both the imposition of authority from above and the joy of autonomy from below. It exemplifies the exploitation of the labour process, even as it delivers autotelic pleasures.

Personally, I am never sure when a pleasure is autotelic; though I take great pleasure in some sports, in the course of my adult life I have been in shape and badly out of shape, and in shape is just better all around. Then again, being in shape is better *for* something – clarity of mind, cardiovascular health, general sense of well-being – quite apart from the question of how quickly one gets to the puck and how effectively one plays when one has it. Still, I like to believe that the pleasure I take in hockey is autotelic. But to say this is only to say that there is in sport – from the ESPN highlight reel to the after-work racquetball match, from the most overpaid, overrated, overhyped celebrity to the humblest weekend duffer – something of the aesthetic, something involving the care of the self, and that this, finally, must be part of its enduring appeal to millions of people who continue to resist the one-dimensionality of high-definition sports capitalism.

Notes

1 A side note on the work of Stephen Ross with regard to sports and labour contracts. When he taught at the University of Illinois School of Law, Ross was my neighbour and frequent interlocutor; he even audited my undergraduate honours seminar in post-modernism in 1991. In 2004–5, after I had moved to Penn State, he sent me an email informing me that he and his partner, Kit Kinports, were considering moving to Penn State, and asking me to compare the two universities. I replied, facetiously, that I could

not in good conscience recruit him to Penn State unless I knew where he stood on the NHL lockout. He promptly replied by sending me a .pdf on the subject: Stephen F. Ross (2004) 'The NHL Labour Dispute and the Common Law, the *Competition Act*, and Public Policy', *University of British Columbia Law Review* 37(2), pp. 343–406. It is a terrific piece of work in its own right, and gave me an insuperable advantage in all my conversations with my fellow Nittany Hockey League players, most of whom were inclined to support management. Steve Ross is now my neighbour in State College, and I thank him for his essay and for coordinating a reading group on *Beyond a Boundary* in Spring 2008, a group led by Grant Farred.

2 See Ben Carrington (2007) 'Merely Identity: Cultural Identity and the Politics of Sport', *Sociology of Sport Journal* 24(1), pp. 49–66.

3 See Grant Farred (2000) 'Cool as the Other Side of the Pillow: How ESPN's SportsCenter has Changed Sports Talk', *Journal of Sport and Social Issues* 24(2), pp. 96–117. Farred has since reconsidered the role of ESPN: 'at the moment I wrote the paper, I believed it raised the IQ, but by now it is responsible for the deterioration of all sports talk. SportsCenter elevated sports talk because it was unique and singular, but now you have stuff like *Rome is Burning*'. *Rome is Burning* is, indeed, a sign of an empire in the final stages of decline. See Vincent Valk (2007) 'Lamenting SportsCenter's Baroque Period', *Gelf Magazine*, 2 August, http://www.gelfmagazine.com/archives/lamenting_sportscenters_baroque_period.php (accessed 14 June 2008).

4 Because my own faculty position – the Paterno Family Professorship – is endowed by Penn State's football coach, I am sometimes asked whether I am not indirectly implicated in critiques of this aspect of the behemoth college sports machine. I suppose I am. But it bears noting that Joe Paterno is, in this as in other respects (such as his BA in Classics and his MA in American Literature), a salient exception to the new rule set by job-hopping coaches such as Nick Saban and Bobby Petrino. (I know of no other football coach in the US who has endowed a chair in Literature; Paterno has also endowed a chair in the university library, and in the 1990s led the capital campaign to double the size of the library overall.) Paterno is a legendary name in college sports, particularly in Pennsylvania. He has coached at Penn State since 1950, serving as head coach since 1966. He holds records for post-season bowl appearances (34) and wins (23), and his 372 lifetime wins are second only to Bobby Bowden's 373. He is also (justly) renowned for running a programme with an exceptionally high graduation rate. Accordingly, observers have generally assumed that Paterno's salary is in the seven-figure range now common among top college football coaches. But thanks to the dogged efforts of the *Harrisburg Patriot-News* in Pennsylvania, which filed suit for 'open records' to disclose the salaries of high-level officials at Penn State, the public now knows that Paterno makes $512,664 annually – a fraction of the salaries of coaches such as Saban – or, within the Big Ten alone, Ohio State's Jim Tressel ($890,000) and Iowa's Kirk Ferentz ($2.8 million). The news made the front page of every newspaper in Pennsylvania, as well as the pages of *USA Today* and the *New York Times*. I am advised (by the editors of this volume) that some readers outside the US might find it hard to imagine that a half-million-dollar salary would be considered modest among leading coaches at the college level – indeed, 'embarrassingly low', as one sports blog put it ('The Big Lead', 30 November 2007, http://thebiglead.com/?p=3798 (accessed 24 June 2008)). Surely, it is hard to fathom that the highest-paid people at American universities generally are the football and basketball coaches, whose salaries routinely outstrip (and sometimes double, triple or quadruple) those of college presidents. And to state the obvious, a half-million-dollar salary puts one among the economic élite anywhere in the world. But Americans, for their part, are generally unaware that there is no comparable phenomenon in international sports, and have come to expect that college football and basketball coaches come with multi-million-dollar price tags. Hence the strange newsworthiness of Paterno's salary in the US media, where the overwhelming response to the long-awaited disclosure was 'Really? Is *that all*?' as people

realized that Paterno was making a fraction of the salaries of far less accomplished coaches. (To my knowledge, the news coverage didn't mention the Paterno chairs or the Paterno Library.) For the record, though, I admit that I accepted the Paterno Family Professorship partly because I admire the man and think that a chair in his family's name is one of the coolest things in American academe.

5 See Michael Bérubé (2002) 'Of Ripped Abs and Sports Bras', *Politics and Culture* 1, http://aspen.conncoll.edu/politicsandculture/page.cfm?key=149 (accessed 14 June 2008).

6 For a recent account of the phenomenon, see Michael Sokolove (2008) 'The Uneven Playing Field', *New York Times Magazine*, 11 May, pp. 54–61. The article is adapted from Sokolove's book, *Warrior Girls: Protecting Our Daughters against the Injury Epidemic in Women's Sports* (New York: Simon and Schuster, 2008), whose subtitle unfortunately carries a strong whiff of paternalism.

Index

References to photos are given in italics

consumption xxiv, xxvi, xxix, 10, 43, 53,
54, 55, 58, 59, 60, 61, 64, 70, 71, 72–4,
75, 84, 142, 146, 163, 205–6, 214,
216–17, 219, 221, 222
contingency 17, 22, 26–7, 37, 42, 171–2,
216, 222–3, 228
*Contribution to the Critique of Political
Economy, A* (Marx) 18
corporate sport 24, 26, 79, 122, 145, 174,
214, 220–3, 223, 225–7, 228
corporatization 52, 81, 213, 221–3, 237
Cosby, Bill 136
Coubertin, Baron Pierre de 88, 96–101
Crawford, Gary 204, 205–6
Crehan, Kate 198, 202
CRG (Civil Rights Generation) 130
cricket 2, 20, 22
critical race theory (CRT) 123–4 *see also*
racism
cultural capital 76, 77, 82, 140, 147
cultural economy 74, 80–4, 214, 220, 225,
226, 228
'cultural economy' (Du Gay) 74
cultural industries 22
Cultural Populism (McGuigan) 73
Cultural Studies: Althusser's influence 68;
Birmingham model criticized 69; and
concrete empirical studies 70;
denigration of 30n5; economy/culture
issue marginalised 73–4; Gramsci's
influence 199; major theorists 26–7;
and Marxism 7, 19–20, 22, 32–3; new
social movements 40–1; shift in
content/analysis 112; a substitute for
Marxism 38–9
culture xxix, 4, 15–16, 27, 34, 35, 39,
43–4, 53, 56, 97, 111, 123, 181, 187
see also celebrity and celebrity culture;
advertising and promotional 78–80;
black 136, 141; capitalist 4, 7, 54,
213–28; and economy 68–84, 217, 218,
223, 224; Hip Hop 130, 131, 147;
industries 10, 217–18, 224; local 8, 54,
58, 60, 64, 237; Marxism and 16–22,
41, 68–72, 197; mass 217, 218, 224;
material 74; middle class 52; Native
American 206; physical xi, 2; popular
xxxi, 5, 8, 9, 19–22, 51, 55–7, 59,
60–1, 62–4, 64, 70, 146, 197, 199, 201,
225; sporting xii, 1, 10, 26, 41, 75, 77,
189, 213–28, 225–6, 236–8

Dalgleish, Kenny 157, 170, 173
Debord, Guy 53–4, 225, 226, 227

DeLuca, Kevin Michael 60
denunciation, sociology of 8, 62
Denver, Broncos 125
Derrida, Jacques 15, 36
determinism 3, 35, 39, 42, 53, 70, 110,
196, 206
Detroit: I Do Mind Dying
(Georgakas/Sarvin) 154
dialectical method 41–2
dialogic 164–7
Diem, Karl 99
disability 199, 207, 238
Discipline and Punish (Foucault) 182
discourse 10, 24, 26, 35, 36, 40, 43, 52, 55,
59, 61, 62, 69–71, 75, 76, 80, 82,
123–4, 132, 134, 139, 181, 185, 187,
188, 189, 216
Discourse on Colonialism (Césaire) 116
disorganized capitalism *see* postmodernism
domination xxvi, xxix, 4, 16, 43, 53, 56,
72, 97, 116, 124, 189, 190, 204, 221
Draper, Hal 35
Du Bois, W. E. B. 147
Du Gay, Paul 74
Dunning, Eric 113, 201, 220
Dworkin, Shari Lee 189
Dyson, Eric 132

Eagleton, Terry 35
East–West Conflict *see* Cold War
economic power 82, 89, 201, 206
Edwards, Harry 2
Edwards, Trevor 142
Eichberg, Henning 43–4
Elias, Norbert 5, 196, 220
Eliot, T. S. 154
Engels, Friedrich 18, 33, 42, 118, 159, 165
ESPN 77, 232, 236–7, 239
ethical charity 141
ethics 21, 162, 165–8, 171, 185–6
Everton Football Club 156, 157, 164,
167–8, 174
evolutionist positivism 208

factory council movement 202
Fanon, Frantz 119
fans xvii, xix, xx–xxi, xxiii–xxiv, xxxii,
23–5, 58, 59–60, 60–1, 61, 62, 64, 76,
83–4, 136, 157–8, 164, 168–72, 172–5,
187, 204, 205, 237, 238; Liverpool FC
159, 162, 163, 166, 167, 168, 173–4
Farred, Grant xvii, xxi, xxiv, 2, 9, 23,
154–75, 237, 238, 240n3
fascism 199

Routledge Sport

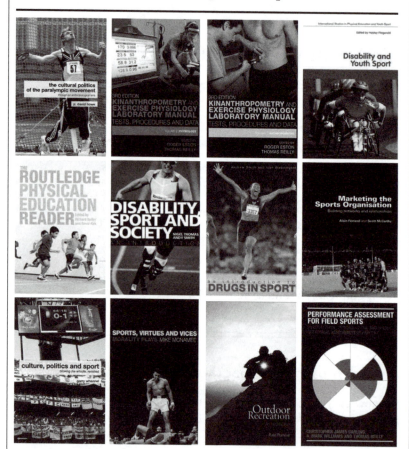

Routledge
Taylor & Francis Group

www.routledge.com/sport

The Routledge Physical Education Reader

Richard Bailey, Birmingham University UK
and **David Kirk**, Leeds Metropolitan
University, UK

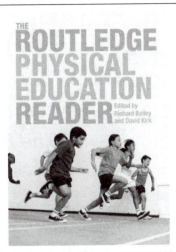

Physical Education teaching and research is fundamental to the physical and social health of our communities. The Routledge Physical Education Reader presents an authoritative and representative selection of the very best international scholarship in PE, drawn from across the full topical range of the discipline.
Containing a rich blend of contemporary, 'classic' and hard-to-find articles, this book helps students gain a full understanding of the historical context in which current issues and debates within PE have emerged.
Leading international scholars Richard Bailey and David Kirk weave a thoughtful editorial commentary throughout the book that illuminates each key theme, making insightful and important connections between articles and approaches. The book is divided into eight thematic sections, each of which includes an extensive guide to further reading:

- Nature and values of physical education
- Physical education and sport
- Physical education and health
- Learners and learning
- Teachers and teaching
- Curriculum and content
- Social construction of bodies
- Researching physical education

Addressing the most important topics in contemporary physical education, and representing a comprehensive 'one-stop' resource, The Routledge Physical Education Reader is essential reading for all serious students of physical education, sport, coaching, exercise and health.

Contents
Introduction
Part One: The Nature and Values of Physical Education
Part Two: Physical Education and Sport
Part Three: Physical Education and Health
Part Four: Learners and Learning
Part Five: Teachers and teaching
Part Six: Curriculum and content
Part Seven: The social construction of bodies
Part Eight: Researching physical education
Conclusion

Routledge
Taylor & Francis Group

September 2008
HB: 978-0-415-44600-6: **£95.00**
PB: 978-0-415-44601-3: **£29.99**

www.routledge.com/sport

Physical
Activity and Health
Second Edition
The Evidence
Explained

Adrianne Hardman, Loughborough University, UK
David Stensel, Loughborough University, UK

Now in a fully updated and revised edition, Physical Activity and Health explains clearly, systematically and in detail the relationships between physical activity, health and disease, and examines the benefits of exercise in the prevention and treatment of a wide range of important health conditions.

The book critically considers the evidence linking levels of physical activity with disease and mortality. It explores the causes of specific health conditions and syndromes prevalent in developed societies, such as cardiovascular disease, Type 2 diabetes, obesity and cancer, and discusses the role of physical activity in their prevention or alleviation. Throughout, the book draws on cutting edge research literature and is designed help the student to evaluate the quality and significance of the scientific evidence. A concluding section explores broader themes in exercise and public health, including therapeutic uses of exericse; exercise and ageing; children's health and exercise, and physical activity and public health policy, and includes a critical appraisal of current recommendations for physical activity. Containing useful pedagogical features throughout, including chapter summaries, study activities, self evaluation tasks, guides to 'landmark' supplementary reading and definitions of key terms, and richly illustrated with supporting case-studies, tables, figures and plates, Physical Activity and Health is an essential course companion. It is vital reading for degree-level students of sport and exercise science, public health, physical therapy, medicine, nursing and nutrition.

R Routledge
Taylor & Francis Group

April 2009
PB: 978-0-415-42198-0: **£29.99**
HB: 978-0-415-45585-5: **£85.00**

www.routledge.com/sport